Law and Justice:
A Strategy Perspective

Sam Muller and Stavros Zouridis (editors)

2012
Torkel Opsahl Academic EPublisher
The Hague

ISBN 978-82-93081-82-1

PUBLICATION SERIES PREFACE

The Hague Institute for the Internationalisation of Law (HiiL) and the Torkel Opsahl Academic EPublisher (TOAEP) are pleased to include *Law and Justice: a Strategy Perspective* in the *Law of the Future Series* established in October 2012.

HiiL – an independent research and advisory institute – is the driving force behind this publication Series, which aims at promoting future-oriented research in the field of law. Thanks to the close cooperation with TOAEP, it is possible to bring such innovative research to persons anywhere in the world who may be interested in it, using an online platform that is open and freely accessible to all.

The *Law of the Future Series* is premised on the assumption that prospective thinking about law and justice systems is not only desirable but also necessary, in order to ensure that they do not become obsolete, ineffective or unjust. The Series primarily features compilations of 'think pieces' about the law of the future and the future of law, but also includes other publications.

The first book in the Series brought together trends from different areas of law. This second book explores what you do with those trends: how does one get to strategise? We utilise the same method we used previously: that of 'think pieces' by thought and practice leaders in different areas.

As will be the case with all future volumes in the *Law of the Future Series*, this book can be freely read, printed or downloaded from www.fichl.org/toaep/. It can also be purchased through online distributors such as www.amazon.co.uk as a regular printed book. Firmly committed to open access, neither TOAEP nor HiiL will charge for this book.

Sam Muller, Larry Catá Backer and Stavros Zouridis
Publication Series Co-Editors

FOREWORD:
WHO STRATEGISES?

After two volumes of *The Law of the Future and the Future of Law*, bringing together 85 think pieces on legal trends in different areas of law, after a little over 10 interviews with key policy makers, and after 15 workshops with different legal and justice actors in different parts of the world, the question arose: what does one do with the different legal futures that emerge, which we captured in *Law Scenarios to 2030*? Or, as we asked Joris Demmink, Secretary-General of the Dutch Ministry of Security and Justice, in an interview in October 2011: *who strategises*?

"Our Ministry certainly does", he said, "we have a directorate for strategy, especially for this purpose". Digging deeper we learned that on the political level there is hardly any time to deal with broad, long-term strategic 'legal system issues'. Occasionally ministers might make time for that, but they are generally caught up in the day-to-day politics of running the country and the ministry. So, the highest civil servant of the ministry of justice strategises, within the parameters that the political bosses set.

Does parliament strategise? Formally, parliament is the law-maker. Here too, the political weather of the day, week, month, or maybe year, seems to determine much of what happens. No looking 10 years ahead. There is, of course, one all-determining moment when parliament strategises, and that is when it adopts, amends, or refuses to amend a constitution. But, again, that is a rare bird: it does and should not happen all that often.

Who strategises on the international plane? We have seen a marked trend towards more law at the international level over the past decades. That must respond to a need, and must be somebody's strategy. However, as the International Law Commission pointed out in 2006, there is little overall strategising regarding the international legal system: fragmentation seems to be prevalent.[1]

---

[1]   "Fragmentation of International Law: Difficulties Arising From the Diversification and Expansion of International Law", Report of the Study Group of the International Law Commission, finalized by Martti Koskenniemi, available at http://untreaty.un. org/ilc/documentation/english/a_cn4_1682.pdf, last accessed on 20 August 2012.

What about non-State actors? Demmink was clear: "Private actors of all sorts have become more important. Also in political and diplomatic terms, private actors make their presence felt, sometimes complicating the work of national governments in international and domestic affairs".

With private parties' big role in globalisation, their quest to find the most reliable and expedient means to obtain justice is becoming ever more relevant to courts, governments and citizens. Private actors rely on public authorities for many of these services and seek out a host State most suited for their purposes. This relationship, where private actors depend on public institutions, is one of the most important and underexplored facts of present-day internationalisation of law. Both hold a degree of dissimilar power (money versus institutions of law).

"Insurance companies are in many ways leading the quest to find justice. Just about every interest imaginable can be insured these days, which is why effective conflict resolution in complex environments and with multi-jurisdictional parties is part of the core business of insurance companies", he said.

So, perhaps the strategist of the legal system does resemble the Wizard of Oz a little: a critical figure but, at the same time, a lot less coherent and imposing than one might wish to imagine.

It was this conversation with a long serving, high ranking civil servant of the Dutch justice system that brought us to this book and, most likely, to much more research to come. The question of *who strategises*, is a fascinating one to which this book and our Law of the Future conferences can only begin to give an answer.

We adopted the tried and tested 'think piece' method and asked thought and practice leaders to reflect on the notion of legal and justice strategies. Is there a strategy? Who makes it? How? In the introductory chapter of this book, we set out our approach in more detail.

Before we get to that, there are many people we need to thank.

It has been a very inspiring endeavour to work with prominent thought leaders from very different fields to explore this question. Deadlines were very tight, which asked a lot from the authors. We thank them for their patience and commitment.

We would also like to thank our copy editing team, Wendy Bremang, Kaitlyn Jones, Sarah-Louise Todd, Lisa-Felicia Akorli, Tsvetelina Mihaylova, Lara Schaefer and Kate Elliot, led by the indefatigable and ever meticulous Alexander Orona. We thank Alf Butenschøn Skre and Morten Bergsmo from Torkel Opsahl Academic EPublisher for their patience and endurance with our inability to stick to deadlines. We treasure your cooperation. A special word of thanks goes to Dessy Velikova, who managed the whole process with both softness and determination.

Lastly, we thank the Dutch Ministry of Security and Justice for the financial support that they have extended to this project. We would not have managed without it and we hope that their expectations were met.

Sam Muller and Stavros Zouridis

TABLE OF CONTENTS

Introduction:
Aligning Legal and Justice Strategies:
On the Benefits of Strategy Theory
to Law and the Justice System

Sam Muller[*] and Stavros Zouridis[**]

1. Connecting Strategy with Law and the Justice System

To lawyers and legal scholars, words like 'law' and 'justice system' will sound familiar. The concept of 'strategy' however, will be rather remote. This volume connects law and the justice system with the concept of strategy. It assumes that law and the justice system may benefit from using strategy theory and strategic models. In fact, we think it is necessary to do so. Societies are highly connected and increasingly interdependent. The constant movement of people, business, and ideas brings much benefit, but also much volatility. Naturally, this also affects law. Law at the national level and law at the international level are increasingly intertwined. The public and the private spheres are also harder to separate: the Internet is run mostly by private rules. In the area of finance, public rules are trying to fight back what were once private ones. Technology constantly creates new questions and matters that need regulation, for example in the area of privacy and data protection. Legal realities in one country can quickly affect another. A national anti-corruption law is sometimes only as good as the laws in the countries with which the State trades most. Law must adapt to all these changes or face irrelevance. Being a minister of justice is no longer a position that keeps you in the capital most of the time. In this complex, often volatile world you need to have a sense of what is going on, and you need legal and justice strategies to deal with it.

[*] **Sam Muller** is the Director of the Hague Institute for the Internationalisation of Law (HiiL).
[**] **Stavros Zouridis** is Professor of Public Administration (Tilburg University), former Director for Justice Strategy at the Ministry of Justice (2005–2010).

To confront this challenge, we set up a process of legal trend watching three years ago. Our method was pragmatic: we asked over 40 leading thinkers and 'doers' in different legal field to write a think piece on what they saw as the main legal challenges for the coming two decades in their field. They were asked to focus on four main questions: (a) what will be the main type of ordering; (b) how are rules made; (c) how are they enforced; and (d) how is conflict resolution organised. In parallel, we held over 15 workshops in different parts of the world with different justice actors. The result was the first volume in our *Law of the Future Series*: the *Law of the Future and the Future of Law* (first volume),[1] a conference held in June 2011, and publication of *Law Scenarios to 2030*, the second edition of which was just released.[2] A second volume of *Law of the Future and the Future of Law* – with new material – was in preparation at the time of writing.

As different legal futures become clearer, the question of how to deal with those different possible futures also becomes more pressing. It was this question that prompted us to bring leading thinkers and doers together around concerns about legal and justice strategy. Our method, again, was pragmatic: we started by asking people to reflect on legal and justice strategies in their field in think pieces. The result lies before you: an eclectic collection of thoughts by leaders in the justice field on strategies in their area of work.

The main questions we asked were: (a) is there such a thing as a justice and legal strategy?; (b) if so, what do they look like?; and (c) who makes them and how?

Thus, the authors were asked to reflect on *what they think* about legal and justice strategies. The think pieces are not meant to be elaborate academic papers, but short essays in which the authors can freely share their thoughts on the topic. Therefore, the authors were asked to minimise the use of footnotes when making references. "Sources and Further Reading" sections included at the end of think pieces list sources provided by

---

[1] Sam Muller *et al.* (eds.), *The Law of the Future and the Future of Law*, Torkel Opsahl Academic EPublisher, Oslo, 2011. Published on the basis of the open access principle, this book is freely accessible and downloadable at: http://www.fichl.org/publication-series/. A hard copy can be ordered through online distributors such as Amazon.

[2] "Law Scenarios to 2030", available at http://www.hiil.org/publication/law-scenarios-to-2030, last accessed on 9 September 2012.

the authors and additional literature for further reading. We think this may strengthen the ability of the book to serve as a catalyst at this stage of development of this new field.

The spread of the invited authors is deliberately wide: law-makers, supervisors, judges, private actors, practitioners and academics. The output, therefore, also covers a wide area.

It shows how diverse strategy making is in the area of justice. Although many use the word 'justice system', and often in reference to a specific country (the Dutch, Tanzanian, or Bolivian justice system), the think pieces collected in this volume show that it is a very loose term. 'The system' seems more like a collection of smaller and bigger systems that interact, in which they can strengthen and weaken each other, without a single 'owner' who develops 'a strategy'. So we have both a sense that legal and justice strategies are needed and indications that there are many strategies and many owners of strategies. That raises a coherency question. Another general issue that arises from the think pieces is related to the data and assumptions on which strategies are based. On what basis does an actor decide to develop a strategy, and how does he assess whether it is working? There seems to be much room for more tools and mechanisms here.

In this introduction we start by exploring the concept of strategy and strategy theory. In section three the concept of strategy is applied to law and the justice system. It appears that goals and actions cannot be defined merely on the basis of legal and political preferences. The environment in which the goals and actions are set should be taken into account in order to achieve the desired goals. Alignment between legal and justice strategies and the environment in which these are deployed is a decisive quality criterion that should be applied by each legislator and legal actor. In other words, the alignment between legal goals, law's design, justice interventions, and the environment of law and the justice system becomes a prime focus. In the final section some conclusions and lessons are drawn for legal theory and practice, thus providing a framework within which to place the think pieces that this book brings together.

2. Strategy Theory and Research: Some Highlights

The concept of strategy has been used in at least three different contexts. Strategy's original meaning refers to the context of war and warfare. For example, in his masterpiece *On War* von Clausewitz explores the dynamics of war and the implications of these dynamics for the planning and execution of wars. He argues that instead of being a contest between individuals, combat in war requires logistics, planning, and so on in addition to the fighting. Von Clausewitz refers to these elements as 'engagements'.[3] Strategy is defined as 'the use of engagements for the object of the war'.[4] As such, it is distinguished from tactics, which 'teaches the use of armed forces in the engagement'.[5] Von Clausewitz proceeds with some famous words:

> The strategist must therefore define an aim for the entire operational side of the war that will be in accordance with its purpose. In other words, he will draft the plan of the war, and the aim will determine the series of actions intended to achieve it: he will, in fact, shape the individual campaigns and, within these, decide on the individual engagements. Since most of these matters have to be based on assumptions that may not prove correct, while other, more detailed orders cannot be determined in advance at all, it follows that the strategist must go on campaign himself. Detailed orders can then be given on the spot, allowing the general plan to be adjusted to the modifications that are continuously required. The strategist, in short, must maintain control throughout.[6]

Accordingly, von Clausewitz defines the constitutive three elements of the strategy concept: the objective to be achieved, a purposeful deployment of resources, and the adaptation of both the objective and the deployment of resources to the context encountered. Within the same warfare tradition, Sun Tzu's text on the art of warfare is much older. One of the central concepts in this text is '*shih*', which among other things refers to the context in which an army or a warrior must fight. '*Shih*' encompasses both the conditions that define the position of the army or warrior and the competitive advantage to be achieved. According to Sun Tzu, a warrior should use the broader environment of the battle as a competitive advantage ('*shih*') in order to win a war.

---

3   Carl von Clausewitz, *On War*, Everyman's Library, New York, 1993, p. 108.
4   *Ibid.,* p. 146.
5   *Ibid.*
6   *Ibid.,* p. 207.

Strategy as a successful course of action has also been used in the context of corporations and executive management. Philip Selznick (1957) has been one of the founding fathers of strategic management. In his classic on institutional leadership, he argues that top management is not primarily about administrative efficiency or about improving the organisation as a production machine. Top management should be regarded as a kind of statesmanship. Top management's primary responsibility is to align the social environment of an organisation and the organisation's internal conditions. Ever since the advent of strategic management, numerous approaches have been developed and lots of knowledge has been gathered. Mintzberg, Ahlstrand, and Lampel have attempted to synthesize the knowledge on strategic management.[7] They have distinguished ten schools of thought on strategic management. Whereas some of these schools focus on goals and design and (strategic) planning, other schools approach strategic management from the perspective of positioning, learning, or culture. Again in their synthesis, one of the core elements of strategic management seems to be the alignment between the organisation and its environment. In order to analyse the interplay between the organisation and its environment they use the concept of configuration. Configuration refers to a stable match of the organisation's characteristics with the environment in which the organisation operates. From a slightly different perspective, Mulgan has analysed how strategy should be organised in public organisations.[8] Whereas most strategic managements focus on successful corporative strategies, Mulgan claims that "all successful governments have created spaces for thought, learning, and reflection to resist the tyranny of the immediate".[9]

Warfare and strategic management are not the only contexts in which the concept of strategy has been used. Perhaps most of the strategy literature nowadays focuses on politics and political communication. Both the stakes and the findings resemble those of warfare and strategic management. In the realm of politics, strategy refers to winning campaigns, gaining and using power effectively, and successful survival in the politi-

---

[7] Henry Mintzberg, Bruce Ahlstrand and Joseph Lampel, *Strategy Safari – Your Complete Guide Through the Wilds of Strategic Management*, Pearson Education Limited, Harlow, United Kingdom, 2009.

[8] Geoff Mulgan, *The Art of Public Strategy. Mobilizing Power and Knowledge for the Common Good*, Oxford University Press, Oxford, 2009.

[9] *Ibid.*, p. 3.

cal arena. Again a major lesson appears to be that functioning strategies are those that are in alignment with the social, cultural, technological, and economic context in which they are deployed. Machiavelli's *Il Principe* provides a famous example. He argues among others that political strategies have to be fitted to the regime of a State, the way a ruler has gained power and the type of position a ruler occupies. Creating 'competitive advantage' in a business environment, creating '*shih*' in warfare and successfully gaining and keeping political power seem to be a matter of aligning one's course of action and the context in which it has to work. Contemporary approaches to political strategy primarily focus on communication.[10]

There are some common denominators of these approaches to strategy. Strategy usually refers to a deliberate and more or less coherent series of goals to be pursued, actions to be taken, and effects to be realised. Strategy is a matter of survival in a competitive environment or winning a confrontation or even war. If it is connected with management, strategy sometimes refers to dealing with difficult problems and unstructured information or dealing with crises and unexpected circumstances.[11] In short, most of the approaches to strategy share some characteristics:

i. Strategy is a more or less deliberate series of actions which are connected with goals or objectives;

ii. The context in which action takes place is continuously changing which creates both opportunities and threats for a given strategy;

iii. Successful strategies appear to be successful because they match the context in which they are deployed.

Strategies do not necessarily have to be rationally chosen in advance. Contrary to a lot of management literature, empirical approaches to strategy show that strategy usually evolves in emergent processes of variation, selection and trial and error. Besides, it is not being designed within the top structure of the organisation. Instead, it evolves out of the actions of frontline professionals and the choices they make. Instead of designing the organisation's strategies, top management makes sense of these actions by codifying the choices already made as the organisation's strategy.

---

[10] Thomas Fischer, Gregor P. Schmitz and Michael Seberich (eds.), *The Strategy of Politics. Results of a Comparative Study*, Bertelsmann Stiftung, Gütersloh, 2007.

[11] Karl E. Weick and Kathleen Sutcliffe, *Managing the Unexpected. Resilient Performance in an Age of Uncertainty*, John Wiley and Sons, San Francisco, 2007.

Even emerging strategies, in which continuous adaptation takes place, can often only be reconstructed in retrospect.[12]

The emergent nature of many strategies has not withheld management scholars from continuously developing strategic design and planning tools, cycles and models. The management literature and theory on tools and models is so extensive that it has become impossible to map. Since most of the literature can be regarded as a variation of the basic model of strategic thought, a mapping of all these theories is not necessary. Three layers are always central:

i.   Many strategy models start with scanning the environment of the actor who wants to develop a strategy. What are the opportunities and threats from the perspective of this actor? Which major trends occur in the market in which he operates? How do competitors behave? Which new technologies have been developed? Which future trends and scenarios are to be expected? The exploration of the environment is believed to reveal the actor's possibilities to manoeuvre. Many analytical tools have been developed to scan the environment, such as market research, positioning techniques and scenario analysis.

ii. The basic model also includes mapping the organisation that has to pursue a strategy. The strengths and weaknesses of the organisation are explored, its mission and vision are laid down, its structure is delineated, its basic technologies and processes are analysed, and its culture and skills are established in order to decide which strategies are feasible and necessary.

iii. The process of developing strategy comes to a climax once these analyses are amalgamated. The confrontation of the opportunities and demand of the environment on the one hand and what the organisation has to offer on the other hand, is used to derive a strategy. The strategy that comes out of this confrontation enables the organisation to seize the opportunities and use the strengths of the organisation.

Mark Moore has developed a variation of this basic model well-suited for public organisations.[13] In his approach, public organisations

---

[12]   Karl E. Weick, *Sensemaking in Organizations*, Sage Publications, Thousand Oaks, CA, 1995.

have to create public value just as private organisations create private value. In order to create public value, public managers have to take into account at least three different considerations that make up the 'strategic triangle':

i. What value does the organisation want to produce? In other words, what is the organisation's proposition?

ii. What sources of 'legitimacy and support' does the organisation derive from the 'authorising environment' in order to produce public value?

iii. What is the operational capacity of the organisation to deliver the results that create public value?

Again, the pattern is familiar. The public organisation's strategy is derived from the consideration of these factors. In other words, the strategy of the organisation is marked by the ambitions and capabilities of the organisation to the extent these are allowed by the authorising environment.

3. Strategic Approaches to Law and the Justice System

So what does all this management speech have to do with law and the legal system? Why should lawyers and legal scholars take notice of strategy theory and strategy methodology? There are at least three reasons that justify serious attention among lawyers and legal scholars. Firstly, the one we set out at the beginning of this chapter: in the volatile, fast-changing world of today, legal systems need strategy if they are to remain relevant and functional. One cannot afford just to let things happen.

Secondly, legislation as a source of law usually expresses a strategy. Even though the strategy embedded in legislation may remain in the background and not even be explicated, legislation instrumentalises political strategies, it is part of a (bigger) political strategy or it symbolises political strategies. Whether law is or is not regarded as a means to an end, as von Jhering once argued and as recently criticized by Tamanaha, legislation and law always serve political or social purposes. From a strategy perspective, it does not matter which goals are pursued. Whether legisla-

---

[13] Mark Moore and Sanjeev Khagram, "On Creating Public Value", available at http://www.hks.harvard.edu/m-rcbg/CSRI/publications/workingpaper_3_moore_khagram.pdf, last accessed on 1 September 2012.

tion is set up to achieve stability, avoid civil war, guarantee human rights or redistribute incomes and create equal opportunities does not matter from a strategy perspective. It does not even matter that many legal systems do not pursue one goal but many, often conflicting goals. Even fragmented and incoherent strategies are strategies, and as argued, strategy does not necessarily require rational and synoptic design. Instead, applying strategy theory to law and the justice system compels legislators and legal institutions to systematically reconstruct their goals and actions. Strategic thinking thus reveals the underlying goals embedded in law, contradictory goals and legal instruments, and inconsistent legislators.

Thirdly, law expresses and embodies (political) strategies, but it is seldom designed by using tools and models derived from strategic management. The design quality of both legislation and legal systems can be enhanced with models and tools that have been developed for strategic management. For example, why should not legislation be subjected to the same quality criteria as corporate strategy? Applying strategy theory to law and the justice system will thus at least produce a more effective law and justice system.

In general, legal and justice strategies occur on at least three levels:

i.   the micro level of legal actors engaging in a legal conflict or a legal process within a given constitutional and legislative context, such as courts or public prosecutors;

ii. the macro level of designing legal systems, legislation and the constitution;

iii. the meta-level of choosing law as a solution for either micro problems or macro problems.

Needless to say that while these levels can be distinguished analytically, they cannot completely be separated in practice. In which direction a legal and justice system moves is a result of all of these three. For example, Supreme Court decisions may have severe design consequences for a legal system. Legislators may engage with micro-strategies as they focus their legislation on individual cases. Even though law as a strategy is a meta-legal issue, it is also directly connected with the strategies embedded in law. If a regulatory framework does not contribute to less environmental pollution, more security or less conflict, it is less likely that law will be an effective and appropriate strategy at all. Legal designs, the building blocks of the strategies embedded in law, are therefore directly connected with the effectiveness and the appropriateness of law as a strategy.

On the micro level of legal actors, strategies refer to litigation strategy (how to litigate effectively?), 'courtroom' strategies (for example, how to select a beneficial jury?) and the legal strategies of transnational corporations (for example, how to avoid taxes or to choose the most beneficial legal environment). Strategies are embedded in the decisions of legal actors, such as whether or not to litigate, whether or not to challenge a member of a jury or a judge, whether or not to settle a dispute outside court and so on. The effectiveness of these strategies can be empirically assessed. Which strategy is the most effective strategy for a client? Which strategies are effective in which legal designs? For example, is convincing a professional judge more effective by using an emotional appeal than convincing a lay jury? Is going to court more effective than using alternative dispute resolution? These strategies can be referred to as *micro legal and justice strategies*.

On a micro level, strategies are developed and implemented in a given legal context. Legal strategies are also embedded in regulatory frameworks. At least two types of choice can be found in legislation. First, the goals, ideals and values that have to be achieved are defined. Should public law be primarily designed to safeguard collective security or should it be primarily designed to safeguard civil liberties and freedom? Is contract law primarily designed to allow maximum freedom for the contracting parties or should law first and foremost create equal positions for the contracting parties? Should competition law protect national economic interests or create as free markets as possible? These choices are political choices and belong to the realm of politics. In general, political choices can be achieved in many ways. A second type of choice therefore has to be made, too. This concerns the legal instruments to be used and the design of legislation and legal systems. First, choices have to be made with regard to the legal instruments deployed. Governments usually have several legal instruments at their disposal that vary from international treaties and legislation (acts of parliament) to administrative acts and powers. Second, law's design requires numerous choices. For example, how to regulate activities (by means of a permit system, a general prohibition, legal obligations and so on), which enforcement mechanism is chosen (private litigation, criminal law, administrative penalties and so on), is legislation being set up on a sectorial basis (for example, separating environmental law, construction law, and urban planning legislation) or does a legislator choose for legislation that transcends specific sectors (for example, integrating building permits, permits prescribed by environmental law and so on)? The same political goal may be achieved with many different legal designs. For example, regulating competition to achieve a level playing field can be achieved with private law and private enforcement mechanisms but it may also be achieved by criminalising and penalising cartels or by creating a system of administrative fines and administrative supervision. Redistribution of income in order to achieve financial equality can be achieved with tax law but also with labour law or even corporate law. High quality education can be achieved by using a permit system that only allows educational institutions that comply with specific norms, but it can also be achieved with detailed regulation on exams and the recognition of diplomas. Whereas the first types of choices belong to the realm of politics, the latter strategic issues belong to the realm of law. The latter will be referred to as *macro legislative strategies*.

Next to micro and macro strategies a third level may be discerned. We will refer to these strategies as *law as a strategy*. Law as a strategy refers to the 'legal way' of organising societies, designing public institutions, settling disputes, and dealing with social and political problems. Whereas many lawyers consider the 'legal way' as the self-evident way that does not require either elaboration or justification, from an extra-legal perspective the 'legal way' is just one way of organising or regulating societies, public institutions, disputes, and social and political problems. In other words, if there is no regulatory or legal problem, why would law be a solution? The 'legal way' does not necessarily have to be the only way or the best way to organise societies and public institutions, to settle disputes, or to deal with social and political problems. In other words, there is no logical necessity to naturalise the 'legal way', even though it is the only way for many lawyers.

4. Law as a Strategy: The Blind Spot of Lawyers and Legal Scholars

Whereas many think pieces in this volume reflect on the micro strategies (for example, the strategies of courts) and macro strategies (for example, program theory underlying legislation) there is much less attention for law as a strategy. It may be both interesting and useful to also discuss legal and justice strategies on a meta-level. As said, this means reflecting on law as a strategy or choosing 'the legal way'. Lawyers, legal experts, and legal scholars may consider the legal way to be a self-evident strategy. Like a fish that does not realise it is swimming in water, many lawyers take the rule of law, the '*Rechtsstaat*', courts as primary dispute resolution mechanisms, and legal solutions to social and political problems as given. A strategic approach to law and the justice system takes a more critical stance. Is law as a strategy really self-evident if we take into account the political, social and economic environment in which law as a strategy has to be effective? Why should a conflict between two citizens be dealt with by law instead of being settled informally if the 'legal' way of settling the conflict is much more expensive, time-consuming, and less satisfactory for both parties? Why should a court deal with a conflict between transnational corporations if both parties agree on informal dispute resolution mechanisms? Why should public administration follow the rather detailed procedures set by administrative or criminal procedure if this kind of 'proceduralism' alienates citizens from the administration and hampers public administration effectively dealing with social problems such as crime, environmental pollution, or unemployment?

The 'legal' way is usually claimed to be a better way to achieve at least four things:

i.   Organising societies. The 'legal way' of organising a society by establishing a legal order is supposed to be a better way to organise societies than to allow spontaneous order. According to many lawyers and legal scholars, the legal way should be preferred above 'chaos' because of the stability of law, its justice or its efficiency. First, law as a strategy reduces social, political, and economic complexity. A well-developed legal order reduces transaction costs and it is therefore more efficient. Because law provides some standardised relationships (from marriage to employment contracts), transactions between people do not have to be reinvented over and over again. Second, the legal way of organising societies is assumed to be a democratic way of organising societies. In most legal systems, legal decision-making is to a large extent transparent. Parliaments decide on regulations, courts extensively motivate their decisions, and because law is published, it is clear for every citizen which rules and principles are valid.

ii. Designing public institutions. The rule of law and its German counterpart the '*Rechtsstaat*' are usually seen as (morally) superior to the rule of men as a design parameter of public institutions. Many lawyers believe that the '*Rechtsstaat*' is a superior model for public institutions, even despite the bureaucracy, inefficiency, 'procedural-ism' and alienation it causes. The rule of law is assumed to reduce the arbitrariness and the whims of government. Because governments are bound by rules and principles and legal institutions guarantee that governments stay within the boundaries set by law, arbitrariness and political interests can be fought.

iii. Settling disputes. Many lawyers and legal scholars prefer law as a strategy for settling disputes among citizens, corporations, and other private bodies. This strategy may be pursued because it is believed that the 'legal way' provides more stability, it is seen as more legitimate, it is regarded as just or fair, and it allows peaceful settlement of conflicts.

iv. Dealing with social, political, technological and environmental problems. The 'legal way' of dealing with these problems is to develop and enforce legislation. There are several reasons to opt for legislation in order to deal with these problems. First, legislation is assumed to guarantee enforcement. In a '*Rechtsstaat*', the coercive power of governments depends upon legislation. Second, legislation is assumed to provide certainty or clarity with regard to what is expected from citizens, corporations, and even governments. Because of the certainty and clarity legislation provides, it is assumed to be an effective regulatory instrument. Third, legislation is usually regarded as a means to protect legal subjects from arbitrariness.

5. A Quality Appraisal of Law as a Strategy

A strategic assessment of law as a strategy requires that this strategy addresses the need for quality criteria derived from strategic thought. Instead of critically questioning the normative (justice) foundations of law, a strategy approach confronts these assumptions with the usual quality standards applied to strategy. A quality appraisal of legal strategies includes integrating the legal strategies with at least three quality standards:

i. Effectiveness

The effectiveness of a legal strategy is the first quality standard that should be taken into account. To what extent should law as a strategy be regarded as effective, and under which (political, social, economic and so on) circumstances is law as a strategy effective? To be more concrete, is the 'legal way' of organising societies, designing public institutions, settling disputes, and solving social and political problems also the most effective way?

ii. Alignment

Alignment between the actor, its strategy, and the context is a second quality standard for legal strategies. Even though alignment also relates to the effectiveness of the legal strategy (if there is no alignment between the legal strategy and its context, it will probably also be ineffective), the assessment of alignment is much broader. Alignment also includes the appropriateness of a legal strategy for a given actor in a given context. Alignment and appropriateness include the legitimacy of a legal strategy and whether a legal strategy actually addresses perceived problems in a society. Assessing the alignment of legal strategies and their environments encompasses legal, moral, cultural and economic considerations. Is law as a strategy appropriate for a specific dispute, political problem, public institution or a society?

iii. Future-Proof

Besides being effective and appropriate, strategies should be future-proof. This does not mean that strategies should survive any given future because no strategy will. It does mean that strategies should be designed in such a way that flexibility is incorporated. It also means that strategies should take into account future contingencies and uncertainties. The only thing we know for sure about the future is that it is uncertain. The literature on strategy has developed methodologies to incorporate uncertainty. For example, scenario methodology explicitly builds on future contingencies and uncertainties. Robust strategies are able to cope with changing environments or even benefit from these changes. Just like well-built airplanes are able to cope with changing weather circumstances (from the freezing temperature at 35,000 feet to tropical heat), well-built strategies are robust enough to cope with different circumstances. For example, a legal strategy that builds on fundamental rights should be designed in such a way that terrorism threats can be dealt with, a legal strategy that builds on privacy and intellectual property should be able to deal with the Internet, and so on. Law as a strategy builds on a legal spirit or ethos in a society and effective legal institutions.

It is impossible to appraise law as a strategy in a general sense. Such an exercise would require mapping the available body of knowledge and probably a great deal of new empirical research. Also the context needs to be taken into account. Perhaps law as a strategy works in Germany, but with regard to the same issues it may not work in Malaysia or vice versa. Any general appraisal of law as a strategy should therefore be rejected. Nevertheless there are good reasons to question or even doubt the assumptions underlying law as a strategy.

First, the 'legal way' is an expensive way. Because of its expensiveness, it also increasingly works as a mechanism of exclusion. In the United States, litigation increasingly requires so many resources that citizens and small companies are *de facto* denied access to justice. In Europe, the European Court of Human Rights is confronted with a caseload with which it cannot cope. The caseload causes huge delays. In general, settling a dispute by asking a trustee to make an authoritative decision on the dispute may be less expensive and time-consuming than going to a court.

Second, the 'legal way' creates artificial procedures and institutions that do not necessarily match any more with the 'life world' of citizens and organisations. In many countries the legitimacy of law's 'proceduralism', formalism and complexity hinders democratic decision-making, thus alienating citizens and politicians from law and the administration of justice. Instead of being a solution for social problems, law may actually have become a hindrance to solving social problems.

Third, creating a rather detailed corpus of rules, principles, rights and institutions stifles decision-making and decisive action by governments, citizens and corporations. In contemporary information society, feedback loops between the preferences of consumers and the actions of transnational corporations are tightly knit. If corporations betray their social responsibilities, market mechanisms may become more severe and unrelenting enforcement mechanisms than fines and penalties. For example, rather huge fines of millions of dollars cannot compete with losing an established reputation in a market that may be worth billions of dollars.

Fourth, law as a strategy has some serious consequences for law enforcement that may have become increasingly untenable. Rule enforcement and coercion may require much bigger enforcement organisations than governments are able to afford. As research has demonstrated, law enforcement therefore focuses on a small proportion of the rules.[14] In re-action to the acknowledgement that legislation can only be partially en-forced, many law enforcement organisations have developed risk control strategies and risk management.[15] Because of this partial enforcement, legislation usually does not provide the certainty it promises. Legislation also does not necessarily provide clarity with regard to what is legally ex-pected from citizens. Most full-grown legal systems are very complex and require in-depth legal knowledge to assess what behaviour is legally al-lowed and what behaviour should be considered as illegal. Moreover, many legal systems are not completely consistent. Contradictory rules are quite common even at a constitutional level (for example, contradictions between fundamental rights). Even court decisions on individual cases do not provide the certainty law promises. For example, a pilot research pro-ject in the Netherlands demonstrated that 31 to 85 per cent of the deci-sions of civil courts had been implemented within three years after the court had decided.[16] Because of the partial enforcement and implementa-tion of law, it may be seriously questioned whether law actually protects against arbitrariness. Even apart from corruption, the idea that legislation actually mirrors real-world practices should be doubted. Despite these findings of empirical research, social and political belief in legislation still seems to be widespread.

Finally, law is usually a rather crude strategy. It works with general rules and principles or with precedents that go along with *stare decisis*. Law seldom provides tailor-made solutions, whereas the increased com-plexity of society may force law to develop these tailor-made solutions.

6. Some Final Remarks

Most think pieces in this volume address micro and macro legal and jus-tice strategies. Law as a strategy should fill the blind spot of many law-yers and legal scholars by reflecting on the meta-level of legal and justice

---

[14] See, for example, Malcom Sparrow, *Imposing Duties. Government's Changing Ap-proach to Compliance*, Praeger, Westport, Connecticut, 1994; and Keith Hawkins, *Law as Last Resort. Prosecution Decision-Making in a Regulatory Agency*, Oxford University Press, Oxford, 2002.

[15] Malcom Sparrow, *The Regulatory Craft. Controlling Risks, Solving Problems, and Managing Compliance*, Brookings Institution Press, Washington, D.C., 2000.

[16] Roland Eshuis, *De daad bij het woord. Het naleven van rechterlijke uitspraken en schikkingsuitspraken*, Ministerie van Justitie, Den Haag, 2009.

strategies. It will not come as a surprise that most of the issues that arise from the quality appraisal point to strategic challenges for law as strategy. Whether or not law as a strategy survives highly depends on whether these strategic challenges are addressed. In other words, the future of law as a strategy highly depends on whether it will become more efficient, whether it will enable public institutions to avoid 'proceduralism' that alienates citizens and effectively address problems, and whether enforcement and compliance are guaranteed. These issues should also prominently figure on the legal and justice agendas.

The think pieces brought together in this volume have shed much light on the notion of legal and justice strategies. There seems to be a shared feeling that more of it is needed. But we can also conclude that more knowledge is needed to understand the concept and to make it work. We will continue our research and we welcome comments and suggestions from the readers of this volume.

7. Sources and Further Reading

Carl von Clausewitz, *On War*, Everyman's Library, New York, 1993.

Geoff Mulgan, *The Art of Public Strategy. Mobilizing Power and Knowledge for the Common Good*, Oxford University Press, Oxford, 2009.

Henry Mintzberg, Bruce Ahlstrand and Joseph Lampel, *Strategy Safari – Your Complete Guide Through the Wilds of Strategic Management*, 2nd edition, Pearson Education Limited, Harlow, United Kingdom, 2009.

Karl E. Weick and Kathleen Sutcliffe, *Managing the Unexpected. Resilient Performance in an Age of Uncertainty*, John Wiley and Sons, San Fransisco, 2007.

Karl E. Weick, *Sensemaking in Organizations*, Sage Publications, Thousand Oaks, CA, 1995.

Keith Hawkins, *Law as Last Resort. Prosecution Decision-Making in a Regulatory Agency*, Oxford University Press, Oxford, 2002.

Malcom Sparrow, *Imposing Duties. Government's Changing Approach to Compliance*, Praeger, Westport, Connecticut, 1994.

Malcom Sparrow, *The Regulatory Craft. Controlling Risks, Solving Problems, and Managing Compliance*, Brookings Institution Press, Washington, D.C., 2000.

Philip Selznick, *Leadership in Administration. A Sociological Interpretation*, Harper & Row, New York, 1957.

Roland Eshuis, *De daad bij het woord. Het naleven van rechterlijke uitspraken en schikkingsuitspraken*, Ministerie van Justitie, Den Haag, 2009.

Sam Muller *et al.* (eds.), *The Law of the Future and the Future of Law*, Torkel Opsahl Academic EPublisher, Oslo, 2011.

Thomas Fischer, Gregor P. Schmitz and Michael Seberich (eds.), *The Strategy of Politics. Results of a Comparative Study*, Bertelsmann Stiftung, Gütersloh, 2007.

PART I:
ABOUT JUSTICE STRATEGIES

1.1.

Thoughts on Legal and Justice Strategies for the Netherlands

Alex Brenninkmeijer[*]

What should a legal and justice strategy in the Netherlands focus on? The central problem facing the legal sector today is the gap between what people expect in terms of justice and what traditional institutions can deliver. Amongst others, this is caused by skewed images of justice created by the media and by ever-increasing specialisation of the legal system. Due to this specialisation, the justice sector and the legal system have become complex systems. This complexity in turn often renders the outcomes of legal proceedings unpredictable; a clear threat to legal certainty. Legal institutions in the Netherlands would benefit from an increased focus on the key public values that the legal system is to provide; procedural justice, legal certainty and trust. An increase in personal contact, fair treatment and participation can act as a bridge between the systems world of legal institutions and lifeworld of citizens. A legal strategy based upon a traditional, deductive, top-down approach of democracy and the rule of law however is likely to exacerbate the tension between the system world and the lifeworld of individuals. We therefore need to move to a more inductive process of norm-setting. Law-making should be based upon intensive interaction with society, for instance by using the wisdom of the crowd: legislation by participation.

1. Introduction: The Problem at Hand

We can see a confrontation emerging over time, between on the one hand, the evolution of the institutions of the justice sector and on the other hand, the societal perspective on the rule of law. The development of traditional legal institutions, is increasingly out of pace with the popular understanding of justice. In the Netherlands, a legal and justice strategy does not exist, at least not a coherent overall strategy. It has become apparent that

---

[*] **Alex Brenninkmeijer** is National Ombudsman of the Netherlands since 2005. He is a specialist in conflict analysis and methods of conflict resolution.

policy-making is one thing, and the way institutions take shape, the daily interactions of all parts of the justice sector with society-at-large and with each other is quite another. The development of the justice sector is in this sense typically a complex process. The legal system as such is becoming a complex system in the sense that the outcome of legal proceedings is often unforeseeable or unpredictable. Why is it then that we trust that law and lawsuits can provide us with legal certainty?

In part, the media is responsible for the perceptions of law we have as citizens. The media project an image of the workings of the justice sector, an image that strongly influences public opinion. Yet it is quite obvious that there is a big difference between the reality of the functioning of legal institutions and the images and impressions in the media. For starters, there is a bias in which part of the justice sector draw media attention. Some areas are interesting to report on, such as the field of crime and punishment, whilst many areas of the law are considered boring by everyone but the legal experts directly involved. Secondly, the media are increasingly visual and oral, whilst the legal sector relies heavily on written documents and formal procedures. These are by definition not easily captured by the visual media. Criminal cases for instance easily attract attention of the media and convictions combined with high sentences are important news items. In the meantime, most people in the Netherlands think that judges only give low sentences – popularly considered too low. Comparative international research shows that, on the contrary, judges in the Netherlands typically give high penalties. The real societal problem behind all this is that most criminal cases are never solved. Yet this problem is hardly addressed in the media.

Another aspect is increasing specialisation, which leads to complexity and can turn into chaos. Areas of law evolve over time through court rulings, additional legislation, lower level legislation, and interaction with international and especially European law. In any field of law only specialists understand the working of the legal system. At the same time, individuals are involved in complex legal structures in their daily life related to work, family life, housing and healthcare as well as consumer issues. Who, for instance, knows what choices he has made by accepting the conditions presented when installing software on his computer? The same applies to the rules related to social benefits, taxation, *et cetera*. In problematic youth care cases sometimes more than ten experts are visiting a family for advice, without knowing from each other what they are doing. Here, too, specialisation may have gone too far.

Specialisation in the legal sector also implies that problems are reduced to singular issues which are solved by specialised procedures and entities. Reality shows that the problems that people face are generally linked to other problems and that the solution of a problem mostly depends on the solution of those other issues. Frequently, a more holistic approach is not possible, because the law does not provide for holistic procedures. Returning to the youth care cases, many institutions can be involved, all of them with their own competence, rules and budgets. In effect, problem solving in serious cases shows that it is necessary to bring all those institutions involved together and find practical solutions within a reasonable timeframe. If a solution is found, it is mostly not because of the rules and budgets but despite them. Good solutions often ask for creative application of the rules. This also applies to families or individuals with debt problems. As National Ombudsman, we published a report with the title *Debts Never Come Alone*. In the meantime, whilst we are quite familiar with so-called multi-problem families, the authorities do not yet use multi-problem-solving methods.

Not too long ago, I picked up on an interesting statement in the newspaper: "Never should the Rule of Law turn up its nose for people's basic sense of justice".[1] Tendencies in the development of legal institutions and societal views on justice seem to move in different directions, thus creating a tension between on the one hand the pretence of the institutions of the rule of law and the craving for justice and democratic influence on the other. I see this as a serious problem that can undermine the trust in and support for the institutions that embody the rule of law. This estrangement between the institutions of the rule of law and people's basic sense of justice is what I see as the most pressing issue for the Dutch 'Rechtsstaat'. Therefore, I will focus on legal and justice strategies that might be helpful in addressing this problem.

---

[1] From a column by René Cuperus in the Dutch newspaper de Volkskrant: "Nooit mag de rechtsstaat zijn neus ophalen voor elementair rechtsgevoel".

2. Justice Strategies

To address this issue, we need to take a closer look at the key public values that the legal system is to provide. My assertion is that in the more or less autonomous development and in particular the continuing specialisation of people and institutions working in the justice sector, these values have increasingly come under pressure. And as a result, the justice system in too many cases does not deliver to people what it promises or should promise.

Let us analyse the public values that the rule of law is to provide as a first step to developing a justice strategy to address the estrangement described above.

2.1. Procedural Justice

I would like to make a difference between the normative approach of 'justice' or 'fairness' as laid down in notions of the rule of law on the one hand, and on the other a more factual approach: what do people consider as 'just' or 'fair'. Research of social psychologists shows us what people find important in their relationships with authorities. *Audi alteram partem* is a familiar part of our legal proceedings. Yet there may be a difference between a legal right to be heard and the factual experience that you are heard. Procedural justice is a serious issue for people. The value of the law on the books for individuals may considerably depend on the actual experiences that people have in their contacts with the institutions of justice.

2.2. Legal Certainty

Strongly related with the problem of complexity of our legal system and institutions is the loss of legal certainty. Providing legal certainty is obviously a key value that a legal system should provide. This legal certainty is enshrined in the law and in the procedures for enforcement of the law. In modern times, it seems to be necessary to make a difference between legal certainty *ex post* or *ex ante*. The legal system does provide for legal certainty but it may take a significant amount of time and money to get it. Important issues often ask for proceedings in more instances. International and European law may make issues more complicated, and, in crucial cases, decisions of the Strasbourg Court or the Court in Luxembourg are indispensable for finding the right interpretation of the applicable legislation. Beside the question whether financial barriers are hindering people from securing their rights, lengthy proceedings put a shadow on the effectiveness of our legal system. Simple rules such as *pacta sunt servanda* may cause serious trouble if things are not going as smoothly as promised in seductive advertisements. And, what was the meaning of the *pacta* that is the basis for my mortgage or other financial product?

2.3. Trust

The functioning of a legal system is strongly related to trust and confidence. Trust in other players in the legal field, confidence in legal institutions and procedures. On the one hand, confidence is related to the reliability of the system or systems. On the other hand, an important issue for trust is the responsiveness of systems to situations where the general rule does not provide the right answer. Do our systems offer room for tailor-made solutions? Or is everybody in the system bound to strict rules? Can we draft systems with considerable discretion for those street-level bureaucrats? Or are policy makers too strongly focused on full control? For example, in the field of taxation and social benefits, administrations are strictly bound, and increasingly so, by rules for recovery and sanctions for faults and abuse. Civil servants complain that those strict rules prevent them from finding just solutions.

3. The System and the Life World of Individuals

At the end of the day the key question is whether our legal system delivers what it promises. What then does the system promise? Answering this question, we can see the gap between the reality of the system on the one hand and the lifeworld of individuals. Especially in this period of economic crisis, growing debt problems, unemployment, costly health care, an aging population and uncertainty about the future of the euro and Europe, individuals face a great deal of uncertainty. Is there a gap between what people expect and what our system, or better, multiple systems, deliver(s)? How can we bridge the gap between the reality of systems and the reality of the lifeworld of individuals? To a certain extent there is a paradox between the two of them. People have a strong need to reduce uncertainty. And systems are set up to create certainty. However, due to complexity and time lags, systems create uncertainty at the same time.

In my experience as National Ombudsman, there is a fundamental misunderstanding about what people expect from our legal system. Do people – as *homo economicus* – always expect that they get what they want? Or are people able to accept negative substantive outcomes? And more importantly: under what conditions do people accept such negative outcomes? Are people primarily driven by financial stimuli, or are they value oriented as well? And what are these values?

4. Bridging the Gap

How then can we bridge the gap between the lifeworld of individuals and the system world of institutions? From my experience as National Ombudsman I see three elements of what I would call the interface between citizens and institutions. They need to be personal, proper and participative. In other words, just as with computer interfaces, in my view the system should accommodate human psychology. Our human tendency to assume that behaviour is intentional and to seek to fathom the mind of the system, is deep-rooted. Kafka describes this beautifully in Joseph K.'s desperate attempts to understand what is happening to him and to discover some logic in the system confronting him. He tries to find out what the system wants of him, because he thinks that by displaying the right behaviour he can "control" it. Citizens are sense-makers. They evaluate the information they can get about a certain issue in order to decide whether what is happening is fair or not. This brings us to the fundamental question of whether humanity should accommodate to the system or the system to humanity. Interfaces are a way for the system world to accommodate to humanity.

4.1. Personal Contact

Experience shows that personal contact promotes good government-citizen relations. It can take many forms. Here are some real-life examples. A person who phones the *Belastingtelefoon* – the support line of the Dutch Tax Administration – and receives friendly and effective assistance will thereafter think more highly of the Tax Administration in general. Indeed, the Dutch Tax Administration recognises this point. Its slogan is "We can't make it nicer, but we can make it easier". Likewise, in complex situations, for example, when a suspect in the case of a child murder gets off scot-free because of mistakes by the justice system, a face-to-face meeting with a member of the Public Prosecution Service may help the victim understand the situation and at least start to come to terms with it. Or take the case of a small municipality that receives only a couple of formal complaints a year because it has installed a telephone help line manned by staff with good communications skills, who listen to people's problems and direct them to the right part of the system.

4.2. Proper Conduct

Proper government conduct means taking citizens seriously and respecting them as individuals. A case in point: an eighty year old woman dashes to the hospital where her husband has just been rushed into intensive care. Finding the car park full, she abandons her vehicle temporarily in a space reserved for the disabled. Having received a parking ticket, she writes to the public prosecutor to explain why she committed this first traffic offence in her whole, long life. The Public Prosecutions Service sends a standard letter saying that the reasons for the offence are irrelevant and the fine must be paid. The deeply law-abiding woman is devastated: she simply wanted to apologise for the offence, not to avoid paying the fine. The Public Prosecutions Service responds to her complaint by waiving the fine: all very well, but that is not what the woman actually wanted!

Over the last thirty years or so, successive National Ombudsmen of the Netherlands have developed a series of general standards of proper conduct based on the hundreds of thousands of real-life cases they have examined. They range from respect for the human right of physical integrity to adequate provision of information, and from promptness to proportionality. Experience shows that complaints and objections tend to be provoked by actions that are not proper conduct. The response of the authorities concerned is usually that citizens are disgruntled because a decision has gone against them. This however is a tragic misunderstanding. Citizens are generally perfectly capable of distinguishing the standard of conduct from the content of the decision. Indeed, citizens who receive very good personal treatment will often take a much more positive view of the final decision, even if it goes against them. The main question is why do people obey the law? It is not for fear of sanctions that they do. Most people are intrinsically motivated.

4.3. Participation

The citizen has a personal stake in everything that happens in his life-world. Government interferes in that world by virtue of its many powers and monopolies. It can do so unilaterally, or it can choose to use its role and powers to deal with the citizen in a participatory manner. The clearest example of this is in the field of spatial-planning, where Dutch law prescribes public participation. Even here, however, politicians and officials often have great difficulty in recognising the value of public participation. In practice, it is reduced to the perfunctory observance of statutory procedures, as described in a National Ombudsman report on the subject (Report 2009/180). However, the government can also choose to create an interface between statutory and administrative procedures on the one hand and individual citizens' lifeworlds on the other by paying genuine attention to their circumstances. It is essential to treat citizens on an equal footing. The role of the administration of the system is obviously different from that of a citizen. However, this difference in role does not imply that citizens should be patronised.

The combination of personal contact, fair treatment and participation is highly effective in reducing the gap between the system, or systems, and the lifeworld of citizens. In effect, it reduces the number of formal legal procedures in a considerable way.

5. Deduction or Induction?

Bridging the gap between individuals and the complex systems of our government asks for a different approach to the concepts of democracy and rule of law. Nowadays, democracy is mostly seen as representative democracy: through elections, citizens decide on the composition of parliament. The Parliamentarians represent their voice and vote on legislation as part of the legislature. This is to a large extent a top-down approach based upon a deductive approach of legal relationships. Rules are made at the top of the system and not bottom-up. In this perspective, the rule of law provides for a complementary system by which legal disputes can be ended by a binding decision of the judge based upon the law. The courts are seen as Montesquieu's *bouche de la loi*. However, case law has to play an important role. Case law shows a tendency to be more inductive than deductive, in the sense that concrete cases inspire courts to decide on rights of parties in the process. The principles of good administration and the interpretation of human rights in concrete cases are based upon case law and not primarily on legislation. Not a deductive but a more inductive process of norm setting. This ties in with the role of the National Ombudsman. His starting point is not the law, but the concrete case and the question of whether the administration has acted in a proper way. The principles of good administration, on propriety, are the result of the case law of the Ombudsman. They are the result of an inductive process of norm-setting.

Democracy and the rule of law have the tendency to work in a deductive way. What we need is a more inductive approach of our legal system. The individual – the citizen – should, if possible, be placed at the beginning of the line and not at the end. Law-making should not be imposing, but be based upon intensive interaction with society, for instance, by using the wisdom of the crowd: legislation by participation. There is quite some literature on this subject. The same turn from deduction to induction can be applied in conflict resolution. To start with, the interface I introduced above, consisting of personal contact, proper conduct and participation, corresponds with the concept of mediation. Not the judge but parties themselves solve the legal dispute, and if necessary, the mediator assists parties in their mutual fair treatment.

In the same way, the Dutch government has started an experiment with effective communication, based on notions of fair treatment, in administrative law cases. According to the General Administrative Law Act, administrative decisions are challenged in procedures for making an objection. An approach based upon the interfaces of the Ombudsman leads to informal personal contact in an early stage of the legal dispute. In up to 60% of all cases, the dispute can be resolved without formal proceedings. This approach has considerable influence on the number of cases brought before the courts. The satisfaction with this approach of both citizens and civil servants is considerably higher than with formal proceedings. Moreover, this approach contributes significantly to the acceptance of negative decisions.

6. Conclusion

A legal strategy based upon a traditional top-down approach of democracy and the rule of law causes more and more tension between the system world and the lifeworld of individuals. There is a gap between what people expect in terms of justice and what traditional institutions can deliver. Legislation should be the result of an interactive process with civil society and should make use of the wisdom of the crowds. However, this is not the focus of this chapter. Procedural justice, legal certainty and trust are key values for citizens. Traditional legal proceedings provide these key values only to a limited extent. How can we bridge the gap between what the legal system delivers and what people expect from it? Personal contact, fair treatment and participation can function as an interface between the systems of government on the one hand and the lifeworld of citizens on the other.

7. Sources and Further Reading

Alex Brenninkmeijer, "Management and Fairness", in *Journal of Public Administration and Policy*, 2012, vol. 4, no. 2, available at http://www.nationaleombudsman.nl/sites/default/files/engels_artikel_web site_2012.pdf, last accessed on 31 July 2012.

Alex Brenninkmeijer, "Een eerlijk process", in *Nederlands Juristenblad* (NJB), 2009, p. 1603.

Alex Brenninkmeijer and Bert Marseille, "Meer succes met de informele aanpak van bezwaarschriften", in *Nederlands Juristenblad* (NJB), 2011 p. 1586.

Kees van den Bos, "Vertrouwen in de overheid", in *Den Haag: Essay Ministerie van Binnenlandse Zaken en Koninkrijksrelaties*, 2011, available at http://www.rijksoverheid.nl/documenten-en-publicaties/rapporten/2011/0 3/01/vertrouwen-in-de-overheid.html, last accessed on 31 July 2012.

Kees van den Bos and Alex Brenninkmeijer, "Vertrouwen in wetgeving, de overheid en de rechtspraak", in *Nederlands Juristenblad* (NJB), 2012, p. 2016.

Ministerie van Binnenlandse Zaken en Koninkrijksrelaties Prettig contact met de overheid 1, 2 and 3, available at http://prettigcontactmetdeover heid.nl/, last accessed on 31 July 2012.

Verslag van de Nationale ombudsman, 2011, available at http://jaar verslag.nationaleombudsman.nl/, last accessed on 31 July 2012.

1.2.

Strategies in Law and Justice in the 18th Century Dutch Republic

Boudewijn Sirks[*]

We see in the eighteenth century, in the judiciary and the legislative bodies, strategies regarding law and justice. Although this was not a very outspoken strategy in the modern sense, they were nevertheless the expression of a persistent wish to provide good law and justice to the people. Next to that, there were informal strategies, which were nonetheless no less effective. Upon consideration the goals were the same, or not much different from present aims.

The Dutch Republic, being a confederation of seven sovereign provinces, does not seem to have been the ideal place for legal and justice strategy. Yet within the province of Holland there was certainly a wish for such a strategy, as we know from the writings of Bijnkershoek, the most important author in this respect: because he published copiously on law and because he was a member and later president of the highest judicial court of Holland and Zeeland for the long period of thirty-nine years, during which he kept account of the court's business. In the last forty years literature on the jurisprudence and justice of the eighteenth century has known a revival. Meijers, after a seminal article in 1918/1919 on published and unpublished court decisions, began to publish Bijnkershoek's account, having discovered it, in 1923, with the last volume appearing in 1962. The accounts of his son-in-law, Pauw, followed in the years 1964–1971. The remaining parts of Bijnkershoek's account were published in 2005 and 2008. Further, letters by Bijnkershoek were discovered, which are for the greater part still unpublished. In some of these he also reports on the court's business. The Court and other eighteenth century judges (Duirkant, Van Bleiswijk) received scholarly attention, and there is a plan to publish the account by Van Bleiswijk. A famous criminal case, against Jacob Muller, was described in 2008 in a biography of Muller. As a result

---

[*]   **Boudewijn Sirks** is Regius Professor of Civil Law in the University of Oxford.

much more material on the justice of the eighteenth century has become available in that period.

How did the judges and law-givers of that time cope with the problems of their times? Like in our times, there was a variety of problems in the legal practice of those days, and some kinds of strategy were developed, sometimes explicitly (for example, by drawing up a rule in a by-law), sometimes implicitly or silently (as a precept of decency, of good judiciary). One persistent problem in the court was the long duration of litigation. Cases could take decades. For example, the case of the moist hay (*liesig hooi*), which occurred in September 1697, was decided in first instance in 1700, in appeal in 1710 and by the Supreme Court in 1717; but the Court wanted to try to have parties settle the case before pronouncing its judgment. Not succeeding in this, it confirmed and issued its judgment in April 1723 (OT 1326). This length was exceptional in view of the value at stake, but considering the time not so exceptional. Another case concerned the sale of an option to purchase whale bones in 1706, decided in first instance in 1706, in appeal in 1713, and by the Court in 1718 (OT 1420). Such a length could be caused by different factors. In the case of the hay, it was the intricate circumstances, which allowed for tergiversation on the part of the advocates, and perhaps the dislike of parties (farmers) of each other. But this does not always have to have been the case in long litigation. As Diestelkamp reminded of when describing cases before the *Reichskammergericht*, it could be in the interest of a party, and sometimes of both parties, to stall litigation for a prolonged time: as long as there was no judgment, there was nothing to pay or return, and on the other side a dubious claim could socially still be more valuable than a claim rejected.

However, there were other factors, which delayed proper justice from being done. One was the propensity of lawyers to make money by writing long memoranda with many articles: they were paid by page. But such long memoranda made the judge's task more cumbersome since all the articles had to be dealt with, and as it was clear, many were merely redundant. The Court's bylaw had set rules about the length of these. Thus in a case in 1726, when the memoranda at both sides exceeded thirty pages, the Court decreed that they could only charge a third (OT 2411). Similarly oral proceedings took time and were profitable for the advocates. Repeatedly, Bijnkershoek refers to days of session over a single case. Although, as we shall see, not all judges shared the same views, we may conclude that in general it was considered necessary that litigation should not be unnecessarily delayed by the advocates and the courts, and certainly not by stratagems. If parties themselves wanted to stall the course of justice it was of course their business.

But fault did not always lay with the lawyers: judges too could prove to be the sand in the machinery. Bijnkershoek relates in a letter that the president Rooseboom was apt to stall cases. In a case in which both litigants had insisted on a quick procedure, he managed nevertheless to keep the case going for two years. That he could do so was due to his position as president. He could set the agenda. We may assume that when Bijnkershoek became president himself in 1724, he looked after it that cases would not be unduly stalled by the court.

Likewise the court tried to cut litigation short by moving parties to an agreement. Sometimes this was because the case was legally very difficult to decide and here the court saved itself time. However, sometimes it was done out of concern for one party, or both parties, to spare them further litigation and costs, and a possible losing face. Thus in OT 1185, one brother sued his brothers and sisters about the division of an inheritance and gained possession in 1693. The Court decided in 1715 to hold a meeting with parties to see whether the assets could be divided between them and the process quickly ended, in order to protect parties against themselves and to spare them further expenses. Or it happened that the object of the quarrel was simply too small compared with the costs: again the Court tried to protect parties against themselves (OT 1233). It also occurred that the Court tried to save socially respected people from the disgrace of losing the law suit. In a case where parents had forced their son to sign an agreement that he would never make contact again with a girl who was considered to be below their status, and where they had requested the Court's confirmation for a title of execution, the Court found that such an agreement was unallowable. It restrained the young man where he should not be restrained, the free choice of a partner (after reaching majority). To spare his parents the shame of a rejection of their request, a judge who knew them would visit them to ask to withdraw the request.

Costs were certainly a factor to be reckoned with in those days. We see a rapid decrease of cases before the Supreme Court from the 1720's onwards. Why this happened is still not known. But in the East Indies a similar decrease took place after 1767 before the Council of Justice. The VOC ordered an inquiry in 1774, but this was only done in 1778. The conclusion of the reporters was that the introduction of the Court procedure had been the cause of it: the average costs had risen from 299 to 414 guilders (a rise by one third!), and many had taken refuge in settlements. The president, Helvetius, had been keen on standing and had argued that the Council of Justice should be ranked higher than a Council of Justice in a Dutch province. Since it had only the High Government as court of appeal above it, it should be ranked as a provincial court (and his own standing accordingly higher): the provincial court of Holland and Zeeland had only the Supreme Court above it, and the other provincial courts could sit in appeal with an extension of judges. Introducing the procedure of a provincial court implied also higher and more fees and this had led to a rapid decline in cases (as Helvetius would have said to the secretary who had complained about his low salary: "We shall introduce the practice of the Court, everything must be done by request then, there will be many court appearances and the recordings give much profit; it will be hard on you in the beginning and entail much writing, but that is nothing: I shall help you".). It follows from the concern of the VOC about this decline that they were unhappy about it and did not want to deny by the sheer costs of litigation the habitants of the East Indies a judicial solution for their differences. It was not their only concern: they sent a minimal number of lawyers, who had to be university graduated, to Batavia to function there as advocates.

As regarding the applicable law, the situation was, as we may expect from the confederate structure of the Republic, varied and complicated. Some legislation was valid for the entire Republic, primarily the ordinances of the Habsburgs, such as the Criminal Ordinances; some for an entire province, such as the Ordinance of Succession for Holland. Provincial states could legislate for their province, too. But within provinces, towns and regions could and often would have their own laws. It was a checkered landscape, as is Europe nowadays. The Supreme Court sailed between Scylla and Charybdis, primarily by taking the Roman law as basis to which the particular laws were considered to be exceptions. But in 1727 the States of Holland asked the Provincial and Supreme Court to draw up a body of the provincial laws, respecting local laws as much as possible (a '*systema Juris Hollandici*'). The Supreme Court replied that in view of the differences in opinion between the two courts the proposed course was very difficult; it would be better to form a committee of representatives of both. However, in the end the States relinquished the idea.

Bijnkershoek was much opposed and this seems strange. He had already long before drawn up two voluminous books on the laws of Holland and Zeeland and was as no other acquainted with these laws: he would have been the ideal codificator. Yet, as he later explained, approval would have been very difficult. The members of the States, representatives of the voting towns, had each their own particular law and, so Bijnkershoek, it would be impossible to expect that they would vote for another law substituted for this. He evidently saw what we now would call the cultural significance of law and the attachment of people to it.[1]

Bijnkershoek also tried to use law to influence public opinion and steer it. The Calvinist church tried to dominate public life through its *censura morum*, its supervision over the morality of its members and in general by taking stand in matters of morality. For example, they were opposed to theatre and tried several times to have the Municipal Theatre of Amsterdam closed. When it burned down in 1772, it was hailed as a just punishment of God for so much depravity. Bijnkershoek, though a judge, did not consider it improper to his station in life and society to publish in 1719 an essay on the cult of foreign religions amongst the Romans, with the very contemporary and actual object to prove to the theologians that religious worship had always been regulated and controlled by the public authorities (he expressly states in the beginning that he has those theologians in mind who try to impose their will on public life). Apparently he did not think his independence as judge was restrained by this. Since he was always very careful and keen to have his independence not curtailed or checked by gifts or other circumstances, his stance here is all the more so remarkable.

Strategies in law and justice may be formulated expressly and by governments, and executed by these; but they may as well be formulated implicitly and by the judiciary itself, or its members, and implemented by these in the course of justice. Though the judiciary should beware of its independence, is this sufficient reason not to partake in any debate on legal strategy? The jurisprudence of the Supreme Court in the eighteenth century and the writings of Bijnkershoek show that there is a long line, not so outspoken perhaps but nevertheless persistent and tenaciously retained, of strategies in law and justice to keep this effective and up to

---

[1] Oncko Wicker Star Numan, *Cornelis van Bynkershoek zijn leven en zijne geschriften*, Leiden, 1869, pp. 247–258.

date. It is up to the reader to decide whether we see this line continued to the present day and whether strategies for the future might be wrapped in the same way.

Sources and Further Reading

Bernhard Diestelkamp, *Rechtsfälle aus dem alten Reich. Denkwürdige Prozesse vor dem Reichskammergericht*, Bech, München, 1995.

Boudewijn Sirks, "Bijnkershoek over de 'quade conduites' van Huibert Rosenboom, president van de Hoge Raad (1691–1722). Een bijdrage op grond van tot dusverre onuitgegeven teksten uit de *Observationes tumultuariae* (als bijlage toegevoegd)", in *Tijdschrift voor Rechtsgeschiedenis*, 2008, vol. 76, pp. 49–94.

Boudewijn Sirks, "Cornelis van Bijnkershoek as author and elegant jurist", in *Tijdschrift voor Rechtsgeschiedenis*, 2011, vol. 79, pp. 229–252.

Boudewijn Sirks, "Een insana Doctorum controversia: de reservatoire clausule", in H. Dondrop e.a. (ed.), *Ius Romanum – Ius Commune – Ius hodiernum. Studies in honour of Eltjo J.H. Schrage on the occasion of his 65th birthday*, Scientia, Aalen, 2010, pp. 263–372.

Boudewijn Sirks, "Gütliche Einigung im Holland des 18. Jh.", in Joachim Hengstl, Ullrich Sick (eds.), *Recht gestern und heute: Festschrift zum 85. Geburtstag von Richard Haase*, Harrassowitz Verlag, Wiesbaden, 2006, pp. 145–150.

Boudewijn Sirks, "Het appèl tegen de veedief Verhoef uit het Schieland (1740)", in Chr. Coppens, J. Hallebeek (eds.), *Fabrica Iuris*, Gerard Noodt Instituut, Nijmegen, 2009, pp. 131–144.

Boudewijn Sirks, "Rode Draad Beroemde en Beruchte Rechters 'Een woelende geest': Cornelis van Bijnkershoek", in *Ars Aequi*, 2010, no. 4, pp. 278–282.

Boudewijn Sirks, "The Supreme Court of Holland and Zeeland Judging Cases in the Early 18th Century", in P. Brand, J. Getzler (eds.), *Judges and Judging in the History of the Common and Civil Law: From Antiquity to Modern Times,* Cambridge University Press, 2012, pp. 234–256.

Christian Brom, "Urteilsbegründungen im Hoge Raad van Holland, Zeeland en West-Friesland" am Beispiel des Kaufsrechts im Zeitraum 1704–1787", in *Rechtshistorische Reihe*, vol. 377, Peter Lang, Frankfurt, 2008.

Cornelis van Bynkershoek, Willem Pauw and Boudewijn Sirks, "Index in observationes tumultuarias", in *Werken der Stichting tot Uitgaaf der Bronnen van het Oud-Vaderlandse Recht*, no. 34, Stichting tot Uitgaaf der Bronnen van het Oud-Vaderlandse Recht, The Hague, 2005.

E.M. Meijers, A.S. de Blécourt and H.D.J. Bodenstein, Cornelii van Bijnkershoek Observationes Tumultuariae, I: 1704–1714 (Harlemi [1923–]1926); *id.*, with T.J. Dorhout Mees, F.J.de Jong, B.M. Telders, II: 1714–1724 (Harlemi 1934); E.M. Meijers, A.S. de Blécourt, F.J. de Jong, K.N. Korteweg, G.J. ter Kuile, W.S. van Spengler, B.M. Telders, III: 1724–1735 (Harlemi 1946); E.M. Meijers, H.F.W.D. Fischer, M.S. van Oosten, IV: 1735–1743 (Harlemi 1962) – cited as OT.

Frans Thuijs, *De ware Jaco: Jacob Frederik Muller, alias Jaco (1690-1718), Zijn criminele wereld, zijn berechting en zijn leven na de dood*, Hilversum, 2008.

H.F.W.D. Fischer, W.L. de Koning-Bey, L.E. van Holk, H.W. van Soest, Wilhelmi Pauw Observationes Tumultuariae Novae, I: 1743-1755 (Harlemi 1964); R. Feenstra, W.L.de Koning-Bey, L.E. van Holk, H.W. van Soest, II: 1756-1770 (Harlemi 1967); *id.*, III: 1771-1788 (Harlemi 1971).

J. van Kan and De Hofpractijk, *Indisch Tijdschrift van het Recht: orgaan der Nederlandsch-Indische Juristen-Vereeniging*, 1930, vol. 130, pp. 497–548.

Lambertus van Poelgeest, "Mr. Johan van Bleiswijk en zijn 'Observationes tumultuariae'", in *Tijdschrift voor Rechtsgeschiedenis*, 1987, vol. 55, no. 1–2, Brill, Leiden, pp. 117–122.

Lambertus van Poelgeest, "De raadsheren van de Hoge Raad van Holland, Zeeland en West-Friesland in de achttiende eeuw", in *Bijdragen en Mededelingen betreffende de Geschiedenis der Nederlanden*, 1988, vol. 103, pp. 20–51.

Oncko Wicker Star Numan, *Cornelis van Bynkershoek zijn leven en zijne geschriften*, Leiden, 1869.

1.3.

Legal and Justice Strategies:
The State of the Art

Linn Hammergren[*]

Starting by defining two critical elements of any strategy (a vision or end state and a plan for getting there), this article argues that we have not one, but multiple legal and justice strategies which vary by level of compliance with these requirements, area of emphasis or prioritisation of values, and intended application. A universal strategy is neither possible nor necessary, but we could advance further by recognising and working around our disagreements. It is generally conceded that all societies need mechanisms to resolve disputes, identify and sanction infractions, and strengthen their normative frameworks. However, these functions can be performed in different ways (and for different sets of rules). Rather than fighting over which existing system is better and merits imitation, it would be more productive (especially for development assistance) to review, discuss and compare the variations of form and results so as to help countries select those most appropriate for their individual situations.

1. Introduction

The editors asked me to comment on the following questions, which are thus the topic of this chapter:

- Does a legal and justice strategy exist?
- What does it look like?
- Who executes it? Is there a clear central strategy leader? Is it more amorphous? Is it national, regional or international, and if all of the above, how do all these levels interact?

I begin with some simple answers and will use the bulk of the following to expand on them:

---

[*] **Linn Hammergren** is an independent consultant specialising in rule of law, anti-corruption, and general governance issues.

- A legal and justice strategy does not exist; instead there are multiple strategies.
- What these strategies look like depends on their origins and purpose.
- Execution, to the extent it occurs, is by the authors of or participants in each strategy. Strategies are of varying degrees of concreteness, and are addressed to or operate at various political levels.

I trust that my unwillingness to be more single-minded about the concept will not be received as a sign of obstinacy. In my defence I would note that for the past half-decade I have been commenting on the multiplicity of approaches to rule of law and the difficulties they pose in moving ahead, particularly, for development assistance. Were everyone singing off the same song-sheet, even if not the optimal one, we might have made more progress, but law and justice, rule of law, judicial reform, justice reform (and the multiplicity of names in some sense conveys the problem) seem to mean something slightly or extremely different to everyone who believes they are pursuing them. Not all of this occurs at cross-purposes, as some "strategies" are aimed at only one level – the implantation of an international, regional, or local system, for example – and thus in practice may never meet. However, there are sufficient inconsistencies among them and enough path-crossings to complicate the issue further – for example, the implications of a regional model or mechanism for the local systems it incorporates. My personal position, as I will elaborate toward the end of this chapter, is that the problem is less sheer diversity than a failure to acknowledge its existence. When people recognise they disagree there is more chance of reaching some operational consensus than when they refuse to acknowledge their differences. Unfortunately, the rule of law community seems to have more than its share of true-believers who find it hard to countenance opposing views or even to acknowledge that any sane person might hold them.

2. Question 1: Does a Legal and Justice Strategy Exist?

As I understand a strategy, it should have at least two parts: a vision of where one is heading (the goal, or for some, the model) and a plan for getting there. Many would-be strategies have some sort of vision, albeit often partial, but no particular plan for achieving it. However, there are also plans that seem to lack a clear final goal. Examples of the former might include many human rights-based proposals, whose accompanying "implementation plans" seem to involve only detailing shortcomings in the status quo and insisting that they would be fixed. Examples of plans without much of a vision include what Tom Carothers has called the "reform template". As used by many donors, this standard recipe incorporates a host of things one might do to "improve justice" in the countries where they work, but retains a certain vagueness as regards the final product (except as the results of a myriad of discrete actions; what I once called 45 activities in search of a purpose). However, whether there are more visions without plans or plans without visions, the larger issue is the sheer multiplicity of both.

This was less evident two or three decades ago, either in the developed or developing world, if only because the reform discourse was dominated by the former, and the former's members believed they were all in agreement. At present, the level of consensus as to where we should head or are heading is far less obvious, and there are clear, growing signs that not everyone shares the same premises. Most would doubtless agree on the need for a dispute-resolution, norm-enforcement system as a basic function of good governance. The contents of that system are far less clear. The "universal human rights standards", the basis for some visions, are increasingly contested, and even presumably homogenous communities (whether single nations or regional groupings) now dispute aspects of their content (the normative and structural details as opposed to the functions). Many strategies are also partial, focusing on more limited functions and rules. Examples include the resolution of civil and commercial disputes, via the Doing Business and other economically driven approaches, or the treatment of criminal matters, as in Latin America's efforts to introduce more "adversarial" proceedings.

In a book published in 2007, I spoke of five approaches to "justice reform", as defined by their area of focus: criminal justice, modernisation or efficiency, professionalism or quality, improved access, and constitutionalism. To this list I would now add human rights, which despite its lack of a real strategy certainly enters the equation, and possibly several more recent restatements of the initial five. These are just the variations in focus, and one could add to them the strategies' target level(s) – international, regional, or purely national systems– and the often radically different values and legal traditions informing each strategic iteration. While presumably both the partial approaches and the strategic levels could be condensed into a single universal strategy to be applied to all nations or eventually leading to one international system, most reform efforts do not attempt this. They instead pick their substantive emphasis, level, and intended range of application, and then of course incorporate the differing value preferences of their individual authors. Moreover, the condensation would be extremely difficult because it would require prioritisation of content (which values trump others?) and levels (does one try for national or regional change only, first, or immediately leap to an international movement?) I am assuming that by international or regional, the editors are referring to a model's application, not to the creation of these supranational systems, but possibly I guessed wrong.

3.   Question 2: What Does the Strategy Look Like?

I am torn between describing the non-existent, ideal strategy or the variety of strategies or quasi-strategies actually in existence. So as not to repeat elements of the prior section, and because I am a social (political) scientist, not a legal advocate, by training and practice, I am choosing a modified version of the first option – what it should look like. However, this has to be done by steps: overall characteristics of a good strategy; general content of the same; and its feasible degree of universality. On the first point, my ideal strategy would have the following characteristics:

- A vision of the end state based on functions or outcomes, not on structures, on the assumption that there are still many roads to Rome, even in the law and justice area.
- A recommended path for getting there, or most likely a series of alternative paths based on the starting point of the (probably national) system. However, for those looking toward a regional or world justice model or even system, alternative paths should also be included.
- While the vision or end state may be an as yet unrecognised ideal, the path should be based on some sort of empirical evidence that it will work. The untried can never be dismissed as impossible, but one should be cautious about basing an implementation plan on sheer wishful thinking or extrapolating from one successful case to the universe.
- Consideration of the degree of pre-existing consensus on the vision and visionary aspects (value elements) of the plan among those who

will be affected by it. Where the consensus is minimal, the plan should also include a process for enlarging its base.

- Recognition that the strategy is open-ended as regards its ultimate aim. Reform or improvement is not a one-time undertaking, but rather an on-going process. It advances by increments or plateaus, but continues once each plateau is reached.

I have some problems regarding content and what is meant by a "legal and justice strategy" inasmuch as the legal portion can be separated, as it is in the thick versus thin rule of law models. My description of an ideal strategy is consistent with both; however, I am more inclined toward a thin model, one that emphasises general functions (for example, dispute resolution) over specific content and structure (including substantive, procedural, and organisational rules). I have my own preferences as to what a normative framework (the law part) would look like, but see this as a second, far more controversial aspect of any legal and justice strategy.

This leads to the third consideration, how the strategy should or could be accommodated to specific contexts. There actually is a strategic choice here – between focusing on the basic functions but not the rules guiding them (thin rule of law model), or instilling the rules first (thick rule of law in its several variations). Here the political scientist prevails, but I admit that the wisdom of 'focusing on function before content' is a hypothesis subject to further testing. If content wins in that contest, then content should go first.

4. Question 3: Who Executes the Strategy? Is There a Clear Central Leader? Is it More Amorphous? Is it National, Regional or International, and if All of the Above, How Do these Levels Interact?

First off, strategies are not the strength of justice systems and the actors within them; a typical judicial development plan can often be described as 'get more money and spend it'. It is only recently that a minority of judiciaries and other sector agencies, largely in developed countries, has begun adopting two very important strategic tools – performance statistics and a definition of results or outcomes – as a means of justifying their budgetary requests, but more importantly, of providing citizens with the services they need and desire most. Most of the judiciaries with which I work (in developing countries) have not progressed that far, and thus remain at the get-it-and-spend-it level. Even when they wish to improve performance, they have little means of devising feasible plans.

Second, some international agencies, and especially the United Nations, have elaborated a series of documents, which they may consider strategic. In reality, these are more accurately described as standards, principles or preferences, rather than empirically based plans for advancing them. In short, if the UN or other international or regional bodies propose to lead the effort, they may be leaving their followers at a loss as to what to do next. One exception may be the EU, but only as regards its actual or would-be members, with the latter having to adopt and try to implement the standards if they wish to join – a goal that some candidates may now be questioning. None of these would-be leaders are currently attempting, and possibly not in a position to, execute anything so execution of their strategies is left to other actors: their own donor agencies, other donors, or the countries themselves. Moreover, as suggested above, it is decreasingly evident that the standard-setters' putative followers are in sync even with the principles set forth. Within the core EU nations, the potential for a single set of standards as the basis for a universal rule of law system may look far more likely than it does from outside.

Not surprisingly, those who execute strategies are those who finance this process – donors or individual countries. These executors may take some recommendations from the others but in the end, what gets implemented is what the implementers are willing to fund – because execution does cost something, often a great deal. The more interesting question, and one not asked by the editors is who *should* devise strategies and on what basis they should do so. Again we have an issue – whether "should" is to be taken as an issue of rights (who has the right to devise a strategy for a nation, a region, the world?) or one of practicality (which author or process is most likely to produce results?). Again, I vote for practicality as rights rarely trump it. In any event, trying to determine who has the right to decide on an international, regional or local strategy is no longer that obvious. Is it the government, the people, the experts or someone else? Logically, the government must be in agreement, but a more implementable plan arguably requires some measure of input from all the others as well.

5.   Where Do We Go from Here?

In my reading of documents by EU authors, I am often struck by what seems to be on the one hand, an unrealistic level of optimism regarding the potential for establishing universal models and standards, and on the other, a relative lack of appreciation for the very different situations in the majority of the world's countries. I say this fully realising the risks of doing so before a European audience, but believe it needs voicing. This EU optimism may be based on its experience with Eastern European countries pursuing accession, but much like the US during our epoch of what critical participants call "legal imperialism", the Europeans may be extrapolating from a situation, which is not only temporally (the US problem), but also regionally limited. At least until recently, Eastern Europe accepted the EU model, in justice as well as in other areas. However, this consensus never extended to common law nations or much of the rest of the developing world. Today, there are a variety of other influences: what Peerenboom and others term the "Asian rule of law model", the resurgence of local traditions and customary justice, and of course Islamic law. Proponents of these alternatives probably would accept the functional requisites of a good rule of law system – a transparent set or sets of norms governing private and public behaviour, widespread access to dispute resolution systems based on this normative framework (although with ample room for legal pluralism), a means to identify and sanction norm violators, and the consequent strengthening of the rules (plural or otherwise). The differences lie primarily in the content of the normative framework and the question (where pluralism exists) as to whom it should govern, and secondarily, in some aspects of the accepted or acceptable procedures and organisational structures.

Although reaching agreement on a single model and strategy is appealing, it may be neither necessary nor advisable at present. As regards necessity, there are clearly different ways of performing the same basic functions and little reason for forcing everyone into the same mould. This fundamental lesson has seemingly been learned and *forgotten* repeatedly over the past three decades of donor assistance, starting with the legal imperialism critique. Advisability hinges on two considerations. First, different contextual settings and institutional capacities make it difficult to apply uniform solutions, but second, and more importantly, since there is still considerable room for improvement in virtually every real system, it seems premature to adopt one of them as the ideal. Even systems generally deemed to function well have traditional elements which at best are unnecessary and at worst reduce their efficiency, efficacy and accessibility.

Aside from recognising and accepting differences of opinion on what works best or what should be (my initial point), what is really needed now is better documentation and discussion of the alternatives of detail. For example, every legal and justice system requires appointment and governance mechanisms, but rather than promoting one model for each (with the usual dose of institutional nationalism), those seeking to help countries develop their own strategies could more usefully lay out the options and the risks and advantages of each. Thus, instead of going to country X to help it adopt the land titling system or commercial code of country Y or Z, expert advisors would define the problem as introducing a system for establishing property ownership, or regulating commercial transactions and disputes, present a variety of alternatives, and help local counterparts design and adopt something that will work for them. Doing so requires a different type of advisor, not one who knows his/her own system extremely well, but rather one who understands the range of options. It also requires the ability to look beyond the specific task (land titling, an appointment system, rules for processing criminal cases) to see how it fits into the larger system and strategy for each country.

Coming from a federally organised country, and having worked in several others, I may be less adverse to diversity than those without this background. Moreover, in a world of imperfect legal and justice systems, diversity has an important advantage. It allows people to experiment with potentially better methods, while leaving room for different preferences as to values and rules. There are some universals of course, starting with the insistence that a strategy have a vision and a plan and extending to the need for greater cross-system consistency in an increasingly interconnected world. Where one draws the line is subject to debate, but promoting reasoned debate is part of the challenge.

Finally, and returning to my five-point characterisation of a good (that is, workable) strategy, a part of this debate might usefully focus on ensuring that candidate strategies meet these criteria, and where they do not, pushing them to do so. It is relatively easy to propose a list of reforms, goals or even activities. However, 'proto-strategies' that do not connect the means-end dots, drawing so far as possible on empirical evidence, are little more than pipedreams. Unlike the debate over values and standards, this part can be conducted more objectively and subjected to the usual scientific, as opposed to legal rules for the use of evidence. Here evidence is used to test and not to prove a hypothesis, fully recognising that the null hypothesis (it does not work) might prevail. "Doesn't work" by no means signifies that an objective is not worth pursuing, but only that we still lack a reasonably reliable plan for its achievement. Where evidence is absent or partial (seems to have worked in one or two countries) experimentation is certainly allowable, but experimental strategies should be presented to adopters in just that light rather than as the time-tested methods they clearly are not. No one can blame the idealist for wanting to forge ahead, but even idealists must recognise the central rule of all assistance – first do no harm – and their potential for violating it in a burst of enthusiasm for what they would like to achieve.

The debates on values (the ultimate objectives) are equally necessary and may indeed be what Hague Institute for the Internationalisation of Law (HiiL) editors meant when they asked about "good" strategies. At the highest level (what is the good system?) I have no easy answers for how to resolve them, but they might be helped along by separating the strategic ends (whether defined as impartial, fair judgments, a reduction in crime levels and violence, or more distant goals like poverty reduction) from the means (laws, structures, practices) believed to advance them and the intermediate goals (like judicial independence) from the societal projects (a more "just" society) to which they are theoretically linked. Doing so will not eliminate the ultimate question – what is a just society? – but it again might allow for a more reasoned discussion on both what it is and what part justice systems and reforms play in how it is achieved.

6. Sources and Further Reading

James Gardner, *Legal Imperialism: American Lawyers and Foreign AID in Latin America*, University of Wisconsin Press, Madison, 1980.

Linn Hammergren, *Envisioning Reform: Improving Judicial Performance in Latin America*, Pennsylvania State University Press, 2007.

Randolph Peerenboom, "Human Rights and Rule of Law: What's the Relationship?", in *Georgetown Journal of International Law,* 2005, vol. 36, no. 3, pp. 809–945.

Thomas Carothers, *Promoting Rule of Law Abroad: The Problem of Knowledge,* Carnegie Endowment for International Peace, Working Paper, 2003.

World Bank, *Doing Business in 2005: Removing Obstacles to Growth,* The World Bank, International Finance Corporation and Oxford University Press, Washington D.C. and Oxford, 2005.

1.4.

Towards a Strategy of Producing and Using Research Evidence: The Role of Empirical Research for Laws, Policies and Programmes of the Netherlands' Security and Justice Ministry

Frans L. Leeuw[*]

Starting with the fact of life that law in action is not equal to law in the books, this paper describes the strategy of the Netherlands' Ministry of Security and Justice to safeguard the production of research, knowledge and evidence needed to understand the complex relationship between the Ministry, its legal strategy and society. Several key organisations and organisational arrangements are discussed. Also, the ways in which the research and evidence produced is transferred to policy makers and other key actors of the diverse organisations of and related to the Ministry are discussed. The conclusion is that a legal strategy and this 'companion strategy' have to go hand in hand for justice ministries in order to reduce the likelihood of (increasing) gaps between law in the books and law in action.

1. Introduction

One of the findings of social and behavioural research regarding laws, regulations and other legal arrangements is the difference between 'law in action' and 'law in the books' (in other words, black letter law). Legal arrangements can be found in treaties, regulations, contracts and in other documents; they try to influence the behaviour of natural and corporate actors, or at least function as 'frameworks' or 'regulatory regimes' for this behaviour. Farnsworth articulated diverse (behavioural) mechanisms that

---

[*] **Frans Leeuw** is Professor of Law in Public Policy and Social Science Research at the University of Maastricht. He is also the Director of WODC, the Research, Evaluation, Statistics and Knowledge Management Institute of the Dutch Ministry of Security and Justice.

are believed to make the 'law in the books' work in reality.[1] To what extent that is happening and to what extent there are unintended side effects, is covered by social and behavioural research. Then the topic is no longer 'black letter law', but 'law in action'.

Differences between the 'black letter' and 'social reality' can be substantial. A classic example can be found in Aubert's survey designed to "establish the extent to which the behaviour of housemaids in Norway conformed to the rules laid down in the 'Law on Housemaids of 1948'".[2] It appeared that there was a huge discrepancy. A more recent example is a systematic review and synthesis of the results of over 50 impact evaluations of Dutch laws spanning the period from 1995 to 2007. It was largely desk research. Klein Haarhuis and Niemeijer not only show that the impact on addressees of laws is often rather restricted, but they also present an explanation, based on an analysis of the behavioural, social and institutional mechanisms that are believed to make laws 'work', but apparently not always do so.[3]

The consequence of the existence of these and many other discrepancies is that organisations active in the world of Justice often are in need of not only a *legal strategy* addressing *which* substantive laws, regulations, enforcement policies and other approaches have to be developed and implemented, but also of a *'companion strategy'* addressing these challenges:

- what are the differences between 'black letter laws' and 'social reality';
- what are the causes of these differences; and
- what can be done to balance them in order to warrant legal arrangements doing what they are expected to do?

2. The Companion Strategy

This paper focuses on this strategy. It has two strands.

---

[1] Ward Farnsworth, *The Legal Analyst: A Toolkit for Thinking about the Law*, University of Chicago Press, 2007.

[2] Vilhelm Aubert, "Some Social Functions of Legislation", in Vilhelm Aubert (ed.), *Sociology of Law*, Penguin Books, Baltimore, 1969.

[3] Carolien Klein Haarhuis and Bert Niemeijer, *Wet en Werkelijkheid*, Boom Legal Publishers, Den Haag, 2008.

The first strand has to do with the *production of knowledge and empirical evidence* on how regulations, sanctions, other legal interventions as well as behaviour modification programmes are implemented in society and how the findings can be explained. Here the role of legal evaluations is discussed, the different types of evaluations (*ex-ante*, process and *ex-post*), the role of data warehouses and data spaces to track and trace key performance indicators of the Ministry and its agencies and the evidence used when forecasts and scenarios are developed. This strand also includes research on how disputes are settled in the Netherlands, which role laws, regulations and courts play in this respect and what is to be said about their efficiency. This strand is oriented towards the production of research, knowledge and evidence.

The second strand focuses on how to safeguard that key policy actors in the diverse organisations of and related to the Netherlands' Security and Justice Ministry and justice ministries in general, are informed about this evidence and are stimulated to use the evidence to reduce the gap between the 'law in the book' and 'the law in action'. This strand is oriented towards knowledge transfer and utilisation and addresses questions like what the best mechanisms are to reach policy makers in time, to prevent them from being confronted with information overload or with answers to questions that they never asked, instead of getting answers to questions they had asked.

3. Content and Characteristics of Strand 1 of the 'Companion Strategy': Producing Research, Knowledge and Evidence

By describing several organisations and organisational arrangements within and related to the Netherlands Security and Justice Ministry primarily active in this strand, the content and characteristics of this first strand will be illustrated.

3.1. WODC: The In-House, Semi-Independent Research Organisation

This organisation[4] was established in the early part of the 1970's and has as its central tasks to carry out and to commission empirical "law in ac-

---

[4] "Wetenschappelijk Onderzoek – en Documentatiecentrum", available at http://www.wodc.nl, last accessed on 11 September 2012.

tion" related studies and evaluations, commission studies to outside organisations like universities, guarantee their scientific quality, take care of the production, systematisation and processing of judiciary statistics and develop forecasts. Longitudinal data on core aspects of the Ministry are readily available such as the 'Reoffender monitor', the 'Organised Crime monitor', the 'monitor of Paths to Justice/Landscape of disputes', including litigation and conflict regulation and many others. A number of other western ministries of justice have similar organisations, for example States such as Sweden, USA, Canada, Australia, Germany and the UK. Part of the research agenda comprises of studies analysing developments in society like cybercrime, fraud, corruption and counter terrorism, while another part of the agenda concerns *ex ante, process and impact evaluations* of sanctions and interventions produced and imposed by the Ministry and the Public Prosecutor and others.

Ex ante evaluations is the *first* type of work. They focus on the validity of the underlying 'legal-behavioural theory' of sanctions and interventions, by articulating the mechanisms believed to make the sanctions and interventions successful after implementation in the real world. Farnsworth gives examples of this work.[5] He unravels legal decisions in terms of behavioural mechanisms that are in part responsible for their 'ineffectiveness'. The book describes mechanisms such as the slippery slope mechanism, cognitive biases and the role of incentives. This type of evaluation is also known as 'theory-based evaluations'.[6]

A *second type of work* that evaluators are doing is to find out to what extent policies, programmes, regulations and other types of measures have been implemented as agreed. This type of work is usually called 'process evaluations'. In this case, evaluators investigate the execution of court orders, including sanctions, behaviour modification programmes and financial penalties. The central question is the following: are the policies and laws and other legal arrangements executed as intended, respectively as was formally agreed upon?

A *third type of work* which evaluators carry out is to find out to what extent the goals of a policy, intervention, law, subsidy, levy and oth-

---

[5] Farnsworth, 2007, see *supra* note 1.
[6] Frans L. Leeuw, "Reconstructing Program Theories: Methods Available and Problems to Be Solved", in *American Journal of Evaluation*, 2003, vol. 24, no. 1, pp. 5–20.

er 'tools' have been attained and to what extent this has been caused by the intervention under investigation. This type of work is called impact evaluations or effectiveness evaluations.

By synthesising the results from these studies and from those done in relevant other countries, WODC makes use of different transfer mechanisms, one of them now under construction, being an evidence repository 'portal' is dedicated to allow for a swift, fast and up to date instrument to be used by policy makers when they think about new interventions by prosecutors when formulating the indictment and by judges when they pronounce sentence.

3.2. NFI: The Netherlands Forensics Institute

The NFI[7] provides services to clients within the criminal justice chain, such as the Public Prosecution Service and the police. A lawyer in a criminal case may also ask the examining magistrate or the public prosecutor handling the case to have the NFI conduct an examination. In addition, NFI provides services to other persons or authorities, such as the International Criminal Tribunal for the former Yugoslavia, the Immigration and Naturalisation Service, foreign police or justice authorities, or to special investigative services.

NFI uses state-of-the-art technology and science to provide high-quality forensic services. The results of the scientific examinations conducted by the NFI may be part of the evidence used in a court case or aid in tracking down suspects. To this end, the experts examine a wide variety of traces, such as flakes of skin, bullets or fibres. The courts regularly call on NFI experts to explain their reports during legal proceedings. The NFI provides a full range of services: from advising on the securing of evidence and examination of evidence at complex crime scenes, to serving as an expert-witness in court.

3.3. An In-House Central Strategic Unit

Part of the strategy on evidence-based policy making in the Netherlands' Ministry for Security and Justice has been the establishment of a central strategic unit. This group has as its core task to think about strategies, cre-

---

[7] Netherlands Forensics Institute, available at http://www.forensicinstitute.nl, last accessed on 1 October 2012.

ate collaborations between the numerous actors in the Justice and Security chains on strategic developments, develop scenarios and organise conferences and symposia.

3.4. Hybrid High-Level Committees Preparing Major Changes in Legal Codes (Like the Penal and the Civil Code)

The Ministry has a long tradition of working with senior professors of Law Faculties that chair or are members of high-level committees when serious and sometimes even paradigmatic changes in legal codes and regulation nationally and internationally are on the agenda. This tradition goes back many decades, if not centuries.

3.5. The Accreditation Committee on Behaviour Modification Interventions

Given the large number of penal sanctions and interventions focused on influencing criminal behaviour, less than a decade ago, an Accreditation Committee was established with the task to sort out which of the then over one hundred intervention programmes warrant the continuation of subsidies or other financial support by the Ministry. Professors in psychology, sociology, penology, bio-psychiatry and methodology are members of this Committee. When an existing or new intervention has passed the first 'stage' of accreditation, the empirical impact evaluation is transferred to WODC, the research organisation of the Ministry.

3.6. The Research and Development Council

Recently, the Ministry has established as one of the main goals of the Research and Development Council the objective of addressing 'grand societal challenges'. The task of this Council which has as members, amongst others, the Director of the Netherlands Forensics Institute, the Director of WODC, the Programme Director of Innovation of one of the Directorates-General and the Director of the central strategic unit, is to formulate these challenges, and to suggest ways as to how to address them.

The very existence of these organisations[8] usually provides for a timely production of relevant evidence to the Justice Ministry. Sometimes

---

[8] Space restrictions prevent describing other organisational arrangements, such as the Netherlands Register of Court Experts.

the evidence is critical, for example when the results of evaluations have become available, showing that things have not worked out as expected and as hoped for. Sometimes the evidence leads to new questions and challenges and sometimes the evidence is largely only there to monitor if an organisation is still 'on track'.

3.7. Content and Characteristics of Strand 2 of the 'Companion Strategy': Towards Knowledge Transfer and Utilisation of Knowledge and Evidence

The production of books and reports alone as a method is definitely no longer able to reach policy makers and other officials, let alone society at large. Other arrangements therefore have to be part and parcel of the transfer and utilisation strategy. One of these arrangements is the *co-creation* of research questions studied by WODC. Co-creation means that the development of the annual research agenda of this organisation is – for a large number of projects – done in collaboration between researchers, civil servants, top management of the Ministry and other actors. They jointly discuss which questions have to be addressed by the institute. The more research topics are considered relevant by the addressees and the requestors, the smaller the likelihood of *l'art pour l'art* research and the larger the likelihood of utilisation of the findings.

However, to prevent the occurrence of a 'sympathy bias' (meaning that only those topics are selected for research that are believed to have positive results), WODC also carries out infrastructural investigations. This part of the research agenda is dedicated to projects, usually of a longitudinal nature such as the 'reoffender monitor', the 'organised crime monitor', the 'path to justice-survey', the 'youth crime monitor' and several other statistical and outcome-oriented oversight reports published (bi-)annually. These studies are carried out regardless of the wishes of policy makers, partly because they go far beyond the usual time horizon of a political appointee. The same is true with regard to programme evaluations; they are often done every five years because of regulations of the Finance Ministry,[9] because Parliament requests them or because the National Au-

---

[9] The "Regeling prestatiegegevens en evaluatieonderzoek rijksoverheid" is a regulation coming from the Dutch Finance Ministry to ensure that occasionally (often every five years) policy programs are evaluated.

dit Office urges the Ministry to ask WODC to carry out an independent evaluation.

A driving force of these and other activities is to stimulate justice ministries to use research results instead of archiving or forgetting them or, worse, file-drawing the reports. Nevertheless, even when research organisations invest in 'translational' activities, utilisation is not guaranteed. Reasons can be that political time is not equal to research time, a study is published way too late to play a role in a crucial political debate, there is a mismatch between expectations and the results of a study or there are doubts about the methodological quality of the study, to list only three explanations from the literature on utilisation of research. An example of a study that attracted serious interests inside the world of justice but did not lead to any response from society at large, was the benchmark of the performance of all forty prisons in the Netherlands. Although the findings could easily have triggered serious debates inside and outside Parliament, with civic society groups and others, nothing of that kind happened. Despite efforts to get translational activities going, sometimes it is still a matter of luck if a study is becoming part of a larger agenda.

Other arrangements to stimulate transfer and utilisation are sessions in which researchers take policy makers more or less by the hand to discuss and show the relevance of their findings in a meet and greet session. The interplay between researchers and civil servants also helps to solve problems of interpretation and the scope of the findings as well as how to explain them. The utilisation of findings from studies using complex methodological and statistical machinery is enhanced by these translational activities. A recent example had to do with the interpretation of the results of a quasi-experimental evaluation of the impact of the "ISD intervention" focused on chronic reoffenders, incapacitated for at the least two years and confronted with several behavioural intervention programmes. As the design of the impact evaluation was quite complicated,[10] and therefore hard to understand, not only a technical document and a reader-friendly fact sheet was produced, but also several 'mini-seminars' and a round table lunch was organised to ensure that to some extent counter-

---

[10] A quasi-experimental design type propensity score matching including next to treatment group, two control groups (a historical and a simultaneous one). See Nikolaj Tollenaar and André van der Laan, *Memorandum 2012-2 Effecten van de ISD-Maatregel. Technisch Rapport*, WODC, 2012.

intuitive results (incapacitation indeed works) were trickled down into the rank and file of the Justice Ministry including its prison agency.

One of the more recent developments is the 'evidence library', a digital repository summarising the results of hundreds of high quality evaluations of the impact of penal code interventions and sanctions on reoffending behaviour. Part of this library contains the results of a meta-analysis of all one-hundred and forty empirical investigations of the impact of Dutch penal sanctions on reoffending behaviour that were published since the 1960's in the Netherlands. However, this will only be a part of the repository; more than one hundred other international meta-studies/ systematic reviews of the impact of penal sanctions published in English will also be part of it.

Another knowledge transfer process that the Ministry has used several times are the so-called 'knowledge rooms'. These are meetings in which the top management of the Ministry, including the Minister and the Secretary of State for Justice meet with research professors in diverse fields like brain and cognition, genetics and social neurosciences, but also robotics and international law to discuss and share viewpoints and future possibilities and limitations of developments for the Ministry. The meetings are chaired by the Secretary-General of the Ministry and usually start by the end of the afternoon and continue till approximately 22.00. There is a working atmosphere without fine dinners, only Dutch *broodjes* are offered as well as one glass of wine at the end of the 'knowledge room'. The central strategic unit usually organises these sessions.

4. Conclusions and Discussion

The Netherlands' Security and Justice Ministry has as its mission and vision the rule of law in the Netherlands, that people can live in freedom, regardless of their lifestyle or beliefs. The Ministry works to a safer and fairer society and has as an important adage that 'law touches people'. Compliance with this mission makes it necessary to be knowledgeable about what laws do to people and organisations. Therefore, the Ministry not only has as a priority a legal strategy but also a companion strategy, addressing the production, transfer and use of scientific evidence on what law does to people and what people do to laws, including criminals and criminals-to-come. Having only either one of them would simply not do.

This brings me to the final question: if and to what extent the ministries of security and justice in general have to be engaged in both strategies in today's world? I strongly believe that the answer is yes. Security and justice policies are often complicated in their designs and impacts, ensuring that exclusively traditional legal knowledge strategies characterised by "ready, fire, go" will be suboptimal for delivering justice in a timely and socially relevant manner. As Smits has argued, the state monopoly in setting the law is rapidly being replaced by a multitude of new law-makers that do not only include European and supranational institutions, but also private organisations.[11] This implies that Security and Justice Ministries need a thorough *understanding* of what is going on in the interplay between regulation by traditional nation states, private regulators, supranational organisations and civilians and corporations. Trying to have this knowledge available cannot be done without a 'companion strategy' as was articulated in this think piece. A third and final reflection is that the justice worlds are getting more and more inter-, if not transdisciplinary. Who would have thought that evidence produced by such diverse scientific fields as socio-neuroscience and behavioural genetics, highly relevant for improving the responsiveness and impact of behavioural interventions directed at – amongst others – chronic offenders,[12] statistics and information sciences, how to use big data and data spaces to track and trace while simultaneously preserving privacy[13] and evolutionary law and economics to understand the development of private law 2.0 and related governance issues,[14] would so rapidly enter the world of justice?

This being the case, it now makes it highly relevant for justice ministries to be *au courant* and able to intervene.

---

[11] Jan Smits, *Private Law 2.0: On The Role of Private Actors in a Post-National Society*, Inaugural lecture delivered by Maastricht-HiiL Chair on the Internationalisation of Law, 2010.

[12] Tracy Gunter et al., "Behavioral Genetics in Antisocial Spectrum Disorders and Psychopathy: A Review of the Recent Literature", in *Behavioral Sciences and the Law*, 2010, vol. 28, pp. 148–173.

[13] Sunil Choenni and Jan van Dijk, "Towards Privacy-Preserving Data Reconciliation for Criminal Justice Chains", in *10th Annual International Conference on Digital Government Research*, ACM Press Puebla, Mexico, 2009, pp. 223–229.

[14] Peer Zumbansen and Gralf-Peter Calliess (eds.), *Law, Economics and Evolutionary Theory*, Edward Elgar, Cheltenham, 2011.

5. Sources and Further Reading

Carolien Klein Haarhuis and Bert Niemeijer, *Wet en Werkelijkheid*, Boom Legal Publishers, Den Haag, 2008.

Frans L. Leeuw, "Reconstructing Program Theories: Methods Available and Problems to Be Solved", in *American Journal of Evaluation*, 2003, vol. 24, no. 1, pp. 5–20.

Jan Smits, *Private Law 2.0: On The Role of Private Actors in a Post-National Society*, Inaugural lecture delivered by Maastricht-HiiL Chair on the Internationalisation of Law, 2010.

Nikolaj Tollenaar and André van der Laan, *Memorandum 2012-2 Effecten van de ISD-maatregel. Technisch rapport*, WODC, 2012.

Peer Zumbansen and Gralf-Peter Calliess (eds.), *Law, Economics and Evolutionary Theory*, Edward Elgar, Cheltenham, 2011.

Sunil Choenni and Jan van Dijk, "Towards Privacy-Preserving Data Reconciliation for Criminal Justice Chains", in *10th Annual International Conference on Digital Government Research*, ACM Press Puebla, Mexico, 2009, pp. 223–229.

Tracy Gunter *et al.*, "Behavioral Genetics in Antisocial Spectrum Disorders and Psychopathy: A Review of the Recent Literature", in *Behavioral Sciences and the Law*, 2010, vol. 28, pp. 148–173.

Vilhelm Aubert, "Some Social Functions of Legislation", in Vilhelm Aubert (ed.), in *Sociology of Law*, Penguin Books, Baltimore, 1969, p. 121.

Ward Farnsworth, *The Legal Analyst: A Toolkit for Thinking about the Law*, University of Chicago Press, 2007.

1.5.

Legal and Justice Strategies:
A Practitioner's Political Perspective[*]

Lousewies van der Laan[**]

This think piece aims to provide greater insight into the strategies of political decision-making. It first explains why notions of legal and justice strategies are, by definition, deeply political, and the implications of that assertion. It then goes on to examine the role of strategies in political decision-making, including how these are influenced by a politician's worldview and by electoral considerations. Finally, the author discusses the lack of media and popular scrutiny at certain legislative levels, such as EU and international legislation, and the impact that this might have.

1. Introduction

Notions of legal and justice strategies have two roots: the law and an idea of what constitutes justice. Laws are adopted and amended by politicians – democratically elected and accountable or otherwise. Notions of what constitutes justice are political as well: one person's freedom fighters are another person's terrorists. Any insights into legal and justice strategies that are, implicitly or explicitly, executed by countries, international organisations, corporations or civil society organisations therefore include a political component. Anyone developing a legal or justice strategy or seeking to change or implement one must be familiar with the political forces at play in order to be effective. Lawyers, judges, lobbyists, media and other parts of society obviously influence politicians, as does public opinion. But the final adoption of laws, as the codification of legal and justice strategies, is the responsibility of politicians. Using my experience as a law-maker, politician and international diplomat, I would like to

---

[*] This article has greatly benefited from valuable discussion and research by Margreet Luth, DPhil in Law at the University of Oxford.

[**] **Lousewies van der Laan** is Vice-President of the European Liberal Democrats and independent advisor on human rights, democracy and the rule of law.

bring a practitioner's perspective to this volume on legal and justice strategies.

What are justice and legal strategies? A justice strategy can be seen as encompassing policy areas far beyond the criminal law; I will define it as any strategy aimed at the creation of a just and fair society. Legislation is a tool to get closer to that goal, which means that a legislative strategy comes into play.[1] These justice and legislative strategies can focus on justice in a narrow sense, aiming to adapt judicial process and crime policy, for example. They can also encompass other policy areas, aimed, for example, at economic and social justice, including education and healthcare. In this article, 'justice strategy' is mainly used in the broad sense of a just and fair society, which of course includes a just and fair legal system. In addition, just and fair societies need effective institutions to support this legal system. For a functioning market economy, for example, efficient tax collectors and a strong competition authority are as important as the letter of the law.

Recent upheavals in North Africa have shown that even in autocratic societies people have strong notions of what is just. The Arab Spring was triggered by the public outrage following the self-immolation of a fruit-seller worn down by corruption. As countries that have known decades of oppression and arbitrary application of justice have to reinvent themselves, justice strategies are a top priority on their list. And the widespread awareness of this need for justice means that no party has a chance of having its candidates elected unless there is a clear vision and articulation of a more just, law- or rule-based society.

Refining justice strategies aimed at building just institutions and societies is work that is never completed. Justice and her sister, democracy, are gardens that need constant tending. Weeds spring up the moment your back is turned and trees that have bloomed for years can fail to bear fruit unexpectedly. At the same time an overly manicured lawn allows little room for exotic flowers to blossom and weed-killing pesticides can do more damage than expected. What grows in my garden may well wither in my neighbour's. I hope this volume will keep all gardeners vigilant.

---

[1] For this reason, I will use the term 'legislative strategy' rather than 'legal strategy'.

2. Vision, Values and Mission as Building Blocks of Political Strategy

In analysing the political aspects of justice strategies,[2] I choose to focus on politicians,[3] but obviously other political actors – including lobbyists, voters and media for example – play a key role in shaping political strategies.[4] I will first explain the building blocks of a political strategy, which will allow me to expand on the dynamics surrounding politics.

Borrowing freely from a business approach to strategic planning, one might distinguish three common ingredients to building a strategy: vision, values, and mission. A politician's vision and values tend to be inspired by his or her worldview, which can be deeply personal. While this is not the place to investigate the real motivation of politicians properly,[5] American cognitive linguist George P. Lakoff has developed an interest-

---

[2] Since legislative strategies follow from justice strategies, I will refer only to the latter throughout most of this article.

[3] In most countries politicians belong to political parties, regardless of whether these are real ideologically based groups with regular changes of leadership or temporary vehicles for individual ambition or greed. The relationship between politicians and their parties merits several volumes of research, so I will use the terms interchangeably here, working on the assumption that politicians both aim to implement their party's electoral platform and also have a role in shaping it. For further reading see Peter Mair, *Party System Change: Approaches And Interpretations*, Oxford University Press, Oxford, 1998; Edward R. Tufte, "The Relationship between Seats and Votes in Two-Party Systems", in *The American Political Science Review*, 1973, vol. 67, no. 2, pp. 540–554. Furthermore, the decline in membership of political parties places a larger importance on personal responsibility.

[4] See for example, Jan Potters, Randolph Sloof and Frans van Winden, "Campaign expenditures, contributions and direct endorsements: The strategic use of information and money to influence voter Behavior", in *European Journal of Political Economy*, 1997, vol. 13, no. 1, pp. 1–31; Dick Morris, *Vote.com: How Big-money Lobbyists and the Media Are Losing Their Influence, and the Internet Is Giving Power Back to the People,* Renaissance Books, 2000; Victoria Nourse and Jane S. Schacter, "The Politics of Legislative Drafting: A Congressional Case Study". in *New York University Law Review*, 2002, vol. 77, p. 575; University of Wisconsin Legal Studies Research Paper Series Archival Collection, available at SSRN http://ssrn.com/abstract=1527 043, last accessed on 20 August 2012.

[5] For further reading see Joseph N. Cappella and Kathleen Hall Jamieson, "News Frames, Political Cynicism, and Media Cynicism", in *Annals of the American Academy of Political and Social Science*, 1996, vol. 546, pp. 71–84; but also David Owen, *In Sickness and in Power. Illness in Heads of Government During the Last 100 Years,* Methuen Publishing, 2008.

ing analogy which will illustrate this point. Lakoff[6] contrasts a strict father model with the nurturing parent model. Using the metaphor of nation as family and government as parent Lakoff argues that conservative politics correspond to the strict father model and progressives are more like nurturing parents. For example, conservatives will be critical of relying too much on the government for assistance, since this might create dependency. Loosely speaking nurturers trust people and believe that empowering them will build effective, cohesive societies, whereas the strict father adherents will want to provide stronger guidance as to the choices that people should be making. It goes without saying that a politician's view of the world and the people in it says much more about the politician him- or herself than the world and the voters that he or she claims to represent.

The relationship between one's worldview (which may be largely passed on from one's parents and surroundings) and personal values is a complex one. Politicians may share a value, such as "no innocent person may be executed", but their worldview may still lead them to have opposing views on capital punishment. Some may accept a certain margin of error because of a strong belief in the unproven preventative effect of executions, whereas others will find the risk of state sanctioned murder of an innocent person an unacceptably high price to pay.

Nevertheless, shared values are the building blocks of political families. In this context, 'values' are beliefs that are shared among the members and elected representatives of the party and, ideally, its electorate. Values drive an organisation's culture and priorities and provide a framework in which decisions are made. One of the pleasures and dangers of being in a political party is being surrounded by many like-minded people.

On the basis of one's worldview and values, a 'political vision' can be developed, which outlines what the party or politician wants to be, and/or how it wants the world in which it operates to be an idealised view of the world. It is a long-term, abstract, often inspirational view of the future: for example, "a world based on biblical values" or "a society where each individual can be free". Certain visions will be considered repellent

---

6   George P. Lakoff, *Don't Think of an Elephant: Know Your Values and Frame the Debate,* Chelsea Green Publishing, 2004.

by many and may well be contrary to international law, such as striving for "an all-White National Socialist America".[7]

This vision can be translated into a political 'mission', which defines the fundamental purpose of the party, succinctly describing why it exists and what it does to achieve its vision. For example the British Liberal Democrats "exist to strive for and safeguard a free, fair and open society".[8] The development and the expression of a political mission are related, yet different enterprises. While the political mission itself defines a party, the expression of the political mission is aimed at rallying like-minded voters to the party's cause, expanding the membership and motivating activists.

To a certain extent, vision, mission and values are deeply ingrained in every politician and political party. Most western political parties have strong historical roots, a clear position on both political axes[9] (social-economic and personal-moral) and a track record of voting. Even parties that are merely guided by a vision of obtaining power or of obstructing the current system still have to present a mission and values in order to attract voters.

In addition, politicians at opposite ends of the political spectrum can find common ground on specific issues, such as a secular, green party working closely with a conservative religious party on environmental issues. Their starting points and vision may be very different, even opposite, but their specific objectives regarding environmental protection can overlap.

3. Political Strategy

In order to turn all these ideas and visions into reality, a political strategy is required. A political strategy is a combination of the end goals for which the party is striving and the means, policies and resources by which it is seeking to get there. For a political party this has to be a combination

---

[7] American Nazi Party website.

[8] As noted in the preamble to the Liberal Democrat Federal Constitution, available at http://www.libdems.org.uk/constitution.aspx, last accessed on 15 June 2012.

[9] See the illustration of the Nypels cross axis in Dennis Hesseling and Herman Beun, "Sociaal-liberalisme, pragmatisme en radicale democratisering: het D66-debat", in Sven Gatz and Patrick Stouthuysen (eds.), *Een Vierde Weg? Een Links-liberalisme als Traditie en als Oriëntatiepunt*, VUB University Press, 2001.

of substance – its electoral programme, which includes policy and legislative priorities as well as the budgetary means available to achieve these – and electoral positioning: which voters to attract, where to focus campaign resources and, once in power, which policies to focus on to ensure that the next elections will be won. Simply put, if you do not win elections, you lack the power to implement your vision.

For politicians, the ideal political strategy is therefore one that will, in their view, make the world a better place and at the same time get them re-elected. This makes the sphere of influence in politics a dynamic between (evidence-based) ideals and electoral considerations. Though ideally the two would always overlap, in practice there are few politicians who would sacrifice their electoral potential in favour of sticking to what they believe to be right. In this way, (perceived) electoral considerations can shape political strategy and politicians' behaviour. This can be a positive force: "bowing to the will of the people" might entail listening to people's real needs and taking them into account, thereby keeping one's political vision in check. However, if political power is viewed as a goal in itself, then the political dynamics will be skewed in favour of electoral considerations and lack a sufficient foundation in vision, values and mission. In my view, politicians should at least try to persuade others of their view, rather than adapting immediately when policy proposals are not (initially) met with public approval.[10] In this dynamic sphere of influence, politicians should be idealists, communicators and listeners. In practice, many politicians will wait until society is ready for change and then codify it, as illustrated by President Obama's support for gay marriage only after polls showed a majority of Americans were in favour.

4. Political Strategy in Action

What implications does this political dynamic have for those seeking to implement effective justice strategies? A fact-based justice strategy could be developed as follows: on the basis of a shared vision – such as 'a crime-free society'– a strategic plan is formed. Empirical evidence would

---

[10] One would hope that politicians would use fact-based, empirically substantiated strategies to work towards their ideal world. In my experience however, often these decisions are not based on factual assessments of the most effective means of achieving an objective, but are mainly guided by perceptions of voters, polling and electoral effect. In a world of 24-hour news cycles and channel-zapping voters, electoral considerations will often win the day. Hence the term 'fact free politics'.

be used to see where available resources could best be applied to reach a maximum of clearly defined targets, from investing in education to repressive measures seeking to deter would-be perpetrators. Next, in order for the thus formulated policy to be implemented effectively (or to continue with this policy after elections), politicians will have to persuade at least a significant part of the public of the merits of this policy.[11] At this point, democracy is uniquely strong but at the same time vulnerable. The dynamics between politicians and the public can lead to better policy decisions because this policy is adapted to people's needs, but it can also entail politicians sacrificing their ideals to stay in power or adapting policy to the loudest voices[12] and/or narrow definitions of self-interest rather than fighting for the general interest.[13]

Criminal justice, justice in the narrow sense of law and order, is especially vulnerable in this respect. The fact that most people can easily imagine themselves as patients in health care, for example, but cannot so easily put themselves in the shoes of a suspect, delinquent or prisoner (and may even only take the imagined perspective of the victim) creates a fertile breeding ground for an 'us and them' narrative. It is this kind of narrative that populism thrives upon, and which may lead to marginalisation of the people defined as 'them' and a neglect of their rights and needs. Yet this is not the way to a just and fair society, and I would argue that it does not lead to a safer one.[14] If *public* opinion – and therefore the political debate – is likely to be unbalanced in this way, this places a special responsibility on those who are active in justice strategies to safeguard the balance in the law, precisely because the public would consider it less of a priority and politicians may find it tempting to follow suit.

---

[11] See Raz' discussion on 'full bloodied normative statements' and Hart's 'internal point of view': Joseph Raz, *The Authority of Law, Essays on Law and Morality,* Oxford University Press, Oxford, 1979, pp. 151–158.

[12] The media and civil society have an important role to play here.

[13] Of course, this refers to a (politician's) *interpretation* of what that general interest might be, but the point remains that general interest is commonly understood to be different from (and broader than) self-interest or the interest of the few.

[14] From the abundance of examples one might consider a policy to supply heroin to delinquent addicts, see Hilde Wermink *et al.*, "Comparing the Effects of Community Service and Short-term Imprisonment on Recidivism: A Matched Samples Approach", in *Journal of Experimental Criminology,* 2010, no. 6, pp. 325–349.

5.   Public Scrutiny in Strategies

One hypothesis that would merit further investigation is my observation that the further one moves away from the national or local arena the more room there is for legislative and justice strategies free of electoral influences. There are two arenas that come to mind: the European Union with its young political structures and, secondly, inter-governmental, multilateral negotiations such as in the UN framework. Both take place in faraway cities in complex international settings where public, political and media scrutiny is much more limited than at local or national level. While this provides an opportunity to adopt complex legislation without the immediate pressures of voter considerations, at the same time it risks undermining popular legitimacy.

Supranational legislation, whether in the form of European directives or regulations or international treaties, usually entails ceding a certain measure of sovereignty. Given that the current notion of the nation state is built on national sovereignty,[15] this means that there is an inbuilt political reluctance to sacrifice sovereignty. Only when there is a clear and perceived self-interest can the public and political support be found to cede power and influence beyond national borders. Despite this, every day, especially in the EU, decisions are being taken of which the electorate has very little knowledge. Politicians have free rein in spinning stories of why they voted in a certain way in Brussels without the scrutiny of media or a parliamentary check.[16]

The European ban on smoking in public areas[17] is an example of a piece of legislation which national health ministers needed for the improvement of national health, but hardly dared to defend before their national audiences for (perceived) electoral reasons. Rather than taking on the discussion at national level, they moved the discussions to Europe, agreed on a law there and then proceeded to blame Brussels for forcing their hand.

---

[15]   See Jürgen Habermas, "The European Nation State. Its Achievements and Its Limitations. On the Past and Future of Sovereignty and Citizenship", in *Ratio Juris*, 1996, no. 9, p.125.

[16]   See the parliamentiary report by Hans van Baalen, "Op tijd is te laat", Kamerstuk 28632/1, 11 April 2002.

[17]   Council recommendation on smoke-free environments (November 2009).

Current media attention on the European economic crisis and the transfer of sovereignty to Brussels, for example on banking and budget matters, may well change this dynamic. Citizens' concerns are stimulating media and politicians to increase their understanding and scrutiny of what happens in Brussels. The tradition in certain EU states of holding referenda when transfers of sovereignty are in play will also raise awareness of and attention to the issues at stake. There is, however, not an immediate indication that more public attention will lead to increased perceived legitimacy.

This process repeats itself beyond the European level when multilateral treaties are in play, with the added difficulty that not only do negotiations take place behind closed doors, but mostly they are done by anonymous bureaucrats. The ratification process will often attract limited attention in a national parliament, be generally ignored by the media and few politicians will be re-elected on a platform of promising to ratify or reject an international treaty.[18]

The question whether it is desirable to have legislation passed without public scrutiny depends, of course, partly on what one's assessment is of the quality and impact of that particular piece of legislation. I am thrilled about the ban on smoking in public places, but still feel it should have been enacted nationally, rather than at European level. In short, it would be of interest to discussions about the future of law to have more comparative research into the interplay between public and politicians, and most notably the level of accountability the latter have at different political levels. Is there more freedom to act – for better or for worse – at European or international level, because of the lack of public scrutiny and its low electoral impact?

6. Conclusions

Politicians play a crucial role in developing and executing justice and legislative strategies. These strategies are developed and implemented in a dynamic sphere of influence in which ideals, electoral considerations, personal motivation and ambition add to the interplay of other forces in a country such as civil society, the media and the public at large. This interplay in turn is set in a specific historical, geographical and cultural context, which helps to determine or limit the range of options available for

---

[18] EU Treaties being a notable exception, as outlined above.

strategising. Whether strategies are executed implicitly or explicitly by countries will be linked to questions of maintaining legitimacy and public support.

Politicians will generally balance two considerations as they determine a strategy: how to implement their vision of a just society and how to get re-elected or stay in power. Ideally, they would be idealists as well as excellent communicators and listeners. Anyone seeking to influence justice strategies needs to take these two, sometimes conflicting, considerations into account. It is easier to convince a politician to implement your strategy if it gets him or her re-elected.

The policy area of justice would seem to be different from other areas related to a just society, such as health or education, because people are more likely to see themselves in hospital than in prison. This makes life more complex for politicians who find it important to protect the rule of law and due judicial process.

Often the next election or even an incident that captures the public imagination can turn the strategy on its head or lead to revisions and, ideally, an improvement. When this interplay works well it is democracy at its best. However, it can also lead to short-term ineffective legislation that erodes the rule of law and undermines the development of just societies.[19] It should be noted that even in non-democratic societies those in power need a certain basis of public support to maintain their current strategies, even if this basis consists of only a small yet powerful group of people who are not at all representative of the public at large.

All those who embark on creating more just societies need to know how to move and influence politicians, so need to understand their considerations, including electoral ones. As brave people across the planet, most notably in the Arab World, are chasing away their dictators and fighting for rule-based just societies, I hope this volume will inspire them on their historic mission.

7.   Sources and Further Reading

David Owen, *In Sickness and in Power. Illness in Heads of Government During the Last 100 Years,* Methuen Publishing, 2008.

---

[19]   Much legislation enacted after the 9/11 bombings is now proving to be either ineffective, counter-productive or used for purposes other than those intended.

Dennis Hesseling and Herman Beun, "Sociaal-liberalisme, pragmatisme en radicale democratisering: het D66-debat", in Sven Gatz and Patrick Stouthuysen (eds.), *Een Vierde Weg? Een Links-liberalisme als Traditie en als Oriëntatiepunt*, VUB University Press, 2001.

Dick Morris, *Vote.com: How Big-money Lobbyists and the Media Are Losing Their Influence, and the Internet Is Giving Power Back to the People*, Renaissance Books, 2000.

Edward R. Tufte, "The Relationship between Seats and Votes in Two-Party Systems", in *The American Political Science Review*, 1973, vol. 67, no. 2, pp. 540–554.

George P. Lakoff, *Don't Think of an Elephant: Know Your Values and Frame the Debate*, Chelsea Green Publishing, 2004.

Hans van Baalen, "Op tijd is te laat", Kamerstuk 28632/1, 11 April 2002.

Hilde Wermink *et al.*, "Comparing the Effects of Community Service and Short-term Imprisonment on Recidivism: A Matched Samples Approach", in *Journal of Experimental Criminology*, 2010, no. 6, pp. 325–349.

Jan Potters, Randolph Sloof and Frans van Winden, "Campaign expenditures, contributions and direct endorsements: The strategic use of information and money to influence voter behavior", in *European Journal of Political Economy*, 1997, vol. 13, no. 1, pp. 1–31.

Joseph N. Cappella and Kathleen Hall Jamieson, "News Frames, Political Cynicism, and Media Cynicism", in *Annals of the American Academy of Political and Social Science*, 1996, vol. 546, pp. 71–84.

Joseph Raz, *The Authority of Law, Essays on Law and Morality*, Oxford University Press, Oxford, 1979.

Jürgen Habermas, "The European Nation State. Its Achievements and Its Limitations. On the Past and Future of Sovereignty and Citizenship", in *Ratio Juris*, 1996, no. 9, pp.125–137.

The Liberal Democrat Federal Constitution, available at http://www.lib dems.org.uk/constitution.aspx, last accessed on 15 June 2012.

Peter Mair, *Party System Change: Approaches And Interpretations*, Oxford University Press, Oxford, 1998.

Victoria Nourse and Jane S. Schacter, "The Politics of Legislative Drafting: A Congressional Case Study", in *New York University Law Review*, 2002, vol. 77, p. 575, available at SSRN http://ssrn.com/abstract=1527 043, last accessed on 20 August 2012.

1.6.

National Responsibility for International Law

Michiel Scheltema[*]

The domestic law of the future will be very different than the law of today. What kind of changes in national legal systems can be expected? Firstly, there will be more internationalisation. However, that internationalisation goes much further than 'more international law'. While international law has certainly grown tremendously in importance, much more is going on. We also see the development of transnational rule-making: rule-making outside the realm of formal international law. Two types of such transnational rule-making appear to be changing the legal landscape significantly: informal transnational law-making (IN-LAW) and transnational private rule-making (TPR). Both types of rule-making will have a big impact on more traditional ideas about rule-making, separation of powers and organising accountability. The growth of international law, IN-LAW and TPR is leading to a rapidly increasing interdependence between national legal systems and between the international legal system and national legal systems. I will argue that in the future national law-makers, and especially national courts, should participate more actively in the development of international and transnational law. This will require new strategies by national ministries of justice and other justice institutions at the national level. It will also necessitate adaptations by international institutions. Lastly, it will mean that legal education and research must change.

1. Introduction

Ten years ago, at the time the first ideas about setting up The Hague Institute for the Internationalisation of Law (HiiL) were developed, it was already becoming apparent that the world of international law was changing rapidly. Most lawyers, on the other hand, are educated within a national legal system and do their work within their own system. Most of them ex-

---

[*] **Michiel Scheltema** was one of HiiL's founders, and since 2006, he has been Chairman of the Programmatic Steering Board of HiiL. Since 1983, he has also been a Royal Commissioner for the drafting of the General Administrative Law Act.

pected – and may still expect – that the domestic law of the future will be very much the same as the law of today. On basis of *the Law Scenarios to 2030* developed by HiiL and research, which has been conducted over the past six years, I will argue that this expectation is unfounded.

2. Scenarios for the Law of the Future

In a way it is surprising that lawyers are not used to thinking a lot about the future of law. Instead, they interpret the law as it is, they deliver judgments on the basis of the present law, and they systemise the rules and the case law in their legal system. Drafting new legislation is supposed to be more the work of politicians than of lawyers. The courts, of course, have a role in adapting the law to new circumstances, but their legal innovations are presented predominantly as an interpretation of the present law, and not as laying down new rules.

This attitude is surprising when one realises that our present rules are meant to function in the future. We expect that people in the future base their decisions and their behaviour on the rules that we have laid down today. So the legal system of today is an important factor in the framing of the future. Consequently, it is important to think about the future. Is our law, our legal system, an adequate answer to the problems of tomorrow?

A serious and unprecedented attempt to instil a more forward-looking attitude in thinking about and working with law, was undertaken by the Hague Institute for the Internationalisation of Law (HiiL). For the first time, different ideas about the way the law can develop were seriously researched and set next to each other. By doing so, a tool was developed, a tool that enables one to think about the functionality of the present legal system in various future scenarios.[1]

This work around the scenarios has strengthened the conclusions drawn from other HiiL research: the law of the future will be quite different from law of today. National legal systems will change dramatically as a result of internationalisation. The initial idea that it would principally affect international law is not correct.

---

[1]   See HiiL, "Law Scenarios to 2030", available at www.hiil.org/publication/law-scenarios-to-2030, last accessed on 11 October 2012.

The scenarios differ from each other in the role they expect national legal systems to play. In two of them, internationalisation leads to an enormous growth of international rules, nonetheless in both cases national legal systems remain of great importance. They differ as to the origin of the international rules. In the first scenario, Global Constitution, those rules are laid down in treaties or decisions of international organisations. In the second scenario, Legal Internet, the rules have no basis in international law, but come from public or private actors that come together to make new rules without any public rule-making power.

I will discuss two questions. What kind of changes in national legal systems can be expected in each of those scenarios? And what role can national law-makers (the legislator and the courts) play to influence the development of the law in the future?

The second question will interest a strategy maker in a ministry of justice most. Such a ministry is among the main guardians of the effectiveness of the national legal system. That ministry and the other national law-makers might have to redefine their role if internationalisation will continue and they should be prepared for that.

3. Growing Importance of International Law

Taking the perspective of six years ago, it seemed logical that the internationalisation of our society would continue and that international law would become more and more important as a consequence of that growth. This has been borne out, but partly in a different way than had been expected. Transnational rule-making outside the realm of international law is becoming very important. I use the word transnational for rule-making across borders that is not based on any power conferred by treaty or other instrument of international law, and international for rule-making according to traditional international law. Two types of new transnational rules can be distinguished.

The first type is where authorities of a number of states come together to coordinate their policies, and decide to develop common rules. They have no formal, treaty making ambitions and consequently their rules are not legally binding. Pauwelyn calls these types of rules IN-LAW, which stands for informal international law.[2] Even though these

---

[2] Joost Pauwelyn, "Informal International Lawmaking: Mapping the Action and Testing Concepts of Accountability and Effectiveness", June 2011, available at

rules are formally not binding, in practice they can have powerful effects. They can be applied by each of the participating authorities as their own rules, they can be adopted in national legislation or they can function as standards that have to be observed. Important examples may be found in the field of safety of airplanes and all kinds of devices, food safety, and financial regulation. Another example is the Basel rules for the supervision of banks, which are decided upon by a committee composed of directors of national central banks. These rules are decisive for the position of banks all over the world.

Pauwelyn comes to the conclusion that as an instrument for transnational rule-making, IN-LAW is developing much faster than rule-making based on international law. He mentions a number of advantages that IN-LAW informal rule-making has, including greater flexibility.

Another trend in international rule-making is when international firms, NGOs, organisations of professionals or experts like technical standard-setters develop rules and standards. This type of rule-making was studied by Caffagi and termed transnational private regulation (TPR).[3] Many of these regimes have their origin in industry; others are driven by NGOs or other actors to serve public goals like the protection of the environment or of human rights. Important examples are the International Accounting Standard Board (IASB), which has great influence on the standards used by accountants worldwide, and the Internet Organization for Assigned Names and Numbers (ICANN).

The development of IN-LAW and TPR make it apparent that a new world of transnational regulation is growing. This new world of rule-making does not fit into our ideas of traditional legal systems. It is not international law, nor is it national law. Is it law at all? Still more important are questions about the legitimacy of all these activities. In practice, they can have great effects. However, who is responsible for them? In how far are stakeholders participating in the preparation of these rules?

---

http://www.hiil.org/insight/making-informal-networks-democratically-accountable, last accessed on 12 September 2012.

[3] Fabrizio Cafaggi, "Private Transnational Regulation: Constitutional Foundations and Governance Design", available at http://www.hiil.org/project/corporate-laissez-faire-or-public-interference-effective-regulation-of-cross-border-activities, last accessed on 12 September 2012.

---

4. The Scenario of Transnational Rule-Making by Public and Private Actors

As a result of these developments the legal profession and all those who are responsible for the legal system have to reorient themselves. Are those new developments acceptable or do they subvert the guarantees of the rule of law?

There are some parallels with developments within national legal systems. The privatisation of public tasks has taken place worldwide. This has as a consequence that we expect that the private sector becomes more active in the promotion of public goods. Corporate Social Responsibility (CSR) is a good example of this line of thought. On the international level we see the same: the protection of human rights – always thought to be at the heart of public government – is now expected from business, too. This is demonstrated clearly by the work of Ruggie in the framework of the UN: international business is supposed to play an important role in the field of human rights. To a certain extent this can be seen as a step in the direction of privatisation on the international level, comparable with what has happened within national legal systems. In my opinion, strong arguments exist to conclude that the public sector is unable to reach the public goals without the participation of the private sector. In the knowledge society we live in, public government needs the knowledge and experience of the private sector as well. This contribution leaves no room for further argumentation,[4] but it strengthens my expectation that transnational law-making by private actors is a realistic scenario for the future.

In research a clear distinction was made between IN-LAW and TPR. Here too, is where things get more complicated as we look deeper. In some cases, public as well as private actors are participating. In many aspects TPR and IN-LAW have much in common, compared with international law-making in the traditional way.

I conclude that internationalisation will have important consequences for legal systems. However, it is too simple to say that internationalisation will lead to more international law and less national law; a whole new category of rules is coming up. It is unclear how they fit into

---

[4] See Netherlands Scientific Council for Government Policy (WRR), *The Future of the Constitutional State*, 2002, available at http://www.wrr.nl/en/publicaties/publicatie/article/de-toekomst-van-de-nationale-rechtsstaat/, last accessed on 17 August 2012, Pauwelyn's concluding remarks.

our legal systems, and it is unclear whether they can even be classified as law(s) at all. In any case they have become too important to be neglected by lawyers.

5. National Legal Systems in an Age of Internationalisation

What will become the role of national legal systems as a result of these developments? This seems to be a key strategic question in light of the conclusion just reached. In the first instance, the inter-relationship between national law and international law has become much more intense. In the past, international law was a separate system of law, regulating the relationship between states, while national law decided over the admittance of international law within the boundaries of a country. Now international law has taken over many of the subjects that were once covered by national law. Today's international law directly regulates the behaviour of individuals and firms, and consequently influences national law much more. Sometimes it is even difficult to see whether a rule belongs to national or to international law. In research on General Rules and Principles of International Criminal Procedure, Sluiter shows that criminal procedure on the international level is largely modelled after the examples of criminal procedures at the national level.[5] At the same time, the international principles of criminal procedure are meant to function as an instrument to review the quality of national procedures. The interaction seems to be so close that it is difficult to say what belongs to national law and what to international law.

The fact that international law is increasingly regulating the behaviour of individuals and organisations like national law has always done, means that both systems of law become interdependent. Application of the law to individuals has to be done by national authorities and legal disputes have to be judged by national courts. So the functioning of modern international law has become dependent on the functioning of the national legal systems. Without the cooperation of national authorities and national courts the international rules cannot be applied to the citizens or the firms within a country. So, the existence of a well-functioning national legal system is crucial for international law to be effective.

---

[5] Goran Sluiter *et al.* (eds.), *International Criminal Procedure. Principles and Rules*, Oxford University Press, 2013 (forthcoming).

For this reason, the international community has a strong interest in the quality and effectiveness of national legal systems. Their role is no longer limited to the shaping of the domestic law of the country but they have become the instrument by which international law can be executed inside the borders of that country. So, if national authorities or national courts are unable or unwilling to execute an international regime, it becomes toothless. As a consequence of this reality, we see more and more that the international community demands that domestic legal systems meet the standards of the rule of law as defined in international instruments. A good example is the European Union, which has a long list of requirements on rule of law and democracy to assess the internal legal system of candidate member states. So too do mandatory requirements of this nature exist in the work of the United Nations (UN), World Bank and International Monetary Fund (IMF) before assistance is given.

On the other side of this coin, one finds national authorities that are in a key position for the effectuation of international law. If they refuse to execute international law then that law is without effect. In developed countries such a refusal is not very likely, because lawyers are used to the idea that international law has to be obeyed by national authorities, including courts. Legal systems in developed countries are also much closer to most international law, which they have helped shape because they had an interest in its development. However, sometimes a good reason exists for a refusal. An illustration can be found in the well-known *Kadi* case. The Court of Justice of the European Union – here in a position comparable to a national court – refused to give effect to a decision of the Security Council to include *Kadi* on the list of terrorists. The refusal was based on the fact that *Kadi* was not given any opportunity to defend himself. As a consequence of this case, the Security Council has changed its procedures and has introduced an ombudsman procedure for the protection of persons and organisations put on the list. This case shows how a 'national court' (here the EU court) can play a role in the shaping of international law.

The above discussion dealt with the interdependency of international and national law. The situation is different for transnational regulation. From the point of view of international law, transnational rules are non-existent as legal rules: a basis for rule-making in international law is lacking. They can enter into a legal system only through national law. Many options are open to this. IN-LAW can have legal effects if national authorities adopt them as their regulations, as is done by central banks adopting the Basel rules. TPR can become binding through contracts or by including them in the bylaws of associations. National legislation can refer to IN-LAW or TPR, making them binding.[6]

Since transnational rule-making falls outside the scope of international law, the rule of law or democratic accountability are not guaranteed on the transnational level in any way. Only the national legal systems are in a position to fill this gap. They can do so by admitting IN-LAW and TPR into national law. They will generally only do so, however, if basic requirements of the rule of law, the participation of stakeholders in the rule-making process and accountability are met. The role that national courts and national legislators are going to choose in this respect is still unclear, since the development is still very recent. However, some steps are taken already. Participation of national authorities in IN-LAW rule-making is made dependant sometimes on prior notice and comment procedures. National courts can scrutinise transnational rules when they are enforced through them, or when citizens want to resist enforcement. The role of national courts and national legislators in judging transnational law could become a crucial one.

6. The Responsibility of National Law-Makers in an Internationalising World

The aforementioned developments show that internationalisation changes the legal landscape rapidly and rather fundamentally. National law and international law become more and more interdependent. Since national legal systems are essential to give effect to international law, national courts and national legislators get a new role. They are no longer institutions of only the national state but also institutions of the international community. Consequently, they are also linked to each other. The courts and the legislators of national states now have a common responsibility for the functioning of the international and transnational legal order.

This change of position diminishes their freedom to organise their own legal system according to their own views. The international community has a strong interest in the functioning of the domestic legal system and will make clear demands. On the other hand, it enlarges their influence as belonging to the law-makers of the international community. If

---

[6] Adoption of transnational rules by an international treaty is possible in theory, but is more complicated than adoption by national rule-makers.

they do not accept an international rule in their country, that rule might become toothless. Since constitutional guarantees are better embedded in national legal systems, national authorities are well positioned to scrutinise international law and even more, transnational law, on these aspects.

This might lead to a less strict hierarchy between international and national law. The *Kadi* case is an example of this. If national courts are accepted as institutions of the international community, than their participation in the international law-making process is more natural. They then are in a position to react to constitutional shortcomings in international and transnational law. The German Constitutional Court has taken that position towards the European Union. Another example of national courts playing an important role in the shaping of international law is the judgments of the Spanish and English courts in the *Pinochet* case. The immunity of heads of states in international law has diminished as a result of these judgments.

In this perspective, the discussion around the European Court of Human Rights (ECtHR) is relevant. The constitutional problem with that Court is that it is not embedded in a clear separation of powers mechanism, as is the case with national courts. In the absence of a countervailing power, it should come as no surprise that the Court would extend its powers. Every court, really committed to its task, would do that. However, this could be perceived as going too far. In such a situation, it might be a solution that national courts – taking note of the absence of checks and balances on the international level – act to some extent as the countervailing power. They might enter into a discussion with the ECtHR by not automatically following all the case law but commenting on judgments that, in their opinion, are overreaching the uniform interpretation of human rights. In this way, the absence of a separation of power mechanism on the international level – a fundamental requirement from the rule of law point of view – could be compensated for on the national level.

National courts act as institutions of the international community are linked with each other. A court of another country is no longer a court of a separate jurisdiction but a court that participates in an international law-making process as well. Since no hierarchy between them exists, a court is not bound by a judgment of another court, but such a judgment cannot be neglected altogether. The courts belong no longer to totally separate jurisdiction, but are a constituent part of an evolving international jurisdiction.

The role of national courts and national law-makers is still more essential when transnational rule-making is concerned. Legislation and case law is needed to make clear what requirements in the field of participation, accountability and rule of law have to be met by transnational law-makers. If not met, then participation of public authorities in the rule-making process could be forbidden, or the enforcement could be withheld.

My conclusion is that national legislators and national courts will have a great responsibility for the law of the future. On the one hand, their autonomy to shape the domestic legal system according to their own preferences diminishes, and the interests of the international community have to be observed as well. On the other hand, they can play a crucial role in the shaping of international and transnational law. That role can only be successful if they realise that they do not act as national institutions, but as institutions of the international community.

7.   Legal Research and Education

In the twentieth century, legal research and education has concentrated on national law. Unlike most social sciences, the international communication among researchers in the field of law was restricted. Public law, private law and criminal law were national law, and so were research and education.

In light of what was sketched above, this is no longer possible. The legal profession has a responsibility for the quality of the law. The growing interdependency of legal systems needs professionals that understand the interaction between legal systems and the growing international role of legal arrangements. Legal education that concentrates on national law is no longer adequate.

Until recently the comparative study of law was of great academic interest but did not have many consequences for practice. That will be different in the future. Since the quality of domestic legal systems is now a reason for international concern, the domestic systems will come under greater comparative attention. Lawyers have not yet developed useful indicators to evaluate the quality and the effectiveness of the law. For instance, constitutional guarantees differ from country to country, and a common framework to assess them is absent. This was not a great problem because lawyers tended to consider their national solutions – the only one familiar to them – as the best in the world. However, the growing international interest for the quality of domestic legal systems leads to the need for better instruments for evaluation. Barendrecht has developed an indicator that measures access to justice in very different circumstances.[7] The development of a much broader indicator to measure the rule of law goes in the same direction.[8] This kind of activity includes empirical based social sciences. I expect that interdisciplinary research will become more important in the field of law. Internationalisation is a relevant factor to advance this process.

Legal education and legal research have to become much more international and interdisciplinary than they have been in the past century. Only in this way can legal professionals organise themselves in an international community, needing to take up the responsibility that the internationalising world expects from them.

8. Concluding Remarks

Despite internationalisation, national law stays important, and national legislators as well as national courts will obtain different roles in the future. Their freedom to shape their own domestic law will diminish, but their contribution to the shaping of law across the borders becomes essential. The ministry of justice is one of the places where ideas and strategies about that role should be developed.

9. Sources and Further Reading

Fabrizio Cafaggi, "Private Transnational Regulation: Constitutional Foundations and Governance Design", available at http://www.hiil.org/project/corporate-laissez-faire-or-public-interference-effective-regulation-of-cross-border-activities, last accessed on 12 September 2012.

Goran Sluiter *et al.* (eds.), *International Criminal Procedure. Principles and Rules*, Oxford University Press, 2013 (forthcoming).

---

[7] HiiL, "Measuring costs and quality of access to justice", available athttp://www.hiil.org/project/measuring-costs-quality-of-access-to-justice, last accessed on 12 September 2012.

[8] World Justice Project, "World Justice Project Rule of Law Index", available at http://worldjusticeproject.org/rule-of-law-index/, last accessed on 17 August 2012. See also thespecial issue concerning means of measuring the rule of law: Julio Faundez and Ronald Janse (eds.), *The Hague Journal on the Rule of Law*, 2011, vol. 4.

Joost Pauwelyn, "Informal International Lawmaking: Mapping the Action and Testing Concepts of Accountability and Effectiveness", June 2011, available at http://www.hiil.org/insight/making-informal-networks-democratically-accountable, last accessed on 12 September 2012.

Julio Faundez and Ronald Janse (eds.), *The Hague Journal on the Rule of Law*, 2011, vol. 4, special issue.

Netherlands Scientific Council for Government Policy (WRR), *The Future of the Constitutional State*, 2002, available at http://www.wrr.nl/en/publicaties/publicatie/article/de-toekomst-van-de-nationale-rechtsstaat/, last accessed on 17 August 2012.

World Justice Project Rule of Law Index, available at http://worldjustice project.org/rule-of-law-index/, last accessed on 17 August 2012.

1.7.

On Legal Strategy in the Netherlands

Krijn van Beek[*] and Bert Niemeijer[**]

In this essay we focus on the big societal challenges for the Dutch legal world: technology, internationalisation, increasingly complex societal dynamics and the economic crisis. We contrast these challenges with the existing legal strategy – more emergent than explicitly defined – which appears broadly to aim at two goals: maintaining a well-functioning legal order and the promotion of a European and international legal order.

We argue that current strategic efforts along these two lines will not face up to the fundamental nature of the societal challenges. Hence it seems necessary to intensify legal strategy-making. We suggest two directions. Firstly, current players should be more connected both within the Netherlands (with other disciplines and centers of strategy making) and with strategy development elsewhere. Secondly, defining more precisely the underlying values and goals of our legal systems might make it easier to think up new forms that may fit new circumstances.

1. Introduction

The notion of a legal strategy raises questions like: what do we mean by a 'legal strategy'? Who are the strategisers and what are they doing when they create or help to create strategy? At the same time we might raise questions about the need for strategy. Why would we strategise? What would be the purpose of a legal strategy? Which challenges would justify what sort of strategising?

In this essay we will address these questions as regards the situation in the Netherlands; first by trying to describe some upcoming challenges that substantiate the need for strategising for the near future, second by

---

[*] **Krijn van Beek** is Director of the strategy unit of the Dutch Ministry of Security and Justice.

[**] **Bert Niemeijer** is Coordinator at the strategy unit of the Ministry of Security and Justice, and part-time Professor of Sociology of Law at the Free University of Amsterdam.

describing the actual practice of legal strategy-making. We will conclude with some remarks on the need for further investments in strategy-making.

2. New Challenges

There are a number of societal changes that make thinking about legal strategy increasingly important for the Dutch legal world. We focus on four of these developments and try to describe their consequences in terms of challenges for the legal order. Not that this list of four is all-inclusive, but it does seem to give an adequate idea of the range and depth of legal challenges ahead.

2.1. Technology

Everything from cybercrime to commercial surrogacy, from robotics to nanotechnology and from net neutrality to psycho-pharmaceutics poses new questions for both regulation and enforcement. It is also interesting to note that new technologies not only may change the nature of social inter-action but also give way to new forms of instrumentation.

Examples of both phenomena may illustrate the kind of challenges that lie ahead. In robotics we see auto-piloted cars just around the corner of development. They will be much safer than ordinary cars driven by humans (otherwise we would not really need them), but still regulators will have to sort out the responsibilities if anything does go wrong. Robot technology in cars is now being experimented with in a sort of legal void where regulation would benefit both developers and the broader public.

An example of new instrumentation can be seen in new techniques of data mining. By combining all sorts of databases and searching through them for suspect or otherwise interesting correlations, whole new policy possibilities become available. But this kind of data use is in strong violation of the principle of purpose limitation. We need somehow to figure out how to deal with such new possibilities while at the same time curbing government powers in a way that adheres to principles of the rule of law.

Both these examples illustrate another important aspect of the inherent legal challenges posed by new technologies. These challenges require hitherto unnecessary cooperation between at least law-makers and engineers. If they do not cooperate and try to figure things out within their own disciplines, they may come up with awkward or unworkable solutions in the other domain. Such cooperation seems to be an integral part of strategy-making for the future legal system.

2.2. Internationalisation

We see increasing amounts of cross-border traffic in people, goods, finances and information which becomes increasingly noticeable in all aspects of judicial attention. Again this has an impact on legal thinking in two ways: firstly it leads to new challenges due to cross-border dynamics; secondly it creates new resources for addressing these challenges.

In the cross-border dynamics section there is international financial regulation that seems to be of the highest priority. The Netherlands with its small size and relative high density of financial players seems to be quite vulnerable to the lack of regulation of new cross-border financial dynamics: American mortgages appeared to be not as trustworthy as assumed; Icelandic banking appeared not to be as adequately regulated as was assumed; and the subsequent euro crisis also seems to be at least partly due to regulations that did not evolve in tune with the banks they were supposed to control. Here we see a European and possibly a global legal challenge of sorts.

Cybercrime is another obvious example of the new challenges that may come from abroad. How do we cope with a bank robbery executed from, for example, the Bahamas? Do we allow our police force to take the culprits out of their cyber hole by means of an Internet attack? And if that were possible, would it be legal? And what if, for example, the Moroccan judiciary wanted to do something similar with a Dutch perpetrator operating from a Dutch Internet access point? What would we think about that? These may be overly simplified examples, but they illustrate how new cross-border phenomena create new legal challenges, also for our local law-makers.

Cross-border dynamics also provide for new resources for developing regulation and enforcement. This can be illustrated by the examples of the aforementioned technological challenges. The Netherlands is not the only country where governments are interested in data mining techniques or where car manufacturers would like to experiment with self-driven vehicles. On the contrary, these challenges are, if anything, global challenges with more or less similar legal consequences across the globe. It seems to be rather foolish to want to tackle these challenges alone. In order to create new legal frameworks for these new societal phenomena it might be a great help to tap into a worldwide cloud of legal knowledge, thinking and creativity. But then again, where is this supposed cloud of knowledge situated? Tapping into that cloud might be easier said than done; it might even be necessary to create it because it is just not there yet.

2.3. Increasingly Complex Societal Dynamics

The third of the big societal challenges that can be identified might be summed up as 'increasingly complex societal dynamics'. Because we are richer, more educated, more mobile, more connected and because our governments are so much more into detail and our legal system is growing so steadily, our interaction with the legal system also becomes increasingly intense.

Maybe the labour market can provide a useful illustration of the new complexities that arise. We used to have employers and employees, and basically all labour market regulation was and is organised around this dichotomy. But somehow the economy evolves in a direction where a growing number of people work for themselves, being neither employer nor employee. What kind of contracts can they engage in, which regulations should they abide by? What is the meaning of a level playing field here? What does workplace regulation mean for the self-employed; if they work from home, or a café? As a case in point, they are represented simultaneously by sections within labour unions and employers' organisations. So if regulators want to talk to representatives of these newly self-employed, whom should they turn to?

This is just a stylised example, which only partly illustrates the growing number of contracts and transactions that people engage in and the growing number and variety of organisations that people form and engage with. If we look at it this way, it is actually quite amazing that our legal institutions are still coping quite successfully. There seem to be two factors at play.

First, we consider the successful empowerment of personal responsibility and trust. Somehow most societal interaction runs amazingly harmoniously. Here we encounter a definite strategy at work: that is, to strengthen people's responsibility, for example, by creating general guidelines, quality standards and regulations, preferably through mechanisms of self-regulation. This is a longstanding strategic orientation in the Netherlands and extremely successful. While at the same time one might wonder if it should not be pursued even more strongly in order to keep the judiciary afloat.

Secondly, and contrary to the idea of successfully coping with these increasing societal dynamics, an increasingly uncomfortable feeling seems to have taken hold of society. Not just in the Netherlands but across the Western world, people seem to believe that there is a growing gap in rightfulness, seem to believe that too many people are allowed to live outside or above the law. It is quite hard to relate these feelings of discomfort to measurable fact. One might, for example, think of growing income differences in many countries, but at the same time poverty has also declined sharply. In spite of feelings of insecurity, violence seems to be ever decreasing. The closest explanatory 'fact' might be that the conspicuous richness of some former bankers could not be challenged in a court of law; this does strike many people as evidence that something fishy has sneaked into our systems.

Anyhow, if hard to measure and hard to concretise, these feelings of discomfort cannot be ignored and in themselves pose a great challenge for the legitimacy of our legal settings. And it may as well be that this feeling of discomfort has a great deal to do with the uses of new communications technologies, bringing all sorts of detail and personal emotions from within the legal system into the view of the people on the outside. Coping with new media pressure can be seen as a specific case of the challenges that technologies and new social dynamics create.

2.4. Economics and Decreasing Budgets

The credit crunch of 2008 and the subsequent Euro crisis of 2011 and beyond are a serious threat to social stability in Europe. There are several possibly very urgent incidents that may require a response from the justice authorities: for example, how should we act on a bank run? Or how should we act against political violence as, for example, displayed by the Greek right wing party 'Golden Dawn'?

Thus far however, the Dutch seem to be blessed with just an 'ordinary' recession which puts a squeeze on policy budgets as the most serious issue to be confronted in the world of safety and justice. This may not even be a bad thing, as it will spur discussions on the effectiveness of interventions and on the possibilities of new technologies working more efficiently.

3. Legal Strategy-Making in the Netherlands

In the previous section we focused on new and arising challenges. In this section we will give a brief description of what is actually being done in terms of legal strategy and how this relates to the challenges ahead.

First, it must be noted that legal strategy in the Netherlands may not be explicitly identifiable in terms of strategic cycles, goal-setting, planning, *et cetera*. One might also rightly question the possibilities of discussing a legal strategy in such traditional terminology. Nevertheless, there does seem to be something like a legal strategy in a more emergent kind of way. It may not be explicitly proclaimed, but is more or less ingrained in the professional education of Dutch lawyers and law-makers, in the system of Dutch law-making, and in the role of law-making in the Dutch policy arena. Two core beliefs of Dutch lawyers then seem to stick out: the belief that it is laws and regulations that ought to govern society and the belief that the existing Dutch legal system is superior to other legal systems. This results in continuous efforts to embed new legal demands in the existing system.

We will get back to these two core beliefs, but first we will describe the actors

3.1. Who Strategises?

In the Netherlands there are no 'think tanks' specialising in systematic multidisciplinary thinking about legal strategy. On the other hand there is a lively academic culture with a wide range of individual scholars contributing to legal thinking. There are, for example, probably more than 100 Dutch legal journals on all aspects of legal thinking and doing. Most of them are for specialists. At the same time there is nowhere where all these individual efforts come together, leaving legal thinking rather fragmented.

There are three places in the Netherlands where thinking about the future of law is more than an incidental activity of individuals. I consider first the initiator of this volume, The Hague institute for the internationalisation of Law (HiiL). With its activities around the *Law of the Future Forum* and the development of the *Law Scenarios to 2030* it earns the honour of putting on the agenda the future of law as such and the fundamental questions that arise from societal developments as, for example, described in our section on new challenges. Secondly, the Netherlands Scientific Council for Government Policy (*Wetenschappelijke Raad voor Regeringsbeleid*) has made a valuable contribution to strategic legal thinking in the Netherlands. Several authoritative advisory reports on the future of law (for example, *State without a Country, The Future of the National Constitutional State*) have been quite influential, especially in the political arena. In the third place the Ministry of Security and Justice can be seen as a centre of legal strategy. We will focus on that, partly for practical reasons – we work there – and partly because the Ministry is the place where thinking and doing actually meet. If there is a place where legal strategy is enacted, it should be the Ministry.

Strategy-making by the Ministry of Security and Justice is – as befits ministries – a multi-layered process in which various actors play a role: the political and governmental top, the various policy-making branches, field organisations, other departments and societal organisations.

Strategic choices, of course, are made by the political (Minister and State Secretary of Justice) and governmental (Secretary-General and the Governing Board) top of the ministry. There is a cycle of strategic and midterm conferences. The rhythm of the conferences is linked to the start of a new government.

Feeding the development of strategy is a small central strategy unit (home to your authors). It reports directly to the Secretary-General, which is crucial for the position of the unit within the Ministry. Within specific parts of the Ministry there are also individual civil servants with strategic tasks. This applies also to field organisations, responsible for implementation.

Legal strategy by the Ministry of Security and Justice is aimed at two broad strategic legal goals: maintaining a well-functioning legal order for a safe and just society and the promotion of a European and international legal order (see Article 90 of the Dutch Constitution). These goals are closely related; all policy domains of the Ministry have important international and European dimensions. At the same time, the advancement of an international legal order is an important goal as such.

3.2. The Advancement of an International Legal Order

The advancement of an international legal order involves the protection of human rights, good relations with other states, especially European member states, good international laws and their compliance and durable international peace and safety. Working at these goals is a shared responsibility of the Ministries of Security and Justice, Foreign Affairs and Domestic Affairs. The Ministry of Foreign Affairs is responsible for coordination.

It is hard to discern an explicit strategy or strategic process to promote an international legal order. But at the same time a more implicit strategy can be identified. A strong belief in the positive forces of international treaties and supranational bodies appears to be the footing of a 'helping to build a proper world government'-type of emergent strategy.

The problems of discerning a strategy which is not explicitly laid down can be illustrated by the Dutch policy in the formative years of the European Union.[1] Whereas most analysts would describe the Netherlands as generally strongly supportive of European integration, historical analysis shows that Dutch governments actually were very reluctant to give up any form of sovereignty. A reluctance which, on closer inspection, has been quite identifiable throughout the decades of growing European institutions, but was never debated in public. Until the 2005 referendum on the European Constitution, European integration was never a political issue in the Netherlands. Thus, notwithstanding evident reluctances in political circles, policy-makers steadily work on and believe in the advancement of an international legal order.

This strong belief and the way it is embodied in the DNA of Dutch legal workers and policy-makers may explain why recent doubts within the population and expressed by some political parties – not about a world government which is not discussed at all, but about several important treaties, and in particular about the process of European integration – provoke such deep and fundamental confusion.

This is a good reason to start thinking anew and more explicitly about the international dimensions of our legal strategy. Further reasons for rethinking legal strategies with regard to internationalisation can be found in the examples we sketched in the preceding section: steadily in-

---

[1] For a short overview and literature see Maarten Muns, "Met frisse tegenzin op naar Europa", in *Historisch Nieuwsblad*, 2011, no. 8.

creasing cross-border traffic in people, goods, finances and information pose all sorts of new questions for our legal order. There are several initiatives to deal with these new challenges. For example, the Dutch are one of the most active members advancing European cooperation for combating organised crime (for example, through the Committee on Operational Cooperation on Internal Security (COSI)). Another example is the launch by the Ministry of a cyber security institute. On a more general level, international strategies have been a leading subject in all strategic conferences within the Ministry since 2005. But it must be noted that it seems hard to come to strategic terms with these omnipresent developments. This recently triggered a joint strategy project of the International and the Strategy division of the ministry.

3.3. Legal Order for a Safe and Just Society

The second great legal strategic goal of the Ministry of Security and Justice implies the advancing of the quality of the general legal infrastructure in the Netherlands. This goal manifests itself in the first place in the constitutionally assigned task of laying down by law the rules of civil (procedural) law and criminal (procedural) law. In the second place, it contains the responsibility for advancing the general quality of laws and for the legal infrastructure in the Netherlands. This implies a continuous effort to adapt the law and the legal infrastructure in the Netherlands to changing trends and needs of society. Current themes are promoting access to law, trust in the law and the quality of law-making, adapting rules to the needs of the economy, promoting respect for human rights, better service by government and implementation of European and international rules.

Under this overarching legal strategic goal we might also understand some more specific strategy-making within the various policy domains belonging to the Ministry. These are domains like (civil, penal and administrative) law-making, criminal law enforcement (the police, public prosecution and prison system), international relations, the judicial system, counterterrorism and security, child protection and juvenile delinquency. From a strategic point of view, various strategic activities can be identified here.

We want to highlight four lines of strategic activity that may illuminate the way the Ministry operates. Firstly, a lot of energy is invested in improving the efficiency and effectiveness of the judicial chain. The main aim is to reduce turnaround times by speeding up information transfer and combating downtime. A prime aspect is the innovation strategy of the judiciary.

Secondly, a recurrent theme concerns the distribution of responsibilities for bringing about a safe and just society. Surely the Ministry has a central role; but what about citizens and corporations? And what is the responsibility of local governmental bodies? How can the Ministry empower other parties to do their bit? As with internationalisation, all strategic conferences within the Ministry address this issue, with an increasingly urgent feeling that its policies should get much better at empowering the widest range of partners.

A third example concerns the position of victims of criminal behaviour. Recent years have seen increasing political attention being paid to victims resulting in cautious policy initiatives regarding the place and role of victims in our legal system. Policy and prosecution, for example, pay more attention to victims and victims have been awarded speaking rights, however limited, in criminal proceedings.

A fourth example concerns the use of new technologies. Increasingly refined DNA techniques have The Netherlands Forensic Institute at the forefront of developments. Dutch Police is also experimenting with social technology. 'Amber alert' uses to all kinds of media in the event of an alarming disappearance of a child. '*Burgernet*' ('citizennet') is a platform to mobilise citizens' information regarding all kinds of criminality.

These four examples illustrate the amount and the direction of effort the ministry invests in dealing with the challenge of increasingly complex societal dynamics, and in which it seeks to use new technologies. At the same time the question arises whether this is good enough, in particular when we take into account the economic challenges ahead.

4.   Investing in Legal Strategy

If we take together the four challenges in the first section and the strategy-making of the second, it does seem that there is serious need for more strategy-making. There is mounting pressure in all dimensions of the system: in the numbers of traditional questions, in the number of new questions that arise from new technologies and their uses, in the changing forums of rule-making, in the way people see and interpret the law, and in squeezed time and budget frames to deal with it all. These challenges are each for themselves enough reason to strategise, taken together even more so.

There is reason to intensify legal strategy-making. The first line of attack is process-oriented: bring together law-makers and experts from varying disciplines around strategic challenges and make them think. More use might be made of the fact that in The Hague so many legal experts from so many different origins and specialisms come together, creating a unique pool of possible new legal concepts. At the same time interaction seems necessary between the legal profession and most other disciplines – which are not necessarily based in The Hague.

The second line of attack is more content-oriented: if we can describe and operationalise and measure more clearly and precisely the underlying values, the fundamentals and the goals of our legal systems, it may be easier to think up new forms that may fit new circumstances. Hence we look at the World Justice Project as one of the most interesting and inspiring initiatives to operationalise the concepts of justice and rule of law across different legal systems. In the same vein, our strategy unit is working on a project called 'societal reference frame' to define explicitly the goals of 'security and justice' within the Netherlands.

The recent appointment of a Council for Research and Development and Innovation within the Ministry is also content-orientated. The Council has the task of providing more direction for a broad range of research and innovation activities scattered across the domain of security and justice. The Council can also be seen as the embodiment of the ambition to speed up innovation processes for security and justice.

Summing up, we see in the Netherlands a lively legal-political debate culture, perhaps even more so than in most other European countries. But most of it takes place between interested individuals within their own fields of legal specialisation, and strategic notions remain rather implicit. And yes, there are at least three centres of legal strategy-making, but their combined clout seems to be rather small with regard to the challenges ahead. Unlike some other countries, we have no 'think tanks' with legal strategy on their agenda. This state of affairs calls for change. In view of the economic situation, we do not see where new capacity might come from, but it should be possible for current players to become more connected. Legal strategy-making should be more connected both within the Netherlands (with other disciplines and centres of strategy making) and with strategy development elsewhere. With regard to the latter, the European Union deserves more attention. After all, the challenges for Dutch society do not seem to differ much from those facing other societies. Moreover, our challenges are so intertwined across borders that it would be foolish to try to answer them on a local or national level. In strategy-making we should seek more connection with an international and at least a European level.

5.   Sources and Further Reading

Maarten Muns, "Met frisse tegenzin op naar Europa", in *Historisch Nieuwsblad*, 2011, no. 8.

Wetenschappelijke Raad voor het Regeringsbeleid, "De toekomst van de nationale rechtsstaat", WRR rapport no. 63, The Hague, 2002.

1.8.

Responsive Freedom

John Braithwaite[*]

A restorative justice strategy is about the idea that because injustice hurts, justice should heal. It should repair harm and meet fundamental needs, such as the need for safety. A responsive strategy is about the idea that justice should be responsive to how actors are behaving in a particular legal environment. Restorative and responsive justice means that a business regulator may be less punitive with a firm that breaks the law if the firm is subject to a self-regulatory regime that disciplines those responsible and repairs harm. This puts restorative and responsive justice in tension with other justice values. For example, will a lawbreaker, who has no access to a self-regulatory scheme, who is not in a position to repair harm to victims, be more vulnerable to the full force of the law? One radical strategy is to give up on the impossibility of reconciling equal justice for lawbreakers and equal justice for victims. Equal concern for the justice claims of all stakeholders to be free from domination by injustice is one alternative.

1. Introduction: Limits of Law in a Justice Strategy

Trained lawyers are a scarce commodity, especially in poorer societies. Legal adjudication is expensive. Consequently, courts do not or cannot provide much of the justice that is done in a society. The challenge for the law is to provide a framework that enables better justice 'in many rooms' beyond courtrooms. This might seem to legal formalists a strategy that gives law a smaller role in our institutional architecture. In fact, it gives law a grander role. This essay considers two strategies for a law that enables continuous improvement in the quality of justice that occurs in other rooms, and in courtrooms. These are restorative justice and responsive regulation.

---

[*] **John Braithwaite** is Professor and Founder of the Regulatory Institutions Network, Australian National University, and former Head of the Law Program of the Research School of Social Sciences.

2. Restorative Justice

Restorative justice is something the law can enable to occur on a much wider front – to deal with school bullies, workplace bullies and bullies in international affairs – to mention just one genre of injustice rarely within reach of the courts. Like therapeutic jurisprudence, restorative justice is about the idea that because injustice hurts, justice should heal. It is a relational form of justice that gives stakeholders opportunities to put their most just self forward in a dialogue about who has been hurt by an injustice, and what might be done to repair the harm and meet the needs of all affected. We entice stakeholders who may have behaved badly in the past to put their most socially responsive self forward. This is accomplished by a move from a jurisprudence of passive responsibility – holding someone responsible for what they have done in the past – to active responsibility – the virtue of taking responsibility for putting things right in the future. After armed conflict, we see important forms of this vision of 'justice as a better future', the way Clifford Shearing expressed the justice aspirations of South Africans.

Formal law brings many assets to the task of encouraging restorative justice meetings. At these meetings all stakeholders are encouraged to sit in a circle to seek a shared view on who has been hurt and what might be a plan to put things right that stakeholders could sign. First, most lawbreakers do not agree to restorative justice in the absence of at least some remote threat of resolution by formal law. Second, formal law brings many rights and imposes many limits on the restorative process. In a visionary legal and justice strategy, restorative justice learns much from formal law, and vice versa.

There is a more important way for a legal strategy of leavening the quality of restorative justice to increase the centrality of law in a society. Part of the aspiration for restorative justice should be to make the judicial branch of governance the branch that does more to energise democratic sentiment than the legislature and executive government. Ordinary people are increasingly jaded and cynical about how much democratic meaning is to be found in electoral politics. Politicians seem remote from them and close to the few who control great wealth.

Now consider the participation of ordinary people in restorative justice circles that are empowered by the state to make important decisions, and which the judicial branch may learn from and vindicate. This gives people real participation rights over things that matter to them personally. The opinion poll evidence shows that community members, victims, perpetrators and their supporters all value this aspect of restorative justice. For children, restorative justice in schools is one of the best ways for them to learn how to become democratic. We are not born democratic. We must learn to be democratic citizens through participation in decision-making. Courts act wisely when they empower children to deal with incidents of schoolyard violence or bullying in a restorative circle, rather than having courts or police impose a solution. One reason is that this strategy implemented by courts nurtures participatory citizenship and democratic sensibility in the society. The strategic vision of the judicial branch acts as the engine room for re-energising wilting democratic citizenship.

3. Responsive Regulation

Responsive regulation is an approach that started with business regulation, but is now applied in some other areas such as tax and child protection. It is about the idea that a regulator should have a strategy that is responsive to how a regulated actor behaves, and that is also responsive to the environment and context that surrounds the regulated actor. The responsive regulatory pyramid is a key idea. The pyramid is also the strategy for integrating restorative justice into responsive regulation. The idea is to organise a variety of different sanctions and supports at different layers of the pyramid. The presumption is to start at the base of the pyramid with strategies that are less interventionist, less punitive and more participatory. At the peak of the pyramid are maximally interventionist and punitive strategies that involve incapacitating or shutting down the actor who continues to pose a risk to the community. Imprisonment and revoking the license of a business or that of a legal practitioner are the classic strategies at the peak (see the example of a pyramid in Figure 1 below).

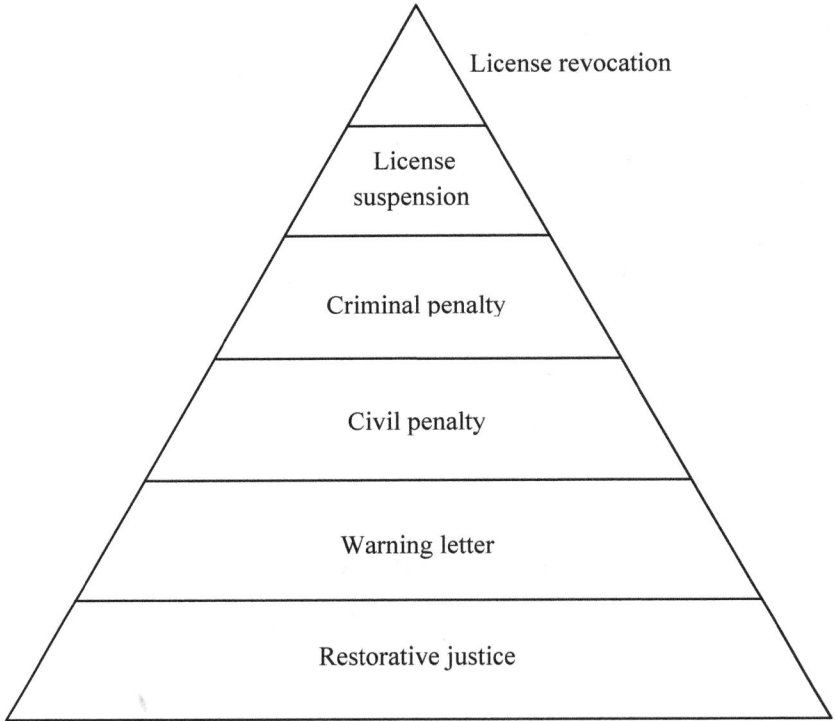

Figure 1: Simple example of a regulatory pyramid.

Restorative justice is the classic strategy at the base of the responsive regulatory pyramid. But there are many layers in a pyramid between, say, incapacitation at the peak, and restorative justice at the base. These might include, moving up from the base to a second or third restorative justice conference with wider participation, a wider circle, after the first circle has failed. Then there might be escalation to different kinds of preventative and deterrent approaches such as cease and desist orders and fines. The idea of the pyramid is that most legal strategies fail much of the time, so the pyramid puts each layer of strategy on top of many others. Each strategy at each layer of the pyramid is crafted to cover the weaknesses of other strategies.

Responsive regulation encourages deliberative, conversational regulation at a wide base of the pyramid. The ideal is to empower victims of injustice around the table with alleged lawbreakers in a conversation as the first port of call. It is only a presumption that it is best to try problem-solving dialogue first. Sometimes responsiveness to extreme circumstances means it is best to override this presumption and start the regulatory response higher up the pyramid. Wherever we start, the ideal is to stick with a determination that serious law-breaking will be made to stop, however many layers we must escalate through. The pyramid is a meta-strategy that allows for the ordering of strategies so that our response can be dynamic and forward-looking toward fixing injustice. Providing for the capacity to escalate to tough enforcement at the peak of the pyramid drives more of the justice down to the base of the pyramid. The paradox of the pyramid is that a benign big gun rests at the peak, which we hope not to use, combined with determination to keep escalating intervention until justice is restored, creating incentives to play the game at the cooperative base of the pyramid.

4.   What about Equality before the Law?

A legal worry concerning both restorative justice and responsive regulation is that these flexible and forward-looking approaches undermine backward-looking equality before the law. Lawbreakers who have perpetrated equal wrongs may get non-punitive restorative justice at the base of the pyramid if they cooperate, while others who resist restorative justice may get prison at the peak of the pyramid. Within a restorative justice conference, one offender may confront a victim who wants to give the gift of forgiveness, whereas another may not.

A broader conception of equality before the law is needed to resolve this dilemma. This conception is of equal concern for the justice claims of all stakeholders in an injustice. If the healing that flows from forgiveness is the justice one victim wants, while the satisfaction of punishment, deterrence to protect future victims, is what another wants, these victim justice claims must be balanced with offender-oriented justice claims. Contemporary criminal law jurisprudence tends to be narrowed to a concern for equal justice for perpetrators in proportion to the wrongs they have committed. Is it just for the claims of criminals to be given more weight than the justice claims of victims? At one level it is. Perpetrators usually, though not always, have more to lose in a criminal process than victims. Here is where the constraining values of the law must impose punishment limits and rights limits on both restorative justice and responsive regulation. For example, the criminal law must lay down that for an offence of a particular level of seriousness (and culpability) punishment beyond a specified maximum is never allowed.

Defending infrangible upper limits on punishment and other interventions does not justify lower limits. It means we might find no fault with the International Criminal Court if it fails to punish one war criminal in circumstances where it imprisons another, if the first offender has submitted to a restorative justice process that has helped to heal victims, and provided practical remedies to repair harm. The normative ideal that can justify the principle of equal concern for the justice claims of all stakeholders is republican freedom as non-domination. This ideal has been developed by the philosopher, Philip Pettit. It is the ideal that a just outcome is that which will maximise freedom as non-domination. So in the balancing above, we weigh the loss of freedom as non-domination a criminal suffers from imprisonment, against the improved freedom as non-domination that past and future victims gain from this outcome.

In this calculus, the freedom from domination of victims counts equally with that of criminals. Pettit's work also gives a republican account as to why no one can be free in a society in which they cannot count on the law to protect them from punishment beyond specified maxima for specified wrongs. Without this, we are subject to the arbitrary power of those who might dominate us. Only the law can be the last bastion of our freedom in this regard. Republican freedom as non-domination in Pettit's account is a subjective value. It is a justified belief that one is assured of legal protection against arbitrary power. This subjective freedom cannot be delivered unless the limits and rights in the law are constraints, which cannot be broken on the basis of some utilitarian reasoning.

5. Conclusion: Continuous Improvement in Delivery of Justice

When courts do a good job of enabling the spread of restorative justice, the hope is that this will put a stop to an increased number of injustices, and more injustices get a remedy. It will mean that some of the caseload pressure is taken off the courts, enabling the courts to allow access to courtroom justice in cases where it is currently denied. When responsive regulation works well, more of the work of regulating injustice will be done through education, persuasion and restorative justice. Again, this frees up the interventionist regulatory tools at the peak of the pyramid for more of the most intransigent cases. But much more importantly, it solves an increased number of problems of injustice conversationally near the base of pyramid.

This is at least the theory of how a more restorative and responsive regulatory strategy should work. One way to evaluate whether any progress is being made in making this theory a reality could start with an annual survey of how many injustices of various kinds people experienced during the year, and whether they got a remedy in each case or saw each problem of injustice solved. If they got a remedy, if the injustice they were suffering ended, they would then be asked how this was achieved: by a court; a problem-solving police officer; restorative justice; some kind of intervention by a family member or a regulatory agency; or by an industry self-regulatory scheme. Over time, this kind of methodology could be refined to monitor continuous improvement (or deterioration) of justice, and to identify which institutions and methods are achieving most success in fixing the injustices that worry people most. If the theory of the legal and justice strategy in this essay is correct, it would show a growth in restorative justice and responsive regulation would deliver more justice to more people. This global legal and justice evaluation strategy is just a tweak to current crime victim surveys, which also ask about each crime suffered whether it was reported to the police and if victims were satisfied with how the police handled it.

6. Sources and Further Reading

Ian Ayres and John Braithwaite, *Responsive Regulation: Transcending the Deregulation Debate*, Oxford University Press, 1992.

John Braithwaite, *Restorative Justice and Responsive Regulation*, Oxford University Press, 2002.

Philip Pettit, *Republicanism: A Theory of Freedom and Government*, Clarendon Press, 1997.

1.9.

A Legal and Justice Strategy towards Strengthening Social Cohesion

Stavros Zouridis[*] and Ernst Hirsch Ballin[**]

This think piece explores the contours of a legal and justice strategy that aims to strengthen social cohesion in society. On the most general level such a strategy is based on a single and simple idea. Law and the justice system should operate as a means of binding citizens instead of antagonistically separating them. At least three principles can be derived from this idea. First, respect instead of tolerance or indifference should guide law and the justice system. Second, social cohesion requires strict but smart enforcement that takes into account individual circumstances. Third, law and the justice system should enable the growth of social capital rather than frustrating it. These principles are illustrated with Dutch law and justice practices during the 2007–2010 government.

1. The Social Cohesion Opportunity

Public discomfort nowadays seems ubiquitous in Western societies. The causes for discomfort are manifold, but these certainly predate the economic crisis that started in 2008. As many sociologists have argued, public discomfort stems from a broader and long-term trend of declining social cohesion and social capital.[1] We are aware of the fact that concepts like these are risky business because their meaning has been debated for

---

[*] **Stavros Zouridis** is Professor of Public Administration (Tilburg University), and former Director for Justice Strategy at the Dutch Ministry of Justice (2005–2010).

[**] **Ernst Hirsch Ballin** is Professor of Dutch and European Constitutional Law at Tilburg University, and Professor of Human Rights at the University of Amsterdam. He is also a Member of the Royal Netherlands Academy of Arts and Sciences.

[1] For example, see Robert Putnam, *Bowling Alone: The Collapse and Revival of American Community*, Simon & Schuster, New York, 2000; Frank Furedi, *Culture of Fear. Risk Taking and the Morality of Low Expectation*, Continuum International Publishing Group, London, 2002; Zygmunt Bauman, *Postmodernity and Its Discontents*, Oxford, Polity Press, 1997; Marc Elchardus and Wendy Smits, *Anatomie en oorzaken van het wantrouwen*, Brussel, VUB PRESS, 2002.

many decades. Many great thinkers have attempted to conceptually capture the mechanisms that keep societies together and they have failed to achieve consensus. Even though social cohesion appears to be a slippery concept, we will argue that it effectively describes a serious challenge for contemporary societies and a great challenge for legal and justice strategies. It can, however, also serve as an inspiring policy goal that strengthens the role of institutions in the service of the rule of law.

In this think piece, social cohesion is defined as a dynamic between humans and the institutions they share. The dynamic is partly maintained by evolving ties between people, such as family ties, friendship, trade and cooperation. These ties are felt and expressed by people with their behaviour towards other people. The ties between people do not tell the whole story of social cohesion, because webs of social ties that connect people also make up an autonomous social fabric. The social fabric can be materialised in a common language, a joint government, sports associations, social organisations or any other social institution. The interplay between the ties felt and expressed by behaviour on the one hand and the social fabric that also develops autonomously, make up the dynamics of social cohesion.

Social cohesion thus defined can be imagined as a double helix of human feelings and behaviour on the one hand and social fabric expressed by institutions on the other hand. The double helix may either spiral towards increasing social cohesion or towards declining social cohesion. We argue in this think piece that law and the justice system should be geared towards propelling the dynamics of increasing social cohesion. In order to find clues as to how law and the justice system may affect social cohesion, we first analyse and reconstruct the problem of declining social cohesion. Section three sketches the foundations of a legal and justice strategy aiming towards social cohesion. We conclude our think piece with some practical implications of such a strategy for law and the justice system. These implications are derived from Dutch practice. The 2007–2010 government in the Netherlands pursued a social cohesion strategy as did the members of government responsible for law and justice.[2] The strategy was designed in order to guide the policies at least until 2011, but

---

[2] See Ellen van den Berg, E. Kaya, Max Kommer, Bert Niemeijer and Stavros Zouridis, *Social Cohesion*, Ministry of Justice, The Hague, 2010.

the government coalition split up in 2010 after a conflict about the continuation of Dutch military activities in Afghanistan.

2. The Social Cohesion Deficit

At least two stories circulate on social cohesion in Western societies. In the top-down story on social cohesion there has been a steady decline of social cohesion for years now. Slowly and gradually, public trust in official, that is, legally established institutions, is declining in many Western societies (for example, as measured by the European Values Study[3]). Individualism has spread among Western societies and challenges authoritarian, self-referential types of institutionalisation. In the top-down story on social cohesion, institutional structures are gradually losing significance because of individualism and group conflict. This concerns not only institutions established under public law (the states and other political institutions) but also religious institutions which like western Christian churches, which have been modelled on public structures.

The basic cause for the decline of social cohesion has been mapped well by Robert Putnam.[4] He observes a long-term decline of social capital in the United States of America. According to Putnam, social capital refers to generalised reciprocity which he describes as "I'll do this for you without expecting anything specific back from you, in the confident expectation that someone else will do something for me down the road". The main cause for declining social capital between 1965 and 2000 in the USA is found in less people 'doing things together'. Social capital is produced if people play sport, eat, work, relax, debate or even shop and fight together. Due to the fact that sporting, eating, working and so on, are increasingly done individually, these activities produce less social capital.

Whereas the top-down story on social cohesion emphasizes its decline, the bottom-up story argues that civic and democratic life is still flourishing. The evidence to support this claim is usually found in local practices of community-building, local support networks, and social media.[5] Taken together it appears that many people still support their rela-

---

3   See http://www.europeanvaluesstudy.eu for more information.
4   Putnam, 2000, see *supra* note 1.
5   See for example the cohesion studies of the Council of Europe. Also, Roel J. in't Veld, *Knowledge Democracy: Consequences for Science, Politics, and Media,*

tives in case of illness or need, many citizens still actively engage in small-scale community work and social and political debate is alive and kicking on Twitter, blogs and other social media. These indications are brought up to prove that Western civil societies still flourish. The picture of individuals who work all day behind their computers and watch television all night appears to be a fable.

Both stories are valid, but media and politics are usually biased towards the top-down story of social cohesion. These perceptions also guide political actions and strategies. At least three political strategies can be witnessed. First, some politicians have chosen to express and emphasise the decline of social cohesion and to draw the conclusion that more social antagonism is necessary. By articulating and emphasizing differences among citizens and groups, they aim at strengthening the 'bonding' processes of social cohesion within groups while simultaneously avoiding 'bridging' between groups.[6] We will refer to this strategy as the *mobilisation strategy*.

Second, other politicians have chosen a '*laissez-faire* strategy'. In this strategy, politics and public institutions should not actively intervene in these processes of declining and strengthening social cohesion. '*Laissez-faire* strategies' only allow for a limited role of law and the justice system. Law and the justice system may peacefully canalise group conflict, but building social ties takes place outside these realms. Law and the justice system should therefore in this strategy become as neutral, distant and indifferent as possible to allow big society to rebuild social cohesion.

Finally, politicians may choose for a strategy towards strengthening social cohesion. This strategy claims an active role for both law and the justice system in order to strengthen social cohesion. A crucial element in these *social cohesion strategies* is the recognition of people in their individual identities, which may contrast or not with that of others. This respectful recognition of the individual is in the end the same thing as paying tribute to human dignity. The next section contrasts these strategies with regard to their guiding principles.

Springer, Heidelberg, 2010; Brian Loader and Dan Mercea (eds.), *Social Media and Democracy. Innovations in Participatory Politics*, Routledge, New York, 2012.

[6] See also Putnam, 2000, see *supra* note 1.

3. Law and Justice towards Social Cohesion

The *social cohesion strategy* assumes that law and the justice system are capable of stimulating both processes of bonding and bridging. On the most general level, a social cohesion strategy is based on a single and simple idea. Law and the justice system should operate as a means of binding citizens instead of antagonistically separating them. For example, Robert Kagan argues that the USA's legal strategy of adversarial legalism does not promote social cohesion. He has analysed the workings of the legal system of the USA and he concludes:

> Adversarial legalism inspires legal defensiveness and contentiousness, which often impede socially constructive cooperation, governmental action, and economic development, alienating many citizens from the law itself.[7]

In a social cohesion strategy the social antagonism that goes along with adversarial legal strategies is replaced by legal and justice repertoires that connect citizens and groups. This basic principle needs to be further refined before it can be deployed as a legal and justice strategy. In general, this legal strategy is based upon three principles.

3.1. Respect Instead of Indifference

Respect has to do with the way that law and the justice system deal with heterogeneity of norms, cultures and customs. Law always expresses a normative reality that is enforced or held up by a justice system. If the normative reality embodied by law is grounded in a normative consensus upheld by a large majority of a society, both law and its application by the justice system will hardly be contested or problematic. Problems arise when law does not embody shared values and norms. Even though some norms are still shared by large proportions of people in Western societies, normative pluralism has become one of the basic characteristics of most European societies.

The strategies described above deal differently with normative pluralism. The mobilisation strategy argues that law and the justice system should embody a dominant set of values and norms. In the German and Dutch political discourse, this set of values and norms has been framed as

---

[7] Robert Kagan, *Adversarial Legalism: The American Way of Law*, Harvard University Press, Cambridge Mass., 2002, p. 4.

the *Leitkultur* or guiding culture, a concept that is often being abused as a means of exclusion, but that is– for instance in the broader sense of a *European Leitkultur* – also suitable for an approach that is receptive to change and respectful inclusion.[8] In this model, law and the justice system will become a political instrument that is either explicitly or implicitly intended to force the *Leitkultur* upon minorities with different values and norms. These politics of exclusion will probably strengthen social cohesion as processes of 'bonding', but they will also lessen social cohesion as processes of bridging. Instead, law and the justice system will become instruments for exclusion and battlegrounds for group conflict.

The *laissez-faire* strategy argues that both law and the justice system embody as little as norms as possible. Law and the justice system merely provide the platform and infrastructure for peaceful settlement of conflict. By focusing on process and procedural values instead of substantial values, law and the justice system are as much as possible detached, neutral and indifferent. This strategy is based on the idea that social cohesion is served best by providing an arena that offers procedural equality and fair trial. Whereas the first strategy contributes to processes of bonding, this strategy is at risk of sliding into a disconnected co-existence.

A social cohesion strategy is guided by a substantive view on human beings who according to the 2007–2010 Dutch government's motto, "Work together and live together" in mutual respect. It puts respect for everyone's human dignity, the principle enshrined in Article 1 of the Universal Declaration on Human Rights and Article 1 of the Charter of Fundamental Rights of the European Union, into practice. It therefore contributes both to bonding and bridging. A true social cohesion strategy therefore does not merely tolerate differences or provide an arena in which individual and group conflicts can be peacefully settled. Instead of accepting normative pluralism, it aims at including and embracing different norms, values and customs. Instead of striving for indifference by banning the normative differences from the law and the justice system, it provides legal status to different sets of values, norms and customs.

---

[8] Ernst Hirsch Ballin, *Citizens' Rights and the Right to be a Citizen*, Brill, Leiden and Boston, 2012 (forthcoming).

3.2. Smart Enforcement Instead of Turning a Blind Eye

A social cohesion legal and justice strategy also affects law enforcement. For decades, law enforcement did not get the attention it needed. Ever since the explosion of law enforcement during the 1990's and the past decade, law enforcement seems to have become a major priority.[9] A social cohesion strategy welcomes the attention for law enforcement. An enforcement policy that is too tolerant threatens social cohesion because it rewards people who violate the law. Law-abiding citizens will lose their confidence in law and in the end, the 'bonding and bridging' functions of law and the justice system will erode. Turning a blind eye also negatively affects social cohesion because it undermines the willingness to obey the law. If crime and fraud pay off, citizens will not be willing to voluntarily comply with legal obligations.

A social cohesion strategy builds upon an effective system of law enforcement, but this does not necessarily mean zero tolerance. Even in the United States, serious doubts have been expressed about the effectiveness of the zero tolerance approach.[10] A zero tolerance strategy consumes a lot of the capacity of law enforcement organisations. As a result more serious violations of law are punished less or they are even not cleared up at all. Citizens who usually abide by the law then observe that their minor offences are punished whereas real criminals get away. Such a policy will undermine social cohesion.

In a social cohesion strategy, law enforcement has to be strict in a sensible way. This means that the more serious the violation of the law, the higher the chance must be that the offender is confronted with a law enforcement response. Penalties do not necessarily have to be severe, but there has to be as much certainty as possible so that serious offences are penalised. Second, smart enforcement also uses extra-legal ways of dealing with everyday conflicts and disputes. If neighbours fight and the police are alarmed, it is possible to treat the fight as a criminal offence and deal with it as such. This will probably worsen the situation between these

---

[9]   As described in David Garland, *The Culture of Control. Crime and Social Order in Contemporary Society*, Oxford University Press, Oxford, 2001; Malcom K. Sparrow, *The Regulatory Craft: Controlling Risks, Solving Problems, and Managing Compliance*, Brookings Institution Press, Washington, D.C, 2000.

[10]   John E. Eck, Edward R.Maguire, "Have Changes in Policing Reduced Violent Crime? An Assessment of the Evidence", in Alfred Blumstein, Joel Wallman (eds.), *The Crime Drop in America*, Cambridge University Press, Cambridge, 2010.

neighbours and it consumes valuable resources of law enforcement organisations. Smart enforcement requires extremely professional law enforcement officers and a managerial and financial system that is not primarily aimed at production figures. Third, smart enforcement means choosing inclusive ways to penalise offenders. The penalty should not only penalise the offender but should also address the cause that led to the offence. For example, if someone with a mental illness or a lack of communicative competences commits an offence, the penalty should be accompanied by a treatment or training. Prevention has to be integrated into law enforcement.

4.   Rewarding and Enabling Social Capital Instead of Hampering It

As argued above, social capital is produced if people do things together. From the perspective of social capital it does not matter what people are doing together. Strictly speaking, even setting up a criminal network will create social capital. Of course that would not be the goal of the legal and justice strategy that we propose. Instead we propose a legal and justice strategy that promotes people doing those things together that contribute to a good and just society. These include supporting neighbours, relatives or friends, neighbourhood activities, working towards a cleaner and more secure environment, building sports associations and so on. We argue that law and the justice system should both be designed and operated as stimuli for these practices.

Many laws in Western European societies are primarily designed to promote people doing things alone. For example, contracts and legal entities as institutionalised forms of cooperation depend on individual agreements between the participants. Sometimes individual ownership hampers the improvement of property. If therefore a minority of owners of apartment buildings in the Netherlands want to improve the joint parts of the building, they are legally obstructed. Especially if many apartments belong to someone who lets out these apartments, the minority of owners is legally stuck. Law could also be designed to stimulate these improvement initiatives by lowering the number of owners required to decide on the improvement of joint parts of the building, which was one of the initiatives of the 2007–2010 government, in response to suggestions on behalf of the local government in the municipality of Rotterdam.

5. Some Dutch Illustrations of an Inclusive Legal and Justice Strategy

We conclude this think piece with some illustrations of the principles mentioned above. These illustrations are derived from Dutch legal and justice practices. In the Netherlands, the 2007–2010 government explicitly chose to work towards strengthening social cohesion. Their policies may therefore function as illustrations of these principles.

Some months after the government started in 2007, it presented its policy program. The government announced a serious policy with regard to *respect*. Although the government could obviously not overlook this concept's elusive nature, it started to identify points of reference in interpersonal relations and in public activities. First, respect became a guiding principle for policy decisions. Among others, these policies implied that religious and cultural organisations were invited to endorse supporting initiatives from their point of view. The government actively approached religious and cultural organisations and appealed to their responsibilities with regard to social cohesion. Even a rather provocative film made by a Dutch politician did not lead to outrage among Dutch Muslims. Instead, government and representatives of many religious and cultural organisations jointly reacted quite moderately, which may have prevented vehement outrage. Many politicians also wanted to abolish the possibility of having a double nationality. If these policies were to be pursued, it would mean that substantial numbers of new Dutch citizens would be excluded. The government therefore explicitly chose to continue to allow double nationalities in situations of family building. Besides these general policies, the government also presented some new policies aimed at improving respect in Dutch society. For example, it announced a policy that should realise codes of conduct in local communities, schools, social welfare organisations and sports associations. Codes of conduct are meant to express norms with regard to behaviour such as how people treat each other and what behaviour is expected from pupils, athletes and citizens. For example, the city of Gouda developed 'ten golden rules':

1. Whatever you break you have to pay for;
2. Do not use violence;
3. Clean up your own litter;
4. Hanging around in an intimidating way is anti-social;
5. Speak Dutch so that we can understand each other;

6. Always respect each other;
7. Driving too fast is dangerous, so don't;
8. Parents teach their children to be good citizens;
9. Do not harass, tease or discriminate;
10. Police officers are here for us all, so please respect them.[11]

Besides the principle of respect, the 2007–2010 Justice members of government deployed the idea of smart enforcement. With regard to smart enforcement, at least two initiatives should be mentioned. First, legislation has been enacted with regard to influencing the behaviour of juvenile offenders. The law on influencing adolescent behaviour, which was enacted on 1 February 2008, expanded the government's possibilities to educate juvenile offenders by creating a new instrument for judges. This new instrument, the behaviour order, aims at improving reintegration of juvenile offenders. Judges who are confronted with juvenile offenders may decide to send them to prison, but they may also choose to use the new instrument. For example, the judge may decide to oblige the juvenile offender to attend a program to learn how to deal with conflict, or the judge may decide that the offender will be closely monitored by resettlement organisations for some time. Besides this new legislation, smart enforcement also extended to the organisation of law enforcement. Smart enforcement means that individual circumstances are taken into account. In order to organise smart enforcement security houses have been set up. 'House', in this respect is referred to in the sense of clearing house. Within these houses platforms have been created to connect the police, the public prosecutor, welfare organisations, healthcare organisations and so on. In these platforms, individual cases are discussed and the platform also decides on a common course of action. The 2007–2010 government actively stimulated the security houses as a means for strengthening social cohesion by smart enforcement. These houses both contribute to more strict law enforcement and to inclusive ways of dealing with crime.

An essential part of social cohesion approach is the view that doing justice requires more than the application of legal rules. Justice is done in the specific, personal experience of right or wrong and therefore always relies on people's understanding of the particular situation in which they

---

[11] Sima Nieborg and Sandra ter Woerds, *De Gouden Stadsregels: op weg naar moreel burgerschap. Product- en procesevaluatie van de implementatiefase van het project Gouden Stadregels van de gemeente Gouda*, Verwey-Jonker Instituut, Utrecht, 2004.

live. In its program on building trust in legislation, the previous government therefore took several initiatives that embody this principle. One of these initiatives aimed at legally promoting citizens and businesses to take joint responsibility to improve their neighbourhoods and public places. As a part of this policy, the government also announced a new legal entity for associations and corporations that implement public and semi-public policies, for example, schools, health care organisations and housing organisations. This legal entity should enable these corporations to engage in entrepreneurial behaviour while simultaneously maintaining a public governance structure and a not-for-profit ethos. Up to now, such legislation has not been implemented. The right-wing government that took office in 2010 and meanwhile has fallen apart chose to withdraw this legislative proposal.

6. Conclusion

These illustrations both demonstrate the principles and action repertoires of a legal and justice strategy that aims at strengthening social cohesion and the feasibility of such a strategy. Any legislator on whatever level be it European, national or local must be able to use these principles to re-think its legislation and its justice action repertoires. Deploying these principles will propel bottom-up social cohesion. As a by-product, public trust in the law and the justice system will rise. We therefore call upon legislators to not hesitate and opt for a legal and justice strategy towards strengthening social cohesion.

7. Sources and Further Reading

David Garland, *The Culture of Control. Crime and Social Order in Contemporary Society*, Oxford University Press, Oxford, 2001.

Ellen van den Berg, E. Kaya, Max Kommer, Bert Niemeijer and Stavros Zouridis, *Social Cohesion*, Ministry of Justice, The Hague, 2010.

Ernst Hirsch Ballin, *Citizens' Rights and the Right to be a Citizen*, Brill, Leiden and Boston, 2012 (forthcoming).

Frank Furedi, *Culture of Fear. Risk Taking and the Morality of Low Expectation*, Continuum International Publishing Group, London, 2002; Zygmunt Bauman, *Postmodernity and Its Discontents*, Oxford, Polity Press, 1997.

John E. Eck and Edward R. Maguire, "Have Changes in Policing Reduced Violent Crime? An Assessment of the Evidence", in Alfred Blumstein, Joel Wallman (eds.), *The Crime Drop in America*, Cambridge University Press, Cambridge, 2010.

Malcom K. Sparrow, *The Regulatory Craft: Controlling Risks, Solving Problems, and Managing Compliance*, Brookings Institution Press, Washington, D.C., 2000.

Marc Elchardus and Wendy Smits, *Anatomie en oorzaken van het wantrouwen*, Brussel, VUB PRESS, 2002.

Robert Putnam, *Bowling Alone: The Collapse and Revival of American Community*, Simon & Schuster, New York, 2000;

Frank Furedi, *Culture of Fear. Risk Taking and the Morality of Low Expectation*, Continuum International Publishing Group, London, 2002.

Robert Kagan, *Adversarial Legalism: The American Way of Law*, Harvard University Press, Cambridge Mass., 2002, p. 4.

Roel J. in't Veld, *Knowledge Democracy: Consequences for Science, Politics, and Media*, Springer, Heidelberg, 2010;

Brian Loader and Dan Mercea (eds.), *Social Media and Democracy. Innovations in Participatory Politics*, Routledge, New York, 2012.

Sima Nieborg and Sandra ter Woerds, *De Gouden Stadsregels: op weg naar moreel burgerschap. Product- en procesevaluatie van de implementatiefase van het project Gouden Stadregels van de gemeente Gouda*, Verwey-Jonker Instituut, Utrecht, 2004.

Zygmunt Bauman, *Postmodernity and Its Discontents*, Oxford, Polity Press, 1997.

PART II:
TYPES OF STRATEGIES

SECTION A: NATIONAL AND INTERNATIONAL COURTS

2.1.

————

Does a Judicial Strategy Exist?

Wilhelmina Thomassen[*]

Developments in our global world have changed the work of the judiciary to such an extent that judicial strategy can be needed for the good administration of justice. Both on a national and international level, courts meet together and try to overcome possible contradictory interpretations of law, applicable in their different legal domains. Selection of cases can amount to judicial strategy when choices are made beyond the merits of an individual case. We do not have much knowledge about how judicial strategy works. Who is in charge? Does judicial strategy amount to a growing power of judges without sufficient democratic control? More judicial strategy calls for more transparency. The right of the citizen to be informed is considered to be a precondition for his or her participation in a democratic society. Why shouldn't this apply to judicial strategy and courts' decisions as well? These are questions that deserve to be discussed.

In this think piece, which deals with the question "does a judicial strategy exist?", I will explore some personal thoughts. These thoughts are mainly based on my experience as a judge and do not have any scientific pretention. They are meant as food for further thinking and discussion.

Do judges and courts have a strategy? I am pretty sure that many judges would answer this question in the negative. They will probably argue that judges have no strategy because the essence of their work is adjudicating the individual cases that are brought before them. It seems to be the very justification of judicial power and of the strong legal position of judges that they have no agendas, no programs and no goals other than to determine independently and impartially the rights and obligations of the

---

[*] **Wilhelmina Thomassen** is a consultant on fundamental law, a member of the Human Rights Commission of the Dutch Advisory Council on International Affairs (AIV), substitute member of the Venice Commission, and former Justice of the Supreme Court of the Netherlands (Hoge Raad der Nederlanden).

parties, or the criminal charge brought against an accused. The law obliges judges to apply the law in individual cases when asked to do so.

1. What Does it Look Like?

Yet some developments in our global world have changed the work of the judiciary to such an extent that judicial strategy can be needed for the good administration of justice. Internationalisation of the law requires harmonisation even beyond the borders of national states, the growing complexity and the growing amount of cases call for selection systems, prioritisation and efficiency measures. The plurality of sources of law and the plurality of judicial bodies encourage courts to exchange views with other judicial bodies and to try to reach agreement on the interpretation of law for the sake of legal security. These activities amount to judicial strategy beyond the merits of an individual case.

Representatives of the four highest courts in the Netherlands, de Hoge Raad (High Court of Cassation), de Raad van State (Council of State), het College voor Beroep en Bedrijf en de Centrale Raad van Beroep meet together on a regular basis in order to try to overcome possible contradictory interpretations of law applicable in their different legal domains. When different interpretations appear in the case law of these respective courts their representatives try to achieve compromises on an interpretation that they both are willing to apply in the future. Although these agreements cannot be binding on individual judges these agreements have a strong *de facto* impact on the deliberations of the chambers of the courts.

Also on an international level the exchanging of views and the efforts to reach agreement are part of the work of judges. The European Court of Human Rights (ECtHR) and the European Court of Justice (ECJ) meet together on a regular basis in informal gatherings to discuss the mutual case law with the aim to avoid different interpretations of fundamental rights and freedoms between the two courts. An example of harmonisation on the European level is the ECJ's judgment *Roquettes Frères*, in which the Court revised its earlier case law in order to bring it into line with the judgment of the ECtHR in the case of *Stés Colas Est and others vs. France* in which the ECtHR brought corporate premises within the concept of 'home' and 'domicile' as protected under Article 8 of the European Convention of Human Rights (ECHR).

Each year the ECtHR organises a seminar in which the ECtHR's case law is discussed with representatives of constitutional courts and high courts, lawyers, human rights professors and NGOs. Moreover, national courts are welcome to come to Strasbourg if they wish to do so in order to discuss the effect of the ECtHRs' case law on their national legal system with judges of the Court.

Also the national courts of different countries of the same level meet together with the aim of harmonisation of the case law.

2. The Selection of Cases by the Dutch Hoge Raad

A courts' activity which clearly implies a form of judicial strategy is the selection of cases because any selection of cases involves choices whether to reject a case or to select it for adjudication.

The need for the selection of cases is considered by both the Dutch legislator and the Dutch Hoge Raad (High Court of Cassation) to be an important means to guarantee the future of the Hoge Raad and the significance of its case law. One of the arguments for the introduction of selection tools is the increase of cases. The input of criminal cases was 560 in 1973, 2069 in 1987 and 3864 in 2007. In order to enable the Hoge Raad to overcome this workload, the legislator, in full agreement with the Raad, has provided the latter with the selection tool of Article 81 of the Judiciary Organisation Act (*Wet op de rechterlijke organisatie*, 'RO'). This provision enables the Hoge Raad to reject appeals which will not succeed and whose adjudication is considered nor to contribute to legal security nor to the development of the case law, without giving reasons. These decisions can be taken after written observations by the Hoge Raad's advocate general on the merits of the case. In fifty per cent of the rejected cases, Article 81 RO is applied.

On 15 March 2012, parliament passed a law that introduces the new provision Article 80a RO, providing the Hoge Raad with more room for the selection of cases. Both the legislator and the Hoge Raad have advanced two arguments for the introduction of the new rule. Firstly the increase of cases and secondly the desirability that the Hoge Raad only deals with cases that matter.

The first argument does not seem to be the most convincing one since the data advanced by the legislator shows that the inflow of criminal cases, representing the Hoge Raads' biggest workload, has diminished compared to 2007. 3683 Appeals were filed in 2008 and 3450 in 2009. Therefore the second argument for the introduction of Article 80a RO seems to be the most important one.

Article 80a RO enables the Hoge Raad to declare appeals inadmissible if the applicants' complaint doesn't justify any further examination because 'apparently the applicant has insufficient interest to have the appeal decided on'. This is my own translation of "klaarblijkelijk onvoldoende belang bij het beroep". In the alternative, the Hoge Raad may declare an appeal inadmissible if 'apparently the appeal will not succeed'. The latter ground for inadmissibility is more or less the same as the one laid down already in art 81 RO, but Article 80a RO decrees that the advocate-general's reasoned conclusion on the merits of the case is not needed anymore before a decision as meant in Article 81 RO is given. This, together with the other component of Article 80a, that an appeal can be declared inadmissible without reasons given if there is "insufficient interest", provide the Justices of the Hoge Raad with ample room for judicial strategy.

The Hoge Raad is of the opinion that the new selection system is in the interest of the development of the law and will enable the justices to fulfil their leading role in the Dutch legal order.

3.   The Selection of Cases by the European Court of Human Rights

The selection of applications filed to the ECtHR is essential as a tool to deal with its enormous workload. Declaring an application inadmissible without giving reasons if it is manifestly ill-founded has appeared to be an effective selection tool. About 90% of the cases are declared inadmissible and about 90% thereof are disposed of by Committees of three judges or a single judge. In order to facilitate a still more efficient selection system, the 14th Protocol enables the Court to reject an application if the applicant has not "suffered a significant disadvantage unless respect for human rights as defined in the Convention and the Protocols thereto requires an examination of the application on the merits and provided that no case may be rejected on this ground which has not been duly considered by a domestic tribunal", as stated in Article 34 of the Convention. The decision to reject an application on these grounds is reasoned.

4. Aggressive Grants and Defensive Denials

Epstein and Knight[1] describe two kinds of strategies towards the positive selection system of the US Supreme Court, the system of *certiori* grant in "aggressive grants" and "defensive denials". An aggressive grant occurs when at least four justices "take a case that may not warrant review" because the case provides a promising tool for the development of doctrine in a way that those justices favour. A defensive denial, by contrast, involves Justices who vote to deny *certiorari*, even when they disapprove of the decision under review and believe it to be significant. They fear that if the case is taken up by the Court, they will lose on the merits, creating undesirable doctrine.

These kinds of arguments which have little to do with the merits of the individual case can also play a role in the ECtHR and the Hoge Raad. A decision ex Article 81 RO can sometimes be the follow up of a vivid discussion on the merits of the case because the chamber is deeply divided and a compromise is difficult to achieve.

5. Selection Beyond the Merits of the Case

An example of how judicial strategy could easily lead to completely different decisions in the same case is *Christine Goodwin vs. United Kingdom*. In this case the ECtHR considered the state's refusal to recognise in law a change of sex on the point of an operated transsexual, an unjustified interference in an important aspect of an individual's personal identity as protected under Article 8 of the Convention. Initially the case had been assigned to a Committee of three judges with the proposal to reject it as manifestly ill-founded without reasons. This proposal was undoubtedly due to the fact that 12 years earlier the Court had rejected an identical application in a largely reasoned judgment, *Cossey vs. United Kingdom*. The proposal in the Goodwin case was clearly inspired by respect for precedent. But one of the judges in the Committee wanted to try to get the new Court to overrule the Cossey judgment and the case was taken out of the Committee and brought before a Chamber. The case ended up in the Grand Chamber who decided that the former Court's case law concerning transsexuals should be changed. The judgment of Christine Goodwin be-

---

[1] Lee Epstein and Jack Knight, *The Choices Justices Make*, QC Press, Washington D.C., 1998.

came one of the Courts' landmark cases. If the composition of the Committee would have been different, the case could have been rejected in a committee. In general, judges are not unfamiliar with the strategy to await a convincing case when they want to try to change the majority on a certain issue, instead of trying to change minds in a border line case or a case which provokes less sympathy.

6. How Does it Work?

We do not have much knowledge about how judicial strategy works. The extent of transparency in this process, the criteria for the selection of cases and the involvement of those others than judges in it, vary. The strategy discussions on the ECtHR seminars are registered and published, whereas its meetings with individual courts are in general confidential. The meetings of the Highest Courts of the Netherlands are only attended by a few judges of the courts concerned, no lawyers admitted and no record published.

The standard of Article 35 of the Convention for declaring an application inadmissible if the applicant has "not suffered a significant disadvantage, unless respect for human rights as defined in the Convention and the Protocols thereto requires an examination of the application on the merits and provided that no case may be rejected on this ground which has not been duly considered by a domestic tribunal", gives more stability and is clearer than the standard of Article 80a RO which enables inadmissibility "if the applicants' complaint does not justify any further examination because apparently the applicant has insufficient interest to have the appeal decided on". In both systems, no systematic and transparent mechanisms seem to be available for the control and evaluation of its application, whereas a large percentage of the applications filed are disposed of on this basis. The granting of *certioria* in the US Supreme Court is carried out by the full court whereas in the Dutch Hoge Raad the selection can be carried out by three judges without other judges being involved and while in the ECtHR these selection choices can be taken by one single judge.

7. More Transparency is Needed

Judicial strategy is an effect of the complicated context in which courts have to work. However, more room for judicial choices calls for more transparency. Judicial strategy can easily affect the democratic rights of the citizens. People have an interest to know how this strategy works, which choices are made and why they are made as they are made.

The extent of transparency of the judicial decision-making process in general seems to be dependent on the system. In the US Supreme Court and in the ECtHR the dissenting opinion is part of a judgment whereas in the Dutch legal culture the minority opinion is seen as weakening the authority of the judgment and therefore not allowed. In my view the possibility of some kind of dissenting opinion system provides for a minimum of transparency. It has proved to work without doing damage to the authority of the judicial system. But the growing room for judicial strategy raises questions that cannot be answered by a dissenting opinion system.

Does judicial strategy amount to a growing power of judges without sufficient democratic control? If so, how can this growing power be counterbalanced in the interest of the citizen? Should strategy discussions within and among the courts be open to other people and if so, how and to whom? Which are the most appropriate ways to realise transparency and accountability in the selection proceedings? Should courts' deliberations be more transparent? Should judges call public press conferences where they themselves explain a judgment and are open for questions? These kinds of questions will not automatically be answered by the courts themselves because judges appreciate confidentiality more than other state powers do, since secrecy is part of their professional attitude and culture. The secrecy of deliberations is likely to influence their views on the transparency of the judicial work in general. The activities of parliamentarians and scholars could be necessary to find answers to those questions.

8.   Do Judges Have Political Agendas?

More transparency can prevent suggestions made by some politicians that judges have political agendas. This is a dangerous accusation because it implies that the courts don't respect the separation of powers and this can provoke initiatives which aim to diminish the influence of the judiciary. For some politicians, it is indeed simply incomprehensible that judges might sincerely care about and be faithful to the law. Especially when the executives' power is restricted by judicial decisions, judges are easily said to be activists or overstepping their legal competences by taking decisions lacking democratic legitimacy, which should have been taken by politicians.

Political speech about judges who overstep their competences can be seen as part of a judicial strategy in the sense of a strategy *towards* judges, a strategy which aims at limiting the competences of the courts. The recent campaign against the ECtHR carried out under the presidency of the United Kingdom and strongly supported by the Netherlands, was aimed at the restricting of the powers of the ECtHR to assess human rights violations. This campaign can be seen as an example of such a strategy. The strategy however failed as during the Brighton conference, organised by the United Kingdom, the different proposals to weaken the Court were rejected by other Member states. Signs of strategies to restrict the judiciary can also be found on the national level. Recent drafts in the Netherlands to introduce minimum sanctions for criminal offences and the substantial raising of court fees could be seen as a strategy aimed at the minimising of judicial power.

9. Stretching Without Snapping

Two American law professors, Malcolm Feeley and Edward Rubin[2] emphasize the role of law in judicial behaviour. They argue that American judges sometimes base their decisions "on their own best efforts to understand an authoritative text" but also sometimes decide on the basis of "their sense of the best public policy". They emphasize that the American Congress sometimes requires such policymaking by leaving gaps in a statutory framework. Feeley and Rubin also observe that judges may become policymakers to address a practice that violates "a widely held principle of social morality" but that has not been addressed by the accountable branches. Regardless, when judges become policymakers, Feeley and Rubin argue, they remain constrained by doctrine and other institutions. They emphasize that the ability of any individual judge or court to create new doctrine or policy is significantly constrained by the need to coordinate their decision-making with other courts. They argue that a judge's "need to maintain contact with existing doctrine, to stretch it without snapping it, is one of several conditions for effective judicial policy making".

---

[2]   See C.K. Rowland and Robert A. Carp, *Politics and Judgment in Federal District Courts*, Kansas University Press, Kansas, 1996.

These observations on United States Supreme Court Justices, even if they date from 1996, are likely to still be applicable and also to judges from outside the US, both on a national and international level.

10. The Right to Know

There is no reason to distrust respected courts in their judicial strategies and the way that they select their cases. At the same time we live in an era where the right of the citizen to know and to be informed is considered to be a precondition for his or her participation in society. In a democratic society governed by the rule of law the question whether this shouldn't apply also to judicial strategy is a legitimate one. Information enables people to have a view on legal issues that can affect their position in society.

Greater knowledge and understanding of strategy will surely have consequences for courts. Exposing the judges' personal policy orientation and their strategic interactions can reduce their power, which rests on a perception that it is above politics. The need for transparency is enhanced by the position of courts as not elected and non-majoritarian institutions in our democracy. Such openness might affect the courts' decision-making. It might reduce the functional role of a high court in society, but perhaps that is not such a bad thing, especially if the openness adds discipline to the judges' legal decision-making and contributes to more consistency and predictability in their case law. Finding new mechanisms of communication between courts and the citizens can contribute to the finding of a balance between the courts need for room for strategy at the one hand and the citizens' interest to be informed at the other. More transparency and participation of non-judges in the work of the judiciary should be part of the scenarios for the future of the law.

11. Sources and Further Reading

C.K. Rowland and Robert A. Carp, *Politics and Judgment in Federal District Courts*, Kansas University Press, Kansas, 1996.

ECJ, *Roquettes Frères*, Case C-94/00, [2002] ECR I-9011, Judgment, 19 October 1982.

ECtHR, *Christine Goodwin vs. United Kingdom,* Series A, 2002-VI, 11 July 2001.

ECtHR, *Cossey vs. United Kingdom*, Series A, 184, 27 September 1990.

ECtHR, *Stés Colas Est and others vs. France*, appl.nr. 37971/97, 16 April 2002.

Lee Epstein and Jack Knight, *The Choices Justices Make*, QC Press, Washington D.C., 1998.

2.2.

Strategic Thinking About National Courts

Elaine Mak[*]

It is hard to imagine a future for the law without national courts which interpret and apply that law in individual cases and which contribute to the development of the law. However, the tendencies of globalisation and privatisation, as well as the increased influence of the social sciences and economic thinking, have had an impact on the role and functioning of the courts in western liberal democracies. Recent developments raise questions concerning jurisdiction, court organisation and judicial decision-making in an evolving legal context. This think piece addresses the issues to be dealt with in future strategies for national courts, the actors involved in policy-making in this context, and the normative framework for this policy-making.

1. Introduction

The design of laws and the promotion of justice in any legal order require policy choices. In western liberal democracies, a policy area that currently poses particular challenges is the one concerning the jurisdiction, organisation and decision-making of national courts. In the globalised and privatised legal context, the judicial function is being redefined. What role do courts play next to private dispute settlement providers, such as mediators and arbitrators, and *vis-à-vis* the other branches of government? Which sources and institutions are authoritative in the courts' decision-making? Which requirements need to be fulfilled in order for judgments to be accepted by society? It seems that new strategies need to be developed in order to ensure the continued relevance and legitimacy of the national courts, in the sense of their utility and the public trust vested in them.

This think piece will address the current debates about the role and functioning of the national courts in western liberal democracies, meaning

---

[*] **Elaine Mak** is Associate Professor of Jurisprudence at the Erasmus University Rotterdam.

states which share the traditions of democracy, rule of law, human rights protection, and open government. The analysis of these debates, firstly, clarifies which issues need to be addressed in a legal and justice strategy for the national courts. Secondly, we will establish which actors are involved in policy-making concerning national courts and what tensions between strategies might occur between different actors. We will then consider which normative framework serves as the context for policy-making in this field. Finally, some concluding remarks will be made concerning the future of strategic thinking about national courts.

2. The Issues

Four specific developments calling for policy choices can be identified when considering current debates about the functioning of courts in western liberal democracies.

2.1. Keeping Public Dispute Settlement Attractive

Firstly, national trial courts have been pushed into a position of institutional competition with private dispute settlement mechanisms, such as mediation and commercial arbitration. The establishment of court-connected mediation in some legal systems, such as The Netherlands, embodies an active policy to transfer cases from the courts to alternative dispute settlement. This policy concerns mainly dispute settlement in private law cases. However, court-connected mediation is also used to promote conflict resolution between citizens and government agencies in administrative law cases and between victims and offenders in criminal law cases. In the field of private law, furthermore, initiatives of private actors, such as 'e-Court' in The Netherlands, claim to provide a qualitatively sound, quick and inexpensive service which can compete with judicial dispute settlement. At the global level, transnational private regulation has increased, and is accompanied by an increase of private enforcement mechanisms. Policy debates focus on the role and the organisation of the courts in light of these changes, addressing in particular aspects of competition and innovation in the area of dispute settlement.

2.2. Reinforcing Judicial Decision-Making

Concerning the content of judicial decision-making, national courts have been faced with the task of including insights from other disciplines in the process of judicial discovery. The emancipation of the social sciences and economics has led to the increased importance of these disciplines in policy-making and to the expectation by society that judges will use insights from these disciplines in fact-finding in individual cases. Moreover, judges are expected to consider the effects which their decisions will have on society. In this light, the system of legal rules provides insufficient guidance for a critical analysis or a weighing of arguments of a non-legal nature, for example the assessment of statistical evidence in criminal cases. Policy-making concerning judicial dispute settlement aims to address the requirements for judicial discovery and the reasoning of judgments in this respect, as well as the skills and training which should be offered to judges in order to meet these requirements.

2.3. Incorporating 'Judicial Dialogue'

In the area of law development, where supreme courts and constitutional courts have become very influential, they have to compete with other institutions involved in rule-making. Part of this interaction concerns the so-called 'judicial dialogue' between highest courts regarding the exchange of legal ideas and experiences concerning questions of substantive law as well as procedural matters. In Europe, the national highest courts have to take account of the case law of the Court of Justice of the European Union (CJEU) and the European Court of Human Rights (ECtHR) when deciding domestic cases. However, it is unclear what the obligations of the national courts in this respect entail exactly. There is a lack of clarity, too, concerning the use of non-binding comparative legal sources by the highest courts. The increased availability of foreign legal materials and the exchange of ideas in judicial networks have stimulated judges to search for inspiration in foreign law when deciding cases. However, this practice has met with criticism and has led to disagreement between judges, legislators and academics in some countries, in particular the United States. The development of the decision-making practices of the highest courts in this context entails further reflection on the legitimacy and the methodology of judicial deliberations and reasoning.

2.4. Rethinking the Judicial Role in the Balance of Powers

The national courts' position in the balance of powers with the other branches of government also remains a much-debated topic, in particular in the field of fundamental rights. The significance of national courts as the ultimate protectors of individual rights at the national level has been emphasised, for example in discussions about the guarantee of national constitutional values and about the legitimacy of the ECtHR. Certain authors have highlighted the potential of the aforementioned judicial dialogue to become a tool for national courts, allowing them to oblige the domestic political branches to account for their actions in light of foreign and international consensus. However, research in the field of political science has suggested that the effects of constitutional courts on distributive justice are limited. Ran Hirschl has argued that constitutional courts seem to be the strategic invention of political and economic elites, who aim to remove political decision-making from the less-predictable representative institutions of government to the judicial branch. These pros and cons of 'judicial empowerment' play a role in policy debates concerning the role of the courts in the development of the public values of the national society.

3. The Actors

Which policy-makers determine the strategy for judicial organisation in a liberal-democratic legal system, either directly or indirectly? Taking examples from national legal systems into account, it can be demonstrated that several actors play a role in this respect. Since these actors have different interests, tensions can occur between their strategies for the national courts.

3.1. Governments

The national government, in particular the Ministry of Justice, can initiate reforms of the court system. Organisational reforms have been introduced in many western legal systems, in particular since the 1980's, concerning *inter alia* the updating of the judicial map, the introduction of more efficient court management and case management, and the further development of specialisation within the judiciary. These reforms aim to increase the effectiveness, efficiency, and client-oriented nature of the courts and to ensure judicial expertise for the judging of increasingly complex cases. In this respect, they embody strategies for the establishment of competitive and innovative public dispute settlement procedures and for the guarantee of qualitatively sound judicial decision-making. At the level of government, reforms such as these need to be discussed by the Parliament and enacted into legislation. In Europe, external influence in this context is exerted by the EU, which has set standards for judicial organisation in new Member States, and by the Council of Europe, which promotes specific policies, in particular through the European Commission for the Efficiency of Justice (CEPEJ).

3.2. Councils for the Judiciary

Another important strategic actor can exist in the form of a central governing organ for the judiciary, outside the Ministry of Justice. In Northern European countries, in particular the Netherlands and Scandinavia, Councils for the Judiciary act as an intermediary between the courts and the Ministry of Justice in decision-making about court management. Their tasks include the negotiation of the annual budget for the courts. In Southern European countries, such as France and Italy, the Councils for the Judiciary are involved in discipline and career decisions concerning judges. When promoting specific policy choices, the Councils for the Judiciary aim to act in accordance with a strategy they have elaborated. The Dutch Council for the Judiciary, for example, published a *Vision of the Judiciary* (Visie op de Rechtspraak) in 2010, in which several 'core values' for the judicial organisation as a whole are identified: independence, impartiality, integrity and professionalism. Similar values can be found at the European level in policy documents issued by the Council of Europe's CEPEJ and the European Network of Councils for the Judiciary (ENCJ). Based on these values, policy advice is prepared concerning a wide variety of issues, including the ones mentioned in the previous section. Together, the national and regional 'intermediary' actors can influence government policies as well as the conduct of courts and individual judges.

3.3. Judges

Thirdly, policy-making for the judiciary is a matter engaged in by judges themselves. In many countries, judges are organised in associations which act as labour unions and as participants in the public debate about the judiciary. These associations, too, follow a specific strategy. The Dutch Association of Judges and Prosecutors, for example, issued a Code of Conduct for Judges (Rechterscode) in 2011. In this Code of Conduct, five core values for the professional behaviour of judges are identified: independence, autonomy, impartiality, expertise and professionalism, and integrity. The Code addresses issues such as the achievement of judicial independence *vis-à-vis* political actors and the efforts to be made by judges to keep their expertise up to standard. Similar codes of conduct have been developed by representative organs of the judiciaries in many other countries, including the UK, France, Italy, and the US. At the international level, the most influential guidelines are the Bangalore Principles of Judicial Conduct, issued in 2002, which were developed by a conference of judges operating under the auspices of the United Nations. Furthermore, judicial cooperation, through coordination between national courts and transnational judicial networks, facilitates the development of strategies for judicial decision-making, judicial organisation and the role of the courts in the balance of powers. Judicial networks also offer a platform for judicial dialogue and for reflection on the usefulness and legitimacy of this dialogue. Examples are the Network of the Presidents of the Supreme Judicial Courts of the European Union and the Association of the Councils of State and Supreme Administrative Jurisdictions of the European Union.

3.4. Private Stakeholders

A relatively new group of actors with an influence on policy-making for judicial organisation are private dispute settlement providers. As was mentioned above, alternative dispute resolution, in particular mediation, has become very popular in many western legal systems. It is felt to provide an easily accessible, not too costly and speedy form of dispute settlement. The influence of private dispute settlement mechanisms on legal and justice strategies is indirect. The main goal of providers of such mechanisms is to offer an economically competitive service. However, the rise of private dispute settlement has pushed courts to innovate in order to remain interesting for parties who can choose between public and private dispute settlement. This concerns predominantly the field of private law cases. Private actors in this way oblige the other identified actors to rethink their strategies and possibly adapt their policy choices in reaction to the actions of the private actors.

3.5. The General Public

An indirect influence on strategies for the national courts is also exerted by the general public. After all, the public trust in the courts forms the basis for their legitimacy in liberal-democratic legal systems. This legitimacy concerns the courts' role as dispute settlement providers in private law cases, their role as law enforcers in criminal law cases, and their role as reviewers of government action in administrative law cases. The courts' legitimacy is assessed on the basis of the classic 'rule of law' principle of the guarantee of judicial independence and impartiality. However, in light of the developments described above, this legitimacy has come to depend as well on the fulfilment of managerial standards regarding the organisation of judicial proceedings and social-scientific standards regarding judicial decision-making. Moreover, expectations of the general public have developed concerning the interaction of the courts with society, through the reasoning of judgments as well as through communication in the media. In order to justify the public trust in national courts, these societal expectations will need to be taken into account in the further development of legal strategies by the actors involved in policy-making for the courts.

3.6. Tensions between Strategies

When comparing the interests of the different actors involved in policy-making for the national courts, a similarity and a difference can be identified. What is similar, firstly, is the acknowledgment by all actors of the importance of judicial awareness concerning the needs and expectations of society. However, different positions are taken concerning the action to be taken to give shape to this responsiveness. An example can make this clearer.

In the published codes of conduct for judges, the associations of judges emphasise the particular responsibility of judges in light of their specific constitutional position and the competences and responsibilities connected with this position. Judges are encouraged to reflect on their position in an evolving societal context, and to engage in discussion with their colleagues about ethical dilemmas that can arise in the adjudication of individual cases. It is pointed out that judges will be able to fulfil their role adequately only if certain constitutional and organisational conditions are met. In this way, part of the responsibility for the proper functioning of the judiciary is attributed to the other branches of government (the legislator and the executive power) and to the authorities involved in the judicial organisation (the Ministry of Justice, the Council for the Judiciary, and the court administrations). Management organs, such as the Northern European Councils for the Judiciary, by contrast, seem to stress the alignment of the judiciary with developments in society. The Dutch Council's Vision of the Judiciary addresses all persons involved in the national judicial organisation. The status of individual judges as members of the judicial organisation is emphasised: the guarantee of judicial independence does not exclude the assessment of the work of individual judges, including the general quality of their judgments, by their superiors in the organisation.

These two approaches reveal a tension between the balancing of values for the organisation of the judiciary and the balancing of values for the professional conduct of judges. In both instances, the roles attributed to accountability (through organisational hierarchy) and autonomy (through discretion in the handling of cases) have to be determined. From the perspective of court managers, agreements concerning the targets to be reached by the courts or concerning the handling of specific types of cases might be favoured. However, individual judges might feel constrained in their ability to deliver qualitatively sound judgments under time pressure and within the parameters set by judicial agreements. This restriction of judicial autonomy could have negative effects on the judges' ability to do justice in individual cases. To resolve this tension between strategies, a closer look can be had at the normative framework within which policy-making for the national courts takes place in liberal democracies.

4. The Framework

What strategies can be developed to ensure the continued relevance and legitimacy of national courts in the evolving legal context? An external constraint is imposed by the budget available for the courts, allocated by the government. Within the limits set by this budget, specific policy choices depend on the weight that is given to different normative values concerning the organisation of the court system and the process of judicial decision-making. The outcome of the balancing of these standards is reflected in the institutional design of the court system as well as in the prevailing organisational culture among judges and in the judicial approaches to discovery and the reasoning of judgments. In this respect, differences can be identified between national legal systems.

4.1. The Public Power of National Courts

In the globalised and privatised legal context, the institutional position of the national courts is being rethought in two ways. The relations between the national judiciary and the other branches of government are reconceptualised in light of the distribution of public power at the national and the supra-national levels. Relations between the institutions of government, including the courts, and private actors are reconceptualised in light of the demarcation of the public space *vis-à-vis* the private space. Aspects of the 'rule of law' are the point of departure for these re-conceptualisations, which are developed first of all in academic research. Research that is currently conducted in Rotterdam, for example, aims to clarify what the constitutional framework for this new distribution and demarcation of public power will look like, both at the institutional level and concerning its output in terms of efficient policies and human rights protection. Concerning the national courts, attention is paid *inter alia* to interaction with private dispute settlement mechanisms and the working methods and legal reasoning of the courts in the multi-level European legal order. Future policy-making for the courts can obtain guidance from the outcomes of this research.

4.2. Judicial Organisation

Current debates about judicial organisation and court reforms in liberal-democratic legal systems do not focus solely on the classic 'rule of law' standards for the judging of cases, such as the principles of judicial independence and impartiality. Beside these standards, which regulate the primary process of judging, standards concerning the organisation of judicial work have become increasingly important. The attention paid to these management standards is related to the effects of New Public Management (NPM) theories, which became influential in debates about the reform of judicial organisation in European countries in the 1980's and 1990's. These theories emphasise the importance of effectiveness, efficiency and a client-oriented approach by the judicial organisation. Under the effects of the NPM, court reforms in European countries have aimed at finding an adequate balance between the classic and the new standards for judicial organisation, *inter alia* with regard to court management and with regard to specialisation within the judiciary.

The inherent tension between the classic 'rule of law' principles and the NPM standards obliges policy-makers to balance these two types of values with every policy choice that is made in the context of judicial organisation. The scope for this balancing is determined by the national constitution in combination with applicable international norms. In European legal systems, Article 6 of the European Convention on Human Rights sets important minimum standards concerning the right to a fair trial. In its case law concerning this Article, the ECtHR has clarified that these standards also concern aspects of court organisation, such as the distribution of cases within the courts.

4.3. Judicial Discovery and the Reasoning of Judgments

Norms for judicial discovery and the reasoning of judgments currently seem to include the expectation that judges can and will take account of non-legal arguments and relevant foreign legal sources in their decision-making. These new demands necessitate the adaptation of the existing methodology for judicial discovery and for the reasoning of judgments. With regard to the inclusion of social-scientific and economic insights in judicial decision-making, several authors have argued that judges could develop a more pragmatic approach to the judging of cases. Judges could be encouraged to learn about psychological processes which influence the assessment of factual evidence and about dealing with 'common sense' arguments in the judging of cases. Indeed, judicial training programmes on these topics have been developed in some countries, for example The Netherlands. Concerning the use of comparative legal arguments in the deciding of cases, some researchers have analysed the current practices of courts, while others have assessed what courts can and may do from a constitutional law and legal theoretical perspective. These empirical and normative approaches can give guidance to the further development of judicial practices in the future.

4.4. Comparing National Frameworks

Differences exist between the strategies promoted by national constitutional frameworks. The constitutional norms and constitutional culture in Germany and France preserve a strong role for the judiciary at the national level. The focus is on procedural safeguards for dispute settlement and constitutional review as a means to guarantee the public values of the national society. The British and Dutch constitutional frameworks, by contrast, endorse the achievement of efficient dispute settlement, not necessarily through courts. Furthermore, these frameworks allow for only limited intervention by the courts in the development of public values through the review of legislative acts.

Concerning the courts' role in the development of the law across national borders, different frameworks exist, too. Rules enabling the judicial use of foreign legal sources can be found in the Constitution of South Africa and in a Practice Direction for the courts in England and Wales. The possibilities for judicial dialogue have been constrained in several US states, which have introduced constitutional bans on the use of foreign law.

The strategies of the actors involved in policy-making for the courts are shaped within these national frameworks. It seems that competition and innovation are higher on the agenda in legal systems in which the role of the courts is less protected by the constitution, such as Britain and The Netherlands. The reinforcement of judicial decision-making is taken up in the same context, with the aim of improving the quality of judicial decisions. Policies concerning transnational judicial dialogue have been developed mostly in legal systems where the courts' role in the balance of powers is debated. The courts' role is facilitated or constrained through strategies concerning the relationship between the national and supranational legal orders and concerning the scope of judicial discretion in the choice of sources for judicial decision-making.

5.   The Future

National courts remain among the most significant institutions of liberal democracies. They deliver justice in individual cases and contribute to the development of the law at the national and supra-national levels. Strategies for the role and functioning of the national courts exist and are of the utmost importance for the further development of liberal-democratic legal systems in the evolving legal context. However, multiple actors are involved in policy-making for the national courts and they represent different interests. Tensions between these actors' strategies should be resolved in a public debate, taking guidance from developed insights concerning the normative framework for the jurisdiction, organisation and decision-making of national courts. Particularities relating to national constitutional frameworks will remain influential in policy-making for the courts in different legal systems; although convergence might occur under the effects of further Europeanisation or globalisation on national legal orders.

6.   Sources and Further Reading

Antoine Hol *et al.*, "Highest Courts and Transnational Interaction", in *Utrecht Law Review*, 2012, vol. 8, no. 2.

Elaine Mak, "The European Judicial Organisation in a New Paradigm: The Influence of Principles of "New Public Management" on the Organisation of the European Courts", in *European Law Journal*, 2008, vol. 14, p. 718.

Fabrizio Cafaggi (ed.), *Enforcement of Transnational Regulation: Ensuring Compliance in a Global World*, Edward Elgar Publishing, Cheltenham, 2012.

Mauritis Barendrecht, *Courts, Competition and Innovation*, The Hague, 2011.

Richard A. Posner, *How Judges Think*, Harvard University Press, Cambridge MA, 2008.

Ran Hirschl, *Towards Juristocracy: The Origins and Consequences of the New Constitutionalism*, Harvard University Press, Cambridge MA, 2004.

Sam Muller and Sidney Richards (eds.), *Highest Courts and Globalisation*, Hague Academic Press, The Hague, 2010.

Tim Koopmans, *Courts and Political Institutions: A Comparative View*, Cambridge University Press, Cambridge, 2003.

Vicki C. Jackson, *Constitutional Engagement in a Transnational Era*, Oxford University Press, Oxford, 2009.

2.3.

Policies, Not Politics:
The Pursuit of Justice in Prosecutorial Strategy at the International Criminal Court

Jan Wouters[*] and Kenneth Chan[**]

This think piece examines how the objective of 'justice' has steered the operation of the Court, and particularly the Prosecutor, in the first decade of its existence. Providing justice to victims of international crime has always been a tremendous challenge for the Court because it does not have the resources to respond to every atrocity that arises on its watch. Consequently, the Prosecutor is bestowed the authority to decide which situations to investigate and which individuals to indict. This paper addresses two main issues related to this problem. First, how should such discretionary powers be employed in pursuit of effective and meaningful justice? Secondly, based on the choices he has made, how successful was the Prosecutor in developing his prosecutorial strategy in accordance with this goal? In particular, is it justifiable to criticise the Office for 'bullying' Africa, and for not being impartial in its investigations?

1. Introduction

> [I]n the face of war crimes, crimes against humanity and genocide, the default position of the international community is no longer impunity but accountability.[1]

The achievement of justice is an ideal to which all legal systems aspire. It is the benchmark against which all the triumphs and failures of the law are

---

[*] **Jan Wouters** is Professor of international law and international organizations, Jean Monnet Chair EU and Global Governance and Director of the Leuven Centre for Global Governance Studies as well as the Institute for International Law at the University of Leuven.

[**] **Kenneth Chan** is a Ph.D. candidate in the research programme "Global Governance and Democratic Government" at the Leuven Centre for Global Governance Studies.

[1] Kofi Annan, Justice vs. Impunity, The New York Times, 30 May 2010, available at http://www.nytimes.com/2010/05/31/opinion/31iht-edannan.html, last accessed on 20 August 2012.

measured. Yet, attempts to define the idea of 'justice' have met with only limited success. One reason for this is that the concept is contextual: it means many things to many peoples in different contexts. In international law, justice could refer *inter alia* to the attribution of responsibility to states for their actions, or to the assurance that fundamental individual rights will be protected. Yet, despite its many connotations in the international sphere, justice is a global public good which remains in dire need of procurement.[2] Indeed, it is the *pursuit* of justice that inspires scholars and lawyers to nurture the practice of law, and to ensure that it does not stagnate in the face of society's ever-changing norms. Thus, it is fitting that this volume seeks to capture the momentum of contemporary legal and justice *strategies*.

In this contribution, we consider how the concept of justice influences the work of the Prosecutor at the International Criminal Court (ICC or 'Court'). The ICC is the first and only permanent international criminal institution in the world, and is bestowed with a jurisdiction vastly greater than its immediate predecessors, the *ad hoc* tribunals. Never before has the notion of individual responsibility been so closely tied to an international body than with the ICC. Consequently, it faces a potentially greater work load than it has the proficiencies to manage. This has forced the Court to adopt a strategic, or selective, approach to its investigations. In fact, both the drafters of the Rome Statute and the Court's Prosecutor (who determines which investigations and prosecutions to pursue) have been at different times responsible for setting the agenda and priorities of the Court. Though this means that many legitimate claimants will inevitably be denied the opportunity to have their situations appear before the ICC, the inability to be completely comprehensive does *not* mean that the institution cannot successfully deliver on its mandate. What is vital is that this process is managed properly, and that it is done in a manner that is consistent, relevant, and consequential. In other words, the Prosecutor must transform selective justice into *effective and meaningful justice*. But what is 'meaningful justice', and what does it entail?

We first consider in Section II why defining the concept of 'justice' and articulating its contours has been such a vexing issue for international

---

2   See *inter alia* Amartya Sen, "Global Justice: Beyond International Equity", in Inge Kaul (ed.), *Global Public Goods: International Cooperation in the 21ˢᵗ Century,* New York, UNDP, 1999, p. 116.

criminal law. The drafters of the Rome Statute were required to craft a specific rubric of justice to operationalise the Court. What has this meant for the work of the Court and for the Prosecutor, who must apply the Statute? Section III examines this question more closely by considering how the Prosecutor, burdened by limited resources, should exercise his discretion by deciding which of the numerous crimes committed under his watch will be investigated and prosecuted. We examine what 'selective justice' means to the Office of the Prosecutor in this role, and what it must strive for in order to ensure victims receive meaningful and representative justice. Finally, in Section IV, we assess how discretion has been used by the Prosecutor in the Court's first decade. During the term of its first prosecutor, the Court was unable to avoid criticisms of 'bullying' and 'prosecutorial bias' – and whilst some of these accusations were unjustified, others were not. How can the Court ensure that prosecutorial strategy in the second decade of its existence does not compromise its vision of justice?

2. A Paradigm of Justice for the International Criminal Court

In December 2011, at the tenth session of the Assembly of State Parties to the Rome Statute, Mr. Luis Moreno-Ocampo (Ocampo) declared in one of his last speeches as Prosecutor that "[a] new global order based on law is coming [...] [because] seventy years ago the crime of genocide did not exist".[3] But what will this 'new global order' look like? The Prosecutor was obviously cognisant of both the difficult history of international criminal law – where for many decades the international community had been unable to provide effective institutions that could bring individuals to account for committing international crimes – as well as the remarkable institution-building successes of the past two decades. However, at ten years old, the ICC remains a fragile institution. To guarantee its long-term success, it must provide effective justice, and indeed, be *seen* to do so by the world at large. But can it do this within the strict limits of its resources?

---

[3]　United Nations News Centre, Support for Ending Impunity for International Crimes Must Grow – ICC, 12 December 2011, available at http://www.un.org/apps/news/story.asp?NewsID=40703&Cr=criminal+court&Cr1, last accessed on 20 August 2012.

In the Preamble of the Rome Statute, there is an unqualified declaration that all states parties must resolve "to guarantee lasting respect for and the enforcement of international justice". However, when this sentence is read in the light of the passage preceding it, it can be interpreted to imply that 'international justice' is a *chapeau* term, a paradigm that incorporates different concepts of justice. Indeed, the framers of the Statute were faced with the difficult task of balancing a number of different values from a variety of stakeholders and interest groups. To do so, a philosophy of selective justice was adopted during the negotiations to weigh these competing interests and to develop a final product. Such iterations of justice can be found in the following preambular paragraphs (emphasis added):

> Mindful that during this century millions of children, women and men have been *victims* of unimaginable atrocities that deeply shock the conscience of humanity, [...]
>
> Affirming that *the most serious crimes of concern to the international community as a whole* must not go unpunished and that their effective prosecution must be ensured by taking measures at the national level and by enhancing international cooperation,
>
> Determined to put *an end to impunity* for the perpetrators of these crimes and thus to contribute to the prevention of such crimes, [...][4]

Let us consider what perspectives of justice emerge from these passages. First, the Statute emphasizes the important role of *victims.* This has had far-reaching implications for the operation of the Court in terms of victim participation, the establishment of a victim's trust fund, and so on. The sudden importance placed on this group's previously unobserved interests (as compared to the *ad hoc* tribunals, for example) by the Statute reflects the increasing significance of human rights in international law. Nevertheless, such decisions were offset by the concern that over-extending the procedures of the Court to accommodate victims' interests could have serious consequences for due process. Secondly, the drive to *put an end to impunity* was the product of a massive global effort, and driven particularly by the fierce punitive force of international criminal

---

[4]   Rome Statute of the International Criminal Court 17 July 1998, UN Doc A/CONE.189/9*, amended January 2002, available at http://untreaty.un.org/cod/icc/statute/romefra.htm, last accessed on 29 August 2012.

law. Thirdly, the Court's (initial) jurisdiction over war crimes, crimes against humanity and genocide as 'the most serious crimes of concern to the international community as a whole' (bolstered by the Statute's expanded definitions of war crimes and crimes against humanity) reflects the conscious decision by the drafters to amalgamate a variety of different norms and values from the disciplines of international humanitarian law, international human rights law and international criminal law.[5]

In light of these observations, it can be concluded that the Statute's ideal of justice has been tailored to fit both the political and practical realities of the ICC. Selective and focused justice is thus a cornerstone principle of the Court. Whilst the Statute provides signposts to guide the Court in its work, it is ultimately the responsibility of the institution to decide how it fills its investigative docket by assessing which of the situations before it will be pursued. The following section therefore considers how the concept of justice should guide the Prosecutor's Office in the selection of situations and cases to investigate.

3. Justice and Prosecutorial Discretion at the International Criminal Court

Though the Rome Statute presents the Court with many jurisdictional hurdles before it may initiate investigations, its biggest challenge lies in managing the volume of potential situations before it that *do* qualify. There are more prospective candidates than the Office of the Prosecutor (OTP or Prosecutor's Office) is equipped to handle. Indeed, the Court's docket is already quite imposing, with the recent additions of Libya and Côte d'Ivoire to existing investigations in Kenya, the Democratic Republic of the Congo (DRC), the Central African Republic (CAR), Uganda and the Darfur region of the Sudan. In addition, the OTP has published a list of seven other situations presently under preliminary examination – Colombia, Afghanistan, Guinea, Honduras, Nigeria, Georgia and Korea – where it is to be determined if these will be turned into new investigations. Mali was recently added to this list when, in July 2012, the situation was self-referred to the new Prosecutor, making it the eighth prospective situation on the investigative docket.

---

[5] See David Scheffer, *All the Missing Souls: A Personal History of the War Crimes Tribunals,* Princeton University Press, 2012, p. 427.

By contrast to the Court's growing workload, the resources provided to it are intended to be stagnant. Because the Court is an independent treaty body (unlike its *ad hoc* tribunal predecessors, which were created by the United Nations Security Council) it does not receive funding from the United Nations. Rather, it is the States Parties that provide the Court's budget. Although it was always anticipated that the investigative docket and caseload of the ICC would expand considerably as it became established, there has never been the political will to index spending to such advancement. Consequently, the Assembly of States Parties (ASP) has established a zero growth budget for the institution. Perhaps most frustrating is the refusal of the Security Council to contribute resources to the Court despite its increasing willingness to engage the ICC as a tool in its security arsenal – as evidenced by its referral of both the situations in Darfur and Libya. For the ICC, the reality is that justice hangs on a shoestring.

Consequently, the Prosecutor now faces a number of difficult decisions regarding the management of his docket. His options are not attractive: he must close existing investigations before they have been properly concluded, or refuse to open new investigations, or – as a Human Rights Watch report warily cautions – be forced to 'hollow out' existing situations under investigation in order to spread resources more widely across new investigations.[6] This is obviously counter-intuitive to the most basic tenets of justice, which demand that the Court actively engage with new atrocities that arise on its watch. Obviously, this requires more, and more effective, investigations to take place.

To aide in this exercise, the chief tool provided by the Statute to regulate the ICC's workload is the discretionary authority delegated to the Prosecutor's Office to determine which of the legitimate situations and cases before it will be pursued. The proper role of the Prosecutor, and the extent of his powers, was of much debate during the negotiations for the Rome Statute. In the initial International Law Commission draft statute in 1994, the Prosecutor had no authority to initiate a case without a referral by the Security Council or a State Party. The push to provide the Prosecutor with such *proprio motu* powers came first from the Preparatory Committee, where delegates championed the need to allow the Office to investigate any information received from non-state sources it deemed to be

---

[6]   Human Rights Watch, Unfinished Business: Closing Gaps in the Selection of ICC Cases, 2011, p. 2.

important. There were fears that such powers would politicise the Court, though this would be a concern irrespective of which position one took on the issue – that is, whilst the Prosecutor *could* be influenced by external political forces undermining his *proprio motu* powers, it would be equally the case that if the Office lacked such discretion, the Court would simply become an extension of the Security Council's political will. Ultimately, the compromise reached in negotiations was that the Prosecutor would have *proprio motu* powers, but the authorisation of the Pre-Trial Chamber would be necessary for investigations initiated in this way.

Consequently, under the Statute, situations can be triggered in one of three ways. They can be referred to the Court via a State's self-referral (Article 13(a)) or through the Security Council (Article 13(b)). Further, the Prosecutor may receive communications about potential situations from individuals, groups, States, intergovernmental or non-governmental organisations (NGOs), and may then initiate investigations *proprio motu* provided the pre-trial chamber gives its authorisation (Article 15). Once triggered, the situations become subject to a preliminary examination to determine whether they meet the criteria for an investigation. The Statute guides this process through a broad legal framework found in Article 53(1). Here, it is stated that the Prosecutor must assess the situation under examination to determine if there is a 'reasonable basis' to believe that a crime within the Court's jurisdiction has been committed, and if so, whether it would be 'admissible'. For an assessment of admissibility, the Article further provides that the prosecutor must decide if there is sufficient situational gravity to move the investigation forward and whether the principle of complementarity is satisfied. Finally, the Prosecutor should decide if it is in the interests of justice to proceed.

This framework is unquestionably ambiguous. Seemingly, its intention was to provide the OTP with a vast, unregulated policy space through which it could define its own strategies under the broad heading of admissibility. The Statute does not attempt to route the Prosecutor's strategies in any way to prevent political or external influence. Therefore, at this point in the examination, the Prosecutor may use whatever criteria he deems necessary to determine whether the referrals/communications received will satisfy the criteria for opening an investigation. That is, the situation must both meet the Statute's minimum standards and pique the Prosecutor's professional interests. It is here where fears of politicisation are most heightened. As Danner explains:

> The ICC Prosecutor sits at a critical juncture in the structure of the Court, where the pressures of law and politics converge. The cases adjudicated by the ICC are infused with political implications and require sensitive decision making by those members of the Court – including the Prosecutor – who are vested with the discretion to exercise its powers. Because of the high stakes of its subject matter and the threat that its decisions can pose to powerful international interests, the ICC will inevitably be subject to charges that it is a purely political institution, remote from both the rule of law and the places where the crimes it adjudicates occur.[7]

The exercise of discretion can fall foul of a number of potential hazards as it is employed at different stages – in the exercise of *proprio motu* investigations, the evaluation of referrals, and in the administration of how such investigations will take place. There is no obviously objective way in which this power can be exercised – personal preference is, after all, the essence of 'discretion'. But it is hard to deny that a decision made not to pursue an investigation where crimes of some calibre have likely occurred is *not* a denial of justice for those victims. So far, the Prosecutor has closed three preliminary examinations in Venezuela, Iraq, and Palestine without opening a subsequent investigation; and in the case of Iraq, the refusal was made despite finding a reasonable basis for the commission of crimes by British Soldiers against victims of Iraqi nationality (this situation is more closely examined later in this chapter).[8] The Prosecutor's dilemma is best described by Louise Arbour, who explained to the ICC's Preparatory Committee in 1997 that:

> [The] criteria upon which such prosecutorial discretion is to be exercised are ill-defined and complex. In my experience,

---

[7] Allison Marston Danner, "Enhancing the Legitimacy and Accountability of Prosecutorial Discretion at the International Criminal Court", in *The American Journal of International Law*, 2003, vol. 97, p. 510. On the eminently political environment in which the Prosecutor and international criminal tribunals operate, see Luc Reydams, Jan Wouters and Cedric Ryngaert (eds.), *International Prosecutors,* Oxford University Press, 2012.

[8] Office of the Prosecutor, Update on Communications Received by the Office of the Prosecutor: Iraq Response, 2006. In Venezuela, the Prosecutor determined there was no reasonable basis to believe any of the alleged crimes had occurred, and the situation of Palestine was rejected because the Prosecutor was unwilling to make a declaration about its statehood, referring the matter instead to the Assembly of States Parties.

based on the work of the two Tribunals to date, I believe that the real challenge posed to a Prosecutor is to choose from many meritorious complaints, the appropriate ones for international intervention, rather than to weed out weak or frivolous ones.[9]

For the OTP, the challenge is then to take the notion of 'selective justice', and through its administration of prosecutorial strategy, secure a regime of 'effective and meaningful representative justice'. But what does this mean, and how can the Prosecutor do this?

First, the Prosecutor must establish his or her own goals for the Office. The Prosecutor's ideal of justice may vary (in broad or subtle ways) from those held by other stakeholders, and even from other Prosecutors who have held the office. For example, at the ceremony for his solemn undertaking as the ICC's first chief Prosecutor, Ocampo famously outlined his vision for the Institution and his Office, stating that "the number of cases that reach the Court should not be a measure of its efficiency. On the contrary, the absence of trials before this Court, as a consequence of the regular functioning of national institutions, would be a major success".[10] For Ocampo then, meaningful justice required that the Court cultivate an atmosphere of accountability at the national level, which would therefore allow his Office to facilitate trials for international crimes in both international *and domestic* fora. This would then allow the Prosecutor to use his discretion to encourage, assist, guide, and direct these local authorities in their pursuit of atrocity crimes. This is a vision of justice that the authors wholeheartedly support – it is ambitious, realistic, and perceptive.

Secondly, as has been already asserted, to fulfil these goals, the Prosecutor would need to approach his mandate strategically, using 'focused investigations and prosecutions' – a term employed in the OTP's 2006 report on prosecutorial strategy.[11] The Prosecutor's strategic plan-

---

[8] Statement by Justice Louise Arbour to the Preparatory Committee on the Establishment of an International Criminal Court, 8 December 1997, pp. 7–8; quoted in William Schabas, *An Introduction to the International Criminal Court,* Cambridge University Press, Cambridge, 2007, p. 160.

[10] Statement by Mr. Luis Moreno Ocampo, Chief Prosecutor of the International Criminal Court, at the ceremony for the solemn undertaking of the Chief Prosecutor at the ICC in June 2003.

[11] The Office of the Prosecutor, Report on Prosecutorial Strategy, 2006, p. 5, available at http://www.icc-cpi.int/NR/rdonlyres/D673DD8C-D427-4547-BC69-2D363E0727

ning can be consequently seen in a number of calculated decisions, for example, in the establishment of 'positive complementarity' (an initiative of the OTP which did not originate from the Statute, though in recent years, he has intimated that it manifests from Part 9 of the Statute on International Cooperation and Judicial Assistance), and in the evolution of his approach to situational gravity as a crucible for evaluating multiple situations. Yet, a degree of inconsistency in the application of these policies had made it unclear whether the Prosecutor had a clear vision of the 'protected interests' he wished to defend. Indeed, the first thing the Office must do when developing a strategic vision is to articulate what and whom it looks to protect, under which circumstances, and from what calibre and forms of criminal conduct. Establishing these core objectives is an essential starting point for the OTP as it rebuilds under Ms. Bensouda.

Within this rubric, there seems to be two different kinds of considerations that arise in the application of discretion. In the first place, the Prosecutor exercises discretion in how it follows the broad legal guidelines located in Article 53(1), as previously outlined. As there is considerable flexibility here, it is critical that the Office makes its decisions with demonstrable wisdom. For example, within Ocampo's vision of a collaborative domestic-international cooperative system of justice, the Office might seek to pursue a specific set of protected interests using a strategy that might involve selecting situations/approving referrals that can *inter alia* act as a model for domestic prosecutions by highlighting certain crimes or kinds of criminality which are often overlooked or should be treated with particular seriousness.[12] This might involve targeting and ending certain violent practices. Alternatively (or cumulatively), investigations may focus on certain intractable conflicts. The Prosecutor may also be inclined to go in the other direction, and attempt to intervene in crimes which are indicative pre-cursors of major conflicts. In such cases, the OTP could target, for instance, countries or regions that are geographically or socially remote – demonstrating that crimes that are committed on the fringes of society's awareness will not go ignored by the Court and its global reach. Although domestic cooperation is still a long way from

---

4B/143708/ProsecutorialStrategy20060914_English.pdf, last accessed on 20 August 2012.

[12] See in particular the important contribution by Kevin Jon Heller, "Situational Gravity under the Rome Statute", in Carsten Stahn and Larissa van den Herik (eds.), *Future Perspectives on International Criminal Justice*, T.M.C. Asser Press, 2010, p. 227.

reaching this point, there have been signs of progress. Human Rights Watch has observed that the investigations of the Court have stimulated interest in seeking national prosecutions of serious crimes in the Congo, Guinea, and Uganda.[13]

The second, and arguably more controversial application of discretion, occurs when the Prosecutor accounts for factors beyond those specifically articulated in the Statute as part of the legal framework. It is, for instance, hard to deny that the ready cooperation of a self-referred State would not be a persuasive consideration for the Court. Neither would it be illogical for the Prosecutor to prioritise a case where a defendant is already in custody. Likewise, a Security Council referral presents a particularly desirable opportunity to extend the Court's reach to situations beyond its typical jurisdiction, strengthening the overall perceived legitimacy of the institution as a whole. These considerations have almost certainly influenced the Prosecutor's assessment of situations and cases in the past. Indeed, William Schabas has argued that the decision to charge Thomas Lubanga was an example of "the exercise of prosecutorial discretion [being] more to do with the fact that this was an accused who was accessible to a Court starved for trial work [than a conclusion naturally reached through an independent assessment of the relevant legal criteria]".[14] This practice is not *per se* inherently objectionable when conducted at the same level of standards and in accordance with the same values expected of the Prosecutor when he assesses the Article 53(1) legal framework. Yet, it should be treated with much more caution, as it is uncertain to what extent such decisions can be made impartially and independently.

Ultimately, as the OTP continues to evolve, its practices must change too. The Office must develop clear and coherent policies that indicate how discretion will be employed to assess merit and discern between situations – and it should make these guidelines (at least partially) publicly known. This can remove some of the sting from what can otherwise be perceived as a failure of independence in prosecutorial decision-making. An entirely articulated strategy need not be published, nor should the

---

[13] Richard Dicker, ICC: The Court of Last Resort, Human Rights Watch, 2012, available at http://www.hrw.org/news/2012/06/29/icc-court-last-resort, last accessed on 20 August 2012.

[14] William Schabas, "Prosecutorial Discretion v. Judicial Activism at the International Criminal Court", in *Journal of International Criminal Justice*, 2008, p. 737.

Prosecutor seek to define his role in such concrete terms that the policy fails to strike a balance with the freedoms, flexibility, and secrecy that is necessary for the Prosecutor to function. However, it must meet minimum standards for transparency and accountability that States Parties (who are the chief stakeholders of the Court) consider essential for the preservation of the institution's legitimacy.[15] For example, it would be particularly useful for the Court to clarify how the Article 53 framework should be used – that is, what indicators make a situation graver than another, when should complementarity be or not be deployed to hold off on further activities, and when is an investigation not in the 'interests of justice'? Though some of these issues have been approached in the OTP's occasional policy publications, these questions have not been dealt with directly by the Court's first Prosecutor.

A final observation is that this framework must be built on the principles of 'impartiality' and 'independence'. The former occurs where allegations against *all parties* are investigated, and the latter where such investigations are free from external (particularly political) influence. The OTP explains that "[the] duty of independence goes beyond simply not seeking or acting on instructions. It also means that the selection process is not influenced by the presumed wishes of any external source, nor the importance of cooperation of any particular party, nor the quality of cooperation provided. The selection process is independent of the cooperation-seeking process".[16] Further principles that have been highlighted by the OTP include objectivity and non-discrimination.[17]

In summary, the Office must bridle the expansive powers given to it to the extent that it can assure the Court's stakeholders that it is not beholden to the whims of any external influence (whether this be other States, non-state parties or even the Security Council), and that the Prosecutor himself is beyond suspicion of personal political machinations. It is a timely reminder to the OTP that the purpose of discretion is to permit the effective administration of policy, not politics. With a properly delineated set of guiding principles that (at minimum) outlines the strategies that will be considered, the Prosecutor can go a considerable way in reconcil-

---

[15] See Luc Reydams, Jan Wouters and Cedric Ryngaert, "Conclusion", in *International Prosecutors*, see supra note 7, p. 929.

[16] Office of the Prosecutor, Criteria for Selection of Situations and Cases, Draft Policy Paper, 2006, pp. 1–2.

[17] Office of the Prosecutor, 2006, see *supra* note 16.

ing the Court's 'selective justice' with the more universal expectations of 'justice' embraced by the international community. If it can embellish further on the contextual meaning and practical implications of its core principles, like impartiality and independence, this will also be a welcome olive branch to the Court's critics. But what do these principles mean, and how have they be woven together to help the Office visualise its goals? The following section considers how discretion has been used in the last decade, and considers the criticisms that have arisen.

4.   Ten Years of Prosecutorial Discretion: Successes and Failures

We are at an opportune moment in the Court's history. Not only has it seen its first case against Congolese defendant Thomas Lubanga concluded, it has also seen the final days of the tenure of its first Prosecutor, and the beginning of Ms. Fatou Bensouda's term in office. How successful has the OTP been under Ocampo, and what liberties were taken to get there? As indicated above, justice must not only be done, but must also be seen to be done. In order to be successful, not only must the Prosecutor's professional conduct and choices have vindicated the law, but he must also have been judged by an external audience of outside observers to have held up those rules. This is not always easy to reconcile with the principle of independence, as it implies that the Prosecutor must respond to specific public outcries for justice in various situations. The Sudan, for example, became the focus of a massive global media campaign in the early 2000's, which played no small role in mobilising international aide and intervention. Thus, it would have been foolish for the Prosecutor to refuse to open an investigation there after the Security Council had referred it, despite having legitimate reasons to do so (for example, because of the many obstacles and dangers for its staff if it were to lead such an investigation). There is no precise science to such an assessment, but it is worth considering some of the choices the Prosecutor has made and the criticisms of the Office that have arisen.

The non-governmental organisation Human Rights Watch has been critical of Ocampo's record in the past. In a recent report, the organisation was particularly damning. It argued that the OTP's investigations had "failed to demonstrate coherent and effective strategies for delivering meaningful justice to affected communities [...] [which would] require multiple investigations, deeply rooted in the country-specific context".[18] These failures, it submitted, "[have] undermined perceptions of independence and impartiality [in the DRC, Uganda, CAR, and Darfur]".[19] For example, the charges laid against Thomas Lubanga caused considerable controversy when they caused a rift between the Office and the demands of victims. After his arrest, expectations were elevated that the accused would be charged with crimes that would reflect the seriousness and violence he had inflicted in the DRC. In fact, during Ocampo's opening statement at the trial, he pointedly noted that "Lubanga's group [had] recruited, trained and used hundreds of children to kill, pillage and rape".[20] Yet, such crimes did not come to pass when Lubanga was indicted. There were no allegations of killings, pillage, or rape included in the charging document. Instead, he would be prosecuted for the war crimes of enlistment, conscription and use of child soldiers – arguably, comparatively less serious crimes.[21] This was met with considerable dismay by observers and victims activist groups such as the Women's Initiative for Gender Justice, who protested the exclusion of rape and sexual violence amongst the charges. The group expressed concerns that "these charges [risked] offending the victims and strengthening the growing mistrust in the work of the International Criminal Court in the DRC and in the work of the Prosecutor specifically".[22] This sense of injustice was only compounded during the trial of the accused when almost all of the prosecution's 30 witnesses, composed largely of child soldiers, acknowledged the wide and pervasive use of rape against young girls by Lubanga's forces on a daily basis.[23] In-

---

[18] Human Rights Watch, see *supra* note 6, p. 2.

[19] *Ibid.*

[20] Prosecutor v. Lubanga (ICC-01/04-01/06-T-107-ENG), Procedural Matters (Open Session), Situation in the Democratic Republic of Congo, 26 January 2009, lines 19–21, available at http://www2.icc-cpi.int/iccdocs/doc/doc623638.pdf, last accessed on 20 August 2012.

[21] Prosecutor v. Lubanga (ICC-01/04-01/06), Joint Application of the Legal Representative of the Victims for the Implementation of the Procedure under Regulation 55 of the Regulations of the Court, 22 May 2009.

[22] Beni Declaration by Women's Rights and Human Rights NGOs from the Democratic Republic of the Congo on the Prosecutions by the ICC, Beni, Democratic Republic of Congo, 2007.

[23] Rachel Irwin, Court Hears Recruits Raped by Commanders, The Lubanga Trial at the International Criminal Court, 26 June 2009), available at http://www.lubangatrial.org/2009/06/26/court-hears-recruits-raped-by-commanders, last accessed on 20 August 2012.

famously, this led the Legal Representatives of Victims to contest the Prosecutor's right to define the scope of charges against the accused (a challenge that was ultimately rejected by the Appeals Chamber).[24]

Suspicions of political influence also arose in 2006, when the Prosecutor announced in an open letter that he was closing preliminary examinations in Iraq without opening further investigations into a number of international crimes allegedly committed by British troops against Iraqi victims. This was despite finding that there was a "reasonable basis" to believe there had been up to 12 victims of wilful killings, and a number of others subjected to inhuman treatment. The Prosecutor explained that the likely gravity of the situation (where only a small number of crimes with only a limited number of victims would be subject to the Court) was outweighed by the gravity of the other situations the OTP was then investigating in Uganda, the DRC and Darfur, which all involved "thousands of wilful killings as well as intentional and large-scale sexual violence and abductions".[25] Yet, in the DRC, Thomas Lubanga was only prosecuted for the use and conscription of child soldiers – crimes that, as we have noted, do not have elements of killings or sexual violence in them. What sets of variables was the Prosecutor actually comparing? If it was the gravity of the prospective crimes involved, then the Prosecutor's argument was undermined by the fact that the crimes investigated in Iraq were more 'serious' than those Thomas Lubanga was charged with. If the comparison was between the levels of violence that had occurred in the entirety of both situations, then this should have been clearly stated. Indeed, if the scale of the atrocities committed was truly a concern to the Prosecutor, why was the degree of violence authored by Thomas Lubanga not reflected in the charges levelled against him? On the face of it, the Prosecutor's use of the justification of gravity does not seem consistent between various situations and cases. It is hard in this case, to avoid the perception of an underlying political motive when the Office has not been more careful in explaining its rationalisations.

These examples highlight the two main allegations that have been made against the OTP during its first decade – that it has been 'targeting' Africa in its strategy, and that it has failed to be impartial in its investigations. Let us consider the validity of such claims.

---

[24] Prosecutor v Lubanga, 2009, see *supra* note 21.

[25] Office of the Prosecutor, 2006, see *supra* note 11.

4.1. Targeting Africa and the OTP's Failure of Due Diligence to Victims of Atrocity Crimes

Ocampo has always insisted that he has acted independently and impartially. Indeed, wanting to avoid the politicisation of his Office was the reason Ocampo in 2012 refused to open investigations in Palestine. He suggested this would require him to engage in a political act by implicitly recognising its statehood.[26] In one of his last interviews in office, with the International Peace Institute, the Prosecutor again insisted that he had always followed the evidence because "[he is] a criminal prosecutor, [...] not a political analyst".[27] Yet, this is clearly not the perception held in Africa, the region where opinions matter the most because the majority of the Prosecutor's activities have been focused there. Ocampo has been famously combative with the African Union (AU), whose Commission Chairman, Mr. Jean Ping, has candidly stated that, "we are not against the ICC. What we are against is Ocampo's justice".[28] In no small part, the AU's discontent comes from the marginalisation of its demands by the Court, which has undermined the sense of local ownership it feels towards countries on the African continent. In particular, the Court's refusal to

---

[26] See International Criminal Court Office of the Prosecutor, Situation in Palestine, 3 April 2012, p. 5, available at http://www.icc-cpi.int/NR/rdonlyres/C6162BBF-FEB9-4FAF-AFA9-836106D2694A/284387/SituationinPalestine030412ENG.pdf, last accessed on 20 August 2012. Amnesty International has notably argued that the decision not to make a determination on statehood for the purposes of the Statute is itself is a political act because the determination of Palestine's Statehood is something that the judges of the Court should do, and not the Prosecutor. As Marek Marczynski, the Head of Amnesty International's International Justice Campaign argues "This dangerous decision opens the ICC to accusations of political bias and is inconsistent with the independence of the ICC. It also breaches the Rome Statute which clearly states that such matters should be considered by the institution's judges": Amnesty International Press Release: ICC Prosecutor Statement: Fears over Justice for Gaza Victims, 3 April 2012, available at http://www.amnesty.org/en/for-media/press-releases/icc-prosecutor-statement-fears-over-justice-gaza-victims-2012-04-03, last accessed on 20 August 2012.

[27] International Peace Institute, Speakers Events: Moreno-Ocampo: 'I Follow Evidence, Not Politics', 20 January 2012, available at http://www.ipinst.org/events/speakers/de tails/338-moreno-ocampo-i-follow-evidence-not-politics.html, last accessed on 20 August 2012.

[28] David Smith, New Chief Prosecutor Defends International Criminal Court, The Guardian, 23 May 2012, available at http://www.guardian.co.uk/law/2012/may/23/chief-prosecutor-international-criminal-court, last accessed on 20 August 2012.

---

heed its calls to postpone proceedings against President al-Bashir of Sudan has been a major point of contention. This, it feels, has damaged its on-going efforts to negotiate a peace accord with President al-Bashir. Consequently, it called for its members to refuse to cooperate with the Court. The Prosecutor's response to this was, quite rightly, that acceding to such demands would be an indictment of his independence, irrespective of the circumstances. As he puts it, "[p]eace is not the responsibility of the prosecutor. The prosecutor has the responsibility to do justice, and judges will review in accordance with critical law".[29] He goes further, stating that, "[w]e cannot decide that when the negotiator says 'okay, now it is better to stop,' I stop. I have no mandate to do that, and I will destroy the Office of the Prosecutor and the Court if people perceive that the Court is just adjusting to political considerations".[30] But is the Prosecutor's failure to widen his vision beyond African situations consistent with an independent focus on the pursuit of justice?

First, it is important to recognise that the accusation of 'targeting' is quite different than that of the ICC 'unfairly or inappropriately targeting' Africa. The OTP is legally entitled to target situations and crimes in Africa, and as part of a broader strategy, is not wrong to do so. As long as each situation and case assessed appropriately complies with the Statute's jurisdictional requirements, there is nothing which specifically prohibits the Prosecutor from targeting certain regions or crimes. Indeed, as we have argued, that is the very point of discretion – to allow the Court to demonstrate its relevance by deciding where it can do the most good. As Ms. Bensouda points out, "[a]nti-ICC elements have been working very hard to discredit the Court and to lobby for non-support and they are doing this, unfortunately, with complete disregard for *legal arguments* [emphasis added]".[31] Admittedly, it is hard to argue that focusing on African cases makes for good strategy when this has weakened institutional ties, undermined the work of regional organisations in Africa, and threatened the ability of the Court to continue its investigative activities on the African continent. However, as a matter of law, there has been no specific evidence to suggest that any of the Court's investigations were wrongly initiated.

---

[29] International Peace Institute, 2012, *supra* note 27.
[30] *Ibid.*
[31] David Smith, 2012, see *supra* note 28.

In our opinion, the real issue with these complaints is that they threaten to mischaracterise the actual victims of inconsistent and incoherent prosecutorial strategy. Such victims are not those States under investigation, as the communities affected by those crimes can find justice through the investigations of the Court. Rather, they are those victims who will not have justice because the OTP has been derelict in its duty to open investigations where the evidence demands that it should have.

At the moment, there are already many victims of prosecutorial case load mismanagement in places where the Court has jurisdiction, but has yet to act on it. Here, the authors would like to draw attention to the situation in Colombia. Colombia is the site of an intractable conflict between its government and numerous violent non-state groups, including the Revolutionary Armed Forces of Colombia (*Fuerzas Armadas Revolucionarias Colombianas* or FARC) and the National Liberation Army. Such groups have led to the creation of a number of paramilitary groups that have been linked to public officials, and who have been equally complicit in the commission of atrocity crimes. In 2009, the OTP made known that the situation in Colombia had been under preliminary examination since 2006. In other words, this situation has been pending a final decision for six years. In its 2011 *Report on Preliminary Examination Activities*, the OTP revealed that the main focus of its analysis has been the assessment of 'complementarity'. It claimed that Colombian authorities had already carried out numerous proceedings against a variety of alleged criminals for crimes against humanity and war crimes. It went on to explain that it still lacked sufficient information to determine if the national proceedings that had taken place there were genuine and carried out in good faith. Thus, it would continue to gather evidence. The report gives the impression that the governmental apparatus for the prosecution of crimes is working successfully and effectively, targeting a range of individuals from both sides of the conflict, including government officials.

There are a number of troubling issues arising from this report. First, it is of concern that the situation has been pending a formal decision for such a long period of time. If the legal system in Colombia is as accessible to the Court as the report indicates it is, then it is inexcusable that the OTP has yet to gather sufficient information about the legitimacy of its operations. Even though the Statute does not require the Prosecutor to make decisions within a specified timeframe, it would be negligent to use this loophole as a means to avoid making a decision either to approve or deny an investigation. Secondly, in his 2011 report, the Prosecutor admitted that the Office had found there to be a reasonable basis to believe that crimes against humanity had been committed.[32] If such crimes are both 'apparent' and 'intractable', then the Office's demonstrated lack of urgency in concluding its initial assessment is egregiously vexing.

But most importantly, the Court appears to have foregone a close analysis of the quality of the national investigations it cites in favour of their impressive quantitative volume.[33] In Colombia, accusations of corruption are rife and real. The fact that the Prosecutor had based his analysis of facts entirely on the prosecutions made under the country's Justice and Peace Law 975 of 2005, which is firmly controlled by the incumbent government, and which has complete control over whom it will and will not process under the law, should be a cause for alarm. There are grounds to believe that this law is being used to deflect accountability away from those architects and engineers of the international crimes being committed in Colombia in favour of a multitude of 'small fish'. Yet, of the numerous criminal proceedings against public officials that the OTP report cites, less than a handful are for crimes falling under the ICC's jurisdiction *ratione materiae*. The majority of these prosecutions focus instead on charges of electoral fraud and conspiracy. As time passes, it will become more and more difficult for the ICC to secure the evidence necessary to reconstruct the truth of what has happened in the country, and provide justice to the victims of the international crimes that the OTP has already stated in its 2011 report that it had a reasonable basis to believe had occurred. The Court must make a decision on the situation soon, and must carefully consider the perception of its independence if it chooses not to act.

4.2. Impartiality and the Failure to Investigate All Sides

Impartiality is a delicate concept, and is often difficult to implement in practice. As an exiled Syrian activist and member of the Syrian National Council was reported to have said, "[in the countries of the Arab Spring,

---

[32] Office of the Prosecutor, Report on Preliminary Examination Activities, 2011, pp. 15–16.

[33] See the report of Avocats Sans Frontières, The Principle of Complementarity in the Rome Statute and the Colombian Situation: A Case that Demands More than a 'Positive' Approach, 2012, available at http://www.iccnow.org/documents/asf_rapport-anglais-complementarity_and_colombia.pdf, last accessed 20 August 2012.

we] have the feeling that international justice is not ruled by law. […] It is ruled by politics, it is ruled by circumstances. It depends on the situation, it depends *how valuable this person is* [emphasis added]. That is not real justice".[34] For the Prosecutor, cooperation by a State being investigated can be the difference between conducting an effective investigation, and being able to even gain access to a region. Securing both documentary evidence and live testimony in regions with obscure local dialects is impossible without such assistance. Thus, the Prosecutor has been particularly eager to put his support behind situations which have been self-referred (as in those situations, the support of the state is essentially secured). However, there may be a cost for such camaraderie. Self-referrals have the potential to be politically charged, in that incumbent governments of referring States can use the process as a convenient way to do away with inconvenient rivals. Indeed, in all three of the self-referred situations that have been investigated (the DRC, CAR and Uganda), all charges have been levelled at rebel groups, and no one affiliated with a government in office has been indicted by the Prosecutor. However, it should also be noted that in the situations of Kenya and the Sudan, public officials have been named in arrest warrants, though in these cases, cooperation by local authorities was dubious at best.

In the past decade, the Office has fallen afoul of the impartiality problem on a number of occasions, where it has appeared to be too close and too reliant on a particular government or faction in a conflict. This has clearly harmed the public perception of the Office's impartiality. It is hard to forget, in this respect, the infamous press conference held in London in 2004 by Ocampo jointly with President Yoweri Museveni of Uganda, who stood by his side as they announced the opening of formal investigations into Uganda. This was widely perceived as prosecutorial support for President Museveni in the region's conflict. Whilst the Prosecutor could have assuaged such concerns by looking into the alleged atrocities committed by the armed forces of Uganda, he instead made a deliberate decision to focus on the crimes of the rebel insurgency 'the Lord's Resistance Army', led by the infamous Joseph Kony.

---

[34] Lydia Polgreen, Arab Uprisings Point Up Flaws in Global Court, The New York Times, 7 July 2012, available at http://www.nytimes.com/2012/07/08/world/middleeast/arab-spring-reveals-international-court-flaws.html?_r=1&partner=rss&emc=rss&from=2, last accessed on 20 August 2012.

The OTP will need to learn from such mistakes in the management of future situations. Consider, for example, Côte d'Ivoire, where the Prosecutor recently opened an investigation *proprio motu* into the crimes committed after the country's contentious 2010 elections. The Office has so far brought former President Laurent Gbagbo into its custody, marking the first head of State to be tried at the ICC. However, it has already been alleged by Mr. Gbagbo's aides that these actions "demonstrate the bias of international players towards former IMF executive Ouattara, who came to power after French soldiers helped him oust Gbago".[35] It is hard to ignore such criticisms when Ocampo continued to demonstrate such an uncomfortably close relationship with members of incumbent President Alassane Outtara's regime up until the end of his term. At the start of 2012, it was reported that Ocampo had written a letter to Guillaume Soro, the former commander of the pro-Outtara rebel group *Forces Republicaines de Côte d'Ivoire*, congratulating him on his election to the country's national assembly.[36] This specific action was particularly galling because Mr. Soro was implicated in a number of international crimes and was a potential prospect for prosecution at the Court. As was stated in a Human Rights Watch report on the violence:

> In one particularly horrific incident, hundreds of ethnic Guéré civilians perceived as supporting Gbagbo were massacred in the western town of Duékoué by a mixture of pro-Ouattara groups, including Republican Forces under the overall command of Ouattara's prime minister, Guillaume Soro.[37]

In the country, such actions were declared to be indicative of "collusion between Ouattara's camp and the ICC".[38] Such criticisms not only harm the Court, but they also threaten to drive deep wedges into the brittle political climate of the state. Ms. Bensouda has considerable work to do if

---

[35] Ivana Sekularac, Gbagbo Faces Charges of Crimes against Humanity: ICC, Reuters, 30 November 2011, available at http://www.reuters.com/article/2011/11/30/us-ivorycoast-gbagbo-daidUSTRE7AS1LO20111130, last accessed on 20 August 2012.
[36] See All Africa, Cote d'Ivoire: Debate on Whether Former First Lady Should Be Transferred to the ICC, 5 April 2012, available at http://allafrica.com/stories/201204060811.html, last accessed 20 August 2012.
[37] Human Rights Watch, Cote d'Ivoire: Ouattara Forces Kill, Rape Civilians during Offensive, 9 April 2011, available at http://www.hrw.org/news/2011/04/09/c-te-d-ivoire-ouattara-forces-kill-rape-civilians-during-offensive, last accessed on 20 August 2012.
[38] All Africa, 2012, *supra* note 36.

she is to patch up the Court's relationship with the people of Côte d'Ivoire, and it is only by investigating crimes committed by supporters of both Mr. Gbagbo and his political rival and current President Alassane Outtara that she can rise above such accusations.

5. Conclusion

The recent referral of the situation in Mali after January 2012 represents the first opportunity for Ms. Bensouda to define the Court's new direction under her leadership. Given the willingness of the referring State, there is a good chance it will become the first investigation to be opened by her. She has noted in particular, the occurrence of "instances of killings, abductions, rapes and conscriptions of children" in the situation, perhaps hinting at a future policy focus.[39] There are of course certain risks involved in this potential investigation of which the Prosecutor will need to be wary. For example, the referral specifically sought the Court's intervention in investigating crimes committed by rebel groups that have taken control of northern Mali. Whilst these groups have seemingly been the primary authors of the atrocity crimes in the country, to what extent would the assumption of this investigation undermine the efforts of Ms. Bensouda to free her office from the criticisms levelled at her predecessor?

In any case, there is good cause to believe that the OTP will go from strength to strength under Ms. Bensouda's leadership. She has been widely reported to be bereft of the kinds of character flaws and poor judgment that made Mr. Ocampo's tenure so tempestuous. Hearteningly, she has already articulated a healthy vision of how justice will be administered under her stewardship, observing that:

> Real justice is not a pick and choose system. To be effective, to be just and to have a lasting impact, justice has to be guided solely by the law and the evidence. Our focus is on individual criminal behaviour against innocent victims.[40]

---

[39] International Criminal Court, ICC Prosecutor Fatou Bensouda on the Malian State Referral of the Situation in Mali Since January 2012, 18 July 2012, available at http://icc-cpi.int/NR/exeres/B8DAF5A7-DD53-43D2-A3A8-0BC30E6D00B9.htm, last accessed on 20 September 2012.

[40] Fatou Bensouda, Law as a Tool for World Peace and Security, Open Society Initiative for Southern Africa, 2012, available at http://www.osisa.org/law/blog/law-tool-world-peace-and-security, last accessed on 20 August 2012.

The critical test will be whether the Prosecutor can take such clarity of vision and apply it in her prosecutorial strategy. The principles which govern discretion – chiefly independence and impartiality – do not require that the Prosecutor be neutral in her course of conduct. On the contrary, as we have stated, the Prosecutor should be encouraged to prioritise and address various forms of criminality and patterns of violence, and target crimes that harm particularly vulnerable groups such as women and children. Thus, Ms. Bensouda should be applauded for her position on gender and sex crimes, which she has indicated will be a central pillar in her Office's work:

> [I will] in particular, also continue to look for innovative methods for the collection of evidence to bring further gender crimes and crimes against children to the court, to ensure effective prosecutions of these crimes while respecting and protecting the victims.[41]

Likewise, in the instances where the OTP has opened investigations *proprio motu* so far, in the Republic of Kenya and Côte d'Ivoire, it should not go unnoticed that both sets of investigations were focused on post-election crimes – that is, those which could likely occur again when future elections arise. If the OTP was looking to develop a strategy where it could potentially end recurring cycles of violence, this is an exciting prospect for the Court, and one that shows real maturation. If the Prosecutor can remain on point, and service these ends alongside the more ambitious goals laid out by the Statute, we may see the Court begin to provide the meaningful justice it has always promised.

6. Sources and Further Reading

All Africa, "Cote d'Ivoire: Debate on Whether Former First Lady Should Be Transferred to the ICC", 5 April 2012, available at http://allafrica.com/stories/201204060811.html, last accessed 20 August 2012.

Allison Marston Danner, "Enhancing the Legitimacy and Accountability of Prosecutorial Discretion at the International Criminal Court", in *The American Journal of International Law*, 2003, vol. 97.

---

[41] BBC, Gambia's Fatou Bensouda Sworn in as ICC Prosecutor, 15 June 2012, available at http://www.bbc.co.uk/news/world-africa-18455498, last accessed on 20 August 2012.

Amartya Sen, "Global Justice: Beyond International Equity", in I. Kaul (ed.), *Global Public Goods: International Cooperation in the 21st Century,* New York, UNDP, 1999.

Avocats Sans Frontières, The Principle of Complementarity in the Rome Statute and the Colombian Situation: A Case that Demands More than a 'Positive' Approach, 2012, available at http://www.iccnow.org/documen ts/asf_rapport-anglais-complementarity_and_colombia.pdf, last accessed 20 August 2012.

BBC, Gambia's Fatou Bensouda Sworn in as ICC Prosecutor, 15 June 2012, available at http://www.bbc.co.uk/news/world-africa-18455498, last accessed on 20 August 2012.

Beni Declaration by Women's Rights and Human Rights NGOs from the Democratic Republic of the Congo on the Prosecutions by the ICC, Beni, Democratic Republic of Congo, 2007.

David Scheffer, *All the Missing Souls: A Personal History of the War Crimes Tribunals,* Princeton University Press, 2012.

David Smith, New Chief Prosecutor Defends International Criminal Court, The Guardian, 23 May 2012, available at http://www.guardian. co.uk/law/2012/may/23/chief-prosecutor-international-criminal-court, last accessed on 20 August 2012.

Fatou Bensouda, Law as a Tool for World Peace and Security, Open Society Initiative for Southern Africa, 2012, available at http://www.osisa .org/law/blog/law-tool-world-peace-and-security, last accessed on 20 August 2012.

Human Rights Watch, "Cote d'Ivoire: Ouattara Forces Kill, Rape Civilians during Offensive", 9 April 2011, available at http://www.hrw.org/ news/2011/04/09/c-te-d-ivoire-ouattara-forces-kill-rape-civilians-during-offensive, last accessed on 20 August 2012.

Human Rights Watch, Unfinished Business: Closing Gaps in the Selection of ICC Cases, 2011.

ICC Office of the Prosecutor, Situation in Palestine, 3 April 2012, available at http://www.icc-cpi.int/NR/rdonlyres/C6162BBF-FEB9-4FAF-AF A9-836106D2694A/284387/SituationinPalestine030412ENG.pdf, last accessed on 20 August 2012.

ICC, "ICC Prosecutor Fatou Bensouda on the Malian State Referral of the Situation in Mali Since January 2012", 18 July 2012, available at ICC Office of the Prosecutor, Criteria for Selection of Situations and Cases, Draft Policy Paper, 2006.

ICC Office of the Prosecutor, Report on Preliminary Examination Activities, 2011.

ICC, Prosecutor v. Lubanga (ICC-01/04-01/06), Joint Application of the Legal Representative of the Victims for the Implementation of the Procedure under Regulation 55 of the Regulations of the Court, 22 May 2009.

ICC, Prosecutor v. Lubanga (ICC-01/04-01/06-T-107-ENG), Procedural Matters (Open Session), Situation in the Democratic Republic of Congo, 26 January 2009, lines 19–21, available at http://www2.icc-cpi.int/icc docs/doc/doc623638.pdf, last accessed on 20 August 2012.

http://icc-cpi.int/NR/exeres/B8DAF5A7-DD53-43D2-A3A8-0BC30E6D00B9.htm, last accessed on 20 September 2012.

International Peace Institute, Speakers Events: Moreno-Ocampo: 'I Follow Evidence, Not Politics', 20 January 2012, available at http://www.ipinst.org/events/speakers/details/338-moreno-ocampo-i-follow-evidence-not-politics.html, last accessed on 20 August 2012.

Ivana Sekularac, Gbagbo Faces Charges of Crimes against Humanity: ICC, Reuters, 30 November 2011, available at http://www.reuters.com/article/2011/11/30/us-ivorycoast-gbagbo-daidUSTRE7AS1LO20111130, last accessed on 20 August 2012.

Kevin Jon Heller, "Situational Gravity under the Rome Statute", in Carsten Stahn and Larissa van den Herik (eds.), *Future Perspectives on International Criminal Justice*, T.M.C. Asser Press, 2010.

Kofi Annan, Justice vs. Impunity, The New York Times, 30 May 2010, available at http://www.nytimes.com/2010/05/31/opinion/31iht-edannan.html, last accessed on 20 August 2012.

Luc Reydams, Jan Wouters and Cedric Ryngaert (eds.), *International Prosecutors,* Oxford University Press, 2012.

Lydia Polgreen, Arab Uprisings Point Up Flaws in Global Court, The New York Times, 7 July 2012, available at http://www.nytimes.com/2012/07/08/world/middleeast/arab-spring-reveals-international-court-flaws.html?_r=1&partner=rss&emc=rss&from=2, last accessed on 20 August 2012.

Rachel Irwin, Court Hears Recruits Raped by Commanders, The Lubanga Trial at the International Criminal Court, 26 June 2009), available at http://www.lubangatrial.org/2009/06/26/court-hears-recruits-raped-by-commanders, last accessed on 20 August 2012.

Richard Dicker, ICC: The Court of Last Resort, Human Rights Watch, 2012, available at http://www.hrw.org/news/2012/06/29/icc-court-last-resort, last accessed on 20 August 2012.

Rome Statute of the International Criminal Court 17 July 1998, UN Doc A/CONE.189/9*, amended January 2002, available at http://untreaty.un.org/cod/icc/statute/romefra.htm, last accessed on 29 August 2012.

Statement by Justice Louise Arbour to the Preparatory Committee on the Establishment of an International Criminal Court, 8 December 1997; quoted in William Schabas *An Introduction to the International Criminal Court*, Cambridge University Press, 2007.

Support for Ending Impunity for International Crimes Must Grow – ICC, United Nations News Centre, 12 December 2011, available at http://www.un.org/apps/news/story.asp?NewsID=40703&Cr=criminal+court&Cr1, last accessed on 20 August 2012.

The Office of the Prosecutor, Report on Prosecutorial Strategy, 2006, available at http://www.icc-cpi.int/NR/rdonlyres/D673DD8C-D427-4547-BC69-2D363E07274B/143708/ProsecutorialStrategy20060914_English.pdf, last accessed on 20 August 2012.

William Schabas, "Prosecutorial Discretion v. Judicial Activism at the International Criminal Court", in *Journal of International Criminal Justice*, 2008.

2.4.

The Supreme Court of the Netherlands:
A Hub of Judicial Cooperation

Geert Corstens[*] and Reindert Kuiper[**]

The central questions raised in this volume (Does a legal and justice strategy exist? What does it consist of? Who executes it? And how does it work?) are approached here from the perspective of the role that the Supreme Court of the Netherlands should play in the evolving legal order. This essay is therefore not about the strategies employed by individual Supreme Court justices to ensure that their legal thinking is translated into precedent – a subject about which so much engrossing American literature exists. Instead, it deals with the strategy of the Dutch Supreme Court on how to play its role as an institution to maximum effect. In particular, it examines the significance of two statutes that came into force on 1 July 2012. The first makes it possible for the Supreme Court to rule a case referred to it inadmissible at an early stage in the proceedings. The second creates a procedure that enables district courts and courts of appeal to apply to the Supreme Court for a preliminary ruling in civil cases. The introduction of these new instruments can be regarded as the result of a strategic analysis designed to improve the way in which the Supreme Court operates.

1. Function and Position of the Supreme Court: Cooperation as a Key Strategic Concept

For a proper understanding it seems advisable to begin with some general comments about the function and position of the Supreme Court in the Dutch legal order. The Supreme Court is the Netherlands' highest court in the fields of civil, criminal and tax law. Jurisdiction at the last instance in administrative cases, other than tax cases, is the preserve of three other

---

[*] **Geert Corstens** is President of the Supreme Court of the The Netherlands (Hoge Raad).

[**] **Reindert Kuiper** is the Law Clerk (gerechtsauditeur) to the President of the Supreme Court of the The Netherlands, and to the President of the Network of the Presidents of the Supreme Judicial Courts of the European Union.

courts. The most important function of the Supreme Court is cassation in the fields of law assigned to it. A large proportion of Dutch law is laid down in international agreements, the Constitution, legal codes, acts of parliament and municipal and provincial ordinances. Cassation means quashing a judicial decision on a point of law, including procedural law. The aim of cassation is to preserve legal uniformity, steer the development of the law and safeguard individual legal protection. Cassation scrutinises the quality of contested judgments of the courts of appeal as regards both the application of the law and the legal reasoning behind it. The Supreme Court is also charged with cassation in judgments in criminal and civil cases of the Joint Court of Justice of Aruba, Curaçao, St. Maarten and of Bonaire, Saint Eustatius and Saba.

The Dutch legal order is interwoven with and forms part of the legal order of the European Union. Moreover, in its relationship with international law the Netherlands has a monistic system: in other words, where a provision of national law conflicts with a provision of international law with direct effect, the latter prevails. This means that the Supreme Court must apply European law and in doing so, take account of the case law of the Court of Justice of the European Union and the European Court of Human Rights. In the system of courts of which it is part, the Supreme Court therefore receives input both from below, especially from the national appeal courts and from above, from the European courts of last resort, to which we have just referred.

This brief description of the role and position of the Supreme Court clearly shows how important judicial cooperation is for it. Judicial cooperation is a key strategic concept for the Supreme Court. This encompasses cooperation not only with district courts, courts of appeal and European courts but also with administrative courts that are outside the system of the civil, criminal and tax law courts.

2. Supreme Court Strategy in an Evolving Legal Order

So how can the Supreme Court discharge as effectively as possible its duties of preserving legal uniformity, steering the development of the law and safeguarding individual legal protection? Deciding on a strategy to ensure that the Supreme Court can perform its role with maximum effect requires an analysis of the setting in which it operates and how it functions within this setting. What are the consequences of ongoing internationalisation, regulation and specialisation and of the growing need for the Supreme Court to act quickly? How can the Supreme Court continue to function authoritatively and with maximum effectiveness in such a highly critical age? Answering such questions provides the insight into internal and external developments that is needed to determine in what respects the organisation should or should not change. The conclusions drawn from such a strategic analysis must ultimately be translated into specific policy.

3. New Instruments as a Product of Strategic Analysis

In 2008 a committee drawn from the Ministry of Justice and the Supreme Court and chaired by Supreme Court Justice Fred Hammerstein, published a report entitled 'Improving cassation procedure'. This report analysed the problems facing the civil, criminal and tax divisions of the Supreme Court and addressed the issue of how it could make better use of existing instruments and what instruments should be added to enhance its performance.

The report noted that civil cassation proceedings were virtually out of reach for people with an average income. For this group, continuing to litigate up to the level of the Supreme Court was too expensive and time-consuming. This limited the ability of the civil division to perform its duties with maximum effect. Questions of law from ordinary litigants reached the Supreme Court too slowly, if at all. Consequently, points of law could be left unresolved for a long time in the lower courts. Not only could this result in long-drawn-out proceedings, but it could also deter parties from referring disputes to the courts at all. As the report pointed out, alternative forms of dispute resolution such as mediation are a welcome addition to the system, but people should not be forced to take this route simply because the ordinary courts are unable to provide an adequate solution to the dispute within a reasonable time and without great expense.

Another finding that concerned both the civil and the criminal division was that a substantial proportion of cassation appeals did not really merit the attention of the Supreme Court because they did not involve issues that needed to be answered in the interests of the uniform application or development of the law, nor did they involve an important aspect of legal protection. The Hammerstein Committee took the view that the cases in which the Supreme Court and the Procurator General's Office whose

Advocates General offer independent advice to the Supreme Court in all civil and criminal cases and in the more complicated tax cases, have no real role to play and therefore must be disposed of at the earliest possible stage of the proceedings in order to minimise the strain on the limited capacity of these two institutions. The fact that instituting cassation proceedings in criminal cases had the effect of suspending execution of the sentence was found to encourage defendants to lodge appeals in cassation. There was also a chance that the proceedings might exceed the 'reasonable time' referred to in Article 6 of the European Convention on Human Rights and that this might result in a reduction of sentence by the cassation court. Besides these perverse incentives for instituting cassation proceedings, the legal aid system enabled convicted defendants to continue lodging appeals right up to the level of cassation also when they lacked the financial means to do so.

The Hammerstein Committee made a number of specific recommendations, each of which has been implemented. Some of them concerned internal measures which the Supreme Court was able to take itself. Others required action by the legislator to make it possible for cases brought before the Supreme Court to be declared inadmissible under the new section 80a of the Judiciary Organisation Act (*Wet op de rechterlijke organisatie*, 'RO') for what is basically 'want of interest,' and for judges in district courts and courts of appeal to seek a preliminary ruling in civil proceedings from the civil division of the Supreme Court. Both these new legal instruments directly affect how the Supreme Court operates. They will change the relationship of the Supreme Court with the courts of fact and provide greater scope for dialogue with the highest European courts and the highest administrative courts. These two new statutory provisions challenge the Supreme Court to provide even more leadership within the legal order.

4. The Strategic Significance of Section 80a of the Judiciary Organisation Act and Preliminary Rulings

In discussing the significance of these new statutory instruments, we consider below the function of the Supreme Court as an intermediary between the highest European courts and the Dutch legal order, the need to cooperate with the highest administrative courts in order to monitor legal uniformity and the growing importance of new forms of cooperation with the courts of fact. We will concentrate on cooperation between the different courts and therefore disregard cooperation with the Bar, the legislature and academia, although they too are naturally important.

5. Cooperation within Europe

The growth of EU law and the case law of the ECtHR are affecting not only the substance of the work of the Supreme Court but also its position in the legal order. The more the law is derived from supranational sources, the more the position of the Supreme Court will become that of an intermediary between the highest European courts and the national legal order. Its responsibility as the highest national guardian of European law and as interpreter of the case law of the European courts will thus grow in significance. This responsibility will be even greater in the light of the excessive caseload of Europe's highest courts. To an increasing extent, national courts – and hence the Supreme Court as well – will become true European courts.

To be able to discharge this responsibility, the Supreme Court requires an excellent knowledge of European law. Ensuring that staff of the court maintains this knowledge should be part of personnel policy, in terms of both recruitment and internal training. Institutionalised efforts should also be made to gather and retrieve information about European law. Naturally, awareness of important judgments of the ECtHR and the EU Court of Justice is a prerequisite. However, knowledge of comparative law and of decisions of other national courts of last resort in Europe would also be useful. For example, in establishing precisely how the case law of the ECtHR should be understood in the national legal order, justices and other staff may find it extremely valuable to know how it has been interpreted by other courts of last resort in Europe. The same applies to the case law of the EU Court of Justice and to the interpretation of terms and concepts derived from European law. In this respect comparative law is a subject that merits constant attention.

To maintain knowledge at the required level and to be able to retrieve information and facilitate its exchange with other courts for comparative law purposes, it would seem advisable to designate a number of specialists for each sector. Law clerks, Advocates General and justices could be specially charged with monitoring developments in European law and making this knowledge accessible to their colleagues, for example through an internal or external database with keyword search capability. This could be based on the concept of similar databases already established for the courts of fact, for example the Wiki Juridica database. Sacha Prechal, who sits on the EU Court of Justice for the Netherlands, recently emphasised that it is important for the judges of the highest courts to engage in dialogue with their counterparts in other countries in a more informal way than through judgments. It would be useful for them to visit one another, hold joint symposiums and contribute to training programmes.

The Network of the Presidents of the Supreme Judicial Courts of the European Union could play a more prominent role in this respect, for example by developing its website to serve as a hub for the easy and rapid exchange of good quality information on comparative law.

The capacity released by the application of section 80a RO both for the judiciary and in the Procurator General's Office should, in our view, be devoted in part to focusing attention on European law and comparative law.

6. Cooperation with District Courts and Courts of Appeal

Section 80a RO and the possibility of seeking preliminary rulings will have a more direct influence on the relationship of the Supreme Court with the lower courts. The introduction of the new selection system warrants a brief description in this think piece. At the level of individual cases, the courts of appeal may well find that their responsibility for providing legal protection increases slightly, notably in respect of the category of cases that do not pass the test of section 80a. Once the contours of this category become clear, it will also be apparent which matters will no longer go to cassation as a matter of course and in which areas the courts of appeal will therefore be obliged to assume final responsibility even more clearly.

As the Supreme Court will concentrate to a greater extent on developing the law and broadly monitoring the quality of the decisions of the courts of fact, in addition to other forms of quality control, the courts of appeal may possibly acquire greater responsibility both for legal protection as the highest courts of fact and for the uniform application of the law. This would be above all in areas most conducive to legal uniformity or harmonisation by the courts of fact, such as sentencing in criminal proceedings and determining the amounts to be awarded, for example as maintenance in divorce proceedings.

The selection of cases on the basis of section 80a RO means that there will also be less detailed feedback for the courts of fact from the Supreme Court and the Procurator General's Office in each individual case. Thought must be given to whether and, if so, how such feedback can still be given. The annual report would be one possibility, but it might be more fruitful to discuss audit results of this kind in more frequent and intensive discussions with the courts of fact. Increasing the frequency of these meetings would seem the obvious choice.

At the same time, section 80a provides greater scope for the Supreme Court and the Procurator General's Office to focus on the development of the law. To make optimal use of this scope it is important to be aware of the wishes of the courts of fact. What issues do they need the Supreme Court to rule on? What do they have questions about? What decisions of the Supreme Court are insufficiently clear or difficult to apply in practice? More frequent meetings with the courts of fact would again provide a forum in which such matters could be assessed. Here too, the new possibility of applying to the Supreme Court for preliminary rulings could be brought to their attention and mutually evaluated. The visits of the president of the Supreme Court and the Procurator General to the district courts and courts of appeal are also useful in this connection.

7. Cooperation with the Highest Administrative Courts

An important development in the Dutch legal order has been the blurring of the boundaries between the traditional areas of the law. In the past 15 years many statutes have provided for the possibility of imposing an administrative fine. The imposition of such a fine can be challenged before the administrative courts. This means that part of the work of adjudicating criminal cases has been transferred to the administrative courts. In consequence, the administrative courts are playing a role in interpreting criminal-law concepts and European case law in this field.

In the field of civil law, there is increasing crossover between private and administrative law through legislation and case law. This is occurring, for example, in competition law, financial law (securities law) and company and commercial law, and it has been under way for much longer in the field of social legislation. Moreover, the administrative courts are also interpreting civil-law concepts, as used in international conventions and otherwise.

Ensuring legal uniformity is a matter that needs to be considered in this connection. From this perspective it is important to give serious attention to the different forms of consultation with the administrative courts and to continue these consultations in a constructive manner. The advisory opinions given by the Procurator General's Office in administrative cases could be a good way of contributing to legal uniformity until such time as provision has been made for this by institutional means.

8. Conclusion

Courts are professional organisations that serve the society in which they operate. If they are to play their assigned role effectively, they must draw up a plan at every level of the organisation for achieving the goals that they have set for each and every element of their work. Strategy therefore plays a role at every level within the structure of a court. In this essay we have examined how the Hammerstein Committee's strategic analysis of the manner in which the Supreme Court performs its tasks has led to the introduction of new statutory instruments designed to enhance this performance still further. We have also discussed the fact that judicial cooperation is crucial in today's complex and specialised international legal order which is so focused on speed and clarity and how the new statutory instruments of the Supreme Court can be of service in this connection.

On the wall of the central hall of the Supreme Court is a saying of Hugo Grotius which serves as our mission statement: *Ubi Iudicia Deficiunt Incipit Bellum*. This can be freely translated as 'where judicial resolution fails, war begins'. For a judicial body such as the Supreme Court, the concept of operating strategically means that although the mission remains unchanged it must constantly be adapted to contemporary demands. So perhaps in a few years' time the mission statement on the wall of the new premises of the Supreme Court will be a neon sign flashing out the message 'Urgent question of law? Try our next-day service!'.

9. Sources and Further Reading

Hoge Raad, "Improving Cassation Procedure: Report of Hammerstein Committee on the Normative Role of the Supreme Court", February 2008, available at www.rechtspraak.nl/Organisatie/Hoge-Raad/OverDeHogeRaa d/publicaties/Documents/ReportHammersteinCommittee.pdf.

2.5.

The ICC and Complementarity:
Support for National Courts and the Rule of Law[*]

Mark Ellis[**]

The International Criminal Court (ICC) was established in 2002 amidst a surge in international criminal justice adjudication. *Complementarity*, the key principle underpinning the ICC, theoretically ensures that the Court's role is strictly complementary to that of sovereign nation states. The ICC adherence to this pivotal principle should play a critical role in this regard, thereby buttressing international justice and the rule of law at the national level. However, the ICC's self-proclaimed commitment to support domestic investigations and prosecutions has languished. As the research will indicate, and much to the dissatisfaction of states whose prosecutorial jurisdiction is threatened, the ICC has yet to develop a uniform, objective method for determining a state's "willingness" or "ability" to prosecute international crimes domestically. Recent challenges brought by Kenya and Libya demonstrate the tensions between domestic and ICC jurisdiction under the current application of complementarity. Both countries have aggressively asserted their right to undertake domestic prosecutions under the complementary principle. However, the Court has demonstrated a lack of consistency when responding to these requests. This has been particularly evident in the case of Libya, where the former Prosecutor and the Pre-trial Chamber has clashed while interpreting the complementary principle. This article focuses on the ICC's approach to complementarity as a way to support the rule of law on the domestic level. It further considers the shortcomings of the ICC's application of *positive complementarity*, and holds that the international community must play a larger role in building rule of law capacity

---

[*] The Author would like to thank Oliver Oldman for his research assistance for this think piece.

[**] **Mark Ellis** is Executive Director of the International Bar Association (IBA) and leads the foremost international organisation of bar associations, law firms and individual lawyers in the world.

and providing technical assistance to states wishing to prosecute international crimes domestically.

1. Introduction

Until recently, grave crimes of concern to the international community were often committed with impunity. The 2002 creation of the International Criminal Court (ICC), the world's first permanent international court, was a turning point in the administration of justice and highlights a growing global commitment to the rule of law. The Court was established to ensure that perpetrators of the most serious international crimes are held accountable.[1] The Court is currently conducting seven formal investigations, and on 14 March 2012 it announced its first verdict, finding Congolese rebel leader Thomas Lubanga Dyilo guilty of war crimes.[2]

Ironically, the most significant change brought about by the ICC could be in making international justice less *international* and more *national*. This is because the principle of *complementarity,* as set forth in the Rome Statute, supports the devolution of judicial authority so that nation states pursue justice against perpetrators of the most injurious international crimes. However, the machinery for prosecuting international crimes is not as well-oiled as the Court would like to suggest. The Office of the Prosecutor has formulated a justice strategy to give life to the principle of complementarity as enshrined in the Rome Statute, but its execution has been staggered largely as a result of it having to compete and negotiate with other players: the Assembly of State Parties, the ICC judiciary and the State Parties themselves. Each of these players has a separate role and a correspondingly differing perspective regarding the implementation of the principle of complementarity. This has meant that, while the principle is rich in potential, its application has been inconsistent and underwhelming.

---

[1] Rome Statute of the International Criminal Court 17 July 1998, UN Doc A/CONE.189/9*, amended January 2002, available at http://untreaty.un.org/cod/icc/statute/romefra.htm, last accessed on 29 August 2012.

[2] Prosecutor v. Thomas Lubanga Dyilo, Case no. ICC-01/04-01/06, Judgment, 14 March 2012, para. 1358, available at http://www.icc-cpi.int/menus/icc/situations%20and%20cases/situations/situation%20icc%200104/related%20cases/icc%200104%200106/court%20records/chambers/trial%20chamber%20i/2842?lan=en-GB, last accessed on 6 August 2012.

2.   The Principle of Complementarity

The Preamble to the Rome Statute sets forth that "the most serious crimes of concern to the international community as a whole must not go unpunished and that their effective prosecution must be ensured by taking measures at the national level and by enhancing international cooperation". Article 1 of the Statute also states that the Court "shall have the power to exercise its jurisdiction over persons for the most serious crimes of international concern [...] and shall be *complementary* to national criminal jurisdiction", since it is "the duty of every state to exercise its criminal jurisdiction over those responsible for international crimes" [emphasis added].[3]

An earlier International Law Commission (ILC) draft of the Rome Statute was careful to give primacy to national courts and only mandated the ICC to assume jurisdiction in specific, limited circumstances.[4]

The importance of the complementarity principle to the rule of law is found in its underlying mandate that it is the duty of nation states to exercise criminal jurisdiction over those responsible for international crimes. It recognises that domestic prosecutions are generally preferable to those conducted at the international level. This too is fundamental to the rule of law principle. No country can purport to embrace and advance the rule of law if it is incapable of holding account those individuals who violate the most basic tenets of this principle. Only in circumstances where a state is genuinely unable to conduct internationally accepted trials should it surrender its responsibility to the international level. One of the reasons is that investigations and prosecutions of individuals by an international court can easily be seen by states as pernicious and as a threat to their sovereignty. Indeed, the ICC' s former Chief Prosecutor, Luis Moreno-Ocampo, has stressed that "national investigations and prosecutions, where they can properly be undertaken, will normally be the most effective and efficient means of bringing offences to justice" since "states themselves will normally have the best access to evidence and witness-

---

3   Rome Statute, preamble, para. 6, see *supra* note 1.
4   Report of the International Law Commission on the Work of Its Forty-Sixth Session, United Nations GAOR, 49th Session, Supp. no. 10., UN Doc. A/49/10 (1994), in Yearbook of the International Law Commission, vol. 2, 1994.

es".[5] It follows that, as Ocampo has famously observed, "as a consequence of complementarity, the number of cases that reach the Court should not be a measure of its efficiency. On the contrary, an absence of trials before this Court, as a consequence of the regular functioning of national institutions would be a major success".[6]

Developed by consensus among State Parties to the Rome Statute, the principle of complementarity addresses the actual and perceived inadequacies of previous international criminal courts and, at its base, is a procedural and substantive safeguard against a supranational, omnipotent institution curtailing the sovereign rights of nations. It ensures that the judgements of a domestic court are not supplanted by the judgements of international courts. It places the ICC in a "complementary" role to national courts and does not bypass the intrinsic responsibility of states to prosecute international crimes.

As a matter of both treaty and customary international law, state sovereignty includes the responsibility of states to punish those who commit serious crimes, including international crimes. States must either prosecute or extradite those who have committed the most serious international crimes. These include genocide; war crimes, whether committed in internal or non-internal armed conflict; torture; and crimes against humanity.

3.   Complementarity in the Rome Statute

Based on Article 17(1) of the Rome Statute, the ICC will not be able to admit a case where "[t]he case is being investigated or prosecuted by a State which has jurisdiction over it, unless the decision resulted from the unwillingness or inability of the State genuinely to prosecute", or where "[t]he case has been investigated by a State which has jurisdiction over it and the State has decided not to prosecute the person concerned, unless

---

5   Luis Moreno-Ocampo, "Paper on Some Policy Issues before the Office of the Prosecutor", ICC-OTP, 2003, available at http://www.amicc.org/docs/OcampoPolicy Paper9_03.pdf, last accessed on 6 August 2012.

6   Luis Moreno-Ocampo, "Statement Made by Mr. Luis Moreno-Ocampo at the Ceremony for the Solemn Undertaking of the Chief Prosecutor of the ICC", 16 June 2003, available at http://www.iccnow.org/documents/MorenoOcampo16June03.pdf, last accessed on 6 August 2012.

the decision resulted from the unwillingness or inability of the State genuinely to prosecute".[7]

The key consideration, therefore, is whether a state is *unable* or *unwilling* to investigate or prosecute a case. The ICC cannot hear a case if a state has made a decision to act, and it is thus prevented from exercising jurisdiction without the consent of a nation state.

However, the terms 'unable' and 'unwilling' remain open to interpretation. Not surprisingly, the Court is struggling to articulate a process for determining a state's willingness and ability to conduct a trial. Recently, the Court demonstrated some confusion over these concepts. In both the *Lubanga* and the *Katanga/Ngudjolo* cases,[8] the Court failed to properly distinguish between the Democratic Republic of Congo's (DRC) unwillingness to initiate trials and its inability to do so. Instead, the Court focused its admissibility standard on the 'same person/same conduct' test; that is, the DRC was not acting in relation to the specific cases before the ICC. Thus, the potential examination of the DRC's willingness or ability to prosecute was avoided.

Statutory confusion notwithstanding, the Rome Statute does set out basic parameters that the Court can follow in deciding whether a state can undertake the investigation and prosecution of a case. Yet, here too the process is rife with ambiguity. The Court's decision in judging a state's willingness and ability to pursue a case is made by several different parties at different stages of the investigative process. The Prosecutor has the first opportunity to assess whether a domestic prosecution is genuine or not. The Pre-Trial Chamber and the Appeal Chamber, however, make the final judgement as to whether the domestic proceedings are genuine. This judgement can also be made at several stages during the process based on a review of progress reports submitted by states on the status of the domestic proceedings. The joint ownership of the complementarity strategy by these separate court players can easily obscure its application.

Although not formally defined, the term 'unwilling' is nonetheless characterised in the Statute by way of *situations*. The language of Article

---

[7] Rome Statute, Article 17(1)(a) and (b), see *supra* note 1.

[8] Lubanga Case, *supra* note 2; Prosecutor v. Germain Katanga and Mathieu Ngudjolo Chui, Situation in the Democratic Republic of Congo, Case no. ICC-01/04-01/07, Confirmation of Charges, 30 September, 2008, available at http://www.icc-cpi.int/iccdocs/doc/doc571253.pdf, last accessed on 6 August 2012.

17 suggests that the Court will consider three distinct measurements to determine 'unwillingness'. Article 17(2) of the Statute provides that:

> In order to determine unwillingness in a particular case, the Court shall consider, having regard to the principles of due process recognized by international law, whether one or more of the following exist, as applicable:
>
> (a) The proceedings were or are being undertaken or the national decision was made for the purpose of shielding the person concerned from criminal responsibility for crimes within the jurisdiction of the Court;
>
> (b) There has been an unjustified delay in the proceedings which in the circumstances is inconsistent with an intent to bring the person concerned to justice;
>
> (c) The proceedings were not or are not being conducted independently or impartially, and they were or are being conducted in a manner which, in the circumstances, is inconsistent with an intent to bring the person concerned to justice.

The second ground on which the ICC can counter a state's inherent right to undertake a trial under the principle of complementarity is declaring that a state is *unable* to undertake judicial proceedings. Article 17(3) of the Rome Statute states:

> In order to determine inability in a particular case, the Court shall consider whether, due to a total or substantial collapse or unavailability of its national judicial system, the State is unable to obtain the accused or the necessary evidence and testimony or otherwise unable to carry out its proceedings.

In determining that a state is unable to prosecute, the ICC will tend to proffer factors that substantiate the collapse of a state's judicial or overall legal system. Although such a determination is imprecise, the targeted state will likely fall into one or more of the following six categories:

1. States entangled in conflict – either domestic or international;
2. States experiencing political unrest or economic crisis;
3. States that lack the type of judicial system that is required under international standards of legal fairness;
4. States in transition;
5. States that have failed to incorporate implementing legislation necessary to cooperate with the Court;
6. States that fail to ensure fair trial proceedings.

In circumstances where at least one of these factors is present, the ICC would likely be able to claim jurisdiction where crimes falling under the Rome Statute have been committed and where the state in question is not able to pursue investigations and trials.

Of course, states may also explicitly declare their unwillingness to prosecute, thereby circumventing the need for ICC to apply these tests.

Importantly, Article 19(2)(b) of the Rome Statute empowers a state which has jurisdiction over a case to submit a challenge to the Court's jurisdiction on grounds that the state "is investigating or prosecuting the case or has investigated or prosecuted".

Despite the theoretical logic of complementarity, there remain serious concerns as to how the principle will be promulgated in future domestic court cases. The challenge for the ICC is to develop the principle of complementarity in a way that preserves the balance between state and international authority while strengthening the rule of law at the domestic level and ensuring accountability for gross violations of international criminal law.

4. Tests of Complementarity

There have been two major tests of the ICC's complementarity regime in the last three years: the cases of Kenya and Libya.

4.1. Kenya: The Ocampo Six

On 26 November 2009, after having received numerous reports alleging crimes against humanity, the ICC Prosecutor sought authorisation from the Pre-Trial Chamber of the ICC to conduct an investigation into the 2007/8 post-election violence in Kenya. The international community, including myself, called for an immediate investigation by the ICC for alleged crimes against humanity.[9] The Prosecutor rightfully argued that there were no active or pending domestic proceedings against "those bearing the greatest responsibility for the crimes [...]"[10] The Pre-Trial Cham-

---

[9] Mark S. Ellis, Atrocities in Kenya Must Not Go Unpunished, London Times Online, 6 February 2008.

[10] International Criminal Court, Situation in the Republic of Kenya, Case no. ICC-01/09, Decision Pursuant to Article 15 of the Rome Statute on the Authorization of an Investigation into the Situation in the Republic of Kenya, para. 183, 31 March 2010, avail-

ber agreed with this position, holding that the Court's jurisdiction had been confirmed because there was "a lack of national proceedings in the Republic of Kenya or in any third state with respect to the main elements which may shape the Court's potential case(s)".[11] Subsequently, the Pre-Trial Chamber authorised an investigation that yielded six suspects, later named the 'Ocampo Six'.

Unsurprisingly, Kenya filed an appeal against ICC investigations pursuant to Article 19(2)(b) of the Rome Statute, as outlined above. The Government argued that it was both able and willing to investigate and prosecute those responsible for the atrocities committed during the country's post-election violence.

The discord between the two legal positions was all too apparent. Kenya's position was uncompromising: "[W]e can say that Kenyan judges meet the best international standards [...] Why on earth should a Kenyan go to The Hague?"[12] The Cabinet Minister's remarks were supported by international observers who reported that "Kenya has strong capacity in many parts of its justice sector" and "all agreed that there are no insurmountable technical challenges to the conduct of credible investigations, prosecutions and trials for international crimes in Kenya".[13]

However, the ICC Appeals Chamber attempted to annunciate more clearly the requirements of complementarity by affirming that the burden lies with the challenging state; that the state must "provide the Court with evidence of a sufficient degree of specificity and probative value that demonstrates that it is indeed investigating the case", and clarified that this is a question of "whether the *same case* is being investigated by both the Court and the national jurisdiction".[14]

---

able at http://www.icc-cpi.int/iccdocs/doc/doc854287.pdf, last accessed on 31 August 2012.

[11] International Criminal Court, 2010, see *supra* note 10, para. 184.

[12] Lucas Barasa, Mutula to Ocampo: Quit Kenyan Probe, Daily Nation, 18 September 2010, available at http://www.nation.co.ke/News/politics/Mutula%20to%20Ocampo%20Quit%20Kenyan%20probe%20/-/1064/1013680/-/b1f4rs/-/, last accessed on 31 August 2012.

[13] Eric A. Witte, Putting Complementarity into Practice: Domestic Justice for International Crimes in Democratic Republic of Congo, Uganda and Kenya, Open Society Foundation, 2011, available at http://www.soros.org/sites/default/files/putting-complementarity-into-practice-20110120.pdf, last accessed on 6 August 2012.

[14] Prosecutor v. William Samoeiruto, Henry Kiprono Kosgey and Joshua Arap Sang, Case no. ICC-01/09-02/11-274, Decision on the Application by the Government of

The Court ultimately dismissed Kenya's admissibility challenge on grounds that Kenya was unable to provide sufficient and convincing evidence that it was investigating the *same* individuals who were suspects before the ICC in relation to the *same* crimes. The decision reflected the view of human rights groups who argued that the Kenyan authorities appeared to have been "remarkably consistent in evading their legal obligations to undertake credible criminal investigations".[15]

After a futile attempt by Kenyan authorities to persuade the UN Security Council to defer the case, Kenyan President Mwai Kibaki once again proclaimed that the government was "pursu[ing] the option of having a local mechanism to deal with any international crimes"; stressing the need for a fair trial and indicating his intention to ensure that the four suspects were tried locally.[16]

The situation in Kenya is of particular interest because it is the first instance in which the ICC Prosecutor invoked his *proprio motu* powers to initiate an investigation. The Court's position illustrated its reluctance to simply permit states to launch domestic prosecutions once allegations of crimes were brought to the attention of the state. As Kenya failed to bring the proper suspects to trial, its continued assurances were not enough to stay the ICC's involvement indefinitely.

Interestingly, when the Pre-Trial Chamber dismissed the admissibility challenge, it disregarded planned investigations by Kenya's Truth, Justice and Reconciliation Commission (TJRC). By omitting the TJRC investigations form its consideration of the admissibility challenge, the Court failed to determine whether a non-prosecutorial mechanism is capable of conducting "genuine" investigations with the intent to bring the persons to justice. This could easily be seen as a missed opportunity to develop the ICC's approach to complementarity.

Kenya Challenging the Admissibility of the Case Pursuant to Article 19(2)(b) of the Statute, 30 May 2012, para. 6, available at http://www.icc-cpi.int/iccdocs/doc/doc1223134.pdf, last accessed on 6 August 2012.

[15] Paul Seils, ICC's Kenya Decision is No Cause for Celebration, Al Jazeera, 31 January 2012, available at http://www.aljazeera.com/indepth/opinion/2012/01/2012128125931617297.html, last accessed on August 6, 2012.

[16] Francis Mureithi, Local Trails for ICC Suspects Still an Option, Says Kibaki, The Star, 24 April 2012, available at http://www.the-star.co.ke/national/national/72787-kibaki-says-ocal-trials-for-icc-suspects-still-an-option, last accessed on 31 August 2012.

The result is an exceedingly delicate political situation. Not only has Kenya expressed its intention to withdraw as a State Party to the ICC, but there have been rumours that the African Union may do the same, favouring a regional court with parallel jurisdiction.

4.2. Libya: The Case of Saif Al-Islam Gaddafi

Libya will be another crucible for the principle of complementarity. On 27 June 2011, the Pre-Trial Chamber issued a warrant for the arrest of Saif al-Islam Gaddafi on charges of crimes against humanity, further to a referral under UN Security Council Resolution 1970. Subsequently, the ICC declared that the Libyan authorities were obligated to cooperate fully with the Court, but should they wish to continue national prosecutions they could submit an admissibility challenge pursuant to Articles 17 and 19 of the Rome Statute.

The Libyan government did file a challenge. Libya argued that the case was inadmissible since Libya was actively investigating Gaddafi for alleged crimes against humanity. The submission further stated that "to deny the Libyan people this historic opportunity to eradicate the long-standing culture of impunity would be manifestly inconsistent with the object and purpose of the Rome Statute, which accords primacy to national judicial systems".[17] The Government forcefully argued that the recent and on-going Libyan judicial reforms affirmed the country's commitment to conducting a fair trial in accordance with the highest international standards.[18]

An interesting twist in this case is that the ICC's Chief Prosecutor has opined that the Libyan judicial system is capable of conducting a fair trial, although human rights groups have steadfastly disagreed.

The Libyan Government's application is, in my opinion, strong. It advances the case that the Libyan Prosecutor-General is conducting an ex-

---

[17] Prosecutor v. Saif Al-Islam Gaddafi and Abdullah Al-Senussi, Case no. ICC-01/11-01/11, Application on Behalf of the Government of Libya Pursuant to Article 19 of the ICC Statute, 1 May 2012, available at http://www.icc-cpi.int/iccdocs/doc/doc1405819.pdf, last accessed on 6 August 2012.

[18] Prosecutor v. Saif Al-Islam Gaddafi, 2012, see *supra* note 17; see also Prosecutor v. Saif Al-Islam Gaddafi and Abdulla Al-Senussi, Case no. ICC-01/11-01/11, Decision on the Conduct of the Proceedings Following the "Application on Behalf of the Government of Libya Pursuant to Article 19 of the Statute", 4 May 2012, available at http://www.icc-cpi.int/iccdocs/doc/doc1407703.pdf, last accessed on 6 August 2012.

tensive investigation of the alleged crimes, emphasising compliance with both domestic and international law. Both of these elements are convincing on the issue of Libya's ability to conduct a fair trial. This is supported by the usual submissions on the independence of the Libyan judiciary and domestic guarantees of due process. The ICC, however, is likely to focus on Libya's unstable political atmosphere and its potential impact on a fair trial.

This most recent test of complementarity is particularly important because, as recognised by former Chief Prosecutor Ocampo, the Libyan admissibility challenge "goes to the heart" of the complementary justice system established by the Rome Statute.[19] The impending decision is all the more significant given Libya's highly sensitive internal situation, which arguably would benefit from justice secured domestically, and its status as a non-State Party to the Rome Statute.

However, the conflict between the Court and Libya has accelerated at a frenetic pace and to a precarious state. As stated above, the Prosecutor made several statements indicating that Libya was capable or trying Gaddafi on its own. However, the Court expressed the exact opposite opinion. In fact, the Pre-Trial Chamber appointed Melinda Taylor as interim counsel to represent Gaddafi because of fears that his rights were being violated by local authorities. She travelled to Libya to meet with Gaddafi and was quickly arrested and detained. Despite accusations by Libyan authorities that Taylor smuggled sensitive documents and recording devices to Gaddafi, accusations vigorously denied by Ms. Taylor, the international community, including the author, called for her immediate release because of the privileges and immunities accorded to ICC staff members under the Rome Statute. Taylor, together with three colleagues, was released on 2 July 2012.

---

[19] ICC Considers Appeal from Libya, UPI News, 17 May 2012, available at http://www.upi.com/Top_News/Special/2012/05/17/ICC-considers-appeal-from-Libya/UPI-10291337274887, last accessed on 6 August 2012; UN Security Council Press Release, International Criminal Court Chief Tells Security Council Libya Wants Domestic Courts to Handle Proceedings against Son of Former Libyan Leader Qadhafi, SC/10651, 16 May 16 2012, available at http://www.un.org/News/Press/docs/2012/sc10651.doc.htm, last accessed on 6 August 2012.

5.   Positive Complementarity

An expansive approach to the principle of complementarity is of paramount importance to international justice and accountability. It is crucial in supporting the rule of law at the national level. Were the ICC to take a 'positive' – or active – approach to complementarity, it would go a long way toward ensuring that domestic criminal prosecutorial institutions flourish.

The Assembly of State Parties has recognised the need to provide assistance to states so that "national jurisdictions are strengthened and enabled to conduct genuine national investigations and trials of crimes included in the Rome Statute [...]"[20] The Assembly of State Parties has also made clear the need to assist states:

> There is also an increasing awareness that building national capacity with regard to Rome Statute crimes requires a targeted approach providing the necessary expertise required in this area. Consequently, there would be a need to ensure that rule of law programmes take into account the specific needs of investigating and prosecuting such crimes and bringing the cases to a successful conclusion. In addition, it would over time, as experience grows, be possible to identify best practices with regard to investigations and prosecutions at the national level and how States can and should assist each other in building capacity in this area.[21]

Positive complementarity is one of four fundamental principles outlined in the Prosecutor's 2009–12 Prosecutorial Strategy and entails a "proactive policy of cooperation aimed at promoting national proceedings".[22] "Positive complementarity" thus flows from the understanding

---

[20]   Assembly of State Parties, Report of the Bureau on Stocktaking, Taking Stock of the Principle of Complementarity: Bridging the Impunity Gap, ICC Doc. ICC-ASP/8/51, 18 March 2010, para. 16, available at http://www.icc-cpi.int/iccdocs/asp_docs/ ASP8R/ICC-ASP-8-51-ENG.pdf, last accessed on 6 August 2012.

[21]   Assembly of State Parties, Report on the Bureau on Complementarity, ICC Doc. ICC-ASP/9/26, 17 November 2010, para. 9, available at http://www.icc-cpi.int/iccdocs/ asp_docs/ASP9/ICC-ASP-9-26-ENG.pdf, last accessed on 6 August 2012.

[22]   Prosecutorial Strategy 2009-12, Office of the Prosecutor, 1 February 2010, p. 5, available at http://www.icc-cpi.int/NR/rdonlyres/66A8DCDC-3650-4514-AA62-D229D11 28F65/281506/OTPProsecutorialStrategy20092013.pdf, last accessed on 6 August 2012.

that the ICC is not a "passive" institution"[23]; it has a responsibility to inspire states to hold accountable those who are responsible for crimes under international law.

But how does this concept require the ICC to act? In a 2003 paper, a panel of experts agreed that the Prosecutor's Office must "actively remind States of their responsibility to adopt and implement effective legislation and encourage them to carry out effective investigations and prosecutions".[24] Specifically, these experts wrote, the Prosecutor's Office must make public statements, arrange private bilateral meetings, work with inter-governmental organisations and build cooperative ties with judicial entities. The Court must also exchange information and evidence to facilitate national investigations, provide technical advice and help to identify the training needs of domestic jurists. This is echoed in the 2009-12 Prosecutorial Strategy, which emphasises a reliance on cooperative networks to encourage genuine national proceedings where possible.[25]

In practice, the ICC's application of positive complementarity has proved elusive. For one thing, it is recognised that the ICC will *not* be involved with "capacity building, financial support and technical assistance", instead "leaving these actions and activities for States, to assist each other on a voluntary basis".[26] For states attempting to bolster their domestic accountability mechanisms, this creates a challenge.

Early in its existence, the Court was criticised for "rarely, if ever" calling on states to produce effective implementation legislation.[27] Indeed, while the Prosecutor's 2003 policy paper recognised the importance of complementary legislation, it stopped short of specifying that the ICC should lobby states to enact such legislation. But most surprising is that the Office of the Prosecutor has restricted its role, making clear that it will

---

[23] Christopher Keith Hall, "Developing and Implementing an Effective Positive Complementarity Strategy", in Carsten Stahn and Göran Sluiter (eds.), *The Emerging Practice of the International Criminal Court*, Martinus Nijhoff, 2009, pp. 163–182.

[24] International Criminal Court Office of the Prosecutor, The Principle of Complementarity in Practice, 2003, available at http://www.iclklamberg.com/Caselaw/OTP/Informal%20Expert%20paper%20The%20principle%20of%20complementarity%20in%20practice.pdf, last accessed on 6 August 2012.

[25] Prosecutorial Strategy, 2010, see *supra* note 22.

[26] Bureau Report on Stocktaking: Complementarity, 2010, see *supra* note 20.

[27] Developing Complementarity Strategy, 2009, see *supra* note 23, p. 221.

not involve itself "directly in the capacity building or financial or technical assistance" required to facilitate national proceedings.[28]

At the June 2010 Review Conference in Kampala, the Bureau of the Assembly of State Parties – another "owner" of the strategy – passed a resolution recognising "the need for additional measures at the national level as required and for the enhancement of international assistance to effectively prosecute perpetrators of the most serious crimes of concern to the international community".[29] However, the emphasis is on the *voluntary* nature of assistance among states. The resolution asks for states to "assist each other in strengthening domestic capacity to ensure that investigations and prosecutions of serious crimes of international concern can take place at the national level".[30] It encourages "the Court, State Parties and other stakeholders, including international organizations and civil society, to further explore ways in which to enhance the capacity of national jurisdictions to investigate and prosecute serious crimes of international concern.

This has caused consternation among some stakeholders that the author has spoken to who argue that the ICC is failing to provide adequate capacity building support to enable national prosecutions of international crimes. Indeed, as James A. Goldston, Director of the Open Society Justice Initiative, has observed, "all too little has been done to enhance national capacity to prosecute and try the many perpetrators of crimes other than those few the Court can address".[31]

The ICC's reticent approach to positive complementarity is perhaps best illustrated by its involvement in the Democratic Republic of the Congo (DRC). A 2004 cooperation agreement between the ICC and the government of the DRC outlined that the Office of the Prosecutor would "co-

---

28 Prosecutorial Strategy, 2010, see *supra* note 22, p. 5.
29 International Criminal Court, Resolutions and Declarations Adopted by the Review Conference, ICC Doc. RC/Res.1, 8 June 2010, part II, para. 3, available at http://www.icc-cpi.int/iccdocs/asp_docs/Resolutions/RC-Res.1-ENG.pdf, last accessed on 6 August 2012.
30 International Criminal Court, 2010, see *supra* note 29, para 5.
31 James A. Goldston, "UN Dialogue with Member States on Rule of Law at the International Level Speech, Strengthening the Nexus between International Criminal Justice and National Capacity to Combat Impunity", Open Society Justice Initiative, 2010, available at http://www.unrol.org/files/James%20Goldston%20Rule%20of%20Law%20Speech%20.pdf, last accessed on 6 August 2012.

operate with the [Congolese] courts and provide assistance to them for[...]investigations, prosecutions, and any eventual trials for crimes that fall within the competent jurisdiction of the International Criminal Court".[32] Despite this agreement, the ICC did not supply Congolese courts with information pertaining to crimes being prosecuted,[33] and neither did it provide national courts with required training.[34] The ICC's failure to enable the prosecution of mid-level perpetrators Thomas Lubanga Dyilo, Mathieu Ngudjolo Chui and Germain Katanga in Congolese courts has been branded a "missed opportunity"[35] to advance complementarity.

6.   Strengthening Domestic War Crimes Courts

Nation states must be competent to prosecute international crimes at the national level and do so consistent with international standards. Yet, many states face daunting challenges, particularly those in post-conflict environments characterised by political turmoil and little will to prosecute alleged war criminals. It is vital that national courts receive discernible assistance to ensure that domestic proceedings are consistent with international norms.

The ICC could play a pivotal role in this regard, thereby buttressing international justice and the rule of law. However, the ICC's self-proclaimed commitment to support domestic investigations and prosecutions has languished. As was reiterated at the Kampala Review Conference in 2010, positive complementarity will be limited in order to ensure that enhancing national capacity does not "interfere with the ICC's judicial function" nor divert funds from on-going ICC investigations and

---

[32]   Judicial Cooperation between the Democratic Republic of the Congo and the Office of the Prosecutor of the International Criminal Court, Article 37, 6 October 2004.

[33]   Pascal Kambale, "The ICC and Lubanga: Missed Opportunities", in *Possible Futures*, 2012, (Interviews with senior military judges, Kinshasa, 2009), available at http://www.possible-futures.org/2012/03/16/african-futures-icc-missed-opportunities, last accessed on 6 August 2012.

[34]   Mission Multi-Bailleurs de l'Audit du Système Judiciaire en RDC, in Rapport Final des Ateliers et du Séminaire pour un Programme Cadre de la Justice en RDC, Kinshasa, 15 November 2004.

[35]   Missed Opportunities, 2009, see *supra* note 33.

prosecutions.[36] This is hardly the stalwart endorsement for assistance that states want and need.

To be sure, the ICC is not a development agency. The international community, including States Parties to the Rome Statute and international and regional organisations, must play a role in delivering assistance through cooperative programmes. There have already been calls for the ICC, the UN, member states, and civil society to develop a "set of common tools" focused on enhancing the capacity of states to carry out genuine investigations and prosecutions, including the provision of technical assistance and capacity building.[37]

I have also called for an international mechanism to strengthen the ability of nation states to conduct credible war crimes trials.[38] The proposed International Technical Assistance Office (ITAO) would be administered by a non-governmental entity and provide unbiased technical assistance to newly formed domestic war crimes courts. It could provide an international perspective on legal issues facing nascent domestic war crimes courts via the provision of advice by a geographically diverse panel of experts; commission trial observers to review and evaluate trials; and provide and coordinate continuing legal education to judges, prosecutors and defence attorneys involved with war crimes trials.

7.   Conclusion

Justice as envisioned by the Rome Statute is guided by the principle of complementarity, which is intended to balance the sovereignty of domestic legal systems with a guarantee that international crimes will be prosecuted. The ICC provides a safety net when states fail or refuse to act, but it is also a custodian of international law intended to facilitate and legitimize the course of genuine prosecutions in national courts. Properly im-

---

[36]   Morten Bergsmo, Olympia Bekou and Annika Jones, "Complementarity After Kampala: Capacity Building and the ICC's Legal Tools", in *Goettingen Journal of International Law*, 2010, vol. 2, no. 2, pp. 791–822, available at http://www.casematrixnetwork.org/fileadmin/documents/Goettingen_Journal_of_International_Law_2__2010__2__791-811.pdf, last accessed on 6 August 2012.

[37]   UN Dialogue, *supra* note 31, pp. 3–5.

[38]   Mark Ellis, "International Justice and the Rule of Law: Strengthening the ICC through Domestic Prosecutions", in *Hague Journal on the Rule of Law*, 2009, vol. 1, no. 1, pp. 79–86, available at http://journals.cambridge.org/action/displayAbstract?fromPage=online&aid=4614164, last accessed on 6 August 2012.

plemented, complementarity is an important safeguard for domestic jurisdiction as well as a catalyst for the rule of law.

However, complementarity has been developed and applied without clarity and as such remains a somewhat stunted justice strategy. The situations in Kenya and Libya demonstrate the challenges and ambiguity associated with the complementary principle. Both states rightfully challenged the Court's jurisdiction. The Libyan challenge is particularly convincing and has earned the support of the ICC Prosecutor. However, current practice indicates that the ICC's decision–making will focus more on factors that denote the disintegration of the domestic legal system than on the promise of future rehabilitation of that system; this does not bode well for post-conflict Libya.

The ICC's approach to positive complementarity has also raised concerns. Bolstering the capabilities of states to conduct genuine domestic prosecutions of international crimes, in line with international standards, is key to delivering justice and developing the rule of law at the domestic level. Yet, even recognising its role as an active court, the ICC, to date, has failed to provide adequate capacity building support to relevant states.

The situation is complicated by the fact that there are three separate "owners" of the strategy, whose perspectives and roles relating to complementarity differ. The Office of the Prosecutor, Assembly of State Parties and judicial chambers of the ICC each play an important part in implementing the principle of complementarity, but their inharmonious approaches threaten its integrity.

The ICC, understandably, does not want to weaken its own judicial function nor divert funds from ICC investigations and prosecutions. These must be the Court's priorities. Therefore, States Parties to the Rome Statute, the United Nations and other international and regional organisations must play a key role in providing technical assistance to states in need.

The vanguard of international criminal law is for international crimes to be prosecuted domestically – in good faith and in a manner consistent with international standards. This is the paradigm shift that needs to take place. However, for this goal to be realized, the ICC (incorporating the Office of the Prosecutor, the Assembly of State Parties, and judicial chambers) and the international community must seek to develop a coherent and objective approach to the principle of complementarity aimed at strengthening domestic legal systems. In so doing, there can be a balance between the ICC's prosecutorial jurisdiction and the responsibility under international law that states too must prosecute international crimes.

8.   Sources and Further Reading

Assembly of State Parties, Report of the Bureau on Stocktaking, Taking Stock of the Principle of Complementarity: Bridging the Impunity Gap, ICC Doc. ICC-ASP/8/51, 18 March 2010, para. 16, available at http://www.icc-cpi.int/iccdocs/asp_docs/ASP8R/ICC-ASP-8-51-ENG.pdf, last accessed on 6 August 2012.

Assembly of State Parties, Report on the Bureau on Complementarity, ICC Doc. ICC-ASP/9/26, 17 November 2010, para. 9, available at http://www.icc-cpi.int/iccdocs/asp_docs/ASP9/ICC-ASP-9-26-ENG.pdf, last accessed on 6 August 2012.

Christopher Keith Hall, "Developing and Implementing an Effective Positive Complementarity Strategy", in Carsten Stahn and Göran Sluiter (eds.), *The Emerging Practice of the International Criminal Court*, Martinus Nijhoff, 2009, pp. 163–182.

Eric A. Witte, Putting Complementarity into Practice: Domestic Justice for International Crimes in Democratic Republic of Congo, Uganda and Kenya, Open Society Foundation, 2011, available at http://www.soros.org/sites/default/files/putting-complementarity-into-practice-20110120.pdf, last accessed on 6 August 2012.

Francis Mureithi, Local Trails for ICC Suspects Still an Option, Says Kibaki, The Star, 24 April 2012, available at http://www.the-star.co.ke/national/national/72787-kibaki-says-ocal-trials-for-icc-suspects-still-an-option, last accessed on 31 August 2012.

ICC Considers Appeal from Libya, UPI News, 17 May 2012, available at http://www.upi.com/Top_News/Special/2012/05/17/ICC-considers-appeal-from-Libya/UPI-10291337274887, last accessed on 6 August 2012.

International Criminal Court Office of the Prosecutor, The Principle of Complementarity in Practice, 2003, available at http://www.iclklamberg.com/Caselaw/OTP/Informal%20Expert%20paper%20The%20principle%20of%20complementarity%20in%20practice.pdf, last accessed on 6 August 2012.

International Criminal Court, Resolutions and Declarations Adopted by the Review Conference, ICC Doc. RC/Res.1, 8 June 2010, part II, para. 3, available at http://www.icc-cpi.int/iccdocs/asp_docs/Resolutions/RC-Res. 1-ENG.pdf, last accessed 6 August 2012.

International Criminal Court, Situation in the Republic of Kenya, Case no. ICC-01/09, Decision Pursuant to Article 15 of the Rome Statute on the Authorization of an Investigation into the Situation in the Republic of Kenya, para. 183, 31 March 2010, available at http://www.icc-cpi.int/iccdocs/doc/doc854287.pdf, last accessed on 31 August 2012.

James A. Goldston, "UN Dialogue with Member States on Rule of Law at the International Level Speech, Strengthening the Nexus between International Criminal Justice and National Capacity to Combat Impunity", Open Society Justice Initiative, 2010, available at http://www.unrol.org/files/James%20Goldston%20Rule%20of%20Law%20Speech%20.pdf, last accessed on 6 August 2012.

Judicial Cooperation between the Democratic Republic of the Congo and the Office of the Prosecutor of the International Criminal Court, Article 37, 6 October 2004.

Mark S. Ellis, Atrocities in Kenya Must Not Go Unpunished, London Times Online, 6 February 2008.

Mark S. Ellis, "International Justice and the Rule of Law: Strengthening the ICC through Domestic Prosecutions", in *Hague Journal on the Rule of Law*, 2009, vol. 1, no. 1, pp. 79–86, available at http://journals.cambridge.org/action/displayAbstract?fromPage=online&aid=4614164, last accessed on 6 August 2012.

Mission Multi-Bailleurs de l'Audit du Système Judiciaire en RDC, in *Rapport Final des Ateliers et du Séminaire pour un Programme Cadre de la Justice en RDC*, Kinshasa, 15 November 2004.

Morten, Bergsmo, Olympia Bekou, and Annika Jones, "Complementarity After Kampala: Capacity Building and the ICC's Legal Tools", in *Goettingen Journal of International Law*, 2010, vol. 2, no. 2, pp. 791–822, available at http://www.casematrixnetwork.org/fileadmin/documents/Goettingen_Journal_of_International_Law_2__2010__2__791-811.pdf, last accessed 6 August 2012.

Lucas Barasa, Mutula to Ocampo: Quit Kenyan Probe, Daily Nation, 18 September 2010, available at http://www.nation.co.ke/News/politics/Mutula%20to%20Ocampo%20Quit%20Kenyan%20probe%20/-/1064/1013680/-/b1f4rs/-/, last accessed on 31 August 2012.

Luis Moreno-Ocampo, "Paper on Some Policy Issues before the Office of the Prosecutor", ICC-OTP, 2003, available at http://www.amicc.org/docs/OcampoPolicyPaper9_03.pdf, last accessed 6 August 2012.

Luis Moreno-Ocampo, "Statement Made by Mr. Luis Moreno-Ocampo at the Ceremony for the Solemn Undertaking of the Chief Prosecutor of the ICC", 16 June 2003, available at http://www.iccnow.org/documents/MorenoOcampo16June03.pdf, last accessed 6 August 2012.

Pascal Kambale, "The ICC and Lubanga: Missed Opportunities", in *Possible Futures*, 2012, (Interviews with senior military judges, Kinshasa, 2009), available at http://www.possible-futures.org/2012/03/16/african-futures-icc-missed-opportunities, last accessed on 6 August 2012.

Paul Seils, ICC's Kenya Decision is No Cause for Celebration, Al Jazeera, 31 January 2012, available at http://www.aljazeera.com/indepth/opinion/2012/01/2012128125931617297.html, last accessed on 6 August, 2012.

Prosecutorial Strategy 2009-12, Office of the Prosecutor, 1 February 2010, p. 5, available at http://www.icc-cpi.int/NR/rdonlyres/66A8DCDC-3650-4514-AA62-D229D1128F65/281506/OTPProsecutorialStrategy20092013.pdf, last accessed on 6 August 2012.

Prosecutor v. Saif Al-Islam Gaddafi and Abdullah Al-Senussi, Case no. ICC-01/11-01/11, Application on Behalf of the Government of Libya Pursuant to Article 19 of the ICC Statute, 1 May 2012, available at http://www.icc-cpi.int/iccdocs/doc/doc1405819.pdf, last accessed on 6 August 2012.

Prosecutor v. Saif Al-Islam Gaddafi and Abdulla Al-Senussi, Case no. ICC-01/11-01/11, Decision on the Conduct of the Proceedings Following the "Application on Behalf of the Government of Libya Pursuant to Article 19 of the Statute", 4 May 2012, available at http://www.icc-cpi.int/iccdocs/doc/doc1407703.pdf, last accessed on 6 August 2012.

Prosecutor v. Thomas Lubanga Dyilo, Case no. ICC-01/04-01/06, Judgment, 14 March 2012, para. 1358, available at http://www.icc-cpi.int/menus/icc/situations%20and%20cases/situations/situation%20icc%200104/related%20cases/icc%200104%200106/court%20records/chambers/trial%20chamber%20i/2842?lan=en-GB, last accessed on 6 August 2012.

Prosecutor v. William Samoeiruto, Henry Kiprono Kosgey and Joshua Arap Sang, Case no. ICC-01/09-02/11-274, Decision on the Application by the Government of Kenya Challenging the Admissibility of the Case Pursuant to Article 19(2)(b) of the Statute, 30 May 2012, para. 6, available at http://www.icc-cpi.int/iccdocs/doc/doc1223134.pdf, last accessed on 6 August, 2012.

Report of the International Law Commission on the Work of Its Forty-Sixth Session, United Nations GAOR, 49th Session, Supp. no. 10., UN Doc. A/49/10 (1994), in *Yearbook of the International Law Commission*, vol. 2, 1994.

Rome Statute of the International Criminal Court 17 July 1998, UN Doc A/CONE.189/9*, amended January 2002, available at http://untreaty.un.org/cod/icc/statute/romefra.htm, last accessed on 29 August 2012.

UN Security Council Press Release, International Criminal Court Chief Tells Security Council Libya Wants Domestic Courts to Handle Proceedings against Son of Former Libyan Leader Qadhafi, SC/10651, 16 May 16 2012, available at http://www.un.org/News/Press/docs/2012/sc10651.doc.htm, last accessed 6 August 2012.

2.6.

The Need for a Legal and Justice Strategy Regarding International Crimes

Fausto Pocar[*]

Due to the internationalisation of law, the role international justice has gravitated toward reflects the mounting significance of the human element in international relations. This has spawned the trend to humanise international law creating the need for states to collectively prevent and repress heinous human rights violations which constitute international crimes, thus establishing international criminal judicial bodies. The variety of models adopted in the establishment and operation of these courts and tribunals manifestly shows the absence of any clear strategy of the international community. In the immediate future, one single actor, the ICC, is due to remain and perform all the functions currently carried out by a plurality of participants. Two key questions emerge: (1) whether the ICC will be prepared and able to stage the entire play and to develop a legal and judicial strategy devised to promote the universal application of international criminal law; and (2) what the international community should do to favour a positive response to the first question or, were a positive response not within reach, to remedy the gap.

1. Towards a Humanisation of International Law

A distinctive feature of legal developments in recent decades is, no doubt, the progressive internationalisation of law and the role international justice has played in the clarification, enforcement, and development of the law. While this phenomenon has characterised all legal fields, including areas related to economic and commercial transactions as well as investments, it is more manifestly apparent in the criminal domain, as a reflection of the increasing importance of the human dimension in international relations. This phenomenon has carried with it a progressive humanisation

---

[*] **Fausto Pocar** is Professor of International Law at the Law Faculty of the University of Milan, and Judge of the International Criminal Tribunal for the former Yugoslavia (ICTY).

of international law and, as a consequence, an emerging approach of states to jointly prevent and repress the commission of serious violations of human rights constituting international crimes. The creation of international criminal judicial bodies, irrespective of their different nature, denomination and legal basis, whether proper international courts, or hybrid and mixed courts and tribunals, has radically changed an earlier approach of the international community, which seemed previously inclined – after the experience of the Nuremberg and Tokyo trials – to leave to individual states the task of repressing international crimes committed by their nationals or on their territory.

2. The Past and the Present: Proliferation without a Clear Strategy

However, this change, which has led to what has been called a "proliferation" of criminal courts, does not appear to have been guided by any planned or coordinated strategy, as far as its judicial and legal dimension are concerned. Indeed, the first step was taken by the Security Council of the United Nations by establishing *ad hoc* international tribunals – the International Criminal Tribunal for the former Yugoslavia (ICTY) and the International Criminal Tribunal for Rwanda (ICTR) – comprised of international judges meant to apply essentially international customary law and international rules of procedure and evidence, adopted by them in plenary session. Subsequently, the Security Council has promoted the creation of mixed or hybrid courts and tribunals by decisions of United Nations bodies or by treaties concluded by the United Nations with the countries concerned like the Special Court for Sierra Leone (SCSL), the Special Chamber of the Supreme Court in Kosovo, the Panels for Serious Criminal Offences in East Timor, the Extraordinary Chambers in the Courts of Cambodia, and the Special Tribunal for Lebanon. Such courts are comprised of internationally appointed as well as of national judges, and form part of the domestic judiciary or operate alongside the national judicial system in each country concerned or in a different location. They apply customary and treaty law as well as domestic law, or primarily domestic law, and follow rules of procedure and evidence, which are either international or the domestic rules in force in the system to which they belong. Other mixed courts, such as the War Crimes Chamber of the State Court in Bosnia and Herzegovina, have been established with the involvement of international authorities other than the United Nations. Lastly, but before the establishment of most of the above mentioned special jurisdictions, an *ad hoc* approach has been set aside in favour of the creation – through a multilateral treaty, the Rome Statute – of a permanent International Criminal Court (ICC), which is comprised of international judges mandated to apply primarily treaty law as set forth in the Court's statute and its annexed documents, including elements of crimes and rules of procedure and evidence, adopted by the Assembly of States Parties, without prejudice to the application of customary international law where appropriate.

The variety of models adopted in the establishment and operation of these courts and tribunals manifestly shows the absence of any clear strategy of the international community in shaping their legal and judicial framework. Rather, it confirms that the only common denominator underlying the creation of these judicial bodies lies merely in an effort to fight impunity, although without a definite vision as to the most appropriate means for achieving such a goal. The absence of a clear strategy is further confirmed by the assignation to these courts of additional tasks, besides the prosecution of the persons allegedly responsible for the commission of international crimes – such as to foster peace in regions where conflict were still going on, to establish the truth about tragic events in the countries concerned, to contribute to reconciliation of populations torn by the conflict, and to make a positive impact on transitional justice. It is self-evident that at least some of these tasks cannot be assigned entirely to a court of justice, but require additional measures.

The absence of a clear legal and judicial strategy has inevitably reflected on the implementation of universal international criminal law, where national, regional and international actors play different roles that frequently lack coordination and even express contradictory approaches, including the actors primarily concerned, in other words the courts and tribunals themselves. Several among them – in particular the ICTY, the ICTR, the SCSL and some hybrid courts – have tried to shape and implement a common legal strategy by building on their respective case law with a view to avoiding legal fragmentation, while still respecting each other's judicial independence. However, this approach has been followed to a lesser extent by other courts, in particular by the ICC, which has deemed it appropriate, in light of its permanent nature and its statutory constraints, to elaborate its own case law without paying much regard to other courts' decisions. The limited consideration given in the recent *Lubanga* case to the previous case law of the SCSL on the subject matter of children's recruitment and use in military operations may serve as an example of this approach.

3.   The Future: From Many Actors to One

Notwithstanding the undeniable success of international criminal justice so far, the current situation strongly invites the international community to devise a comprehensive strategy, aimed at improving the legal and judicial framework for combating impunity and at promoting its universality, which is far from a reality. A plea for such a strategy is especially momentous as the above described judicial scenario is going to change dramatically in the years to come. Failing always possible but unlikely surprises, the courts' proliferation which started in 1993 appears to have come to a halt. The *ad hoc* tribunals established in the first fifteen years since 1993 have either closed or are about to close, and in a few years they will have completely left the scene. One single actor, the ICC, is due to remain and perform all the functions currently carried out by a plurality of participants, which have until now occupied a stage where the role of the ICC has been increasingly relevant but still marginal. The obvious questions that arise in this prospectively changing scenario are twofold. Firstly, whether the ICC will be prepared and able to stage the entire play and to develop a legal and judicial strategy devised to promote the universal application of international criminal law and an efficient judicial guarantee thereof, as envisaged by the Rome Statute. Secondly, it raises the question of what the international community should do to favour a positive response to the first question or, were a positive response not within reach, to remedy the gap and devise alternative means to replace, at least temporarily, the inability of the Court to pursue entirely its goals.

The difficulties faced by the ICC throughout its almost ten years of pursuing its objectives are visible to everybody – it is not helpful to highlight them for the purpose of criticising the institution, as it is frequently done. Rather, a constructive strategy should be adopted, consisting of identifying the issues that may hinder the Court's activity and proposing adequate and viable solutions. In this context, it is more than obvious that the experience of other courts should be taken into account, and that the Court should avail itself, or be put in the condition of availing itself, of such experience. Continuity in the vision of law and justice between the *ad hoc* courts and tribunals and the ICC will only benefit the role of the latter, as the continuity in the legal vision of the post WW II tribunals has benefitted the more recent *ad hoc* tribunals.

4. Several Legal Areas of Attention

Several legal areas should be explored with a view to development in the sense indicated in the first question above, both concerning the procedural framework within which the Court operates and the law that it applies.

The first area concerns the rules of procedure and evidence of the Court, which were adopted by the Assembly of State Parties and are subjected to the power of amendment by the same body, the Court enjoying only the power to propose amendments and, in particular cases, to enforce them temporarily. In contrast, a different course of action was followed for the *ad hoc* international tribunals, which were given the power to adopt and amend their own rules, and have indeed done so. Irrespective of the reasons that determined this course of action, which may have simply been practical ones due to the short deadline within which the Statute of the ICTY had to be drafted and submitted to the Security Council, it is a fact that the ICTY has made large use of its power and has added a number of amendments, including the insertion of some forty additional rules. This was done with the goal of rendering its procedure more efficient and to prevent excessive delays, without detracting from principles of fair trial. In other words, by allowing a small group of competent and experienced people, consisting of the judges who daily faced the challenges of an international procedure, to revise the rules as necessary, a degree of flexibility was introduced in the legislative process, which contributed to more expeditious adjudication of the trials and appeals. The rigid approach of the ICC, where any amendment has to undergo political negotiations between State Party delegations, cannot allow for similar flexibility and will hinder, or at least delay, any change in the rules that the judges may identify. Whilst it is true that some trials in the ICTY have been lengthy and have suffered delays, one may wonder how frequently this would have occurred had the rules not undergone continuous adaptations. It is submitted that the Assembly of State Parties should perhaps change the current approach and entrust the judges with more responsibilities in shaping the Court's rules of procedure and evidence. This will allow the rules to reflect the judges' daily experience and the new challenges that arise in dealing with international procedure, which have delayed proceedings in the past, such as victims' participation and the delicate relationship between the prosecutor and the chambers. This change will also allow the Court to avail itself to a larger degree of the experience of the tribunals that preceded its judicial activity. The efficiency of the Court could only benefit from an increased flexibility in the shaping and application of its rules of procedure and evidence.

Another, and even more important issue from the point of view of a legal strategy, relates to the law applicable by the ICC in terms of its universality. When establishing the ICC, the international community undoubtedly set amongst its goals the universalisation of international criminal law and its enforcement. Such a goal is clearly instrumental to eradicating impunity and ensuring that perpetrators of heinous crimes against humanity do not find any safe haven among states. To this end, the international community adopted the Rome Statute, a treaty listing the crimes over which the Court has jurisdiction, as well as a document describing the elements of those crimes in order to assist the Court in the interpretation and application of the Statute. By nature, a treaty is not a universal legal instrument. It is only binding on the states that have accepted it and does not produce effects on third countries. Admittedly, in the future a treaty like the Rome Statute may be universally applied. However, this can only be achieved if all states ratify it, or if the provisions of the treaty become customary international law, as happened for example for the Geneva Conventions on international humanitarian law of 1949 or the Convention on the Prevention and Repression of Genocide of 1948. Without these developments, a treaty goes in the direction of fragmentation of the law rather than universalisation.

Nevertheless, if the task of interpreting a treaty is given to an international court which is also mandated with the application, as appropriate, of customary international law – which is by definition universal, unlike treaty law – that court can play a significant role in merging the provisions of the treaty into the general customary legal framework, making the applicable law truly universal. The potential role of an international court could be to help make a treaty universal, and if given this role, it should not be underestimated. Whilst a judicial decision based only on treaty provisions represents but a limited precedent for the states that are not parties to the treaty, the application of customary international law by a court makes that precedent significantly more valuable to all states. Although formally only binding on state parties, the decision will have to be taken into account as a precedent in assessing the rights and duties of all states under general international law. Thus, its value extends far beyond the limited circle of the state parties to the treaty, which establishes the court and the geographical boundaries of its jurisdiction.

International criminal law has been regarded as universal since its foundation, in light of the human values that it protects, and has developed as a universal body of law through its judicial interpretation and application by the *ad hoc* tribunals, which were mandated to apply customary law provisions. It would be odd and paradoxical if the ICC, as the body tasked with fostering universality within the scope of its jurisdiction, were to favour fragmentation of the law by adhering to a strict application of the statute rather than placing it within the framework of customary international law. The Court should be encouraged to rely on general law to the largest extent, as the Statute permits, with a view to bridging, at least in terms of the development of the law, the gap created by the lack of ratification, and to bringing about the universality of its role. This approach will also establish a continuity between the role played by the *ad hoc* tribunals, which has produced an abundant case law that currently represents almost the entirety of international jurisprudence on international criminal law, and the role which will be played in the future by the ICC as the sole jurisdiction dealing with international crimes at the international level.

So far, the universality of the Court has been pursued essentially by encouraging ratifications of the Rome Statute, with significant but limited results, since, notwithstanding the ratification of around two thirds of the states forming the international community, more than a half of the world population is still not protected by its provisions. Pressure for ratifications should continue, but the universality of the law should also be pursued through developing jurisprudence in which a more significant role would be played by customary international law.

Finally, turning to the second question posited above – what action should be taken in the case that the ICC is not in the position of taking up all the burden of ensuring the universal application of international criminal law and an efficient judicial guarantee thereof? It has to be recalled that the Rome Statute itself contains provisions aimed at permitting the Court to exercise jurisdiction even beyond the boundaries of states parties. The referral of situations by the Security Council is precisely intended to fill in the gap in the universal jurisdiction of the Court deriving from the lack of ratifications by a number of countries. However, as the implementation of these provisions depends on the special majority required under

Chapter VII of the UN Charter, it is possible only if the permanent members of the Council reach an agreement thereon. Furthermore, once the referral has been authorised, the continuous support of these members is critical for a successful activity of the Court. Unfortunately, on the occasion of the two referrals authorised so far, this support – and indeed the support of other countries, including states parties to the Statute – has been provided but only to a certain extent, and the investigations of the prosecutor have only resulted in the approval of arrest warrants that have never been carried out. This situation is far from satisfactory, and requires a careful analysis by the UN bodies involved and the Court to find more convincing solutions. In any event, the question could only be raised whether referrals to the ICC represent the only means to deal with situations connected with states that are not parties to the Rome Statute, or whether other forms of intervention could be envisaged to ensure that justice is done when crimes occur in such states. Various models could be considered, including existing and new ones, and a serious study should be conducted in order to identify their possible features, bearing in mind that any solution should take into account not only the nature of each situation, but also the desirability to shape a legal and judicial strategy more comprehensive and coherent than has been done so far in pursuing impunity for international crimes.

2.7.

Legal and Justice Strategies: An ICTR Perspective

Adama Dieng[*]

Why is it important for an international justice institution to have a legal and justice strategy? Or to put it differently what role does it play? In this contribution, it is contended that legal and justice strategy is critical for the realisation of the objectives underpinning the existence of the institution in question. In other words, for a justice institution to effectively discharge its functions must be predicated on the legal and justice strategy that identifies both challenges and opportunities that may arise in the implementation process. Citing the International Criminal Tribunal for Rwanda (ICTR), this think piece will show that its legal and justice strategy was critical in addressing various challenges that had the potential to significantly impact the work of the Tribunal in the beginning, during the course of its work, and as it completes its tasks. Its strategy had to be innovative enough to identify and address both immediate and long term challenges of the ICTR as a justice institution.

1. Introduction

Legal and justice strategies may be understood as an attempt to undertake specific initiatives in advance to inform future decision-making of an institution concerned with justice administration. It requires an institution to clearly define its objectives or goals and parameters within which it will attain them based on the available resources, both financially and technical. It is challenging for a justice institution at the national level to make such a strategy. It is even more difficult in the international context: the International Criminal Tribunal for Rwanda (ICTR) was a new type of institution, one that was set up *ad hoc* to address quite specific legal challenges with both local and global emotional and political ramifications.

---

[*] Adama Dieng is Under Secretary-General and Special Adviser of the United Nations Secretary-General on the Prevention of Genocide, and former Registrar of the International Criminal Tribunal for Rwanda.

The temporary nature of most international justice institutions in existence today, made it essential for them to clearly define their objectives and time limits within which objectives underpinning their existence can be achieved. Similarly, the strategy had to elaborate how resources needed to attain the stated objectives will be acquired. This think peace intends to discuss these issues in relation to the work of the ICTR established by the United Nations Security Council to specifically address the mass crimes committed in Rwanda.[1]

Any institution established, whether within the international or national context, is charged with specific role to play or objectives to accomplish. The ICTR's mandate was determined by the UN Security Council. It was exclusively limited to Rwandans, in or outside the country. It was limited to a pre-determined list of crimes, and to events occurring within a set period of time. Lastly, the ICTR was not setup as permanent body (unlike the ICC), even though its impact was meant to be permanent (peace and stability through justice). From this, the ICTR strategies had to be developed.

2. Why Legal and Justice Strategy?

Why is a legal and justice strategy necessary? It can be argued that it essentially guides and directs the work of the institution in question. One of its key attributes is that it must define a framework within which its beneficiaries – victims and alleged perpetrators of crime – can access justice. A good strategy will ensure that key questions or challenges likely to impact the quality of justice delivered are identified from the beginning and appropriate mechanisms to address them are developed. Examples of such challenges are: delivering high quality justice within available resources that may not be adequate for the task; identifying those likely to be tried by the Court; transferring alleged perpetrators to the custody of the court; and putting in place mechanisms to allow victims to rebuild their lives, with impact and relevance even after the Court has closed down. For example the strategy can identify the creation of victim trust fund to raise resources from different sources both private and public to guarantee

---

[1] United Nations Security Council Resolution 955 Establishing the International Tribunal for Rwanda (with Annexed Statute), S.C. res. 955, U.N. Doc. S/RES/955, 8 November 1994.

compensation for the victims most affected in accordance with criteria set by the justice institution concerned.

3.   Stronger Legal Framework

An international justice institution must be predicated on a strong legal framework to enable it undertake its functions effectively. As indicated in the previous paragraph, the ICTR was founded on United Nations Security Council Resolution 955 adopted under Chapter VII, which also included its Statute. This is significant because from the beginning it enabled the Tribunal to undertake its functions under the direct authority of the Council. Decisions of the Council undertaken under Chapter VII bind all States and this ensured that the Tribunal enjoyed stronger international cooperation in discharging its functions. One level underneath the Statute, and based on the Statute, the judges adopted the Rule of Procedure and Evidence.

It is worth examining the nexus between a legal and justice strategy and the legal framework on which the ICTR was based a little closer. An effective strategy should take into account the nature and extent of the mandate of the institution in question. The stronger the legal framework, the more likely it is that the objectives underpinning the institution would be achieved. If the institution is predicated on a weak legal framework it may, for example, be difficult to obtain critical cooperation or assistance from states.

4.   International Support to the Tribunal's Strategy

For a good legal and justice strategy, the ICTR did not only need to ask the right questions, to develop a strategy and have a sound legal framework as a foundation, it also needed to garner critical international support for its successful implementation. The extent of the Tribunal's success has been highly dependent on the measure and nature of support extended by the international community. This observation emanates from the reality that while international justice institutions can issue indictments and render judgements, they lack means to enforce their decisions. For that, they must solely rely on the political commitments and good will of member States to carry out their international responsibilities as outlined in their founding instruments. This situation also exists for the permanent international justice institution, the International Criminal Court and is therefore a key strategic consideration for all international justice institutions.

The fact that the ICTR mandate is based on the aforementioned Chapter VII resolution does not automatically mean that States have been willing to transfer all those indicted by the Tribunal and present on their territories to Arusha. Indeed, seventeen years after the adoption of the Resolution 955, ICTR is still grappling with significant instances where some States have been reluctant to apprehend and transfer to the Tribunal those accused of crimes.

What can be done to address this challenge? One way is to create allies that can help confront inadequate or non-cooperation with political and other forms of opposition. Such a strategy must reflect different mechanisms or options that can be used to achieve this objective. From the outset, the ICTR put strong strategic emphasis on state cooperation. Senior officials of the Tribunal such as the President, Chief Prosecutor and the Registrar have played a key role in engaging states and international institutions to seek their cooperation in locating, arresting and transferring the accused to the seat of the Court.

5.   Challenges to the ICTR Legal and Justice Strategy

While the ICTR adopted its own legal and justice strategy as part of its efforts to establish an overall framework within which to effectively conduct and conclude its judicial activities, external factors also dictate whether the strategy will succeed or fail.

For example, the UN Security Council compelled the Tribunal to develop a 'completion strategy' for its activities.[2] This requirement has had profound implications on the overall functions of the Tribunal. The major challenge has been the need to comply with the directive of the Security Council without compromising the primary role of the Tribunal to render impartial and effective justice to both victims and the perpetrators.

Another challenge relates to the question of how to deal with those acquitted by the Tribunal. This aspect is significant because the Resolu-

---

[2]   ICTR adopted a 'Completion Strategy' as part of the requirement of UN Security Council Resolution 1503 (2003) which among other things argued ICTR "to formalize a detailed strategy modeled on ICTY Completion Strategy to transfer cases involving intermediate and lower rank accused to competent national jurisdiction to allow ICTR to complete all its work by 2010".

tion establishing the Tribunal does not designate a specific country to undertake to admit such persons. There are instances where states are not willing to accept certain individuals especially when they feel that such persons may pose danger to their national peace and security. While the Resolution obliges all States to cooperate fully with the Tribunal in discharging its functions, relocating those acquitted has been and continues to be a major challenge. Indeed, the Tribunal in consultation with the Office of the High Commissioner for Refugees has had to seek assistance from the Security Council to determine the fate of some of those acquitted by the Tribunal.[3] This aspect is especially important for a permanent justice institution such as the International Criminal Court, which is more than likely to conduct trials for high profiled criminal suspects.

6. Enhancing National Capacity to Complement the Work of the ICTR

Given the temporary nature of the ICTR and the limited nature of its resources, it is evident that it cannot investigate and prosecute all the alleged perpetrators of crimes. It is this aspect that provided a compelling need for the Tribunal to adopt specific measures or strategies to ensure that those that cannot be tried by the Court receive fair trial within their own jurisdiction.

The ICTR as an international judicial institution is required to comply with the highest standards of human rights and fair trial that are the hallmark of its Statute. As such it has an obligation to ensure that before it transfers any suspect in its custody, necessary conditions exist in a country concerned to achieve a fair trial.

The Tribunal cannot transform overnight the national judicial system of a UN Member State to ensure full compliance with international standards, so it has to make do with clear assurances from the country concerned to undertake necessary reforms to achieve this objective. For example, because of the need to comply with the Security Council directive to complete all the work of the tribunal within the specified period

---

[3] This was included in the Report of the President of the Tribunal to the Security Council 2011. The close cooperation between ICTR and UNHCR is based on the reality that the Tribunal neither has mandate nor means to address the plight of those acquitted by the Tribunal. It therefore remains the role of UNHCR as the primary UN refugee agency to assist them seek asylum in other countries.

of time, it has been necessary for the Tribunal to transfer some cases to the Rwandan judiciary. For this, the Tribunal needed guarantees that the accused would receive fair trial guaranteed under the ICTR Statute and that all relevant international human rights instruments would be respected. Similarly, the Tribunal has had to address the challenge related to the criteria used to decide which cases would be tried by the Court in Arusha and which ones would be transferred to the national jurisdiction. The key reference points for such decisions, as developed by the Court, were the nature of the crimes committed and a determination as to whether such transfer will advance the interests of justice as per Resolution 955.

The ICTR legal and justice strategy has also focused on how to enhance cooperation with regional and international human rights institutions to ensure that they work and support the government of Rwanda to create necessary conditions to ensure fair trial for those accused transferred to the Rwandan judicial authorities. As part of this, the Tribunal has also worked to enhance its cooperation with the African Commission on Human and Peoples rights, headquartered in Banjul Gambia, to ensure that the latter works closely with the Rwandese authorities to guarantee fair trial to the already transferred cases to Rwanda.

7. Conclusion

Coming back to the question with which this think piece started out, the ICTR case has shown that a legal and justice strategy is crucial for successful functioning of any judicial institution to effectively fulfil its mandate, in particular an international institution like the ICTR. It has further been shown that while a strong mandate is important for its successful functioning a lot also depends on the political will of Member States to actually fulfil their obligations. Senior officials of the Court have had to play a more proactive role to engage both international institutions and individual states to cooperate with the Tribunal for it to effectively and successfully carry out its mandate.

8. Sources and Further Reading

Adama Dieng, "Capacity Building Efforts of the ICTR: A Different Kind of Legacy", in *Northwestern Journal of International Human Rights*, 2011, vol. 9, no. 3, pp. 403–422.

Chile Eboe-Osuji (ed.), *Protecting Humanity: Essays in International Law and Policy in Honour of Navanethem Pillay*, Martinus Nijhoff, 2010.

Daphna Shraga and Ralph Zacklin, "The International Criminal Tribunal for Rwanda", in *European Journal of International Law*, 1996, vol. 7, pp. 501–518.

Djiena Wembou, "The Rwanda Tribunal: Its Role in the African Context", in *International Review of the Red Cross*, 1997, vol. 37, no. 321, pp. 685–693.

Erik Møse, "The ICTR's Completion Strategy: Challenges and Possible Solution", in *Journal of International Criminal Justice*, 2008, vol. 6, no. 4, pp. 667–679.

Jamil D. Mujuzi, "Steps Taken in Rwanda's Efforts to Qualify for the Transfer of Accused from ICTR", in *Journal of International Criminal Justice*, 2010, vol. 8, no. 1, pp. 237–248.

Hassan B. Jallow, "Justice and the Rule of Law: A Global Perspective", in *International Lawyer*, 2009, vol. 43, pp. 77–82.

Mathew Saul, "Local Ownership of the ICTR: Restorative and Retributive Effects", in *International Criminal Law Review*, 2012, vol. 12, no. 3, pp. 427–456.

2.8.

Complementarity, Local Ownership and Justice Sector Assistance in Future Legal and Justice Strategies

Erik Wennerström[*]

Unlike traditional forms of justice sector-assistance, complementarity-assistance strives towards compliance with a singular norm. Complementarity-assistance is not intended to enhance the capacity of the local judiciary in general, but to ensure that it conforms to standards ultimately set by the International Criminal Court (ICC). However, the positive effects of complementarity-assistance naturally transcend the parties immediately concerned with the processes of international criminal law. In this think-piece, some of the challenges in this encounter between the traditional rule of law assistance offered to affected countries, and the proponents of the normative prerogative of the ICC are described, drawing on the pioneering legal-political facilitation, for example, of the International Center for Transitional Justice (ICTJ), and the advanced legal-technical development of tools spearheaded under the ICC Legal Tools chapeau.

1.   Introduction

Complementarity-assistance differs in certain ways from traditional forms of justice sector-assistance. First of all, complementarity-support is not intended to enhance the capacity of the local judiciary in general, but to ensure that it conforms to standards ultimately set by the International Criminal Court (ICC) as regards the small group of serious crimes covered by the Rome Statute. Secondly, complementarity-support focuses on a group of crimes that are for most states extraordinary and not on the volume of crimes processed at all times in any national system. Thirdly, the positive effects of complementarity-support transcends the parties immediately

---

[*]   **Erik Wennerström** is Director-General of the National Council for Crime Prevention in Sweden, and former Principal Legal Adviser in International Law for the Swedish Ministry of Foreign Affairs.

concerned with the processes, and feeds into the transition of the state, as the processes are often part of the healing and exaction of accountability following conflict.

The resonance in local society of complementarity-support may, in spite of the potential benefits, be less than enthusiastic, or rather the enthusiasm is not necessarily where it has conducive operational implications. While a programme on enhanced court efficiency or the launching of a professional training programme in a recipient country has the potential of coinciding well with the 'organic' interests of any judiciary, as well as with those of its political masters in the Ministries of Justice. The handover from the donor to the local partner can occur at an early stage, once satisfying structures for programme management have been installed. Complementarity-support does not necessarily trigger the same amount of autonomous interest or enthusiasm.

An additional dimension with regard to capacity-building for complementarity is the strong normative element that sets this type of assistance apart from other areas of justice sector (or rule of law) assistance. Whereas most efforts to support capacity-building in the justice sector are at best benchmarked against measures of progress set by the donor community, if the donors are not directly involved in individual projects, complementarity-assistance is – whether the assistance actors like it or not –ultimately "benchmarked" against legal norms by a judicial body. Neither the assistance actors nor the local owners can autonomously determine with certainty when their efforts meet the standard. In order to meet the challenge posed by this fact, new ways of bridging assistance interests with normative imperatives need to be identified.

2.   Complementarity and Normative Imperatives

The complementarity principle, as it appears in the Rome Statute, was constructed for vertical application. The International Criminal Court – resembling the role of the European Court of Human Rights or the Court of Justice of the European Union, which have *vis-à-vis* national court systems – would monitor the proceedings of states and act as a state only when those proceedings fall below the standards set by the Statute, as interpreted by the ICC. The principle stipulates that when a state party to the Rome Statute, through inability or unwillingness, fails to carry out its obligations under the Rome Statute, the ICC may assert its jurisdiction instead of that state.

When designing domestic mechanisms, aimed directly or indirectly at fulfilling national obligations, under international law and particularly under the Rome Statute, it is essential to ask: "when are investigations and prosecutions carried out by a state sufficient to render a real or potential case before the ICC inadmissible?" Only the International Criminal Court can answer this question with any degree of certainty in each case brought before it, although with each such answer the case law will present an ever widening and fuller guiding jurisprudence, in addition to individual cases.

Trial Chamber II of the ICC issued a decision on 16 June 2009 in the case of *The Prosecutor* v. *Germain Katanga and Mathieu Ngudjolo Chui*, rejecting a motion by one of the accused challenging the admissibility of the case on the basis of national proceedings for similar crimes, as the Court deemed the national efforts unable to succeed. The Court adds that the ICC may pursue a case that is being processed in a national jurisdiction, as long as that state does not object and prove to the Court that it is indeed able and willing to carry out the proceedings. In this case, the Democratic Republic of Congo (DRC) had not objected to the ICC proceedings.

Important guidance was also given by the Court in the 30 August 2011 case *The Prosecutor* v. *Francis Kirimi Muthaura, Uhuru Muigai Kenyatta and Mohammed Hussein Ali*, in which the Appeals Chamber dismissed an appeal brought by Kenya, suggesting national investigations having been initiated would render the case inadmissible. The Appeals Chamber confirmed that it is the state that challenges the admissibility of a case that carries the responsibility of providing the Court "with evidence of a sufficient degree of specificity and probative value that demonstrates that it is indeed investigating the case". In the case, the Court also stresses that having an identical national investigation and a genuine investigation are two separate issues for the Court to examine, adding further guidance to national jurisdictions for future cases. As these and other decisions of the Chambers and statements of the Prosecutor have suggested, a case will be deemed admissible before the ICC unless a state is able to persuade the Court that it is carrying out national proceedings in relation to the same case, and that these proceedings are genuine. This 'complementarity test' under Article 17 of the Rome Statute is crucial to keep in mind, whenever designing support for national capacity in the area of international criminal law. If overlooked, negligence or over-simplification of the steps and challenges contained herein may render huge assistance efforts futile. For the test, Article 17 of the Rome Statute should be read together with Article 53(1)(b), and with Rule 48 of the Rules of Procedure and Evidence of the Court.

While the vertical nature of the principle as outlined in the Statute appears to suggest a negative interpretation, i.e. it focuses on the role of the ICC when subsidiary efforts in states are insufficient, much emphasis has, since the Office of the Prosecutor presented its *Report on Prosecutorial Strategy* in September 2006, and even more so since the Kampala Review Conference in 2010, been placed on the 'positive approach to complementarity' or positive complementarity. Positive complementarity, according to the Office of the Prosecutor, "[...] encourages genuine national proceedings where possible; relies on national and international networks; and participates in a system of international cooperation". While still a vertical principle it permits movement in both directions.

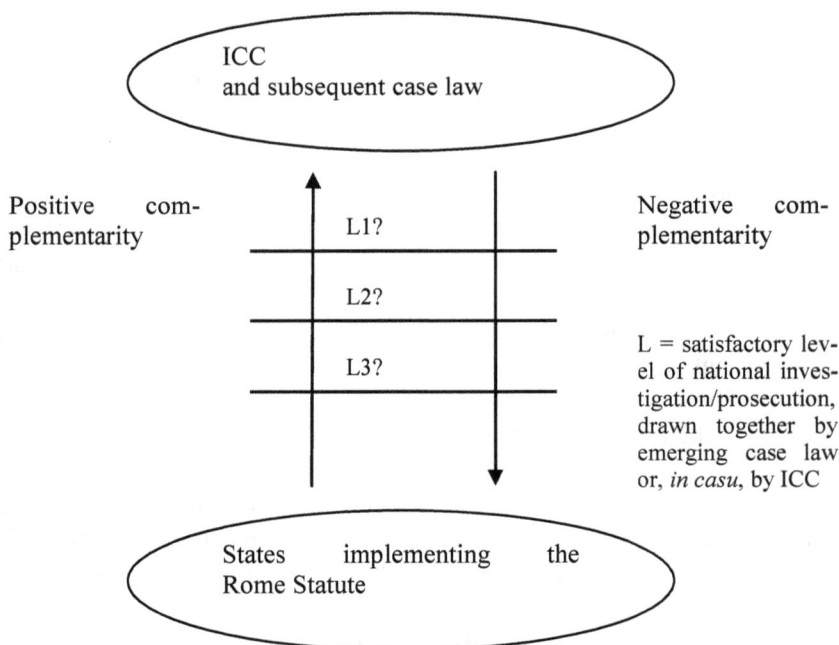

ICC
and subsequent case law

Positive com-
plementarity

L1?

Negative com-
plementarity

L2?

L3?

L = satisfactory level of national investigation/prosecution, drawn together by emerging case law or, *in casu*, by ICC

States implementing the
Rome Statute

Figure 1: Positive and Negative Complementarity as Opposite Directions under Vertical Principle.

3. Integrating Complementarity into Rule of Law Assistance?

3.1. The Shift from International to National Capacity Building

As the *ad hoc* and hybrid tribunals are slowly closing down and the ICC assumes its role as the sole authoritative court for international criminal law – albeit with little prospects for budgetary growth – it is in the effected states that the future capacity for processing international crimes is needed. This redirection of focus from capacity building at international to national level must be considered especially by donors that already have rule of law-assistance in their development aid portfolios. In this endeavour, much can be learned from the experience of the International Criminal Tribunal for the Former Yugoslavia (ICTY), and its closing strategy that imposes positive complementarity by returning cases to national courts and simultaneously supporting these courts in a way consistent with international law, as well as from the legacy of the International Criminal Tribunal for Rwanda (ICTR) that started to return cases to the Rwandan justice system in a similar way, once it was convinced that Rwanda had the capability and intention to apply the international law concerned.

Although the ICC and its bodies neither were designed, nor have the capacity or resources to act as traditional agents for strengthening national capacity, there are ways in which it can make crucial contributions. The Greentree process on complementarity, as well as the discussions taking place at the Assembly of States Parties (ASP) to the Rome Statute, has produced several suggestions to facilitate this knowledge-sharing and technical assistance. On the margins of the ASP, the principle of ensuring accountability for serious crimes has seen a major breakthrough at a high-level meeting at Greentree, New York, in 2011, generating proposals for a broad reference group of states to develop policy approaches to complementarity as well as the creation of a group whose role would be to develop strategies and country-specific plans on the delivery of complementarity assistance. The process seeks to ensure that plans for delivering accountability for mass atrocities are developed in accordance with national development planning, and *vice versa*, thereby supporting and being supported by the sustainable development of rule of law objectives. The process strives towards the co-ownership and coordination between development and rule of law sectors in the implementation of complementarity.

The process has identified the greater need for more concrete plans of action to ensure effective implementation in relevant situations. The challenges herein should not be underestimated, such as the need for broader political support for the complementarity agenda, as well as the need for greater coordination of assistance offered by different actors, particularly from the rule of law and development spheres. The creation of a coordination group of stakeholders in the development and rule of law fields, as well as recipient states, ICC and UN representatives, expert organisations, and donor agencies has been proposed. It would be responsible for developing strategies and country-specific plans on the delivery of complementarity assistance. The establishment of such a group has the potential of meeting some of the operational challenges, while the political side of the process will continue at future ASP meetings and at the General Assembly High Level Rule of Law Debate in September 2012.

3.2. Maintaining the Normative Imperative

As complementarity-related capacity building and assistance will be subject to another form of audit than most other types of assistance, namely the potential legal audit by the ICC, local ownership should be seen as an instrumental factor, and local owners identified accordingly. Complementarity needs to be acknowledged as a political and legal process, with relevant parts of the executive designing and promoting it to make sure that parliament, the judiciary – possibly also the security sector and parts of civil society – are included as required by the local context. Complementarity can only be implemented by an authority that controls both the legislative and budgetary processes, and that is furthermore also the administrative master of the judiciary.

Efforts to include complementarity in general rule of law assistance programmes could ensure greater participation from development actors in complementarity initiatives, as their programmes are developed to advance justice, security, and development simultaneously, thereby assisting not only with adequate resources and an integrated approach to programming, but also ensuring national ownership and facilitating better coordination of all actors involved. Few results will, however, be obtained without efforts to work on the specific crimes concerned, mainly because the guiding norms for these crimes are not found in the general development strategies, nor in the recipient countries legislation or policies, but outside the 'jurisdiction' of both donors and recipients.

3.3. The Actors and Tools at Local Level

Local ownership in the justice sector alone is not necessarily a recipe for success, as there is too little organic interest in the sector itself for the required reform to be implemented, as part of the country's international obligations. The fulfilment of complementarity obligations under the Rome Statute may not be obvious in the technical long-term interests of the justice sector in a particular country. It creates capacity for dealing with out-of-the-ordinary cases, in a way that creates a risk of diverting resources from the volume activities of a judiciary. It is politically perhaps more of an interest to ministries for foreign affairs, which is the part of the administration that is likely to feel the external pressure of complementarity. As the ICC is the ultimate arbiter regarding whether efforts to avoid the complementarity threshold have been sufficient, one of the central goals can never really be owned by any local entity, nor by any donor for that matter. In time, the case law of the ICC will cover an ever larger part of the normative canvas, possibly permitting states party to the Rome Statute, to integrate the norms flowing from that case law in their domestic law, processes and apparatus—as states have done, with varying degrees of success and assiduity, with international law in general. For the foreseeable future, however, with case law consisting of relatively few guiding decisions made by the ICC, the only source of normative guidance is the ICC itself.

Sector responsibility

Normative and political responsibility

```
┌─────────────────────┐        ┌─────────────────────────┐
│                     │        │                         │
│  Ministry of Justice│        │ Ministry for Foreign Affairs │
│                     │        │                         │
│           ┌─────────┼────────────────┐                 │
│           │    Relevant  local  ow-  │                 │
└───────────│    nership?              │─────────────────┘
│           │                          │
│   ┌───────┤                          │
│   ▼       │                          │
│  Judiciary└──────────────────────────┘
│                     │
└─────────────────────┘
```

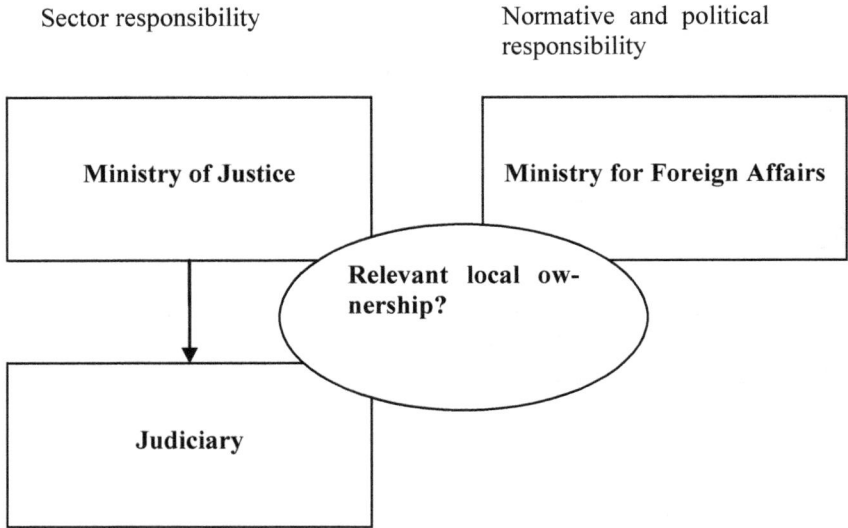

Figure 2: The Potential "Mismatch" between Political-Normative Responsibility and Practical Responsibility for Reform.

For local ownership to have a constructive role in complementarity-related assistance, the inclusion of local civil society actors needs to be considered with care. Local non-governmental organisations (NGOs) may or may not be in a position to assist in the establishment of judicial mechanisms, as so much depends on the state taking steps to ultimately meet the requirements of international law. The ultimate test as to whether the assistance project was "right" or "wrong" does not depend on local ownership; instead it depends upon whether the threshold established by the ICC is met or not. While several international NGOs have considerable knowledge and experience in the field of international criminal law, some may find that their advocacy work will prove difficult to combine with national capacity building, while organisations such as the Coalition for the ICC (CICC), Parliamentarians for Global Action (PGA), the International Center for Transitional Justice (ICTJ) and the International Legal Assistance Consortium (ILAC) will be ideally placed to support and carry out several of the capacity-building steps, either through implementation or through legitimating consultation.

Many donor-supported rule of law programmes have focused on strengthening state justice sector institutions through capacity building and transfer of know-how. While the legal empowerment agenda may lead to a shift away from this practice in general, it is vital for complementarity-related assistance to maintain a strong point of gravity in the state justice sector. The European Union has embarked on a process of improving its aid delivery approaches to include:

> [...] a problem solving and service delivery approach in the support to the justice sector, so as to combine institutional building support with legal empowerment of people and strengthening accountability aspects of the justice sector by increasing support to oversight mechanisms.

The idea of empowerment is a useful metaphor also in relation to complementarity, although here it is the state that needs empowerment to build, with assistance, the mechanisms required of it under the Rome Statute.

Apart from the legal necessity of ensuring the national responsibility for processing crimes under the Rome Statute, there are several practical advantages in doing so that in turn will enhance the positive results of capacity-building. National proceedings facilitate victim participation in the proceedings, evidence gathering, hearing of witnesses, and enforcement of arrest warrants. They can also be expected to be faster and cheaper than international proceedings. The strengthening of national capacity for processing the Rome Statute crimes can also have several positive effects in healing the social wounds of war, ending a national culture of impunity and at the same time strengthening the general respect for the rule of law with effects way beyond the area of international criminal law.

The tools developed by the European Union (such as the ICC Complementarity Toolkit), the ICC Legal Tools Project and the Case Matrix Network (such as the Case Matrix), in order to facilitate national capacity building in full compliance with the normative prerogative of the ICC (and the case law of the *ad hoc* tribunals), will undoubtedly play an important role in years to come, and attention should be paid to their importance in all efforts purporting to support complementarity. These tools are key in transferring know-how compatible with international legal requirements and making national practitioners, in particular those that are assisted by interventions, self-sufficient.

4.   Conclusion

There is currently no sole strategy guiding the efforts undertaken to promote complementarity-support, although several assistance actors have included activities in their broader rule of law strategies that will support capacity building for complementarity purposes. The actors in the field of justice sector assistance are actors that will also occasionally act for these purposes *vis-à-vis* the type of recipient institutions implicated by future complementarity-assistance (inasmuch as such institutions exist). The actors carrying the normative guidance for successful capacity building for complementarity are not, however, necessarily the same actors, and these two groups of actors are following different strategic imperatives and work under very different distributive conditions. In short, traditional assistance actors possess the resources whereas the complementarity actors possess the normative know-how to make this work.

We are dealing with obligations or benchmarks mainly located *outside* the main area of legal and justice strategies, in areas where local ownership in the sector concerned can be a deflecting or centrifugal force, rather than a constructive guarantee for sustainability. Calls for enhancement of local ownership need to be balanced by the need for normative stringency; empowering local actors through robust and endurable methods of information-sharing related to legal development, such as the Case Matrix Network, appears to be a realistic ambition to pursue, in order to make it as easy as possible to integrate international obligations in the local justice sector. This will, naturally, present challenges for donors, recipients, and for the ICC as well as for those supporting its activities, but the reward is the transformation of the verticality of the complementarity principle into a genuine two-way street and the inclusion of a normative component into rule of law assistance. Through the Greentree process, strides are being taken to bridge the interests of the two sets of actors, which can pave the way for a future strategy that combines the broader assistance goals with the narrower complementarity goals.

5.   Sources and Further Reading

Bartram Brown, "Primacy or Complementarity: Reconciling the Jurisdiction of National Courts and International Criminal Tribunals", in *Yale Journal of International Law*, 1998, vol. 23, p. 383.

Chris Stephen, *Clarifying the Principle of Complementarity: The ICC Confirms Admissibility of Case Despite Investigation by Kenya*, EJIL, 2011.

Daniel Benedix and Ruth Stanley, "Deconstructing Local Ownership of Security Sector Reform: A Review of the Literature", in *African Security Review*, vol. 17, no. 2, 2008.

Frederic Megret, "Why Would States Want to Join the ICC? A Theoretical Exploration Based on the Legal Nature of Complementarity", in *Complementarity – Views on Complementarity*, T.M.C. Asser Press, 2005.

ICTJ document for ICC ASP Ninth Session, "Making Complementarity Work: The Way Forward", 2010.

ICTJ document, Synthesis Report on "Supporting Complementarity at the National Level: An Integrated Approach to Rule of Law", December 2011, pp. 7–9.

James Boughton and Alex Mourmouras, *Is Policy Ownership an Operational Concept?*, IMF, 2003, Working Paper, WP/02/72, available at http://www.imf.org, last accessed on 6 August 2012.

Jann Kleffner, "The Impact of Complementarity on National Implementation of Substantive International Criminal Law", in *Journal of International Criminal Justice*, 2003, vol. 1, no. 1, pp. 86–113.

Mohamed el Zeidy, "The Ugandan Government Triggers the First Test of the Complementarity Principle: An Assessment of the First State's Party Referral to the ICC", in *International Criminal Law Review*, 2005, vol. 5, no. 1, pp. 83–120.

Morten Bergsmo, "Complementarity after Kampala: Capacity Building and the ICC Legal Tools", in *Göttingen Journal of International Law*, vol. 2, 2010, pp. 791–811. (with Bekou, O., and Jones, A.)

Morten Bergsmo, *Complementarity and the Challenges of Equality and Empowerment*, Policy Brief Series No. 8, Torkel Opsahl Academic EPublisher, Oslo, 2011.

Morten Bergsmo, "Complementarity and the Construction of National Ability", in *The International Criminal Court and Complementarity, From Theory to Practice*, Volume II, Cambridge University Press, 2011, pp. 1052–1070.

Morten Bergsmo (ed.), *Active Complementarity: Legal Information Transfer*, Torkel Opsahl Academic EPublisher, Oslo, 2011.

Morten Bergsmo, "New Technologies in Criminal Justice for Core International Crimes: The ICC Legal Tools Project", in *Human Rights Law Review,* 2010, vol. 10, no. 4, pp. 715–729.

Morten Bergsmo, "Preserving the Overview of Law and Facts: The Case Matrix", in *Collective Violence and International Criminal Justice*, Intersentia, 2010, pp. 413–435.

SECTION B: INTERNATIONAL ORGANISATIONS

3.1.

A Master Plan

Robert Visser[*]

A strategy is a plan to reach a result. It is thinking before doing. Looking at legal and justice strategies it is important to understand the environment and context in which strategies have to be realized. Hard and soft facts influence the implementation of a strategy. A successful strategy should be comprehensive, realistic and flexible. As the concept of strategies is the same, nevertheless different dynamics can be distinguished as the national level, the European Union level and the international level are concerned. On the EU level some interesting developments on strategic approaches can be noticed.

1.   Towards a Legal and Justice Strategy

The first reaction to this might be: that seems like a good idea. But what is a legal and justice strategy? How does it work? Who is in charge of it? What does it need to be successful? These questions are central to this contribution, as well as an example of some developments on a European level.

The first question is of course what is a strategy? According to the dictionary, a strategy is: a plan of action designed to achieve a long-term or overall aim. A more simple way to describe it is: a strategy is a pre-planned way to reach a result. It is thinking before doing.

The main characteristic of a strategy is that it is orientated towards the future insofar as it aims to reach a certain result at a later time. In that sense, it is about shaping the future. Some would claim that a strategy is a vision, a vision of the future and on future developments. Some would say that a strategy is a 'Master Plan'. In any case a strategy is more than just a goal. A strategy is a plan, a preconceived plan to realise a goal.

[*]   **Robert K. Visser** is Executive Director of the European Asylum Support Office, and former Director-General for the department of Legislation, International Affairs and Immigration at the Dutch Parliament.

Why do strategies deserve our special attention? Is it because in modern times quick decisions are daily practice? Is it because we think that external circumstances are dictating our future? Is it because we no longer feel in control? Is it because we think that we should think first before acting? Is it because we think that strategies produce better results than normal decisions and "just" realising goals? To many this seems to appeal to reason. I do not seek to pursue this point if indeed it is true and evidence based. However, the least one could say is that a strategy puts matters into perspective, that it can also take into account the environment and the side effects. As such, a strategy could lead to a more balanced decision.

At this point it is good to realise that a strategy by itself is a neutral term. A strategy is not by definition something positive. History provides ample examples of strategies used for bad and sometimes dramatic goals.

2. Legal and Justice Strategies

The legal and justice area has its own context that should be taken into account. Also legal systems have an environment. Most important in that environment are the facts. Facts should not be underestimated. They determine to a large extent our possibilities. Facts are the geographical position of a country, the composition of the population, natural resources, climate, but also history, past events and the geopolitical situation.

Then there are the 'soft facts' – 'soft' because they can be changed to a certain extent and over time. But in a given moment they are in general taken for granted. Examples of soft facts include the cultural environment, the financial situation and certain traditions. Also the legal tradition of a country can be such a soft fact.

Yet there is also another environment to take into account. Countries and people are influenced by other legal systems. Changes in those legal systems influence us, as well as changes in our system influence the world around us. We can claim to be autonomous or even sovereign, but in fact we are not. For a strategy to be successful it is important to keep all this in mind. Let's call this a realistic strategy.

There are different types of strategy. We can distinguish between explicit strategies and implicit strategies. We can also see incident driven strategies, or to put it nicely, topic-focused strategies.

3. A Successful Strategy

What does it take for a strategy to be successful, what are the elements of a successful strategy?

A number of elements can be mentioned without being exhaustive. As indicated previously, a very important element is that a strategy should be realistic. This means that it takes into account the relevant environment of facts and circumstances. Part of this, but worth mentioning separately is taking into account the collateral effects. Side effects of a strategy can make or break the success of a strategy.

It is also essential that the approach is a comprehensive one. This means that it takes into account the wider area of law involved. Also the general legal context is relevant, as well as the constitutional setting, the governmental and parliamentary unwritten laws and traditions. Therefore, a successful strategy should have a well-conceived goal, and be realistic, coherent and comprehensive. A specific point still to mention is the need to be flexible. A strategy is a plan based on a certain situation. If the situation changes, the strategy might have to be adapted accordingly.

4. Does a Legal and Justice Strategy Exist?

Ask this question in government circles and the answer would very likely be that of course they exist. Everything we do in government is well thought of and thought of well in advance. However, is this always the case? We all know of projects of law that originate in a quick reaction to an incident, or projects of law designed to serve a specific occasion and not necessarily a general problem. We also know of laws that are only symbolic and have no real effect. I would not honour these categories with the label of legal or justice strategy.

In reality, legal and justice strategies may not always be so common. At this point of the discussion, it is useful to distinguish between different types of governing systems and levels.

On the national level, there is an overall system of law in place. New and changing laws are, so to speak, on-going business. Here strategies are often implicit. There is a certain context, there is a tradition. Proposals tend to be in line with that context even if not explicitly addressed. Of course there are also explicit legal and justice strategies on the national level. Mostly those strategies originate and result from an election period. Election promises and government negotiations, certainly for coalition governments, often lead to new strategies. Changes of government are the source of new strategies. This does certainly not imply that they are by definition successful. Not all of them are realistic or take other elements of success into account.

On the level of the European Union, the situation is different. Here legal and judicial strategies are more explicit, well known and well developed. The European Union is a legal concept and basically a legal community. Legal basis and legality are part and parcel of every discussion about new EU laws. The notion of subsidiarity and proportionality asks for explicit strategies. One might say that the European Union is still in the process of creating itself and at the same time in parallel working on its operational structure and adapting to changing circumstances. That is why the EU process often starts with a general strategic plan, or programme, followed by a strategic green book or white book. This process will then result in concrete proposals of legislation that are linked in the broader strategic framework. A new policy is based on a common feeling of a subject, but certainly not as a quick reaction on an incident. Many different views and traditions have to be discussed before a common line can be agreed upon. Take as an example the developments in the area of migration. The first step towards EU-competence on migration was set with the Treaty of Maastricht in 1992. It took until 1999 to have a general strategic programme on migration, the Tampere programme. This programme drafted the broad lines for this new area, the perspective of a Common European Asylum System. After 11 September 2001 it took speed. Three years later, there was the first set of EU laws implementing the original framework of Tampere. The strategic programme of The Hague in 2004 and the Stockholm programme in 2009 set the framework for further development in this area. At this moment this process is in full discussion. A planned process and step by step, that is the way in which the EU built its legal and justice area.

5. Different Actors, Different Realities

As a strategy is a preconceived plan, it must have a master and a master mind. There must be someone behind the strategy. Someone must have created the idea, the master mind. However, it only becomes a real strategy if there is someone who takes the responsibility to realise it, the master. A strategy without a master, without a guide that leads cannot exist. A strategy is different from an incident, a coincidence. An incidental development is nice to discuss afterwards as a brilliant development, but it is not a strategy, it is not a planned development.

We can easily decide that the master mind can be anyone. Anyone can have a brilliant idea. More important is the question of who is the master of the master plan? Who is the captain? Who is driving the train?

From a formal point of view this question is not difficult to answer. Constitutional law provides a clear answer as to who the actors are as far as legislation is concerned, as well as when policy is concerned. However, if there are several levels of government the answer might be more diffuse. Politicians have a natural inclination to claim the father or motherhood of good ideas and good results. At the same time they just as easily deny responsibility or involvement in what turns out wrongly. Reality might be different.

On the national, regional and local level, a vested situation exists. Laws are the prerogative of the state. The discussion is primarily political even when it is sometimes heavily influenced by civil society. The argument for doing something is that 'society needs this'.

From a constitutional point of view, the situation on the level of the European Union is the same as on the national level. There are formal authorities that play a role in the process of legislation: the European Commission, the Council of Ministers and the European Parliament. However, there is a different political situation and a different playing field. The relations are less crystallised. Discussions are more focused on juridical and legal aspects. The discussion before doing something is "why do we need this".

The situation on the International level shows yet a different view. In theory this is about relations between equal sovereign states. In reality real power plays a big role and so does relative dependency. This creates a very diffuse situation. Here the main discussion is not to change something in the own situation. The background of the discussion is "we want the others to accept this and act accordingly, or the others need to accept this".

All of these situations have an impact on the instrument of legal and law strategies. All strategies start by explaining the need for something. However, the process and arguments differ widely. On the national level the strategy will be directed to explaining the needs of society. Times have changed and so adaptation to it is needed. Also the argument of promises made to the electorate may be used. Often the public itself is addressed and can become part of the discussion.

On the EU level the debate is more technocratic and sounds formal. Certainly the debate is mostly less a public debate. The first stage often is not the question if there is a need of society, but if there is an EU competence to deal with the matter.

6. Bottom-Up: A New EU Strategy?

It is time for a short case study. In the area of EU practical cooperation, new developments deserve our attention as far as legal and justice strategies are concerned. The history of the European Union is one of mutual feeling with regards to the need for cooperation for the benefit of all. In that sense there is nothing new in any sort of cooperation within the EU context. Yet there are two reasons to pay special attention to the developments on practical cooperation in the field of the Justice and Home Affairs area.

The first is the differences between this area and the classical EU area of economics. In the economic area the traditional strategy is to decide on common rules on the EU level and to leave the implementation and enforcement to the Member States. The European Court of Justice plays an essential role in ensuring uniform implementation in the different Member States. This means that the European Commission can remain in the second line and that the heavy infringement procedure can remain an *ultimum remedium*. The fact that the main actors in this field are economic actors who profit from a level playing field and are willing to go to court in order to ensure their rights, certainly does contribute to the success of this system. Where this system proved to be not flexible enough, it was extended by the system of mutual recognition. This mutual recognition was first introduced by the jurisprudence of the European Court of Justice in the famous *Cassis de Dijon* judgment. This mutual recognition turned out to be a practical instrument that could be and is since applied in other areas as well.

In the relatively new area of justice and home affairs, the situation turned out to be different. Also here common rules on the EU level were installed. Yet, no real role for the European Court of Justice was foreseen. It is only with the Treaty of Lisbon that the full role of the European Court of Justice has been introduced. Common rules were put into place, but the reality in this area was one of diverging practices. This meant that the European Commission had to use its infringement procedure in a way that it was not intended to be: to be in the first line. Rather soon another strategy was launched: this was the creation of operational agencies to stimulate practical cooperation. One of the first was the EU border agency, Frontex. More recently the EU asylum agency EASO was established. Such forms of practical cooperation did already exist, for example, Europol. However, this form of practical cooperation was still based on an intergovernmental treaty. Since the Treaty of Lisbon, Europol has been transformed also into an EU Agency.

Do agencies work as a way to organise practical cooperation? Is it possible to stimulate practical cooperation and to enhance common practice by way of an operational agency? What could be the effect on the policy level?

First let's look at the effect on practical and the operational level. Here the answer is as simple as clear. The motto of EASO is: support is our mission. If an agency can make that a reality and show added value, it can prove itself. At the same time it is essential to understand the context of a European agency. An agency clearly works within the EU legal framework. As such it is an instrument of European policy and part of the European strategy.

There is also a secondary effect, an explicit or an implicit effect or a strategy. That is the bottom up effect of practical cooperation within the EU context. Operational cooperation and improvement of working methods can provide evidence-based input into the policy process. This might come in as a welcome side effect in times where the debate on migration in most Member States is not an easy one. Effective practical cooperation and evidence based input into the policy process can ease the sometimes difficult discussion about the needs and necessary measures on the EU level. Is it a strategy or a solution born out of need? Anyhow it is an interesting development on the European level.

To summarise: looking at the situation on the EU level, three different strategies can now be distinguished:

1. Top-down: legal harmonisation: this is the traditional strategy. It will remain essential to realise EU-policies. In the migration area this is expressed in the Common European Asylum System (CEAS).

2. Horizontal: practical harmonisation: this is the operational and practical cooperation. It is a very strong strategy once it is organised; bringing the work floor as well as the practitioners together and actively involving them in the process of working to the same common objective. Examples of inclusive methods include common training, common assessment of the situation in countries of origin (COI) and also sharing the analysis and trends of the external dynamics and trends in migration flows, how they change, what their impact is on other Member States and how the Member States are much more interdependent than generally realised. The horizontal strategy is not restricted to specific areas. It also can be effective when operational agencies like EASO, Frontex and Europol work closely together.

3. Bottom-up: this is supporting policy harmonisation: providing evidence-based input for the policy process. This also is a very strong strategy. If it is properly organised it will provide proposals based on the real and practical day to day needs. As such it is less controversial and at least easier to explain. It might at certain moments contribute to change the nature of the political debate to a more practical and realistic level.

All we have seen on the EU level is not new. In different forms and intensity it can be found in different administrations in Europe and beyond. The debate on the primacy of policy and on the relation between policy and operational levels is well known. The establishments on the national level of more independent operational services and of ex ante assessments of draft laws testify for that. The interesting situation that we see at the EU level is the way in which these ideas take shape in a different dynamic. Experiences from different sides lead to a new dynamic and show a new interpretation and implementation. In this respect we might see here just another example of the Law of the reversed advantage.

3.2.

A 21st Century Paradox: Proliferation of Rules, Weakness of Laws

Ana Palacio[*]

Peace without strife, and enjoyment without work, belong to the days of Paradise. History knows both only as the result of painful, uninterrupted effort. That, to struggle, is, in the domain of law, what to labour, is, in that of economy, and that, in what concerns its practical necessity as well as its moral value, that struggle is to be placed on an equal footing with labour in the case of property [...].[1]

Today's legal landscape can be characterised by an overwhelming proliferation of rules emanating from competing, and sometimes conflicting sources which coupled with the multiplication of sources they derive from, form a complex multi-level/multi-plane amalgam of rules and norms. Whereas their sheer volume may seemingly imply that this is a peak for the law as such, quite the contrary is true. Regulatory abundance has in fact undermined the systemic coherence of the law, which today is at its lowest point.

The implications of this are manifold. On the one hand, the legal order is undermined at the state and national levels, whereas at the international level, actors increasingly avoid the law and its struc-tured mechanisms, resorting rather to *ad hoc* solutions and ar-rangements. Although both are critical, the latter development is tangibly more important as it stalls the top-down process of legal consolidation, whereby observance of the law at the international level trickles down to observance of the law at the national level.

---

[*] **Ana Palacio** is a member of the boards of different companies, think tanks and public institutions. In March 2012, she was appointed a member of the *Consejo de Estado*, the supreme consultative body on legislation and governmental acts in Spain.
[1] Rudolph von Ihering, *The Struggle for Law*, Callaghan and Company, Chicago, 1879, p. 4.

1. Introduction

Far from being the spontaneous, rational product of the historical process of development, law is, like Rudolph von Ihering aptly put it, a struggle. The law is not a given. It is not the perfect product of an ethereal collective conscience. Rather, it is a collective achievement, the fruit of a constant desire to struggle against injustice. Those who have experienced different political realities and the transition from autocratic to democratic regimes are more sensitive to this fact than those whose life, in the words of the Göttingen master, "passes away, within the limits imposed by the law to human action; and if we were to tell them: The law is warfare, they would not understand us, for they know it only as a condition of peace and of order".[2]

Jurists, irrespective of their conceptual differences, see the law as a system bound by the coherence of its elements under common principles and through a set of techniques. As such, the law organises counterweights, checks and balances which domesticate power and thereby eliminate the 'survival of the fittest' principle from our societies. This universal identification of the rule of law encompasses the rejection of the 'rule of man' and the notion that law should be prospective and accessible, the idea that the law applies to all, including the sovereign and that it has to apply to all persons equally, offering equal protection without discrimination against the backdrop of respect for human rights. In this regard, the state governed by the rule of law is the label that every liberal democratic regime aspires to. Ever since it appeared in the work of the great German jurists at the turn of 20th century, who pitted this concept against that of the 'police state', this formula has broadened in scope. However, it remains faithful to its original purpose; the state governed by the rule of law is a state in which power encounters its limits in legal norms to which it submits, thus protecting citizens against arbitrariness.

Nevertheless, in order for this purpose to be fulfilled, law has to be recognisable by those for whom it is designed. Although one cannot presume that every citizen would be intimately familiar with the relevant rules and laws, legal norms must be at the very minimum, comprehensible.

---

[2]   von Ihering, 1879, p.3, see *supra* note 1.

In this context, numerous factors surface that erode the intelligibility of rules – from linguistic factors arising from the sudden influx of arcane scientific vocabulary, to the formal aspects of legislative technique, the abusive use of certain omnibus laws, or the emergence of laws that fail to establish real, immediately effective rights.

The severity of these factors notwithstanding, the most significant problem is the proliferation of legal norms. This is certainly the case in Europe where supra-national institutions are gripped by a rule-producing frenzy and where numerous countries are undergoing a process of political and administrative decentralisation, prompting the generation of even more legal norms, both at the local and regional levels.

2. The Proliferation of Norms

Although an often forgotten fact, the warning signs for the proliferation of legal norms go back to Article 5 of the 1789 Declaration – *"la loi n'a le droit de défendre que les actions nuisibles à la société"*, suggesting that the excessive proliferation of regulations may constitute an interference with individual freedoms. Today there is an exponential growth in the number of legal regulations determining every single aspect of individual behaviour, even when it bears no direct legal connection to the rights of others or the proper functioning of society or the economy.

The proliferation of legal norms is partly explained by the multiplication of legal sources. For example, the development of international law is superimposed upon national law. In the European context, this superimposition occurs at the level of the European Union institutions, which never cease designing new rules and which, to give an example, elaborately postulate on obscure matters such as the proper shape of bananas and courgettes, on the assembling of tractor sockets, or the proper dimensions of the cages of egg-laying hens, all under the authorising pretext of the rationalisation of subsidies.

A seemingly reasonable counterargument is that these are examples of issues which may give rise to public expenditures and which may consequently incur damage to society as a whole and therefore constitute grounds for intervention. But where is the limit? The law is no panacea against hazard, nor can it serve to eliminate risk from every sphere of life. Another aspect encouraging regulatory excess is social anomia, or the absence of common morals which underwrite behavioural norms. This leads to an expansion of the law's ambit, regulating on hitherto unimaginable aspects of life, from parental rights to teachers' independence.

Against the backdrop of the proliferation of regulatory texts and their parallel opacity, the jurist has been placed in a dominant position. The recourse to his or her competence has become indispensable in every aspect of today's life while the age of the honest generalist lawyer has given way to highly-specialised legal practices.

Most critically, the sheer volume of rules and the proliferation of norms are indicative of the fact that the systemic coherence of the law is critically undermined. The legal structure is porous at best, characterised by numerous gaps and *lacunae*, which further exacerbate the absence of a coherent unifying framework.

3. The Evasion of Law and Other Challenges to International Law Today

In the late 19th century, the German experts in administrative law coined the expression "evasion of the law" as an efficiency-maximising technique which manifests itself in the expansion of resources and the emergence of subterfuges. This was specifically designed to evade the techniques of administrative control that previously ensured the transparency of decisions through formality and procedural accountability.

This phenomenon is reflected in equal measure at the national and international levels. Whereas both are critical, the latter development is tangibly more important as it affects the core functioning of states and stalls the top-down process of legal consolidation. Observance of the law at the international level trickles down to observance of the law at the national level.

In the former case, this is manifest in the reluctance to create strong institutions and procedures in the international space, with actors increasingly avoiding the law and its structured mechanisms, approaching it instead as little more than a toolbox and resorting to *ad hoc* solutions and arrangements.

3.1. Law as a Toolkit/Law as a System

It is a widely accepted truth that law is a mirror for the values and mores of society; it is a moderating force against the political wishes of the majorities and, in effect, enables democratic rule. But above and beyond this, law provides the key system of social organisation. It is the vehicle that governs the relationships between individuals, individual relationships with the authorities and those of the authorities among each other.

It is also an essential tool for the functioning of the economy, not only because it provides a framework propitious to the exercise of economic activities, but also because of the legal certainty it confers, guaranteeing the stability and predictability of conduct. Today, the world's thriving economies are those with strong and effective institutions, backed by legal frameworks that guarantee the rule of law.

This approach, however, has been undermined for decades from the bully pulpit of the Washington Consensus. Conventional wisdom has long assumed, partly due to the philosophical rift borne out of the Cold War, that the market and the state, long pitted against each other, provide for conflicting and irreconcilable forms of social organisation. For decades the free world hailed the market as a superior framework for the blooming of the individual while it remained suspicious of any effort to strengthen the state. A lingering consequence has been the fact that, for years after the fall of the Berlin wall, law has been relegated to little more than a toolkit, secondary to the dictates of furthering the market.

Now, however, the economic tumult shaking Europe, the erosion of the middle class in the West, and the growing social inequalities worldwide are undermining the pure market approach claims to universal triumph. The pervasive soul-searching prompted by these developments has nurtured a growing recognition that capitalism's success depends not only on macroeconomic policy or economic indicators. It rests on the bedrock of good governance and the rule of law – in other words, a well-performing state.

The standard bearers of the Cold War were not just the United States and the Soviet Union, but in ideological terms, the 'individual' and the 'collectivity'. When competing in newly independent or developing countries, this ideological opposition became Manichean, fostering a fierce suspicion, if not outright rejection, of rival principles. As a result, strengthening state institutions was too often seen in the West as communist subterfuge, while the Soviet bloc viewed the slightest notion of individual freedom and responsibility as a stalking horse for capitalist counter-revolution.

Leading economists have long argued that the West's greater reliance on markets resulted in faster and more robust economic growth. But viewing the state and the market in terms of their inherent conflict no longer reflects reality (if it ever did). Indeed, it is increasingly obvious worldwide that the threat to capitalism today emanates not from the state's presence, but rather from its absence or inadequate performance. What the crisis has demonstrated, in unequivocal terms, is that the rule of law and its integration in the international arena are indispensable for shared prosperity in a globalised world.

The Arab uprisings of the past year and their impact on the region have thrown into sharp relief not only the human strive for freedom and economic opportunity, but also for the need of a coherent growth and development policy that in order to be effective, rests on a systemic legal approach. Another example is the recent events in Argentina. Argentina is facing certain economic losses as anxious investors have second thoughts about the country in the aftermath of the government's nationalisation of energy giant YPF, in full-blown dismissal of legal principles. That response is only logical, as investors seek the security of a well-functioning legal system to protect them from capricious political decisions.

It is only by strengthening law and institutions on all levels that powerful interests can be prevented from exerting undue influence on discourse or society. Latin America and Africa are not the only examples that prove the point. The European Union's internal problems, and the ongoing sovereign-debt crisis, are clearly linked to the weakness of its institutions and on its periphery, Europe still confronts feckless democracies that show worrisome disrespect for the legal foundations of the European construction.

The World Bank, among other international institutions, not only promoted the Washington Consensus, but has been, until recently, unable to pursue the goals of development and the rule of law coherently or in any meaningful, mutually-reinforcing fashion. Acknowledging the relevance of the rule of law to the Bank and integrating it into its work is an important element in the efforts to step up the Bank's promotion of good governance and its global fight against corruption. Indeed, in substantive terms, these areas share common legal principles, making an even stronger case for the need to have a coherent systemic approach, under the arc of law.

Thus, law as a system is at once a framework for regulating society and, at the same time, it is an enabling mechanism for the functioning of democracy and the economy. For law to serve as a vehicle for such advancement, it cannot remain subordinated to politics. Jurists and judges must have a recognised, independent space like "the political influence of jurists", as explained by Alexis de Tocqueville in his work *Of the Spirit of the Jurist in the United States and How It Serves as Counterweight to Democracy*.[3]

3.2.   The Evasion of Law, *Ad Hoc* Style

On a fundamental level, law is an expression of societal values which permeate not only its black letter form, but also its practical enforcement. In this context, western states are bound by a value framework that forms the foundation of our legal systems and the West's general approach to the law both at the national and international levels. However, one has to remain mindful of the fact that law as a system is not embedded in the same fold in other states equally powerful and important in geopolitical terms.

Without a real international community and states as major actors concentrating on safeguarding immediate interests, this would lead to the evasion of the law, an approach whereby law's relevance is displaced by power relationships, seen as paramount, with negotiation replacing justice as the means to overcoming conflict. This approach is rooted in, but also feeds into, a genuine mistrust in the global legal architecture as a reliable mechanism based on permanent commitments and foreseeable rules.

Fitting illustrations of this point are China, Russia, and to a lesser extent India. These countries practice a type of diplomacy and demonstrate an understanding of international relations and law that is exclusively based on the pursuit of immediate interests. They seek to attain objectives with the lowest level of legally binding multilateral commitments possible, seeking benefits by establishing alliances with the most dubious regimes when suiting their interests, with little criticism or pressure to improving the situation of the populations at large. Syria is a particularly poignant case, as is Sudan, although the latter is not currently in the spotlight of public opinion.

---

[3]   Alexis de Tocqueville, "Of the Spirit of the Jurist in the United States, and How It Serves as Counterweight to Democracy", in Eduardo Nolla (ed.), *Democracy in America: Historical-Critical Edition of De la Démocratie en Amérique*, Liberty Fund, Indianapolis, 2010 [1835], vol. 2.

Neither China nor Russia show strong interest in developing international law or in utilising the UN system, resorting instead to informal forums such as the G20 and *ad hoc* negotiation as means for overcoming differences. The failures of the post-Kyoto negotiations or the Doha Round provide stark examples of this evasion of law. An even more illustrative example is the concept of 'Chinese multilateralism', elaborated in the statutes of the Shanghai Cooperation Organization.

In stark opposition to this conception of evasion of the law stands the competing notion that strengthening the law is essential for the functioning of the international order. The Western world has always borne the yardstick of the law, although not all of our actions have lived up to pre-established principles. The legal approach has been and remains a prominent benchmark for the West and constitutes a vital prerequisite for effective governance and the rule of law and thus for the consolidation of well-functioning states.

4. Conclusion – The Legal Order Ahead

The above-mentioned risks and threats notwithstanding, there are numerous opportunities ahead. Today's world of instant communications, the rapid growth of economic exchange, migration waves as well as the emergence of new actors on the international scene are all factors which modify the position of states. A first order of consequences would include the attainment of greater freedoms by populations *vis-à-vis* states, prompting the latter to converge on a path towards democratic coexistence.

Furthermore, the increasingly complex nature of problems facing the international community today throws into sharp relief the need to articulate international solutions on issues that cannot be addressed in isolation through fragmented or local solutions. Naturally, *ad hoc* solutions have salience within the context of bilateral relations or well-defined groups, but the character of today's global problems makes it inconceivable that conflicts can be managed using provisional mechanisms lacking transparent rules.

Neither of these foreseeable developments will be the result of historical determinism, but rather a consequence of the struggle for law. Its future trajectory will be neither linear nor swift, but full of doubts and reversals, more reactive to circumstances than proactive in the face of the challenges that we are facing. Nevertheless– and this is the great contribution of approaching the law as a system– the aim of rationalising international relations is best met through a permanent and predictable legal framework.

5.   Sources and Further Reading

Alexis de Tocqueville, "Of the Spirit of the Jurist in the United States, and How It Serves as Counterweight to Democracy", in Eduardo Nolla (ed.), *Democracy in America: Historical-Critical Edition of De la Démocratie en Amérique,* Liberty Fund, Indianapolis, 2010 [1835], vol. 2.

Rudolph von Ihering, *The Struggle for Law*, Callaghan and Company, Chicago, 1879.

3.3.

Legal and Justice Strategies
in the Council of Europe:
Cooperation with the European Union[*]

Guy De Vel[**]

The Strasbourg-based organisation comprises today, in 2012, 47 Member States, covering nearly the whole of the continent and all Member States of and all candidate States to the European Union (EU) are members of the Council of Europe (COE). The Warsaw Declaration and Action Plan adopted at the third Summit of Heads of States and Government (2005) aimed at the "progress in building a Europe without dividing lines". Furthermore, the cooperation between Brussels and Strasbourg has considerably increased in recent years, in particular as regards fundamental rights, the rule of law, justice and the judiciary implementing a Memorandum of Understanding between the COE and the EU of 2007. In search for a legal and justice strategy, this think piece describes the content of the Warsaw Declaration and Action Plan and the way these have been implemented not only in standard setting, monitoring and assistance programmes, but also regarding new trends and future prospects. It will do so by providing answers to the following questions: Does a legal and justice strategy exist in the Council of Europe; what are the sources of the strategy; what does the strategy look like; and who executes the strategy? Furthermore, the first steps towards a Council of Europe neighbourhood policy with countries around the Mediterranean and Central Asia in cooperation with the European Union; the state of play of the accession of the European Union to the European Convention of Human Rights; and the necessity of further reforms to the European Court of Human

---

[*] This contribution was written in a strictly personal capacity and does not necessarily reflect the official position of the Council of Europe or the Agency of Fundamental Rights of the European Union.

[**] **Guy De Vel** has a Diploma in Philosophy and Literature from St Ignace, Antwerp, 1962 and received a Doctorate in Law from the University of Leuven, 1966. De Vel is a former member of the Management Board and Executive Board of the Agency for Fundamental Rights of the EU in Vienna, representing the Council of Europe.

Rights as a follow-up to the Brighton Declaration (2012) will be discussed. The author stresses the importance of on-going reforms, both in the Strasbourg Court and in the other activities of the Council of Europe, and expresses the firm hope that these reforms will not weaken the action of the COE in the fields of human rights and the rule of law.

1. Introduction: Does a Legal and Justice Strategy Exist in the Council of Europe?

In replying to the question, does a legal and justice strategy exist in the Council of Europe, one has to take into account that the Strasbourg-based Organisation is comprised of forty seven member states to date (2012). It covers nearly the entire European continent with the exception of Belarus. One has also to take into account that all candidate states to the European Union (EU) are members of the Council of Europe (COE). Furthermore, it is important to note that the cooperation between Brussels and Strasbourg has considerably increased in recent years, particularly as regards fundamental rights, the rule of law, justice and the judiciary. There is no single, comprehensive document containing a "legal and justice strategy of the Council of Europe". However, one can perceive such a strategy through the combining of several documents, such as the Warsaw Declaration and Action Plan adopted at the third Summit of Heads of State and Government (2005), and through the programmes of activities of the Organisation. Additionally, in 2011 Thorbjørn Jagland, Secretary-General of the COE, proposed Outline Priorities 2012-2013, which were subsequently endorsed by the Committee of Ministers in the Programme of Activities for the biennium. Other important sources for a strategy are the documents concerning the relations between the Council of Europe and the European Union, following the Warsaw Summit. It was here where Jean-Claude Juncker, Prime Minister of Luxembourg, was asked to prepare in his personal capacity a report based on the relationship between the COE and the European Union. The report was developed in order to initiate political debate on how a more democratic and secure Europe could result from improved cooperation between the two organisations.

Following the presentation of his report, "A Sole Ambition for the European Continent", in April 2006, a Memorandum of Understanding (MoU) was signed between the two organisations in May 2007, providing a new framework for their cooperation, stating that:

9. The Council of Europe and the European Union will develop their relationship in all areas of common interest, in
particular the promotion and protection of pluralistic democracy, the respect for human rights and fundamental freedoms, the rule of law, political and legal cooperation, social
cohesion and cultural interchange. In doing so, they will follow the guidelines adopted by the Third Summit in Warsaw
which called for the building of a Europe without dividing
lines.

10. The Council of Europe will remain the benchmark for
human rights, the rule of law and democracy in Europe.

11. On the basis of enhanced partnership and complementarity, the Council of Europe and the European Union will take
all the necessary measures to promote their cooperation by
exchanging views on their respective activities and by preparing and implementing common strategies and programmes for the priorities and areas of shared interest set out
below.

12. The cooperation will take due account of the comparative
advantages, the respective competences and expertise of the
Council of Europe and the European Union – avoiding duplication and fostering synergy –, search for added value and
make better use of existing resources. The Council of Europe
and the European Union will acknowledge each other's experience and standard-setting work, as appropriate, in their
respective activities.

13. They will extend their cooperation to all areas where it is
likely to bring added value to their action.

The MoU was in 2008 supplemented with an "Agreement between
the European Community and the Council of Europe on Cooperation between the European Union Agency for Fundamental Rights and the
Council of Europe", establishing a cooperation framework between them
in order to avoid duplication and ensure complementarity and added value.

2. What Does the Strategy Look Like?

The Warsaw Declaration summarises the strategy as follows:

The Council of Europe shall pursue its core objective of preserving and promoting human rights, democracy and the rule
of law. All its activities must contribute to this fundamental

objective. We commit ourselves to developing those principles, with a view to ensuring their effective implementation by all member states. In propagating these values, we shall enhance the role of the Council of Europe as an effective mechanism of pan-European cooperation in all relevant fields. We are also determined to strengthen and streamline the Council of Europe's activities, structures and working methods still further, and to enhance transparency and efficiency, thus ensuring that it plays its due role in a changing Europe.

After the Warsaw Summit the activities of the COE where continuously more concentrated on the above priorities: human rights, the rule of law and democracy. In doing so, the organisation continued to use the tools, which proved very successful in the past, and adapting them to cover new needs:

- standard setting;
- monitoring of legal instruments;
- assistance programmes.

Each of these methods can be perceived as new "strategic" trends.

2.1. Standard-Setting

The COE continues its standard setting work, as it has since 1949, and continues elaborating conventions (treaties) and Recommendations of the Committee of Ministers to Member States (soft law). It seems not necessary, in the framework of this volume, to dwell on the two hundred and thirteen treaties drafted in Strasbourg. However, it is interesting to note some recent "strategic trends" in this normative work. A clear recent trend, following the Warsaw Action Plan, is not only to concentrate on human rights, democracy and the rule of law but also, within these fields, to focus on problems that constitute a real danger for these values – terrorism, corruption, money laundering, cybercrime, trafficking in human beings, sexual exploitation of children, violence against women, counterfeiting of medical products – or which constitute a challenge for fundamental rights in our 21st century: biomedicine and data protection.

Another trend is to open treaties more widely and going beyond member states – some of them even world-wide – mainly because of the fact that the matter dealt with cannot be dealt with only in a limited continental context. This is manifestly the case for the more recent conventions on terrorism, cybercrime and medicrime – the Convention on the Counter-feiting of Medical Products and Similar Crimes Involving Threats to Public Health – but work is also underway in order to modernise the 1981 Convention for the Protection of Individuals with Regard to Automatic Processing of Personal Data (ETS 108) and to open it up beyond Member States.

Part of the COE's strategy is also to promote the accession of the European Union to its treaties, as already foreseen in an agreement concluded in 1987 between Strasbourg and Brussels. Since then, most of the COE conventions contain "accession clauses", but unfortunately until now the Union has acceded to only eleven and signed four of them. On the other hand it should also be pointed out that some thirty Council of Europe Conventions have been incorporated into the so-called "EU-*acquis*" and that they frequently acted, and continue to act, as a springboard to EU membership. The Union has furthermore, at several occasions, expressed its support to COE treaties by adopting common positions promoting their adoption, signature or ratification by member and candidate states, for example in the fields of cybercrime, corruption, money laundering. The entry into force of the Lisbon Treaty opens new prospects in this regard. First of all, because it grants legal personality to the Union (Article 46A), which will technically facilitate accession to treaties and participation in their monitoring systems. Secondly, because the Lisbon Treaty (Article 6 para. 2) expressly provides that the Union "[...] shall accede to the European Convention on Human Rights and Fundamental Freedoms [...]". This is probably the most significant element, not only in the present COE legal and justice strategy, but it constitutes also a major step in the development of human rights in Europe.

2.2. Monitoring

The long and wide experience of the Council of Europe has shown that many treaties remain "death letter" if their implementation is not monitored by international independent bodies. Of course such monitoring mechanisms were already set up in the past. The most known and successful are, of course, the Strasbourg Court of Human rights and the Committee, set up under the European Convention for the Prevention of Torture and Inhuman or Degrading Treatment or Punishment (ETS 126). However, the trend in the last decades is to more systematically assort new treaties with monitoring systems; some of them have proved to be very efficient, for example GRECO (Group of States against Corruption), MON-EYVAL (Committee of Experts on the Evaluation of Anti-Money Laundering Measures and the Financing of Terrorism) and GRETA (Group of Experts on Action against Trafficking in Human Beings). Here one can also perceive a tendency to open up such systems to non-members, or at least to some of them.

The participation of the United States of America, as a full member in GRECO, is an interesting example. Participation of the EU in such monitoring systems is also encouraged, and discussions take place concerning accession to GRECO.

The backlog of the Strasbourg Court of Human rights has made it necessary – beside the reform of the Court itself – to assist member states in the reform of their legal systems and in particular of their judiciary. One of the means to implement this strategy is the assistance programmes, which were developed after the fall of the Berlin wall. However, this was not sufficient and ten years ago the COE had set up an intergovernmental body, the European Committee on the Efficiency of Justice (CEPEJ), with the aim to improve the efficiency and functioning of justice in member states but also the implementation of the instruments adopted by the Council of Europe to this end.

Its tasks are:

- to analyse the results of the judicial systems;
- to identify the difficulties they meet;
- to define concrete ways to improve, on the one hand, the evaluation of their results, and, on the other hand, the functioning of these systems;
- to provide assistance to Member States, at their request; and
- to propose to the competent instances of the COE the fields where it would be desirable to elaborate a new legal instrument.

In the Action Plan adopted at their Warsaw Summit, the Heads of State and Governments decided to develop the evaluation and assistance functions of the CEPEJ in order to help member states to deliver justice fairly and rapidly. They also invited the COE to strengthen cooperation with the EU in the legal field, including cooperation with CEPEJ. Furthermore, in order to help member states to deliver justice fairly and rapidly, and to develop alternative means for the settlement of disputes the Council of Europe has developed a strategy to step-up its cooperation with legal practitioners making proper use of two bodies which are the Consultative Council of European Judges (CCJE) and the Consultative Council of European Prosecutors (CCPE).

3. Programmes of Assistance

The COE, well known for its standard setting and monitoring work, has since the fall of the Berlin Wall and the dismantling of the Iron Curtain developed a thorough strategy to improve legal systems and the functioning of the judiciary in candidate and Member States and sometimes – more recently – beyond. This strategy was based on cooperation or assistance programmes and has helped many countries to reform their legislation and institutions in order to comply with the values the COE and the EU stand for and share: human rights, the rule of law and democracy. The programmes dealt with topics such as the reform of constitutional law (European Commission for Democracy through Law, better known as the Venice Commission), of the judiciary, fight against corruption, money laundering, cybercrime but also with training of practitioners such as judges, prosecutors, advocates and police as well as prison staff.

For over 15 years, the COE and the EU have implemented numerous joint programmes to promote respect for human rights and the rule of law without dividing lines. This is one of the most visible parts of the very tight network of relations and cooperation links existing between the two partners. The joint programmes format was initially intended as a tool to facilitate cooperation with countries, which had joined the Council of Europe since 1989. They have paved the way for accession of countries not only to the Council of Europe but also, later on for some of them to the European Union. There have been approximately 180 joint programmes of cooperation and joint actions over the past fifteen years. They were recently extended outside Europe. However, the main goal of the present programmes is to continue to assist member states of the Council of Europe, especially Russia, Ukraine, Moldova, Armenia, Azerbaijan, Georgia and countries of South-eastern Europe in their reforms.

4.   Future Prospects

4.1.   A Neighbourhood Policy?

The COE's core mandate is, and will, remain geographically focused on Europe. This clearly follows from its Statute as well as from the political expectations and priorities of its member states. However, this did not prevent the development of wide-ranging political and legal arrangements with a number of non-European countries. This includes countries which benefit from the Observer Status under Statutory Resolution (93)26 of the Committee of Ministers (Canada, Japan, Mexico and the Holy See as well as the United States of America) but also those who have links based on participation in COE conventions or partial agreements (for example, the Venice Commission and GRECO). In the past, these relationships have developed largely on an *ad hoc* basis, without an overall strategy, criteria and priority objectives.

In today's interdependent world, the COE's core mission of promoting democracy, human rights and the rule of law, cannot longer be carried out without greater consideration given to what is happening outside Europe, and especially in its immediate neighbourhood, the Southern Mediterranean and the Middle East, but also in Central Asia. This is why the COE included, in 2010 the development of a neighbourhood policy as one of its main priorities. The three objectives of such a strategy in countries in the Council of Europe neighbourhood are:

i.   To facilitate democratic political transition (constitutional process, elections);
ii.   To promote good governance in the countries on the basis of the relevant COE standards, mechanisms and instruments (independence and functioning of the judiciary, fight against corruption, money laundering, *et cetera*);
iii.   To reinforce and enlarge the COE's regional action in combating trans-border and global threats such as trafficking in human beings, cybercrime, organised crime, terrorism, *et cetera*.

The Secretary-General of the COE, Thorbjørn Jagland, and the Commissioner for Enlargement of the EU, Štefan Füle, signed on 17 January 2012 a joint programme for an amount of four million eight hundred thousand euros to strengthen democratic reforms in the south Mediterranean.

4.2. Accession of the European Union to the ECHR

The EU's accession will strengthen the protection of human rights in Europe, by submitting the EU's legal system to independent external control. It will also close gaps in legal protection by giving European citizens the same protection *vis-à-vis* acts of the EU as they presently enjoy from member states. Accession is the best means of achieving a coherent system of fundamental rights' protection across Europe. As the Union reaffirms its own values through its Charter of Fundamental Rights, its accession to the European Convention on Human Rights (ECHR) will give a strong political signal of coherence between the EU and "greater Europe".

Negotiations started in 2010 and the draft legal instruments for the accession have now been transmitted to the Committee of Ministers of the Council of Europe. Further negotiations are currently on-going with a view to the finalisation of the instruments. It is of course encouraging that the Brighton High-level Conference on the Future of the European Court of Human Rights (19–20 April 2012) stated in its *Declaration* that it "[...] notes with satisfaction progress on the preparation of the draft accession agreement, and calls for a swift and successful conclusion to this work".

4.3. Reform of the European Court of Human Rights

This brings us to another important element of the Council of Europe's strategy: the reform of the Court of Human rights. The reform of the Court – which is clearly overloaded as its considerable backlog shows – started with the adoption of Protocol No. 14 to the Convention for the Protection of Human Rights and Fundamental Freedoms, amending the control system of the Convention (ETS 194) but later developments have shown the need for further reforms.

At the beginning of 2012, the turning UK chairmanship of the Committee of Ministers of the COE convened the contracting Parties to the ECHR at the Brighton Conference. Some far-reaching proposals ran the risk of weakening the right of individual application and the protection of human rights, but at the end of the day the adopted Declaration strengthened the role, and the authority, of the Court. Further reforms will start and will have to tackle remaining shortcomings.

States also will now need to step up to the challenges of improving the implementation of the European Convention on Human Rights at national level and making sure they acted quickly and effectively on the

Court's judgments, so as to both meet their obligations and cut the Court's backlog by putting a stop to repetitive applications.

Another element of the strategy, in order to protect human rights and to complement the role of the Strasbourg Court, was the undertaking of the Warsaw Summit to strengthen the institution of the COE Commissioner for Human Rights, which has proven its effectiveness. One of the results is that, according to Article 36 of the ECHR, the Commissioner can take part in the proceedings of the European Court of Human Rights, either at the invitation of the President of the Court or, since the entry into force of Protocol No. 14 to the Convention on 1 June 2010, on his own initiative.

4.4. Accession of the European Union to the Council of Europe?

We have seen that as a follow up of the Juncker Report and the subsequent Memorandum of Understanding the cooperation and synergies between the COE and the EU have considerably been stepped up. However, an important recommendation of the Juncker Report has not yet been implemented: the accession of the Union-as such- to the Strasbourg Organisation by 2010. President Juncker considered that:

> […]It follows logically from the complementary relationship between the Council of Europe and the EU […] and from the increased cooperation between the two bodies, which is necessary for the democratic security of people in our continent, that a further step in the relationship should be envisaged, once the EU has acquired legal personality – EU membership of the Council by 2010.
>
> Why membership?
>
> If the EU accedes to the ECHR, if it participates, as such, in the debate on democracy in Europe, if it joins in establishing a pan-European legal and judicial area with appropriate sharing of standards, if it plays a synergetic part in the Council's projects in the fields of education, youth and culture, if it commits itself to inter-cultural dialogue in Europe, if its approach to inter-institutional [cooperation] deepens and diversifies towards building a Europe without dividing lines, if it continues to evolve in this direction – then there is nothing to stop it acceding to the Council. This will allow it to speak directly for itself in all the Council bodies, on all issues which affect its interests and which fall within its area of compe-

tence –all within the context of a pan-European dynamic which it will help to push ahead in the general interest of the continent.

5. Who Executes the Strategy? Is there a Clear Central Strategy Leader? Is it National, Regional, International, and if All of the Above, How do All these Levels Interact?

As in other international organisations the strategic decisions are taken by the executive body of the COE: the Committee of Ministers following proposals or initiatives coming from the Parliamentary Assembly, member states the Secretary-General or other sources such as the Conferences of Ministers of Justice. The activities of the COE are implemented as follows:

- Intergovernmental activities such as drafting of legal instruments are carried out under the authority of the Committee of Ministers by expert committees, comprising delegations from member states with the assistance of the Secretariat;
- Conventional activities are implemented through committees provided for specifically by international treaties (conventions). These committees comprise representatives – or for some of them – independent experts of the contracting parties and generally have the task of monitoring compliance with conventions, for instance, on torture, corruption, cybercrime, trafficking in human beings;
- Cooperation or assistance programmes are implemented by the Secretariat General directly in cooperation with government authorities of the benefiting States and, where necessary, with the assistance of experts from other countries.

6. Conclusion

A strategy of the Council of Europe exists. It is inspired by the Declaration and Action Plan adopted at the Summit of Heads of State and Government in Warsaw (2005). It aims at "progress in building a Europe without dividing lines which must continue to be based on the common values embodied in the Statute of the Council of Europe: democracy, human rights, the rule of law". The Warsaw documents are largely complemented by the subsequent Memorandum of Understanding with the European Union and programmes of activities.

The entry into force of the Lisbon Treaty opens new possibilities for cooperation between Strasbourg and Brussels, and for accession of the EU to COE treaties and monitoring systems, especially in the field of judicial cooperation and criminal law in which the COE has acquired for decades an incomparable experience and where the Lisbon Treaty gives new competences to the Union. The Accession of the EU to the European Convention of Human Rights will constitute a major step forward in the development of a European space, governed by human rights and the rule of law. Although perhaps we are still waiting for a greater step to be taken: the accession of the European Union to the Council of Europe?

However, the Council of Europe is – like most international organisations but maybe even more so – affected by severe budgetary constraints due not only to the on-going economic crisis but also due to the success of the Strasbourg Court! This situation and the increasing number of individual applications to the Court have caused a considerable backlog in their handling and some criticism in some member states. This has led to the Brighton Conference and to some far-reaching proposals, but at the end the Declaration adopted has strengthened the role and authority of the European Court of Human Rights and has paved the way for further reforms, and has improved the implementation of the European Convention on Human Rights at national level. As Secretary-General Thorbjørn Jagland stated:

> Member states have themselves freely chosen to submit to an international judicial control mechanism, because they are deeply convinced that this is a vital safeguard for democracy, freedom and peace across our continent. Basic human rights do not come from any majority or any authority. They come from the fact that we are all human beings and that every nation has an obligation to uphold these rights by law.

Nonetheless, one has also to take into account that the Council of Europe's contribution to the safeguard of democracy is not limited to the case law of the Court. Under the pressure of budgetary constraints reforms have started and touched upon all the activities in the various fields of competence of the Council of Europe. One can only express the firm hope that these reforms will not weaken the action of the Council of Europe in the fields in which it has an incomparable experience such as human rights and the rule of law, where its standard-setting and monitoring activities together with its assistance programmes, contribute considerably to the setting up of a European space of democracy, human rights and rule of law without dividing lines.

7. Sources and Further Reading[1]

Council of Europe, Warsaw Declaration, 16–17 May 2005, available at http://www.coe.int/t/dcr/summit/20050517_decl_varsovie_en.asp, last accessed on 11 October 2012.

Council of Europe, Action Plan, CM(2005)80 final, 17 May 2005, available at http://www.coe.int/t/dcr/summit/20050517_plan_action_en.asp, last accessed on 11 October 2012.

Jean-Claude Juncker, "Council of Europe – European Union: 'A sole ambition for the European continent'", 11 April 2006, available at http://assembly.coe.int/Documents/WorkingDocs/doc06/EDOC10897.pdf , last accessed on 11 October 2012.

Memorandum of Understanding between the Council of Europe and the European Union, 11 May 2007, available at https://wcd.coe.int/com.instra net.InstraServlet?command=com.instranet.CmdBlobGet&InstranetImage =1555975&SecMode=1&DocId=1104084&Usage=2, last accessed on 11 October 2012.

Agreement between the European Community and the Council of Europe on cooperation between the European Union Agency for Fundamental Rights and the Council of Europe, OJ L-186/7, 15 July 2008, available at http://eurlex.europa.eu/LexUriServ/LexUriServ.do?uri=OJ:L:2008:186:00 07:0011:EN:PDF, last accessed on 11 October 2012.

Guy De Vel, "L'Agence des Droits fondamentaux de l'Union Européenne et son interface avec le Conseil de l'Europe", Collection Les Grandes Conférences publiques du Centre d'excellence Jean Monnet-Faculté, Droit-Université Pierre Mendès France–Grenoble, 2009.

Council of Europe, Outline priorities 2012-2013, SG/Inf(2011)4 FINAL, 17 February 2011, available at http://www.coe.int/t/dg4/cultureheritage/ culture/cdcult/plenary_session/session10_mai11/SG_Inf(2011)4fin_EN .pdf, last accessed on 11 October 2012.

Steering Committee for Human Rights (CDDH), Report to the Committee of Ministers on the elaboration of legal instruments for the accession of

---

[1]   Following the expressed wish of the author, references in this Section have not been alphabetised, and are instead ordered chronologically.

the European Union to the European Convention on Human Rights, CDDH(2011)009, 14 October 2011, available at http://www.coe.int/t/dg hl/standardsetting/hrpolicy/Accession/Meeting_reports/CDDH_2011_009 _en.pdf, last accessed on 11 October 2012.

Council of Europe, High Level Conference on the Future of the European Court of Human Rights: Brighton Declaration, 20 April 2012, available at http://hub.coe.int/20120419-brighton-declaration, last accessed on 11 October 2012.

Guy De Vel, "Conseil de l'Europe et Union européenne: deux institutions pour un continent", Collection Les Conférences publiques du Centre d'excellence Jean Monnet-Faculté, Droit-Université Pierre Mendès France–Grenoble, 2012.

3.4.

How to Approach European Union Criminal Law: International Law, National Law, or Something in Between?

Håkan Friman*

Criminal law and criminal procedures traditionally belong to the sovereign realm of state regulation and multilateral legislative efforts follow traditional negotiation patters. Within the EU, however, the intense and rather successful regulatory work in the area of justice and home affairs has transformed traditional international negotiations into a legislative process. Using international criminal cooperation as an example, this paper explores how a traditional 'damage control' approach has shifted into something more like a domestic legislative process, albeit in a different forum and with different features. Now producing 'superior' laws with 'direct effect' in the member states, preserving the legislative role of national parliaments is also held out as a challenge. Focusing on Sweden, the paper discusses an emerging strategy as how to approach an international legislative process that produces national laws, which must fit into existing domestic decision-making processes, and the existing penal and procedural systems.

1. Background

Since the establishment by the European Council in Tampere, Finland, in 1999 of 'mutual recognition' as the key concept for the European Union's development of European criminal law, there has been an amazing development. The need to address this area of law is obvious in order to advance the freedoms of movement (of people, goods, services, and capital) within the Union, counter-acting the negative effects of these freedoms. The concept of 'mutual recognition', which first appeared at the Cardiff European Council, is a clever compromise between those member states

---

* **Håkan Friman** is Deputy Director-General in the Swedish Ministry of Justice (on leave), and former head of the division for international judicial cooperation and criminal cases.

that want further harmonisation and supra-nationalism and those that do not but still cherish interstate cooperation. Whilst the concept leans towards the latter position, it is almost inevitable that at least a level of harmonisation is necessary in order to create workable EU-wide solutions. This has also been acknowledged in the Lisbon Treaty, where moves towards harmonisation – or 'approximation' – are explicitly foreseen. Also Sweden, which traditionally favours inter-state solutions over supranational ones in this field, accepts this development as necessary and desirable.

Since the advent of 'mutual recognition', numerous instruments have been adopted by the European Union. Perhaps the most progress thus far has been made, within the field of police and judicial cooperation, in criminal justice matters. The format for these instruments – under the 'third pillar' of the Maastricht Treaty[1] – is that of so-called 'framework decisions'. The Council adopted this peculiar legislative act without any real influence from the side of the European Parliament. Often the original proposal, or at least the final content, stemmed from member states rather than from the European Commission. The framework decisions are binding upon the member states 'as to the result to be achieved', and these must be implemented (no 'direct effect'), with the states retaining the freedom to choose the 'form and methods'.[2] The framework decisions are not subject to enforcement proceedings before the European Court of Justice by the Commission. The Court's role is limited to resolving disagreements between member states concerning the interpretation of the decisions, and to hear annulment proceedings regarding their validity.

With the Lisbon Treaty,[3] however, the pillar structure was abandoned; police and justice cooperation is now governed by the same institutional principles, types of legal instruments and decision-making procedures that apply to other policy areas (that is, the third pillar merged into the first pillar). Hence, the Commission and European Parliament will part-take in future police and criminal law legislation. In addition, nation-

---

[1] Treaty on European Union (as amended by the Nice Treaty), Article 34, 24 December 2002, available at http://eur-lex.europa.eu/LexUriServ/LexUriServ.do?uri=OJ:C:20 10:083:0013:0046:en:PDF, last accessed on 13 August 2012.

[2] Treaty on European Union, Article 34(2)(b), see *supra* note 1.

[3] Consolidated Versions of the Treaty on European Union and the Treaty on the Functioning of the European Union (as amended by the Lisbon Treaty), 2008 O.J. (C 115), 9 May 2008.

al parliaments are more closely involved with the European Union legislative process.[4] Resolutions, directives and decisions will be utilised also in these fields and the unanimity requirement for decision-making no longer applies.

2. The Matter

To use criminal cooperation as an example, framework decisions have been adopted to address good parts of the criminal justice process. They reach from pre-trial matters – such as the arrest and surrender of suspects (the European Arrest Warrant)[5] – to post-conviction cooperation with respect to recognition and enforcement of custodial and non-custodial sentences, fines and forfeiture orders. The coverage is quite comprehensive, with the exception of the collection of evidence where the adoption of the rather dismal 'European Evidence Order' is to be substituted by the 'European Investigation Order', which is currently being developed.[6] International cooperation in criminal matters is the external side of criminal procedural law, and due to greater mobility, this has become increasingly important for the ability to effectively investigate, prosecute and punish crimes. The cooperation is important not only for accessing evidence, suspects and assets, but also for other substantive issues. For example, the availability of enforcement mechanisms for non-custodial sentences against a defendant living abroad may enhance the opportunities to choose such a penalty instead of a custodial one.[7] Similarly, if it were possible to enforce this abroad, orders restricting the liberty of a suspect, without detaining him or her, can sometimes substitute for the deprivation

---

[4] Protocol No. 1 on the Role of National Parliaments in the European Union, and Protocol No. 2 on the Application of the Principles of Subsidiarity and Proportionality, 2008 O.J. (C 115/203), 9 May 2008.

[5] Council Framework Decision 2002/584/JHA of 13 June 2002 on the European Arrest Warrant and the Surrender Procedures Between Member States, 13 June 2002.

[6] Compare: Council Framework Decision 2008/978/JHA of 18 December 2009 on the European Evidence Warrant, 18 December 2009; and Initiative for a Directive of the European Parliament and of the Council Regarding the European Investigation Order in Criminal Matters, Inter-institutional File 2010/0817 (COD).

[7] Council Framework Decision 2008/947/JHA of 27 November 2008 on the Application of the Principle of Mutual Recognition to Judgments and Probation Decisions with a View to the Supervision of Probation Measures and Alternative Sanctions, 27 November 2008.

of liberty of a suspect living abroad (due to a flight risk or otherwise).[8] Hence, the new mechanisms are aimed at improving equal treatment in the criminal process of EU citizens, regardless of where they live.

Consequently, the instruments on international criminal cooperation aim at key functions of the domestic criminal justice process, issues that are traditionally reserved for national considerations as well as the sovereign sphere of state legislation. Such cooperation has been addressed earlier in international instruments, but in much less intense and imposing forms. These are voluntary undertakings and the preceding instruments leave ample room for discretion as to whether to provide assistance in the case at hand. The grounds for refusal are manifold. The 'mutual recognition' instruments, on the other hand, establish an obligation to cooperate and limit the grounds for denying cooperation. The latter also provide for direct contact between the national authorities concerned with different states, as well as simplified procedures and time limits. In short, they aim to make the cooperation schemes a natural part of domestic national procedures and, hence, the seeking and provision of assistance should be part of the day-to-day operations of police, prosecutors, judges and others authorities.

Clearly, the European Union schemes must be integrated into the existing national criminal procedural system. Quite apart from the problem of the piecemeal introduction of new elements into established domestic systems, are the numerous differences between them, which complicate and hamper the negotiations. In order to make progress, States must be prepared to accept results that require amendments to their laws of criminal procedure, at least in the context of cooperation, and perhaps also in the general procedural scheme. In addition, national differences may be so large that harmonisation of the procedural laws is required. Consequently, the work towards an EU instrument requires in itself close cooperation between member States, in order to identify and address procedural difficulties that the proposed European Union regulation may cause for the different States.

---

[8] Council Framework Decision 2009/829/JHA of 23 October 2009 on the Application, between Member States of the European Union, of the Principle of Mutual Recognition to Decisions on Supervision Measures as an Alternative to Provisional Detention, 23 October 2009.

3. Challenges

The discussion above indicates that the process of developing EU instruments with respect to criminal law, criminal procedures and inter-state cooperation in this field, bears more resemblance to (domestic) legislative processes than to traditional international treaty making negotiations. The latter are normally *ad hoc* for a particular issue and often approached with the view of promoting certain interests (which motivate the international efforts), but also to exercise 'damage control' in other areas. Multinational instruments rarely, if ever, seek to regulate domestic criminal procedures but instead give states great latitude to implement the treaty obligations in a way that suits their existing criminal law and criminal procedure systems. Regularly, the negotiators cautiously guard and steer the negotiations toward solutions that will require no, or minimal, amendments to existing domestic law. Consequently, they are often also prepared to allow such solutions when proposed by others. The result is often rather watered-down provisions which state the core of the issue, but leave most of the details and the implementation to the individual judgment of member States.

The 'third pillar' system already created an international legislative process much more intense, and intrusive, than 'normal' international treaty negotiations. The discussions lasted longer, covered broader areas in consecutive instruments, and the solutions were based on stricter obligations. The basic idea was, and still is, to create 'freedom of movement of judicial decisions and orders' with respect to criminal justice. Experts on the different substantive legal areas, rather than generalist diplomats, meet regularly in Council working groups and have gotten to know and trust each other. The dynamics of the work have changed over time and, in this author's opinion, the quality of the output has improved. Instead of essentially protecting the *status quo* of one's own domestic system, many state representatives have increasingly worked toward solutions that will improve intra-EU cooperation, even if this in the end will require amendments to the domestic criminal or criminal procedure system. Cooperation in criminal matters has also served as an engine for harmonisation of criminal law and criminal procedural law.

The framework decisions, however, were consciously construed in such a way that national differences and state sovereignty in the justice and home affairs areas were largely safeguarded. In effect, the member states could negotiate these instruments with the confidence of knowing that the less than perfect solutions could often be remedied later. With the Lisbon Treaty, this has changed, for example by introducing majority decisions, a new role for the European Parliament, and judicial control by the European Court of Justice. Hence, the EU member states must take a stance as how to approach this legislative process, and ensure domestic democratic control and involvement.

Of importance here is the fact that directives also in this area under certain conditions will have 'direct effect', that is, if the member state does not implement the directive within the deadline provided (and the rule must meet the normal requirements for 'direct effect'). Regulations, which may also be utilised, have 'direct effect'. Moreover, the principle of primacy of the law adopted by the EU under the treaties over the domestic law of the Member States, as established in the jurisprudence of the European Court of Justice, will extend to this policy area as well.[9]

Whilst it is clearly a legislative process from the perspective of the European Union, this might not be as obvious at the national level. Hence, the challenge is to develop a national strategy for 'multilateral legislation' in the field of criminal law, procedures, and cooperation, which resembles the approach to domestic legislation rather than international negotiation.

4. Emerging Strategy

At the outset, Sweden (and other states) approached the 'third pillar' work on legal instruments as international negotiations, conducted by Governments. Regularly, references to incompatibility with (existing) domestic law were made when opposing rules were suggested. While aiming to create a workable EU-wide cooperation system, the preservation of domestic procedural law was given preference.

However, already the framework decisions have created some uneasiness and a challenge to the Swedish concept of parliamentary involvement. Whilst constitutionally the Swedish Government possesses the power to negotiate and enter into international agreements, the Swedish Parliament also plays a certain controlling role. To exclude the national parliament in the legislative process of the implementation stage, when the framework decision was adopted and 'a done deal', would relegate its

---

[9] Conference of the Representatives of the Governments of the Member States, Declaration Concerning Primacy, 23 July 2007.

role to a weak form of *ex post facto* control. The Swedish solution was to seek the authorisation of Parliament before the framework decision was adopted (in case the implementation would subsequently require amendments to Swedish law). In practice, this resulted in a rather odd process where the Government had to produce a bill to Parliament with a preliminary assessment of the legislative amendments required. This was to be followed by a full proposal. The process delayed both the adoption and the implementation of the framework decision. Nonetheless, the required process meant that the Swedish representatives were more or less forced to consider the effects on national law throughout the negotiations. In turn, this often led the representatives to prepare thorough analysis of the material not only through the prism of domestic law, but also with a view to explore generally acceptable solutions. In addition, the work was often organised in such a way that the Swedish negotiators (and their superiors) would be responsible for the work towards the implementation of the instrument; they would be the first to suffer the consequences of unclear language or sloppy analytical work. This acted as a great incentive on an individual level, pushing those involved to make the efforts sooner rather than later. Often, the Swedish representatives took active part in the work (also by taking or supporting new initiatives) and played an influential role in the negotiations.

This active approach thus led to an internal discussion within the Swedish Ministry of Justice, concentrating on how to relate to the work of the EU in the field of criminal justice. It is clear that the work has long moved beyond traditional international (legislative) treaty negotiations. Should we then consider it as something similar to the domestic legislative process, albeit in a different forum and with different features? This question has become increasingly more relevant with respect to the systemic changes created by the Lisbon Treaty.

In essence, what has traditionally belonged to international law and inter-state negotiation has now, with the Lisbon Treaty, turned into a multilateral legislative process, which may produce law with 'direct effect' domestically. Logically, processes and principles that apply for domestic legislative work should also be considered when approaching the legislative work within the European Union.

In a legislative process, holding the initiative is key. Many legislative initiatives were undertaken by member states during the 'third pillar' regime. Although the prerequisites have changed, this is still possible under the Lisbon Treaty. Sweden has continued to be active in this regard, particularly in the area of international judicial cooperation in criminal matters. As is the case of domestic legislation, a legislative initiative is made in promotion of distinct interests. While the EU legislative process should not be used in an attempt to resolve essentially domestic problems in another forum, a consequence of a legislative approach to the negotiations would be to more actively promote domestically relevant issues on the European Union agenda. The member states have a choice whether to pursue a particular legislative issue in the domestic or in the European Union arena.

Despite this, the political appetite for such a strategy also depends upon both arenas being politically relevant in the eyes of the electorate (and opinion-makers); it must be possible to also 'score political points' when the law is achieved at the European Union level. This is not yet the case and, generally, a level of scepticism exists concerning EU-intervention in these traditionally national subject-matter areas. Giving priority to an 'international agenda' is also not a traditional feature of the national justice and home affairs policies. Hence, brave politicians and good odds for success are required. Moreover, an active and legislative approach means that the results sought cannot be viewed merely through a domestic lens. Of course, it must also be possible to implement the rules in the various domestic systems and serve different national interests, such as an improved ability to conduct criminal investigations and proceedings. In the case of international criminal cooperation, there is always a 'price tag', namely the commitment to provide assistance: you get what you are prepared to give. Departing from traditional assistance – where the assistance mirrors measures taken in domestic investigations or proceedings – the concept of 'mutual recognition' views the measures as part of the criminal process of the investigating or prosecuting state. Complications due to national differences may thus be reduced. The de-linking of assistance measures from the ordinary national process is easier to achieve through an international legislative process than in the domestic one.

Even more radical would be to enter into harmonisation, which necessitates a multilateral legislative process. The work under the 'third pillar' has also forged closer ties between national authorities in the different states and cross-fertilisation with respect to issues of criminal law and criminal procedures. Even if not prescribed, harmonisation may also make good sense in terms of cooperation. The Lisbon Treaty moves this ambition further. In turn, however, this will naturally restricts the scope for successfully bringing domestic issues onto the EU legislative arena.

The bottom line is that European Union legislation should be useful in practice and provide an added value. Measures that are limited, *ad hoc*, and foreign to the basic criminal and criminal procedure system are seldom effective in practice. In order to achieve real improvements, one must also be prepared to amend the domestic law, and to make systemic changes, if this is motivated by the greater good. To adapt to more mainstream European solutions, and thus increase the possibilities to cooperate effectively, may in itself be worth more fundamental amendments to the domestic system. Within the Swedish context, for example, are the directives to the legislative committee for the reform of criminal penalties, which underlined, *inter alia,* that the penalty system should not, substantively and in isolation, depart from the systems of other European Union member states.[10]

Within these parameters, the member states should arguably adopt strategies that coordinate the European Union and domestic legislative arenas, not only for the implementation of EU instruments in the domestic system, but also for pursuing a coordinated legislative agenda in both forums. Sweden has begun thinking and acting along these lines in terms of the policy areas of criminal law, criminal procedures, and police and judicial cooperation. As outlined, however, the political attractiveness is not yet high enough for a fully-fledged commitment to the strategy. In addition, the strategy requires appropriate involvement of national Parliament, possibly stretching beyond the current consultations, primarily between the Government and the Committee on European Union Affairs, before and during the EU legislative process and, subsequently, when the EU instrument is implemented into national law. Indeed, this is an exciting outlook which has the potential to bring international law and national law much closer together.

5. Sources and Further Reading

Conference of the Representatives of the Governments of the Member States, Declaration Concerning Primacy, 23 July 2007.

---

[10] Sweden, Ministry of Justice, "En översyn av påföljdssystemet", Dir. 2009:60, p. 9.

Consolidated Versions of the Treaty on European Union and the Treaty on the Functioning of the European Union (as amended by the Lisbon Treaty), 2008 O.J. (C 115), 9 May 2008.

Council Framework Decision 2002/584/JHA of 13 June 2002 on the European Arrest Warrant and the Surrender Procedures between Member States, 13 June 2002.

Council Framework Decision 2008/947/JHA of 27 November 2008 on the Application of the Principle of Mutual Recognition to Judgments and Probation Decisions with a View to the Supervision of Probation Measures and Alternative Sanctions, 27 November 2008.

Council Framework Decision 2008/978/JHA of 18 December 2009 on the European Evidence Warrant, 18 December 2009.

Council Framework Decision 2009/829/JHA of 23 October 2009 on the Application, between Member States of the European Union, of the Principle of Mutual Recognition to Decisions on Supervision Measures as an Alternative to Provisional Detention, 23 October 2009.

Initiative for a Directive of the European Parliament and of the Council Regarding the European Investigation Order in Criminal Matters, Inter-institutional File 2010/0817 (COD).

Protocol No. 1 on the Role of National Parliaments in the European Union, and Protocol No. 2 on the Application of the Principles of Subsidiarity and Proportionality, 2008 O.J. (C 115/203), 9 May 2008.

Sweden, Ministry of Justice, "En översyn av påföljdssystemet", Dir. 2009:60.

Treaty on European Union (as amended by the Nice Treaty), Article 34, 24 December 2002, available at http://eur-lex.europa.eu/LexUriServ/LexUriServ.do?uri=OJ:C:2010:083:0013:0046:en:PDF, last accessed on 13 August 2012.

3.5.

Legal and Justice Strategies:
The Commonwealth as an Agent of Change

Akbar Khan[*]

The modern Commonwealth, represented today as an intergovernmental body of 54 sovereign States, has its roots in the world's oldest political association and exists as a 'trusted partner' for promoting democracy and development. A defining and unifying aspect of
the Commonwealth is its shared common law tradition, offering the
opportunity to develop a coherent legal and justice strategy across
the Commonwealth. However, significant challenges remain in developing and implementing such a strategy given limited resources,
the diversity of the Commonwealth's membership, the tension between adopting a pan-Commonwealth or a regional approach, uneven levels of development and the need for greater coherence, coordination and impact. This think piece will critically examine these challenges and the role the Commonwealth has played, and continues to plays, as a change agent in the legal and justice field.

1. Introduction

Today, the Commonwealth is the world's oldest political association of
sovereign states, with 54 members representing more than two billion individuals – almost one third of the world's population – and every major
world religion. Eight hundred million Hindus, five hundred million Muslims and four hundred million Christians live in the Commonwealth. It includes India, one of the world's most populated nations, and Nauru, one
of the least populated.

Thirty-three of the Commonwealth's member states are republics,
five have their own monarchs and 16 have Queen Elizabeth II as Head of
State. Its roots go back to the British Empire, which once covered a quarter of the world's land area and about the same portion of the world's
population.

---

[*] **Akbar Khan** is the Director of the Legal and Constitutional Affairs Division and
Principal Legal Adviser to the Commonwealth Secretary-General.

The Commonwealth Secretariat is the primary intergovernmental organisation of the Commonwealth, committed to working as a 'trusted partner' for peace, democracy, equality and good governance, as a catalyst for global consensus building, and as a source of assistance for sustainable development and poverty eradication. The two main external faces of the Commonwealth are the Secretariat and the biennial Commonwealth Heads of Government Meeting (CHOGM). The Secretariat was established in 1965 as "the visible symbol of the spirit of cooperation which animates the Commonwealth" at the service of all Commonwealth governments, while the CHOGM constitutes the largest regular meeting of Heads of Government in the world.

It is worth noting that 32 of the 54 member states are deemed small jurisdictions and these states, many of them island states, are given a special focus within the Commonwealth's programme of work. Through the Commonwealth's extensive network, small states are given a platform to raise concerns, a platform that is often unavailable to them in larger multilateral settings where their voices are drowned out. At the same time, the Commonwealth working as a group can often help to mould and influence the contours of discussions being undertaken in other fora. In this context, Sir Shridath Ramphal QC, Commonwealth Secretary-General (1975–1990) aptly observed: "The Commonwealth cannot negotiate for the world but can help the world to negotiate".

2. The Commonwealth and the Rule of Law

One of the main challenges facing Commonwealth countries today is developing and maintaining strong democratic and accountable governance underpinned by the rule of law. The Commonwealth Secretariat's rule of law programme therefore aims to achieve this objective through a variety of legal and justice strategies.

As recently as 2009, the CHOGM in Port of Spain, Trinidad and Tobago, reaffirmed the rule of law as a core value of the Commonwealth. Heads of Government reiterated that each country's legislature, executive and judiciary are the guarantors of the rule of law, and that access to justice and an independent judiciary are fundamental to the rule of law, enhanced by effective, transparent, ethical and accountable governance. The rule of law is also expected to feature prominently in the Charter of the Commonwealth, the text of which is currently being considered by member governments. The relevant extract from the draft approved by the Ministerial Task Force reads as follows:

> We believe in *the rule of law as an essential protection for the people of the Commonwealth and as an assurance* of accountable government. In particular, we support an independent, impartial, honest and competent judiciary and recognise that an independent, effective and competent legal system is integral to upholding the rule of law, engendering public confidence and dispensing justice.

There is a general consensus that the rule of law and good governance are necessary foundations for efforts to achieve sustainable development and growth. It is therefore clear that the promotion of the rule of law is more than the provision of technical legal expertise. The Commonwealth Secretariat therefore supports, promotes and strengthens the rule of law, and the administration of justice that underpins strong democratic and accountable governance. In doing so, the Commonwealth Secretariat works with member countries to develop legal, judicial and constitutional reform and strengthen both legal and regulatory frameworks that protect and promote the rule of law.

3. Does the Commonwealth Secretariat Have a Legal and Justice Strategy and, if So, What Does it Look Like?

In considering this question it is worth recalling that the Mission Statement of the Commonwealth Secretariat is to: "work as a trusted partner for all Commonwealth people as a force for peace, democracy, equality, equity, respect and good governance". In order to affect sustainable impact in the area of legal development as a 'trusted partner', the legal and justice strategy that has been developed by the Commonwealth Secretariat embraces several strands. The highest-level strand is essentially directed to political standard setting and is the role of the CHOGM, which historically has promulgated the Commonwealth's core or fundamental values and principles. Earlier statements through which the Commonwealth's values and principles have been defined and strengthened over the years include the Singapore Declaration, the Harare Declaration, the Millbrook Action Programme, the Latimer House Principles and the Aberdeen Principles.

The next strand or level of the strategy is at the ministerial level, where the Secretariat is privileged to exercise high-level convening power

– it is the only global organisation that regularly convenes meetings of law ministers. The triennial Commonwealth Law Ministers Meetings (CLMMs), together with the meetings of Law Ministers of Small Commonwealth Jurisdictions (LMSCJ) and of Senior Officials of Commonwealth Law Ministries (SOLM), provide an opportunity to confer mandates on the Commonwealth Secretariat which seek to implement the Commonwealth core values of respect for the rule of law and human rights. Examples of mandates to assist member states might include the creation of legal toolkits and/or legislative and policy guidance to harmonise states' national laws with the international frameworks to which they are party, developed either by the Secretariat or in other fora such as the United Nations.

Alternatively, mandates may seek to promote best practice and norms across the Commonwealth in a specific legal area, such as international cooperation, as demonstrated by the establishment of the Harare Scheme on Mutual Legal Assistance in Criminal Matters aimed at promoting and sharing best practice in the field of mutual legal assistance. Such voluntary, non-binding schemes are in the best tradition of Commonwealth, reflecting shared principles and practices, and the consensual nature of the organisation. One might even conclude that such instruments, while legally non-binding, nonetheless have normative significance between the parties regarding their behaviour and can therefore be regarded as 'soft law'.

Other mandates have sought to place focus on combatting or mitigating specific threats and challenges within the Commonwealth at any particular time, such as developing a new legal architecture with regard to displaced migrant populations and access to vital natural resources arising from the impact of climate change. The meetings also provided an opportunity for law ministers and other senior officials to exchange experiences of good practice and peer-learning among Commonwealth members, and to focus on the particular needs of small jurisdictions. At the lowest level or strand of the legal and justice strategy lies the programmatic level, which implements activities at the national, sub-regional, regional and pan-Commonwealth level aimed at fulfilling the mandate, which in turn promotes adherence to the rule of law.

Commonwealth civil society organisations operating in the fields of human rights and international law, to mention but two, have also played a vital role in articulating standards. A significant example of such a contribution was the articulation of the Commonwealth (Latimer House) Principles on the Relationship between the Three Branches of Government (CLHP). These principles, developed from a private initiative by four Commonwealth Associations, were subsequently endorsed by the 2003 CHOGM at Abuja and constituted by the Malta 2005 CHOGM as an integral part of the Commonwealth's fundamental political values, as set out in the Harare Declaration.

4.   Who Executes the Legal and Justice Strategy?

The position would seem that execution is amorphous between national, regional and at the pan-Commonwealth level, depending on the particular issue at stake. This approach reinforces the 'trusted partner' status of the Commonwealth Secretariat with its member states. However, the importance of forging strategic partnerships with other international/regional organisations and other partners is gaining importance in order to promote the Commonwealth's values and principles, to minimise duplication of effort and resources and to maximise sustainable impact.

As an international organisation tasked with delivering on the various mandates conferred by CHOGM or other ministerial meetings, the Secretariat is primarily responsible for execution of the various programmatic activities that fulfil specific mandates, which in turn underpin good governance and the rule of law. On occasion, however, CHOGM and other ministerial meetings have delivered high-level statements aimed only at action at the national or regional level. For example, at the 2011 Commonwealth Law Ministers Meeting, concerning the issue of conventional weapons and promotion of international humanitarian law, ministers resolved to encourage states to actively consider ratification of outstanding weapons and related treaties, to incorporate the provisions of these treaties into their domestic law and to report on progress as required by the conventions.

The Secretariat's work on strengthening the rule of law enjoys the comparative advantage of the commonality of the legal systems within the Commonwealth, occasioned by a shared history of common law. The similarities provide a basis for facilitating the exchange of best practice and replication of successful models from one jurisdiction to another, based on shared Commonwealth fundamental principles such as the Harare Declaration and the Latimer House Principles. The Secretariat focuses its technical assistance on key actors in the justice delivery chain, who underpin the rule of law from an institutional perspective, for example, judges, investigators, prosecutors, legal drafters and registrars.

In particular, the Commonwealth Secretariat supports member countries in strengthening the independence of the judiciary through the promotion of the Commonwealth (Latimer House) Principles on the Accountability of and the Relationship between the Three Branches of Government. The Commonwealth High Level Review Group Report recommendations adopted in 2002 by Commonwealth Heads of Government noted that, in the promotion and enhancement of the Commonwealth fundamental political values, greater priority should be given to the review and strengthening of democratic institutions, including constitutions, judiciaries and judicial processes. Commonwealth declarations also seek to promote the independence of the judiciary as pivotal to strong, democratic and accountable governance underpinned by the rule of law.

The Commonwealth Secretariat also receives requests for technical assistance from its member states, linked to the mandates conferred in support of the rule of law. Most such requests from member states revolve around strengthening court registries, effective case-flow management, training for judicial officers, prosecutors and other court staff, and legislative drafting. These elements help to promote and embed the rule of law at the national level.

Across the Commonwealth, the Commonwealth Secretariat has responded to the diverse challenge of strengthening the rule of law as a principle of good governance through a range of technical support and capacity building measures. By these and other practical measures, the Commonwealth helps to build a stronger, resilient and more progressive family of nations founded on enduring values and principles.

5. How Are the Rules Enforced?

Traditionally – and still to a large extent today – the Commonwealth does not generally favour a coercive process of enforcement, preferring to operate on the basis of consultation and consensus in accordance with the organisation's preference for friendship and cooperation, thereby eschewing highlighting member states' non-compliance with values and principles. However, values and principles that were previously seen as merely 'non-binding conclusions', without articulating any further standards or commitment to implementation, have through the passage of time become regarded as the standards by which members should abide. Today, these fundamental political values have become the focus of the Commonwealth's machinery on enforcement. Adherence to Commonwealth fundamental political values remains with member states, which have committed themselves to various high-level declaratory statements of principle, including recently in the 2009 Trinidad and Tobago Affirmation on Commonwealth Values and Principles.

The 2009 text states: "We solemnly reiterate our commitment to the Commonwealth's core values […]", which clearly places a political obligation on the part of member states to adhere to the organisation's agreed values and principles. The first step towards a more coercive process, with the intention of ensuring greater adherence to Commonwealth values and principles, was originally created by Commonwealth Heads of Government under the Millbrook Action Programme of 1995, which established a Commonwealth Ministerial Action Group (CMAG) comprising nine foreign ministers with the power to sanction a fellow member government for serious and persistent violations of the fundamental political values of the Commonwealth.

Since its creation, CMAG has been the custodian of the Commonwealth's fundamental political values. CMAG's scrutiny of countries that are deemed to be in serious or persistent violation of such values has always included an appraisal of the extent to which the rule of law is respected. In all instances where CMAG has suspended a country from the Councils of the Commonwealth or from membership, the rule of law has been a relevant factor – one that is taken into account in addition to other considerations such as adherence to the constitution, elections, the proper functioning of the legislature and human rights. In 2011 at the Perth CHOGM, Heads of Government approved an enhanced role for CMAG. A number of considerations were spelt out which would trigger an assessment by the Secretary-General of the situation in a particular country and his/her bringing the matter to the attention of CMAG. Notably, these considerations include the abrogation of the rule of law or undermining of the independence of the judiciary.

Fiji was suspended in 2009 by CMAG following the failure of the interim military government to meet the Commonwealth's deadline to restore democracy, after taking power in a bloodless coup in 2006. Suspension is a public indication to the rest of the world of the failure of a member state. Other instances of suspension include Nigeria in 1995, after the military government ordered the execution of nine dissidents. Occasionally, governments have chosen to withdraw from the Commonwealth. Examples include Pakistan in 1972, after other member states agreed to recognise Bangladesh. Pakistan re-joined again in 1989. Following suspension in 2002, Zimbabwe withdrew its membership in 2003.

A further tool for the enforcement of fundamental political values is the holding of election observations each year. Commonwealth observer teams assess various factors in determining whether an election is credible and adequately reflects the will of the people. These factors include the electoral laws of the country, as well as the adjudication of election-related disputes. One might conclude, therefore, that even though declared Commonwealth fundamental values and principles are not legally binding in the conventional sense on member states, taken together with CMAG they nonetheless provide a normative framework of behaviour and a mechanism for enforcement. As Rosalyn Higgins QC has stated:

> International law is not rules. It is a normative system. All organised groups and structures require a system of normative conduct – that is to say, conduct which is regarded by each actor, and by the group as a whole, as being obligatory, for which violation carries a price.

6. Conclusion

This short article is intended to address two main questions: (i) does the Commonwealth Secretariat as an international organisation actually have a legal and justice strategy and, if yes, what does it consist off; and (ii) who or what executes this strategy and how does it work?

In concluding this article the answers are clear. The Commonwealth Secretariat does indeed have a legal and justice strategy for its member states, one that consists of declaratory core values and principles articulated at a high political level and buttressed by the provision of practical measures of technical assistance and capacity building. Fundamental values of respect for the rule of law and human rights are implemented through a number of mandates and other interventions at the national, regional and/or pan-Commonwealth level by the Commonwealth Secretariat working as a 'trusted partner' with its member states and other partners. These fundamental values and principles are also enforced by the Commonwealth Ministerial Action Group (CMAG), which serves as the custodian of Commonwealth fundamental political values.

In my view, the effectiveness of Commonwealth legal and justice strategies is not generally premised on any coercive processes of compliance, or 'conditionality' as followed by other organisations and governments, but rather on the Commonwealth notion of 'shared principles and practices'. These serve to underpin a pragmatic approach to addressing the complex legal problems faced today by so many Commonwealth member states, which are at different levels of development and hold different resources.

The need for greater co-ordinated development of legal and justice strategies by international organisations, like the Commonwealth Secretariat, has grown steadily over the past decades, as more rule of law challenges become 'global' or 'transnational' in character – like cybercrime and climate change – which require coherent and concerted efforts of international cooperation in order to combat or mitigate their impact.

Another increasingly important area requiring international cooperation and regulation is trade. Within the Commonwealth trade is now worth over three trillion pound every year, with more than half of all Commonwealth countries now exporting over a quarter of their total exports to other Commonwealth members. This in turn has fuelled greater demand for regulation, through harmonised national laws and efficient dispute resolution mechanisms. This is where international organisations have a vital role to play by facilitating agreement on proposed 'model legislation' and 'schemes' aimed at promoting closer international legal cooperation, economic and regulatory integration, and dispute resolution.

Looking to the future, it would seem that demand for the Commonwealth to widen and deepen its legal and justice strategies will only increase in time as more pressure is placed on already overburdened national legal systems to find solutions. Given this likelihood, it is no surprise that Lord Howell, the UK Foreign and Commonwealth Office Minister for the Commonwealth, speaking in July 2011, stated that: "The Commonwealth is the soft power network of the future. The sheer breadth and diversity that the Commonwealth typifies is extraordinary and is something to be celebrated".

7. Sources and Further Reading

Rosalyn Higgins, *Problems and Process: International Law and How We Use It*, Clarendon Press, Oxford, 1999, p. 1.

3.6.

The UN: A Law-Maker on the Move

Willem van Genugten[*]

Despite manifold efforts to make things change for the better we are living in a world full of structural poverty and conflicts. That will not easily change. Even if we should (and will) see positive trends in the field of poverty alleviation, there will always be a 'lowest level'. And conflicts do belong to human nature.

Stating my 'world view' this way – which is in no way meant to be cynical, but rather realistic – I will focus on the role the United Nations should play as a law-maker with an ambitious 'global justice agenda'. The underlying question will be: how to strengthen the international legal order, while recognising the variety of powerful and less powerful actors and the diversity of perspectives visible in today's world. This short article is about the UN as an international law-maker and as an organisation which finds itself strategically between adaptation to changing circumstances and the risk of becoming obsolete if the adaptation fails.

1. Understanding the UN and its Membership

It might look strange to focus on the UN as a possibly proactive maker of strategy and law. Is the UN not seen by many as a consensus machine, a brake, a failure? Think of Somalia, Bosnia, Rwanda, sometimes called "black pages in the UN history". And rightly so. But how did and does the UN move forward, while taking these failures seriously? Starting from there, the challenge is to my mind a) to see and strengthen the UN along the lines of its original ambitions as expressed in the 1945 UN Charter, b) to scrutinise the way it has been able (or not) to adapt to new challenges, in terms of content and procedures, and c) to see to what extent it has been able to link its activities to non-state actors who ask for the floor and are able and willing to co-exercise the UN's ambitions, thus also bringing in and strengthening a bottom-up perspective to the realisation of these (enormous) ambitions.

---

[*] **Willem van Genugten** is Professor of International Law at Tilburg University and Dean of the newly established *The Hague Institute for Global Justice*.

Having said that, one enters difficult ground: the United Nations, currently composed of 193 Member States, is not a homogenous body with one overriding agenda. It is not like a company with a specific product to sell and with a limited number of share- and stakeholders. On the contrary. The UN is rather a 'club' where variety is dominant and which tries to make the best out of issues that in many ways transcend its capacities as well as its convening power. In addition, the manifold UN ambitions and the objectives linked to them (see the UN Charter, especially the Preamble and Article 1) are paradoxical things. Objectives are very much needed to bring focus into activities, but if taken too literally they often also contribute to controversy. Those who would ask the question what the UN and, by implication in many ways, international law are meant for would receive totally different answers, depending on whether the question is addressed to, for instance, a human rights NGO, a conservative US citizen or a CEO of a multinational company. There would be some shared answers, such as that the UN has a (co-)responsibility to protect populations against genocide, to act in the event of natural disasters or to block acts of terrorism. However, such answers would immediately provoke the next questions: how about reality and how about the power of the UN to contribute effectively to the realisation of such objectives?

When characterising the UN, it has of course also to be underlined that some UN Member States are more equal than others. As regards the non-equality of states one can obviously refer to the position of the P-5 in the Security Council, but also to, for instance, the 'power of the payers' in UN specialised agencies like UNESCO or UNICEF. Adding a historical note might help in understanding the UN in this sense. As early as in the early 1940's, US President Roosevelt expressed his ideas about the UN, as a successor to the failing League of Nations, but he was not thinking of a world government or a supranational organisation. He rather emphasised the responsibility of separate states for the healthy and peaceful life of their inhabitants, with the UN as a facilitator, initiator and coordinator. Simultaneously, however, he helped to create differences amongst the UN Member States. In his eyes the four allied powers – China, Great Britain, the Soviet Union and the United States, later on joined by France as a reward for De Gaulle's opposition to the Axis powers – should safeguard the protection of his Four Freedoms like four police officers. For that reason they were entrusted with a special position in the UN.

Time has passed, and we now have a discussion on power sharing with other economically and/or geopolitically strong states of today's world, such as India, Brazil, South Africa/Nigeria, Japan and Germany. That discussion has been going on for decades, and will not materialise, since changing the UN Charter requires ratification by all of the P-5 (Article 108 of the Charter). Against that background, the P-5 have been asked by the Secretary-General to the UN and by at least 35 governments to refrain from using their veto in situations of, for instance and especially, actual or impending atrocities, *id est* in situations of applying core notions of international law, related to what are generally called 'the most serious crimes'. In relation to that, it is also important to know that Article 27 of the UN Charter asks for an "affirmative vote of nine members including the concurring votes of the permanent members". In the reality of Security Council (SC) decision-making, however, it is accepted that abstention from voting by one or two of the P-5 no longer blocks a resolution, as long as nine out of 15 SC members vote in favour. To illustrate: the US and China abstained from voting in the case of the referral of the case of Sudan to the ICC (2005), while The Russian Federation and China did something similar as regards the military intervention in Libya (2011). All this can be characterised as a creative way of adapting the formal system to political realities in situations where changing the formal system is not an option.

Finally, it has to observed in this short, legally oriented section on the UN and its Member States that the status of international legal person is still primarily reserved for states, while all other participants in international law derive their legal status (and competence to act thereupon) from states, and therefore from national law and not from international law. Worldwide, the exception to this is the UN itself, as stated by the International Court of Justice in its 1949 Advisory Opinion in the case on the *Reparations for Injuries suffered in the service of the United Nations*. According to the Court, the founders of the UN "had the power, in conformity with international law, to bring into being an entity possessing objective international personality, and not merely personality recognised by them alone, together with capacity to bring international claims". For some it might look too nuanced, but it is the way it is: the UN is like a *primus inter pares*, legally speaking.

2. The United Nations as a Law-Maker

The UN plays an enormous role in international law-making, including the progressive development of international law, through the International Law Commission, the International Court of Justice, the Security Council, or one of its Specialised Agencies like the World Health Organisation and the International Labour Organisation, or through, for instance, one of the (many) supervisory bodies in the human rights field. Here, one can also refer to the UN General Assembly (GA), which often takes the first steps in the field of law-making concerning a specific topic. In numerous cases, a group of states, inspired or not by civil pressure, has started discussing something in the context of the GA, followed by the adoption of a GA resolution, and thus creating soft law as a first step to what later on often becomes a convention. A good example is the GA run-up to the 1984 Convention against Torture and Other Cruel, Inhuman or Degrading Treatment or Punishment. Another example to illustrate the initiating role of the GA is the beginning of the long way to the establishment of the International Criminal Court in Rome in 1998. Following the Second World War, the GA in 1947 adopted a resolution (number 177), asking the International Law Commission to "prepare a draft code of offences against the peace and security of mankind, indicating clearly the place to be accorded to the [Nuremberg] principles [...]". The Nuremberg Principles, often characterised as 'guidelines' and therefore as soft law, although with some characteristics of customary international law, thus obtained support from the GA, which by its resolution marked the way towards (further) codification of international criminal law and the establishment of an international criminal court (not yet mentioned in the 1947 resolution).

A recent example to illustrate the nuanced law-making role of the UN is the concept of the 'responsibility to protect' (RtoP), as recognised in paragraph 138 the 2005 World Summit Outcome document. It can be observed that putting RtoP in the 2005 document was quite a progressive (and unanimous) act of the UN GA, while the GA simultaneously and strongly underlined that the responsibility to protect does *not* transfer state sovereignty to the UN, but that the concept helps re-characterise 'sovereignty as control' to 'sovereignty as responsibility' in both internal functions and external duties of the UN. In other words: the concept of RtoP, as recognised by the GA, helps to move away from an exclusive focus on state sovereignty in a traditional sense ('mind your own business') to a focus where human dignity is (one of) the load star(s). This is sometimes called a paradigm shift, but that is incorrect to my mind. In the UN Charter one can already find the duty to stand up for human rights, but this duty is placed in a horizontal relationship to other obligations, such as the duty to respect the sovereignty of states. The Charter does not address the question of prioritisation or hierarchy in the event of clashing rights and principles. The 2005 RtoP formulation changes that only a little, and not radically in a way that would qualify as a paradigm shift, especially because the third pillar of RtoP can be invoked by the UN SC only, thus not authorising states to act outside the framework set by the UN Charter. Further to this, the RtoP legal development can be seen as the filling in of the contentious Article 48 of the Draft Articles on the Responsibility of States for Internationally Wrongful Acts, as developed by the International Law Commission, and in 2001 "commended to attention of Governments" by the UN GA. Article 48 speaks of "obligations owed to the international community as a whole", and was and is clearly controversial (and not reflecting customary international law, as most other articles do), but the RtoP concept is clearly fitting as part of the legal puzzle. The same goes for the remarks on the SC made in the Rule of Law report of the UN Secretary-General of March 2012: the Council is called upon in paragraph A (1)(a) "to fully adhere to applicable international law and basic rule of law principles in order to ensure the legitimacy of [its] action". That sounds logical, is correct as such, but also leaves us with one core question: what do we do if the applicable international law, as arranged for in Chapter VII of the UN Charter, orders the SC to refrain from action, because the right to veto is used by one or more of the P-5?

In other words: what do we do in situations in which the UN SC is paralysed? That question is discussed extensively in legal literature and publications on morality, as well as in governmental and non-governmental policy papers and position-taking statements, but is not dealt with in this article with its focus on the UN. The only UN-linked question is whether or not the organisation is able to adapt itself to such 'cries for action' coming from outside the UN, otherwise running the risk of another 'black page' in its history or becoming obsolete. At the moment of writing, Syria is a case in point – 13 members of the SC voted in favour of a draft resolution, while China and the Russian Federation used their veto power – but it is too early to say whether or not the SC strategy is wrong, even if it feels that way. It is clear, however, that also in the case of Syria the argument of sovereignty is no longer accepted; the discussion is rather about the instrument to be used – military or not – while trying to combine the notion of friendly relations, the risky geopolitical situation, manifold economic interests and the rights of the victims, all that in different sequences and with different priorities. In more conceptual terms, the notion of sovereignty is no longer as 'holy' as it might have been in 1945, when the UN Charter was adopted (see especially Article 2 (7)), and in, for instance, 1970, when the famous 'Friendly Relations Declaration' was adopted (see especially Article 1, *passim*), after the decolonisation process. State sovereignty is still the leading concept, but it is clearly perforated, as confirmed by many (quasi-)law-making acts and (quasi-)legal decisions and judgments by and in the context of the UN, and backed by numerous acts in national contexts.

3.   Civil Society, from Horse-Fly to Co-Constituent and Co-Law-Maker

NGOs often take the lead in identifying problems, confronting states with their shortcomings, and urging them to come up with better rules, or rules at all. Difficult as it may be, NGOs often help the UN fulfil its core tasks, while their role also adds to another debate: the non-democratic character of many UN decisions. Structurally linking the world of the civil society to the government oriented work done within the UN would at least bring in a bit more democratic legitimisation, even if many NGOs have a legitimacy gap themselves. The late American philosopher John Rawls, for instance, argued time and again for more democracy by focusing not on states but on peoples, because in his eyes peoples – unlike states – have moral motives and a moral nature, and wish to survive and to cooperate, among other goals. And peoples must be represented in one way or another, be it in principle or for practical reasons: one simply cannot imagine participation by everybody on every issue. There, NGOs enter the scene. In addition, and at least as important: the capabilities and political will of states' governments are often falling short, while the NGO world can bring in additional expertise in order to help the UN 'land' in the daily realities of populations. They also make the organisation more 'outward-looking' in an era in which effectiveness, legitimacy and accountability are the core words. The UN itself came up with very good reports on the issue – such as: *We the peoples: civil society, the United Nations and global governance* (2004), the title of which refers to the opening of the UN Charter: 'We the peoples of the United Nations [are] determined to

[....]" – stating that the constituency of the UN should comprise and already comprises three broad sectors: civil society, the private sector and the State. States would then no longer be the exclusive owners of the organisation, but should share that core position with the other core actors of today's international arena.

It sounds as it should sound, although one should keep in mind that not all UN Member States are equally fond of the civil society and that the words, as used on many occasions, should be followed by action. Embracing the civil society requires a constant review of the UN and its role in the international order, of the role the civil society can play not only as 'starter' for legal development but also as part of the enforcement of it, and the transformation of traditional international law as the domain of states into a domain of and for – at least *also* – peoples. Especially since the fall of the Berlin wall, a lot has happened in this field, conceptually as well as in daily legal practice. But this is about a long-term process rather than about static givens.

4.   It's the Economy, Stupid! The UN and Economic Issues

Over the years, it has become clear that enterprises are needed to make human rights flourish in many ways. Think of creating jobs and of providing tax revenues to governments which can be used for public investments, but also of providing access to affordable essential drugs in developing countries and making available the benefits of new information technologies. It is also broadly recognised that negative economic growth increases the risk of civil conflicts dramatically. In sum, private investment is in many ways good for human rights, although one should not fall into the trap that trade should replace aid: trade reforms will always have to be complementary to other development policies, not replace them. That is in line with the UN Millennium Development Goals (see especially MDG number 8) and the discussion on the Doha Round, starting in 2001 and so far not very successful, to say the least.

Having said that, let us return to the issue of the UN as a lawmaker. As regards the relationship between the 'UN at large' and standard-setting in the field of economics and financial matters, it can be observed that the drafters of the UN Charter understood that peace and security were inseparable from economic development, and that the UN should have a task in that respect. However, while the UN Charter allowed for the creation of specialised agencies independent of the principal

UN organs, the role of the Economic and Social Council was reduced to one of light coordination only. The Council was not allowed to become the centre of the world's decision-making on matters of trade and finance, as was the SC for peace and security issues. The UN framers were aware of the need to link economics to development and human rights, but did not allow the Economic and Social Council to play a steering role in that. The core reason was that economics and finances were – understandably, to my mind – considered to belong to the core domain of 'the haves'. In these fields, the UN has in the meantime been bypassed by, *inter alia*, the G8 and the G20, while for instance the IMF and the World Bank, although formally part of the UN family, act in a rather autonomous way, making use of the special decision-making rules developed for them.

It is illustrative that the G20 is composed of 19 Member States plus the EU, but not the UN. Despite that, the UN is taking numerous steps in the domain of economics and economic actors. Apart from the field covered by its development programme (UNDP), one can primarily think of the 2000 Global Compact initiative of the then Secretary-General to the UN (Kofi Annan), which proclaimed a series of universal principles of responsible corporate citizenship, accompanied by a self-regulatory system of participation and control, currently including about 6,000 businesses in 135 countries. In 2011, this was reinforced by the adoption of the "Guiding Principles on Business and Human Rights" (the 'Ruggie Principles'). I myself strongly support Ruggie's protect, respect and remedy framework, as developed especially in his 2008 and 2009 reports, while to my mind he also deserves praise for further paving the way conceptually and practically, even if he stays on the traditional side as far as the state–companies–human rights triangle is concerned. On a critical note, I think Ruggie could or should have done more with the concept of *ius cogens* and the specific rights belonging to that category, as well as with the concept of extraterritoriality, but also in his approach misbehaviour-across-borders-escapes become less and less possible. In that field, there is again a long way to go, no doubt, but the developments underway are to my mind more about speed than about direction, again backed by numerous legal and policy developments in national contexts.

5. Final Observations

The UN is by aspiration an organisation with global coverage, meant to keep the world moving, with all its controversies and different views and cultures. Making a blueprint for another UN-type organisation would get us nowhere, to my mind, as long as that blueprint ignored the 'real issues', some of which have been touched upon in this article. The one and only logical alternative to my mind is to make the UN move ahead, challenged by the manifold challenges the world is confronted with.

The UN is a law-maker and 'legal developer' in many ways, either because it takes the initiative itself or offers a platform to others to do so. It is also a law-maker if and when one of its decision-making or supervisory organs does not abide by the traditional division of roles as provided for in Montesquieu's *Trias Politica*, and takes the lead in legal development. In the eyes of many that is not (or never) enough, while in the eyes of others that goes too far, but in both cases it makes sense to look at it from an evolutionary perspective, as pleaded for in this short article. Doing so, one must also understand issues 'under the radar', which can only been seen by not looking at the UN with legal eyes only.

The UN is often blamed for adopting 'broad consensus documents', reflecting either the lowest common denominator on a specific issue at a specific moment, or for adopting rather vigorous but open terminology while the cameras and the stage-lights are on. Nevertheless, such documents later often serve as benchmark documents, even given their open formulation. They are often followed by detailed policy documents, treaties, judgments and quasi-judgments, linking the aspirations mentioned in the documents to more concrete action.

Finally, on the actor side, the UN no longer wants (and does not have) to walk alone. Keeping their different starting points and interests in mind, and aware that their interests are often not overlapping and sometimes are even contradictory to each other, it is clear that the UN has to join forces, and actually is joining forces, with the civil society and the business sector in order to realise its manifold objectives. From a law-making perspective, I see a common public–private approach to the major problems of today as a highly necessary, although not necessarily sufficient condition. Translating that into a better understanding of international law and of the interaction between players and legal layers, from traditional and local to formal national systems and rules and principles of international law, is already going on in many ways. For an elephant halfway through a narrow gate, there is no way back.

6. Sources and Further Reading

Alfred van Staden, *Between the Rule of Power and the Power of Rule. In Search of an Effective World Order*, Martinus Nijhoff, Leiden, 2007.

Andrew Clapham, *The Human Rights Obligations of Non-State Actors*, Oxford University Press, Oxford, 2006.

Anne-Marie Slaughter, *A New World Order*, Princeton University Press, Princeton and Oxford, 2004.

Bernard Berendsen (ed.), *Common Goods in a Divided World*, KIT Publishers, Amsterdam, 2011.

Brian Tamanaha, *The Perils of Pervasive Legal Instrumentalism*, Wolf Legal Publishers, Nijmegen, 2006.

Cardoso *et al.*, *We the Peoples: Civil Society, The United Nations and Global Governance*, 2004 (A/58/817).

David Kinley, *Civilising Globalisation*, Cambridge University Press, Cambridge, 2009.

Jared Genser and Irwin Cotler (eds.), *The Responsibility to Protect. The Promise of Stopping Mass Atrocities in Our Time*, Oxford University Press, Oxford, 2012.

Jeffrey D. Sachs, *Investing in Development: A Practical Plan to Achieve the Millennium Development Goals*, Earthscan, Millennium Project, London/Sterling, UNDP, 2005.

John Rawls, *The Law of Peoples*, Harvard University Press, Cambridge, 1999.

John Ruggie, *Final Report, Including the "Guiding Principles on Business and Human Rights: Implementing the United Nations 'Protect, Respect and Remedy Framework'"*, A/HRC/17/31, 21 March 2011.

Joseph E. Stiglitz, *Globalization and Its Discontents*, W.W. Norton and Company, New York/London, 2002.

Martti Koskenniemi, "What Is International Law For", in Malcolm D. Evans (ed.), *International Law*, Oxford University Press, Oxford, 2003, pp. 89–114.

Malcom Langford, Wouter Vandenhole and Martin Scheinin, Willem van Genugten (eds.), *Global Justice, State Duties. The Extraterritorial Scope of Economic, Social, and Cultural Rights in International Law*, Cambridge University Press, Cambridge, 2012 (forthcoming).

Paul Collier, *The Bottom Billion: Why the Poorest Countries Are Failing and What Can Be Done About It*, Oxford University Press, Oxford, 2008.

Thomas Weiss, Tatiana Carayannis, Louis Emmerij and Richard Jolly, *UN Voices. The Struggle for Development and Social Justice, United Nations Intellectual History Project Series*, Indiana University Press, Bloomington, 2005.

UNDP, *Sustainability and Equity: A Better Future for All. Human Development Report 2011*, UNDP, New York, 2011.

Willem van Genugten and Camilo Perez-Bustillo (eds.), *The Poverty of Rights; Human Rights and the Eradication of Poverty*, Zed Books, London/New York, 2001.

Willem van Genugten, Kees Homan, Nico Schrijver and Paul de Waart, *The United Nations of the Future; Globalization with a Human Face*, KIT Publishers, Amsterdam, 2006.

Willem van Genugten, Rob van Gestel, Marc Groenhuijsen and Rianne Letschert, "Loopholes, Risks and Ambivalences in International Lawmaking: The Case of a Framework Convention on Victims' Rights", in *Netherlands Yearbook of International Law*, 2006, The Hague, 2007, pp. 109-154.

Willem van Genugten, "Protection of Indigenous Peoples on the African Continent: Concepts, Position Seeking, and the Interaction of Legal Systems", in *American Journal of International Law*, 2010, pp. 29-65.

3.7.

The Expanding G-Universe and its Justice Challenges

Sam Muller[*]

In light of the interconnectedness of the world economy, the G20 has led to a new paradigm of multilateral cooperation that is necessary in order to tackle current and future challenges effectively.[1]

In parallel with three serious global crises – the oil crisis in the early 1970's, the collapse of communism and the Asian financial crisis of the end of the 1980's–1990's, and the financial crisis of 2008 in which we now still live – a new governance universe has slowly opened up around the G20. At its core, the UN-universe is about inclusion and participation, for which a rule-based approach was chosen. The G-universe is different. It is not about inclusion but about leadership. At its core it is informal and with that, less rule-based. Given these differences, the G-universe has very different rules than the UN-universe and requires different legal and justice strategies in order to maintain its legitimacy and effectiveness. The G-Universe is not an alternative to the UN-Universe; both complement each other, and if they do so well, then global governance will fare better.

1.   A New Form of Governance

In the past four decades, slowly at first, but at ever greater speed as time passed, a new form of global governance has emerged, centred on the G20. It is part of a broader phenomenon: informal, meaning not based on a law or a treaty, networked forms of governance, around challenges that transcend borders, international, local, or disciplinary ones, bringing together public and public, public and private or private and private actors.

---

[*]   **Dr. A.S. Muller** is Director of the Hague Institute for the Internationalisation of Law (HiiL; www.hiil.org).
[1]   G20 Leaders Declaration at the G20 summit of Los Cabos, Mexico, 18–19 June 2012, para. 181.

G-governance, as the G20 universe will be called in this think piece, is very different from UN-governance. Legal and justice strategies of most States seem to generally only relate to the UN-universe. This is not only a missed opportunity; G-governance can be very effective and citizens and companies are clearly taking to it. Thinking UN-universe only is also bad for justice/rule of law; G-governance must also meet basic justice standards and States must be part of shaping that.

In the following, a concise history of G-governance will be given to illustrate how it has evolved and what its main strengths and weaknesses are. This will be followed by a brief assessment of G-governance against the most fundamental justice requirement for government: that it is legitimate, in other words that it is transparent, open, participatory, rule-based, and effective. Based on this, some thoughts on justice strategies for G-governance are developed.

2.   From Five Stars to Twenty

The 'big bang' of the G-universe was the oil crisis and the unstable economic period of 1973. The ministers of finance of the UK, Germany, France, and the US took the initiative to meet periodically to informally discuss economic policies. When the Japanese minister of finance also joined the group, the meeting got branded the 'Group of Five', or 'G5'. The French President, Valery Giscard d'Estaing, saw something valuable emerging and called a conference of the Group in 1974 at Rambouillet, also asking Italy and Canada to join. The G7 was born.

So things remained for two decades. The G-members were democratic, largely Western or Western in focus, rich, and military allies of the US. It was a small, coherent group, informally organised, in which the members addressed each other on a first name basis and which did not have detailed agendas before each meeting.

The 1990's brought expansion. The disintegration of the Soviet Union, the fall of the Wall, violent demonstrations at the G7 summit in Toronto and the financial crisis in Asia required a change of approach. First, the G7 became the G8 with the addition of Russia. There was experimentation with a G22, which ultimately met twice at the level of the ministers of finance and the directors of central banks. In 1999, two seminars on the same level were held as a G33. This not only brought more inclusiveness, but also created meetings that were harder to handle. There was a desire for somewhat more structure in order to keep the G-method working.

At the end of 1999, the outlines of the current G20 were more or less in place. The ministers of finance in Berlin decided on the G20's mandate: being the central coordinating body for sustainable global economic development, for all. The 'the' was reiterated in 2009 at the third G20 leaders' summit in Pittsburgh ("We designate the G20 to be the premier forum for our international economic cooperation").

Its membership was fixed at nineteen states and the EU: Argentina, Australia, Brazil, Canada, China, France, Germany, UK, India, Indonesia, Italy, Japan, Mexico, Russia, Saudi Arabia, South Korea, Turkey, the US, South Africa, and the EU. About 90% of worldwide GDP, more than 80% of world trade, and governments who represent two-thirds of the world's population. To quote Maria Monica Wihardja: a club that brings together full-market advanced democracies, emerging-market democracies, and emerging–market-non-democracies. It's a careful balancing act: all the countries of systemic relevance for the world economy, a broad regional spread, and a group that is big enough but not too big.

The presidency was also organised a little more. An executive 'governing board' was agreed on, consisting of a troika of the past, sitting, and future presidency (now: France, Mexico, and Russia; in 2013: Mexico, Russia and Australia; and in 2014: Russia, Australia, and Turkey). The sitting presidency keeps things going through its own diplomats and experts. Informal working groups of ministers of finance, directors of central banks, and civil servants prepare and work out summit decisions. There is much room for the troika-presidency to take initiatives. In 2010, chair Korea worked to connect the G20 more to emerging economies and development. Mexico has accentuated food security, commodity prices and the transparency of G20 decision-making.

3. After the 2008 Crisis

In the eye of the financial storm of 2008, the heads of government meeting was institutionalised (in G-style, not through a treaty or other formal document); it came together for the first time on 15 November 2008 in Washington and it has met frequently since then. With that, the G20 universe was expanded with a layer above the ministers of finance and the directors of central banks. The leaders' summit took more of a political consensus, building and leadership: a forum for breaking deadlocks, for setting priorities, providing a vision, and for giving direction. Based on this, the ministers of finance, the directors of central banks, the heads of inter-governmental organisations, and other stars, planets, and moons in the G-universe (see below) do the rest. At the level just below the heads of government, a flexible system was created to prepare the summit meetings and to ensure the implementation of decisions. This system included technical working groups around topics, chaired by different G20 members and the 'sherpas' – the personal representatives of the heads of governments. They don't deal with financial-economic technicalities but are responsible for the politics of the G20 universe; the oil in the machine.

The expanding continued. Every year five non-G20 states from the five regional groups of the UN are invited to participate in the summits and their preparation. The French invited Equatorial-Guinea, Singapore, Ethiopia, the United Arab Emirates, and Spain. The current Mexican presidency invited Benin, Cambodia, Chile, Colombia, and, again, Spain as guests.

And it continued. The international organisations that work with the G20 now have a more defined role: the bosses of the IMF and the World Bank, together with the chairs of the International Monetary and Financial Committee and the Development Committee of the IMF and the World Bank were given the status of permanent participants. The UN, the WTO, the OECD, and the ILO are slightly less permanent participants, although the UN Secretary-General is always present. Within the G20 presidency, more attention is being given to relations with international organisations and the legal frameworks within which they need to work. Existing international organisations now have two main roles. Firstly, they provide key analysis in decision-making processes (at the end of the report of the G-20 Development Working Group gratitude is expressed to 26 international organisations and 'structures' – from the African Development Bank and UNDP, to the Task Team on South-South Cooperation and the Consultative Group to Assist the Poor). Secondly, they are key implementers of G20 decisions and policies, including standard setting.

In line with their increased relevance, non-state actors are now also being given an explicit place. In Toronto, Seoul, and Cannes the Business 20 (B20) emerged: the employers' organisations of the G20 states that bring together around 140 companies. The emergence of the B20 recognises, numerically, that an increasing number of global companies have a larger 'economy' than many states, politically, that many global challenges need cooperation between the private and public sector, and factually, that in some areas, industry organisations and cooperative arrangements between companies and civil society organisations are far ahead of states in terms of practical solutions. Cannes saw a further innovation, which the Mexican presidency strengthened: the Labour-20, or L20. This network brings together the employers organisations of the G20 states, and both the G20 and the B20 recognised its importance in dealing with the fall out of the current global crisis. Both the French and Mexican presidencies met with both groups in both the Cannes and Los Cabos final communiqués of the heads of government the importance of a social dialogue is emphasised and the consultations with the B20 and L20 are welcomed. (UN Secretary-General Ban Ki Moon actually addressed the L20 in Cannes, which also made clear that the L20 is, for now at least, slightly less equal than others: unlike the B20 it was not permitted to hold its meetings within the security zone of the summit meeting, so Ban Ki Moon had to take a motorcade to get there, a distance he could have walked.) Mexico is innovating further: a Youth20 (50 million Mexicans are younger than 25) – a special meeting to which each G20 member can send seven students – and a Think20 (T20) to involve think tanks and academia in the G-processes. Both initiatives were praised by the leaders at the Los Cabos summit. Lastly, the Mexican presidency has stressed the need that the chairs of the different technical working groups involve relevant societal organisations in their work.

As can be seen from the outcome documents of Cannes and Los Cabos, a careful, subject matter expansion is also emerging, with a more holistic definition of 'economic governance'. Corruption, preventing social exclusion, and the environment, also pushed by the B20, are more and more visible on the G20 agenda. As a first, the Mexican presidency chaired a meeting of the G20 ministers of foreign affairs, not to compete or replace the world's executive board on peace and security – the UN Security Council – but to help coordinate where peace and security, and economic policies touch each other. It remains to be seen what contribution this forum will make.

4. How to Assess All This?

Firstly, we see a clear and fairly sustained G-trend. The networked, informal executive board on economic governance is about half the age of the UN system but seems just as 'here to stay'.

Secondly, with periods of less and periods of ADHD level activity in times of crisis, the overall picture is one of an expanding G-universe. The ADHD is also important to know: the G-20 works most in times of crisis. When there is no imminent and urgent need to work something out, the G-approach can flounder, and lose coherency and effectiveness.

Thirdly, 'informality' is its First Principle: a very particular, networked form of international governance, focusing on global economic challenges, albeit more and more holistically defined. The G20 has very consciously not become a treaty organisation with a secretariat, a budget, a building, and a secretary-general, although there is talk of a small secretariat, but it would be quite small and staffed by people seconded from the Presidency. It has not created 'specialised agencies' or entered into 'agreements' with international organisations and others. And yet, a clear universe is visible – with a forum for government leaders, ministers of finance, directors of central banks, heads of the international organisations, and frequent consultations with regional organisations, business, civil society, academia, and with *ad hoc* bodies like the Financial Stability Board and the Basel Committee – all somehow working together. In his Governance for Growth report to the 2011 Cannes summit UK Prime Minister Cameron heralds this "power of informality". It is referred to as critical for leadership. And for flexibility: the ability to quickly draw in the most relevant expertise and participation, the ability to quickly decide. For trust: an environment in which relationships count more than formal structures, one in which you can say and do things off and on the record.

Fourthly, the G-universe has not sought to displace the formal UN-universe and its Stately stars. The G20 recognises that it needs them, so it works with them. Inversely, organisations like the IMF, World Bank, UN, ILO, and OECD have recognised that they need the G20 to get certain things done.

Fifthly, saying that the G-universe is here to stay does not mean that it stays as it is: the G-idea has shown remarkable powers of adaptation. It quickly adapted its structures to be able to deal with the turmoil of the 1990's and the 2008 crisis by enlarging, adopting some basic rules for its meetings, drawing stars from elsewhere into the universe, like the IMF, the World Bank, the UN, the OECD, the WTO, and the ILO, and by creating new stars, like the revitalised Financial Stability Board, the B20, the L20, the T20, and the Y20. Compare that to the UN system, which is perpetually working on reform but which never seems to get it done, except in the margins of informality.

Lastly, the G-universe is not that alien after all: it shares one basic need with States and the UN: the need for legitimacy. Cameron: "informal does not mean less relevant [...] nor [...] being unstructured and unengaged with the rest of the global system". It means "delivering its past commitments and managing its agenda more closely through time" and giving "clearer and stronger political direction" to existing international institutions. This not only goes to the core of the justice strategy required for the G20, but also for those that want a role in its universe because they are the ones who face the consequences of what it decides. In the concluding paragraph below, this final issue will be looked at.

Before we do that, one important preliminary remark about 'strategy' itself: 'government' in the traditional State sense is a fairly well-defined thing, with limited players, who can be identified quite well, such as the government, parliament and the judiciary. G-governance is more fluid, more chaotic, and more multi-level. It is therefore much more difficult to have one strategy, aimed at one actor. Justice strategies in the G-universe will by definition involve more actors, more levels, and small contributions by many, not one by a few. Secondly, the G-universe is not a legal universe; the term 'justice strategy' is therefore used, rather than 'legal strategy'.

5. What About Legitimacy?

Tools for legitimate government are being transparent, allowing participation, being at least somewhat rule-based, and being effective. How does the G-universe do in respect of these elements and what justice strategies are needed for G-legitimacy?

5.1. Transparency

Informality and transparency don't always go together. However, formal rules don't always guarantee openness either. It is probably a good thing that nobody knows what was said by whom to Italian Prime Minister Berlusconi at the Cannes summit, but his replacement 10 days later by Mario Monti was good for the global economy. At the same time: at Los Cabos the leaders agreed that more work is needed here. The inhabitants of the G20 universe – parliaments, civil servants, businesses, civil society organisations of both G20 members and non-members – should never stop reminding leaders of just how important transparency is. The Presidency websites are adequate but not more than that, there are quite a few serious G20 watchers like the Centre for International Governance Innovation, the OECD and OECD Watch, the World Economic Forum, the B20 has an acceptable website, but not more than that and institutions like the FSB and Basel Committee are fairly open in their communication as well. The many participants in G-governance may make things more chaotic, but also contribute to transparency: it's hard to keep a secret. There are less formal rules on 'closed' meetings, and 'confidentiality regimes'.

Much more use can be made of websites and other fora: sharing agendas, outcomes of meetings, exchanges between participants at meetings of which the World Economic Forum website may serve as a good example. National parliaments, participating non-members and international organisations should demand this. Every presidency now sets up a new website, which is complicating and annoying. More transparency can also be organised in the 'sherpa' institution: who they are, with whom they meet, what topics are on the agenda. The Los Cabos summit refers to 'practices' which sherpas will develop but does not specify.

5.2. Participation

Only about a tenth of the total number of States in the world is a member. But, as said: they cover two-thirds of the world population, 80% of world trade, and around 90% of world domestic product. There has also been structured involvement of non-member states, via regional organisations and based on prevailing political needs and a stated commitment to this. There is civil society involvement that is in some ways more promising than what the formal UN system has. Employers, workers, academia, have ways to really participate and certainly much more room to develop creative strategies so that they can do so. While the Dutch government was being sore about the fact that 'the Dutch state' could no longer participate in G20 meetings after 2010, Dutch businesses, Dutch employees organisations, and Dutch academics were already engaged in the G20 universe through for instance the B20, the L20, advisory bodies in the OECD, and the World Economic Forum network.

The justice strategy that fits with this: participate and have something to offer to improve decision-making. There is much room for creativity in the G-20 universe; more than in the formal, state-UN one. Why don't parliamentarians set up a P20? Can a U20 of leading universities be envisaged? Or a CSO-20 of leading coalitions of civil society organisations? The G20 yearns for good analysis on which to base decisions, good standards it can work with and good tools with which to make things work (see the Cameron report). These are all grounds for participation.

5.3. Being Rule-Based

The G20 has no constitution, no written rules of procedure, and no constitutional court. At the same time: 16 G20 states are from more or less working democracies, based on various degrees of rule of law, including the EU. The heads of the participating international organisations also work within structures where democracy and rule of law are fairly well embedded. In respect of all G20 decision-making, there is therefore always a large group of participants that feels the breath of voters and other stakeholders on their necks and that are limited in what they can do by forms of rule of law. Moreover, the absence of formal rules can be beneficial in some respects: the prime ministers of the strongly democratic G20 states cannot hide behind rules when a decision is forced though (the famous: "sorry, I was outvoted", when an international deal needs to be explained before parliament). They must always be able to explain what they did.

G20 rule of law anchoring lies in participating and in national rule systems and the rule systems of international organisations. Make sure your prime minister does not come home with a G20 deal that has no constitutional basis or that violates basic rights. Parliaments: wake up to this universe and define an effective role for yourself. The G20 has recognised that it must have more respect for the mandates and work methods of the international institutions through which its decisions are implemented. General assemblies and governing boards of international organisations: wake up to this. The G20 has however also been clear: international institutions should not get tied up in their own rules and must reform if needed.

5.4. Effectiveness

Whether something is 'effective' largely depends on what it has been created for. Paul Heinbecker said it beautifully: "The larger story of the G20, including its much criticised performance at Seoul, is not that the G20 is failing to resolve intractable issues, but that the issues are intractable and that the G20 is trying to solve them". The effectiveness model of the G20 places emphasis on 'leadership'; leaders that coach, strategically direct and coordinate existing international organisations and others. Another component is bringing in the best expertise: the best people and organisations contribute the best analysis, on the basis of which there is a better chance that the best decisions emerge. When reflecting on effectiveness, it is also important to realise that the G20 is a process, rather than a summit with results. And not all of its results are easy to measure or communicate. Knowing and trusting each other is a good result but it cannot be quantified or easily made visible. Finally, a word on effectiveness and crisis. The more informally organised G-universe is in many ways faster than the more formal UN universe in responding to needs. It is quite astounding how much G20 activity the current financial crisis has led to. We however also see – and that is a typical feature of networked governance – that without an acute crisis, the risk of floundering is always there. Without the pressure of a crisis, the G20 model can cause processes to lose momentum and concentration to fritter away.

The justice strategy on effectiveness should not be to institutionalise the G20. Global governance – in the economic sphere or elsewhere – benefits greatly from both formal and informal systems. The UN universe has the formal governance guarantees. The G20 model is a good corollary to that. I would say, and with this I end this think piece: the core effectiveness strategy is very much connected with the strategy on participation and with maintaining focus. Everybody with something to offer: participate. And leaders of the G20: keep focusing on focus.

6. Sources and Further Reading

Andrew Sparrow, Politics Live: G20 Summit – Thursday 3 November 2011, The Guardian, 3 November 2011, available at http://www.guardian.co.uk/world/blog/2011/nov/03/g20-summit-live-coverage, last accessed on 10 September 2012.

Anne Marie Slaughter, *A New World Order*, Princeton University Press, 2005.

Bruce Jones, Making Multilateralism Work: How the G-20 Can Help the United Nations, The Stanley Foundation, 2010, available at http://www.stanleyfoundation.org/resources.cfm?id=416, last accessed on 10 September 2012.

B20 and L20 Joint Statement, 2011, available at http://www.ilo.org/wcm sp5/groups/public/---dgreports/---dcomm/documents/meetingdocument/w cms_166713.pdf, last accessed on 10 September 2012.

Conclusions of the T20 Meeting Convened by the Mexican Presidency, available at http://g20mexico.org/en/press-releases/259-la-reunion-think-20-concluye-exitosamente, last accessed on 10 September 2012.

David Cameron, Governance for Growth: Building Consensus for the Future, 2011, available at http://www.number10.gov.uk/wp-content/uploads/2011/11/GovernanceForGrowth_acc.pdf, last accessed on 10 September 2012.

David Frum, For World Leader, G-20 – An Enormous Waste of Time, 7 November 2011, available at http://www.cnn.com/2011/11/07/opinion/frum-g20-bloat/index.html, last accessed on 10 September 2012.

Discussion Paper by Mexico's Presidency, January 2012, available at http://www.g20.org/images/pdfs/disceng.pdf, last accessed on 10 September 2012.

Draft HiiL Trend Report on Multilevel Rule Making, June 2012, available in final version on the HiiL website by mid-October 2012 (http://www.hiil.org).

Gordon S. Smith, G7 to G8 to G20: Evolution in Global Governance, CIGI G20 Papers no. 6, 2011, available at http://www.cigionline.org/publications/2011/5/g7-g8-g20-evolution-global-governance, last accessed on 10 September 2012.

Jonathan Kopell, *World Rule – Accountability, Legitimacy, and the Design of Global Governance*, Chicago University Press, 2011.

Leaders Declaration, Los Cabos Summit under the Mexican Presidency, available at http://g20.org/images/stories/docs/g20/conclu/G20_Leaders_Declaration_2012_1.pdf, last accessed on 10 September 2012.

Maria M. Wihardja, "The G20 and Global Democracy", in Wilhelm Hofmeister, Susanna Vogt (eds.), *G20 – Perceptions and Perspectives for Global Governance*, Konrad Adenhauer Stiftung, available at http://www.kas.de/wf/en/33.29099/, last accessed on 10 September 2012.

Max Brem (ed.), *Prescriptions for Growth, The Cannes Summit and Beyond*, CIGI, 2011, available at http://www.gppi.net/fileadmin/media/events/2011/CIGI-2011-program.pdf, last accessed on 10 September 2012.

Paul Heinbecker, The Future of the G20 and Its Place in Global Governance, CIGI Paper no. 5, 2011, available at http://www.cigionline.org/publications/2011/4/future-g20-and-its-place-global-governance, last accessed on 10 September 2012.

Perspectives on the G-20 Foreign Ministers' Meeting, available at http://www.brookings.edu/opinions/2012/0217_g20_mgo.aspx, last accessed on 10 September 2012.

The Group of Twenty: A History, Study Prepared by the Deputies of the of Group of Twenty under the Chairmanship of South Africa to Commemorate 20 Years of the G-20 (1999–2009), 2008, available at http://www.g20.utoronto.ca, last accessed on 10 September 2012.

The G-20 Mutual Assessment Process (MAP), IMF Factsheet, available at http://www.imf.org/external/np/exr/facts/g20map.htm, last accessed on 10 September 2012.

Website of the G20-G8, available at http://www.g20-g8.com, last accessed on 10 September 2012.

Website of the G20 Mexico summit, available at http://www.g20.org/en/home, last accessed on 10 September 2012.

3.8.

European Justice and Legal Strategy

Bernard Bot[*]

Officially the first day of spring. I had to climb a few steep stairs to the first floor of the 17th century house in which Dr. Bernard Bot holds office and was met by a smiling, former Minister of Foreign Affairs and one of the longest serving Dutch ambassadors to the European Union. Few people have been as close to legal and justice strategy as he has.

The European Union is perhaps the most impressive piece of legal and justice strategy project in history. In 1951, six countries started with a shared management agreement regarding their coal and steel industry. The road they took was legal from the outset: a strong treaty which created supranational institutions. They transformed this first cooperation effort into an economic community in 1957 in which people, goods and services could move around unhampered. Again, law was used as the tool to solidify political agreement. Now, the EU has a solid legal infrastructure around issues such as human rights, immigration, crime, market regulation, finance, and data protection. Additionally, it has a firm governance structure with a very peculiar form of federalism, well embedded in law.

"The approach of enshrining political agreement in legal structures and rules was always very strategic and deliberate. It started out with a relatively blank piece of paper, on which the overarching, supranational structure was first written down. From there, the European Union was developed, with the European Court of Justice as one of the most important engines. Through its judgments, the Court created far-reaching precedents, many of which later on found their way into legal texts."

1. Who Makes Strategy?

"Legal strategy finds its origin mainly in Brussels. Ministers are generally not in a good position to be strategy-drivers. They are in Brussels once a month, with around 5 hours of effective meeting time. Generally speak-

---

[*] **Bernhard Bot,** former Dutch Minister of Foreign Affairs and Ambassador to the EU, interviewed by Sam Muller on 20 March 2012.

ing, Ministers are not always that interested in legal strategy and sometimes even look at the EU with negative connotations as something to fight against or something that interferes with the national legislative process. Therefore, much of the effort originates from the civil servants of the Commission and the diplomats of the member states. They prepare in most cases the ministerial meetings and filter out what can already be decided at their level. Even for issues that are left for the political level, the ambassadors are on occasion asked to sit in the minister's chair. Matters are often simply so complex that they have to be prepared and finalised on a technical level. I do recall moments when I wondered whether a judge would ever be able to fully understand the complex texts we sometimes adopted."

"The Court is now definitely less of a driver. More generally, one can say that the supranational structure of the EU has lost ground in favour of a more intergovernmental approach to shaping the EU legal order. This development started already around ten years ago. It goes hand in hand with the change from a European governance structure dealing with more technical issues to an EU that deals with matters much closer to the social and economic lives of people. Organising trade, for example, could more easily be dealt with at a supranational level. However, dealing with taxes, health, finance, and pension systems touches more directly the lives of people and national politicians. It is probably true that legal strategy regarding issues that have a direct impact on the lives of people requires rule-making that is equally close to the people."

2. The Relationship Between the Different Strategy-Makers

"Convincing the EU to incorporate the so-called third intergovernmental pillar on justice and home affairs into the Union was a hugely significant breakthrough. That was not an easy process; the Netherlands and France, for example, initially opposed this proposal. They were convinced that they had the best legal systems imaginable and that 'unionising' justice and security would be damaging to their systems. However, the hurdle was taken and with that, the legal order of the EU took another important step in its development."

"When I started out in Brussels, between 1964 and 1970, it was not done to even ask the Commission to see a draft of a legislative proposal before it was put before the Council. Only when it was felt that the draft was ready, it was shared with the member states. When I came back to Brussels in 1992 that attitude had completely changed. Now, the Commission gladly shares its ideas and drafts as early as possible and welcomes input by the member states at various entry points of the process. And when we, as ambassadors, assessed these proposals we would also check whether the Commission had consulted the member states. Occasionally, we did send proposals back for lack of prior consultation. Why? Because whatever the Council and the European Parliament decide upon has to be implemented by all the member states without too many reservations. And for that, you need buy-in. It is fair to say that parallel to this strategy, the decision-making process has become more 'intergovernmental'. During my time as ambassador to the EU, I made sure that on the one hand I connected the country that I represented to the Commission's proposals from as early on as possible, while on the other, I always remained in close contact with the national ministers so that I understood their concerns. That was essential for being successful."

"Connecting to the citizen has always been and probably will remain the biggest challenge of the European Union and the legal and justice strategies that it aspires to achieve. There are so many beneficial things that the EU has accomplished; but these results are not always visible and understood."

What emerged from our conversation on that first day of spring is that justice strategy in the European Union was and remains in essence a complex process of aligning the interests of multiple stakeholders around a few big ideas. First, the idea between six countries that there should not be another war between the two main European powers. Then the idea that the citizens and companies of a handful of European States should be able to move freely in a shared economic space. When the Berlin Wall and communism fell, the big idea became to fully absorb the new East European democracies in the European project. Now that that has been achieved, the EU seems to be somewhat adrift, although today's financial crisis seems to be focusing the minds again and new structures and processes are being added to make the Union more of a solid player in today's global economy. The blank piece of paper on which the first pencil strokes of the European legal order were drawn has now become a very complex work of art. It has developed into an intricate system with many owners, including an almost federal European Minister of Justice in the Commission. Many owners often mean no owner. So strategists need to create them. Were the steep stairs into his office a metaphor? All that has been done to shape the European Union till this point and all that still remains to be done?

3.9.

Strategy by Stealth: The Security Council

Kimberly Prost[*]

The Security Council, in the context of counter terrorism sanctions, has an ombudsperson. In many respects, that's justice strategy of almost Chinese Wall proportions. A body that represents the quintessence of power politics has agreed to provide for an objective assessment in the exercise of that power, not through judges or anything radical like that, but through an ombudsperson with carefully defined powers. So, as such a small step. But as a principle and as a potential foundation for more, a huge leap for mankind. Like most justice strategies, this one was not driven necessarily by benevolence but by the necessities of power politics itself. And, interestingly enough, by a chunk of justice that lay outside the UN system.

The European Union, through its Court of Justice, was the main driver. With its Kadi judgments – that covered 27 UN Member States which represent a sizeable and highly influential part of its membership particularly in the context of financial sanctions. – aspects of the Security Council's Al-Qaeda sanctions regime were not implementable. Kadi raised issues at two levels. Firstly, at a more micro rule of law level. A serious court across the ocean was saying that there were human rights issues with putting people on sanction lists based on information they do not know about, without any means of redress. The second issue concerned rule of law at a broader level: it is a problem if the Security Council's resolutions are – at least in part – not enforceable. That could start to undermine the authority of the Council. Sanctions are increasingly seen as an effective tool, so it is important that they can continue to be used.

More rule of law around the Security Council: a milestone by all accounts, but one that is implemented by stealth, quietly step-by-step. The Security Council members like their political room for manoeuvre and

---

[*] **Kimberly Prost**, Ombudsperson for the United Nations Security Council Committee pursuant to resolutions 1267 (1999) and 1989 (2011) concerning Al-Qaida and Associated Individuals and Entities, also known as the "The Al-Qaida Sanctions Committee", interviewed by Sam Muller on 25 June 2012.

would not easily give in to a grand long-term justice strategy that could tie their hands in the future. So how did this happen?

"There were many factors which led to the adoption of this particular mechanism – an Ombudsperson – in response to the fairness and due process issues in the use of targeted sanctions. There was the criticism coming from academics, NGO's/civil society and importantly Member States who were facing significant challenges in implementation. Finally the Courts – particularly in the European Union – added their voices to the chorus of concern. But it is one thing to criticise and another to come up with proposals – particularly in such a highly charged political context – to respond to the problem. Here there was a like-minded group of States," commented Kimberly Prost, the Ombudsperson "mostly from the EU, that very cleverly and effectively translated the academic and judicial writing that was being done around the principles enshrined ultimately in Kadi into what it would mean for the Council itself. They put forward practical proposals which were realistic in a political context. Even though the ultimate result may not have mirrored exactly those suggestions, it certainly contained elements of them and was instrumental in informing the thinking of the Security Council members on the issue. That was an effective strategy".

It is interesting to consider this particular development in the broader context of the Security Council's recent activities. It appears the idea of reinforcing credibility is not an isolated one. What you see over the past years is a Council that devotes much more time to regional consultations before it acts. You clearly saw that in Libya, where the Arab League was extensively consulted in steps that were taken and in the context of crisis in Kenya and Cote d'Ivoire where the African Union played a role. Clearly that is also about legitimacy, about ensuring that the Council does not issue resolutions that are not implemented. It is about the same ideas as with rule of law.

What comes together in the Ombudsperson's work are individual human rights, rule of law, and geopolitics. Strategies at all these levels, simultaneously. That is rather unique.

"It's not always easy". Prost is clear on that. "I am not only dealing with individual cases, I am also trying to build a system, to build support for a rule of law approach in the consideration of petitions for delisting. I have adopted certain strategies myself. Firstly, when I started I made it clear what I saw as the basic principles of due process: right to know the case against you, to be notified of it, to be able to answer it and be heard by the decision-maker, and independent review of information and finally a reasoned decision. I had help in this respect from the Secretary-General who had outlined previously in a speech his view on the fundamentals of fair process in this very particular context. I used that as my starting point. These principles then formed the basis upon which I could evaluate the process I was implementing and publically comment to a broad audience, including the courts, on whether it meets the fundamentals of fairness. It is of course ultimately for others to decide if it is sufficient or not but I was best placed to advance the process in accordance with those principles and to comment on it factually".

"It is important to understand that I do not have a judicial role in this process and the ultimate decision still rests with the Al-Qaida Sanctions Committee. Rather I am there to provide the Committee with an objective, independent assessment of the information in the case. I make my case by saying that in this particular instance, today, based on the material gathered through my process; the information is or is not sufficient to provide a reasonable and credible basis for continued listing. I do not review the Committee's decision to list nor presume to know the information upon which that was based. I focus solely on the information I have and render my analysis and recommendation on that. The Committee can then draw its conclusions".

Prost continues, "I like to think that the incremental approach I have taken – staying within my mandate but using it as aggressively as possible to advance those fundamental principles – engendered some basic trust and confidence on the part of the Committee and the Council. I hope this contributed to the developments last year when the Security Council renewed and expanded my mandate, allowing me to move from only making observations, to making recommendations in each case which can only be set aside by a consensus decision of the Committee or if a State refers the matter to the Security Council for a vote. Twice a year, I report publicly to the Security Council and that's where I have a chance to report openly on my activities, in a broad fashion, including providing my comments on the evolution of the process in terms of fairness".

Despite these changes in New York, the issue of targeted sanctions and fair process remains before the Courts in Europe. A second challenge by Mr. Kadi – Kadi II – is currently pending before the Grand Chamber of the European Court of Justice. There is also a case pending before the European Court of Human Rights, the Nada case, coming out of Switzerland. He is off the list now, but he brought an action that was argued before the Strasbourg court. That may enlarge the scope of the justice issue at stake here considerably, namely to over 50 UN member states. It will be interesting to see the results and also to see what if any impact the Office of the Ombudsperson has on the same.

But strategies by one, creates strategies by others. Some states choose to make extensive use of both domestic listings and the UN targeted sanctions Lists. Other States take a more cautious approach relying primarily on a domestic or regional system to deal with terrorists – individuals, groups and entities – and pursuing international listings in only the most egregious cases.

Moreover, all strategies have their limits. Kadi just lost a case in the US, with the US court showing great deference to the executive under a due process regime that is quite distinct from that employed in other judicial contexts such as the European Court of Justice.

Another developing issue is whether this Ombudsperson process should be extended to other regimes beyond Al-Qaida. The obvious question which arises is why individuals on the Al-Qaida list are accorded these rights and remedies while those on other targeted sanctions list are not. A recent case highlighted the issue when an individual was delisted from the Al-Qaida list through the Ombudsperson process and on the same day relisted by the Somalia/Eritrea Sanctions Committee. "That subsequent listing may be entirely justified", explains Prost, "but what it demonstrated to me is the fair process problem that arises. I had to explain to the individual that I had no mandate with respect to this new listing. While it is entirely a decision for States as to the scope of the Ombudsperson mandate, this is an issue which is clearly going to start to arise".

There will, again, have to be strategy. Five years ago, the idea of an ombudsperson for a Security Council sanctions committee was a complete no-go. Now it's there. While the debate about a strategy to enlarge the Security Council continues and goes nowhere, the Council consults extensively with regional groups and in that way, partly enlarges itself. Strategy by stealth can lead to remarkable results. This example shows that individuals play an important role in such situations. Individuals who push the envelope, but who do not overplay their hand. It also shows the importance of leverage that has to be seen and put to use. Something in the

EU changes the UN. Something what the Council wants to do needs the Arab League or the African Union.

3.10.

Environmental Justice
and Corporate Responsibility

Birgit Spiesshofer[*]

Environmental Justice is above all *iustitia distributiva* (Aristotle), claiming the fair distribution of environmental benefits and burdens, complicated by the fact that existential resources like water, sunshine, fertile soil and mineral resources are unevenly distributed, and that scientific knowledge regarding cause-effect-relationships is limited. Besides social, territorial and inter-species aspects, environmental justice encompasses also a time dimension, that is, intra-generational and inter-generational justice. Some of the characteristics of the globalised economy are that benefits and burdens do not match, external cost are only partly internalised, benefits are privatised, burdens tend to be socialised. Too big to fail situations, like the Fukushima accident, show that the attribution of corporate responsibility on the basis of causation and 'polluter pays' strategies is insufficient. Climate change proves to be an enormous challenge for environmental justice in a multitude of respects. Procedural aspects, like the fair participation of potentially affected parties, ombudsmen for nature in decision-making processes, and the adequate access to courts and remedies, are crucial elements in achieving environmental justice.

1. Introduction

Is environmental justice an impossible claim, as all of the natural resources like water, sunshine, land, food, fertile soil, vegetation and mineral resources are unevenly distributed over the earth? Can environmental justice be achieved at all in light of limited scientific knowledge about complex cause-effect-relationships such as climate change, and, in particular, with regard to damages emanating and discoverable only in the long run? Can corporations take the popular standpoint that 'the business of business is business' and that environmental justice is an issue to be taken

---

[*] **Birgit Spiesshofer** is an Attorney-at-Law, and an Of Counsel at Salans LLP.

care of by (only) governments and supranational organisations? Or do they have to bear their fair share in the environmental justice scheme? And how, and by whom, is it defined?

2. Environmental Justice

Environmental justice encompasses various dimensions and points of reference: social and territorial justice, time dimensions in the form of intragenerational and inter-generational justice, inter-species justice including the environment at large, *iustitia distributiva* (just distribution of environmental benefits and burdens), procedural, participation, enforcement and adjudication aspects.

2.1. Social and Territorial Justice

In the United States, the Environmental Justice Movement developed in the early 1980's out of the Civil Rights Movement. It raised at first mainly two issues: (1) the socially uneven distribution of environmental burdens, for example, highly polluting facilities were mostly built in areas where coloured and low income citizens lived, and (2) the right to participate in and influence the decision-making process. It later developed into a broader scheme, encompassing all ecological, economic and social conditions for the right to a healthy environment.

2.2. Intra-Generational and Inter-Generational Justice

The responsibility not only for the present generation but also for future generations was already a concern of the Roman politician and philosopher, Cato, who stated that an 'après nous le déluge' attitude was unacceptable for a wise man and dismissed by public opinion.

In the ecological debate, the *Brundtland Commission*[1] was among the first to claim not only a just distribution of environmental benefits and burdens within one generation (intra-generational), but also to take into consideration the needs of future generations (inter-generational), and to respect their right to the same or equivalent living conditions. Both aspects are encompassed by the term 'sustainable development', established by the Brundtland Commission, with a certain emphasis on the future impacts of present activities. John Rawls defined the relationship between

---

[1]   See WCED, *Our Common Future*, 1987, p. 43 et seq.

the generations as a contractual band between equals, and the Wissenschaftlicher Beirat der Bundesregierung Globale Umweltveränderungen (WBGU) entitled its latest report Gesellschaftsvertrag für eine Große Transformation (Social Contract for a Large-Scale Transformation), emphasising the obligations towards future generations. The Rio Convention on Climate Change of 1992 referred also to both the intra-generational as well as the inter-generational aspect, stating:

> The Parties should protect the climate system for the benefit of present and future generations of humankind, on the basis of equity and in accordance with their common but differentiated responsibilities and respective capabilities[2] [...] The Parties shall take full account of the specific needs and special situations of the least developed countries in their actions with regard to funding and transfer of technology.[3]

The Rio Convention does not follow a purely retro-oriented causation and compensation based approach – that is the industrialised states that contributed most to the climate change effect should compensate for their past behaviour – but a differentiated approach, taking into consideration not only the responsibilities, but also the remedial capabilities of states, and the specific needs of the poorest countries. Past behaviour is only one equity criterion for the distribution of the burdens each state should bear; another is the capability to care and the specific need for help.

Regarding the problem of limited scientific knowledge about complex cause-and-effect relationships in climate change scenarios, affecting in particular the protection of future generations, the Rio Convention provides for the following guidance:

> The Parties should take precautionary measures to anticipate, prevent or minimize the causes of climate change and mitigate its adverse effects. Where there are threats of serious or irreversible damage, lack of full scientific certainty should not be used as a reason for postponing such measures, taking into account that policies and measures to deal with climate

---

[2] United Nations Framework Convention on Climate Change, available at http://unfccc.int/key_documents/the_convention/items/2853.php, last accessed on 1 October 2012, Art. 3, para. 1.

[3] *Ibid.*, Art. 4, para. 9.

change should be cost-effective so as to ensure global bene-fits at the lowest possible cost.[4]

The precautionary principle is at least one answer to limited scientific knowledge. The measures to be taken depend on the severity of potential damages, the likelihood of their occurrence, the global benefits of their prevention and the costs entailed.

2.3. Inter-Species Justice

The prevailing justice doctrine follows an anthropocentric approach, that is, justice, particularly according to Rawls' contract scheme, requires mutual obligations that exist only between human beings, and not between human beings and other species or nature as such. The eco-centric approach is wider as it claims that the environment as such can be an independent addressee of environmental justice. Both opinions agree that laws shall protect other species and nature. The eco-centric approach, however, is more supportive of instruments like citizen suits and ombudsmen taking care of the 'rights' of other species and the environment.

2.4. *Iustitia Distributiva*

Environmental justice is primarily a question of what Aristotle called *iustitia distributiva*, that is, the fair and just distribution of benefits and burdens, resources and chances within a society or between societies and generations.

One of the characteristics of our globalised economy is that environmental benefits are usually privatised whereas burdens tend to be socialised. The internalisation of external cost, that is of damages to the environment and of the often barely foreseeable long-term impacts, is incomplete.

This is obvious in cases like Chernobyl and Fukushima, where the operators of the nuclear power plants (and their shareholders) had the benefits and profits of the operation, whereas the consequences of the accidents for the population (also of other countries) and the environment are of a magnitude that neither insurance companies nor the operators, in case of Chernobyl not even the state, can cover them. In these "too big to fail" situations the polluter pays principle, which is otherwise an equitable

---

[4]   *Ibid.*, Art. 3, para. 3.

and just concept for the attribution of burdens and responsibilities, in particular, with regard to corporate activities, is inadequate. The state or the international community has no choice but to take over at least part of the burden because the bankruptcy of the operator would cause even more problems and would not avert the danger to human beings and to the environment. Although it is extremely unjust that 'innocent' parties – parties who neither contributed to nor benefited of or had any influence on the damaging activities – should bear the burden of the remediation and compensation, they have no other option because the alternative would be even worse. Germany is still suffering the impacts of the radioactive fallout of the Chernobyl disaster. However, instead of claiming compensation, it had no choice but to co-finance the 'sarcophagus' and its supervision.

In the Fukushima accident, the Japanese government did the inevitable: it rescued the operator Tepco by injecting capital combined with a claim for more control, it shut down all nuclear power plants for thorough inspections, revised the structure and operations of the supervising authorities to enhance their independence and efficiency, it introduced stricter requirements for the layout and the safety systems of the facilities, and finances the clean-up of the contaminated land and the compensation for the people who lost their basis of living. Despite these measures, full environmental justice will never be achieved as the contamination of the aquatic environment, the loss of income of the population, the damage to the fauna and flora, the long term effects of radioactive contamination, in particular for future generations and other countries, the higher cost to produce energy in conventional power plants and other consequences, will not be (fully) compensated. Even in the long run, the operator will barely be capable to take over the burden that the state has shouldered on its behalf.

Whereas most countries ordered the operators of nuclear power plants to shut down their plants, execute thorough check-ups and increase the safety requirements (to avoid accidents like Fukushima), the German government adopted a more radical strategy, ordering the nuclear power plant operators to exit nuclear power technology by 2022, as the burdens of potential accidents are of a magnitude that cannot be counterbalanced with the benefits of this technology. The operators challenge this exit decision and claim multi-billion euro compensation for damages and frustrated investments in German courts as well as the World Bank arbitration court. The Federal Constitutional Court will have to decide whether the exit order is a mere definition of the social limits of the use of private property or an expropriation of the operators.

Another example of an obvious incongruence of environmental benefits and burdens is climate change. To achieve environmental justice in all respects described above, issues with global impact such as climate change, should be handled by international bodies and regulated by global legal instruments. There are, however, only few international environmental treaties regarding the atmosphere. An example of a successful one is the Montreal Protocol on Substances that Deplete the Ozone Layer[5] prohibiting the production, trade and use of Chlorofluorocarbons (CFCs). In most cases, however, international law is non-existent, insufficient, too slow, or too limited in terms of scope. An example in that regard is the Kyoto Protocol, regulating national greenhouse gas emissions. It took a long time until it entered into force and did not find a successor so far, although scientists describe drastic scenarios of global warming if the greenhouse gas emissions are not significantly reduced in the foreseeable future.

The main reason why the international community cannot find an agreement, despite striking and acknowledged scientific evidence is justice, is due to emerging economies like China and India, which consider it unfair that they should curb their industrial production and the living standard of their people, whilst the United States– who were for a long time the main contributor and beneficiary of air pollution – do not accept to submit to restrictive standards.

The European Union (EU) decided to step forward and to introduce an Emissions Trading Scheme (ETS), which was extended as of 1 January 2012 to all aircrafts starting or landing at EU airports. It required the airlines to obtain emission certificates for the carbon dioxide (CO_2) emissions for all flights arriving in or departing from the EU. The European Union justified its unilateral move as all attempts to find an international

---

[5]   United Nations Environment Programme, "The Vienna Convention for the protection of the Ozone Layer and its Montreal Protocol on substances that deplete the Ozone Layer", available at http://www.unep.org/ozone, last accessed on 13 September 2012.

solution had previously failed, despite the fact that aircraft emissions had increased since 1990 by eighty seven per cent.[6]

This measure encountered harsh critique from non-EU air carriers, their trade associations and their countries. They filed lawsuits as well as threatened with severe sanctions against EU airlines and the European Airbus industry.[7] They considered it unfair that their airlines should be subject to the EU Emissions Trading Scheme, in particular, also with regard to CO_2 not emitted over European territory.

The European Union reaffirmed that it will revise its Emissions Trading Scheme when a solution is developed on the international level, in particular, in the context of the International Civil Aviation Organisation (ICAO). With regard to the indivisibility of the atmosphere, in order to reduce aircraft emissions to the utmost extent possible, and in favour of an equal burden for all air carriers, the EU would have preferred an international solution. As this was not achieved, the EU tried (not for the first time) to lead by example in order to force non-EU states and their air carriers into negotiations.

With regard to environmental justice, emissions trading schemes are a step forward insofar as they internalise (at least) part of the external cost, that is, atmospheric pollution, and they are designed to reduce the total amount of the emissions over time. They are insufficient, however, as most of the emission certificates are handed out in the first phase for free, allowing the companies to even make a profit, if they sell such emission certificates. Regarding the indivisibility of the atmosphere, they are of limited efficiency if they have only a regional scope. They lead to a distortion of competition and a disadvantage for those companies, which are subject to the scheme. The European Union tried to optimise its scheme in

---

[6] Directive 2008/101/EC of the European Parliament and of the Council of 19 November 2008 amending Directive 2003/87/EC so as to include aviation activities in the scheme for greenhouse gas emission allowance trading within the Community; see also: Commission Decision 2009/450/EC of 8 June 2009 on the detailed interpretation of the aviation activities listed in the Annex I to Directive 2003/87/EC; Commission Regulation (EC) No. 748/2009 of 5 August 2009 on the list of aircraft operators which performed an aviation activity listed in Annex I to Directive 2003/87/EC on or after 1 January 2006 specifying the administering Member state for each aircraft operator.

[7] Frankfurter Allgemeine Zeitung 23 February 2012 and 2 March 2012; Case C-366/10, press release No. 139/11, available at http://www.curia.europa.eu, last accessed on 13 September 2012.

favour of the climate to the utmost extent possible by expanding it beyond its territory as the emissions of the entire flight starting or landing at a European airport are subject to the EU Emissions Trading Scheme, not only those generated over its territory. The European Union ETS has, however, a limited effect if the emissions reduced in Europe are overcompensated by an increase of aircraft emissions in China and India as is to be expected. It is therefore understandable that European airlines question the justification of their sacrifice for the environment if it does not have a tangible effect.

One of the most important, and still unresolved, issues of environmental justice and corporate responsibility is the insufficient internalisation of environmental cost. The World Business Council for Sustainable Development noted, in its *Changing Pace* policy, recommendations for the Rio+20 conference that there should be a budget established through fiscal reforms to price scarce natural resources and negative externalities.[8]

2.5. Procedural Justice

Besides the material aspects of environmental justice, adequate procedural provisions and participation rights play an important role for the acceptance of decisions as to what is just and what is fair. The procedural requirements can have a broader scope encompassing also inter-species and nature protection aspects, which aren't connected with personal and property rights of individuals. Complex zoning procedures and industrial facility permitting procedures according to the Directive on Integrated Pollution Prevention and Control (IPPC-Directive)[9] and the respective national laws,[10] require that Environmental Impact Assessments (EIA) – encompassing also species and nature protection issues –are executed. Not only for the EIA but in all planning and zoning procedures, it is mandatory that all material aspects are noticed, respected and taken into considera-

---

[8] World Business Council for Sustainable Development, available at http://www.wb csd.org, last accessed on 13 September 2012.

[9] Directive 2008/1/EC of the European Parliament and of the Council, 15 January 2008.

[10] See, *e.g.*, § 10 Gesetz zum Schutz vor schädlichen Umwelteinwirkungen durch Luftverunreinigungen, Geräusche, Erschütterungen und ähnliche Vorgänge (Bundesimmissionsschutzgesetz – BImSchG) of 26 September 2002 (BGBl. I S. 3830), last amended 24 February 2012 (BGBl. I S. 212); 9. Bundesimmissionsschutzverordnung (Verordnung über das Genehmigungsverfahren - 9. BImSchV) of 29 May 1992 (BGBl. I S. 1001), last amended 23 October 2007 (BGBl. I S. 2470).

tion. They have to be adequately assessed and weighed and balanced in a proportionate and equitable way. Potentially affected parties, such as neighbours, have to be heard; their comments have to be taken into consideration. They may not agree with the result, but transparency and adequate participation as well as representation in the procedure, warrants that all people who eventually have to bear consequences also have a say.

In a disastrous situation like Fukushima or Chernobyl, a lot of people, companies and states have to bear the consequences of such accidents, despite not having had any say regarding the establishment and operation of these facilities. Again there is incongruence: the 'neighbourhood' has been extended to entire continents and even beyond, at least with regard to the negative effects, not, however with regard to the participation rights. There are certain international treaties like the Aarhus Convention,[11] which provides for information and participation rights and access to court in environmental matters, or the Espoo Convention,[12] regarding Environmental Impact Assessments in trans-boundary contexts. They do not cover, however, phenomena like Fukushima or climate change.

The incongruence is even more severe regarding the adjudication of environmental matters. Whereas adequate remediation may be warranted in a national context, and in cases with limited territorial effect (like the clean-up of soil contamination), it is difficult in international settings, in complex cause-and-effect relationships and in situations where the environment at large is at stake, for example as it is with climate change. The environment and other species do not have standing, and environmental NGOs are granted standing on behalf of nature only under specific and limited conditions. Damages, as the result of Climate change, can barely entitle damaged parties or insurance companies to sue those contributing to climate change globally. The limitation of the access to courts and to adjudication has the effect that the burdens are warded off from the polluter and remain with the victims, the general public and the environment.

Procedural and adjudication aspects are thus Janus-faced: on one hand they enhance environmental justice, on the other they socialise envi-

---

[11] Convention on Access to Information, Public Participation in Decision-making and Access to Justice in Environmental Matters, done at Aarhus, Denmark, on 25 June 1998, available at www.unece.org/env/pp/treatytext.htm.

[12] United Nations Economic Commission for Europe, "Convention on Environmental Impact Assessment in a Transboundary Context (Espoo 1991)", available at http://www.unece.org/env/eia, last accessed on 13 September 2012.

ronmental burdens, and discharge individuals and companies of the consequences of their actions.

3. Corporate Responsibility for Environmental Justice

As indicated above, corporations face environmental justice questions in a multitude of ways. Although they cannot be held responsible for the entire picture, they have to play their role in the environmental justice scheme, with regard to the procedural and adjudication aspects they are subject to and with regard to their contribution to the material aspects of justice. Based on the findings above, it is not unfair to say that corporate responsibility, for various reasons, does not encompass (at the moment) all of the consequences of corporate operations. The existing legal attribution and adjudication schemes do not have adequate answers for the most disastrous issues such as the 'too big to fail' cases and the complex cause-and-effect situations, like climate change. The lack of adequate justice schemes results in a (partial) discharge of responsibilities - benefits are privatised whereas burdens tend to be socialised.

4. Conclusion

Regarding environmental justice and corporate responsibility, no coherent legal and justice strategy exists. Certain principles like the Polluter Pays Principle and the Precautionary Principle have been widely accepted and transposed into law. There is no strategy in place, however, for the complete internalisation of the environmental damage and cost caused by industrial operations. Moreover, not all aspects of environmental justice are covered by the existing legal frameworks. The overall picture resembles rather a patchwork carpet consisting, in particular, of international treaties covering only specific aspects of global environmental issues and addressing mainly the states, and European directives and national laws, which spell out material and procedural environmental responsibilities of enterprises but carve out major corporate impacts. The implementation and enforcement of environmental justice is mostly left to national governments and courts.

What could a coherent legal and justice strategy look like? A coherent strategy should achieve maximum avoidance of corporate environmental impacts, both with regard to the operation and the product, and, to the extent this is not achievable, a full internalisation of external cost to reflect the real efficiency and cost and to direct government and corporate policies. Zoning and permitting procedures can warrant that industrial facilities are located in specific areas adequately separated from residential and other sensitive neighbourhoods, environmental impact assessments make sure that impacts on other species are taken into consideration, in particular, when they are assisted by efficient ombudsman and citizen suit schemes. Permits should follow a 'cradle-to-grave' approach, that is, the full range of operation, its emissions, waste treatment, water usage and effluent discharge is regulated including the closure, clean up, re-cultivation and insurance coverage in case of default. Besides administrative enforcement orders, criminal sanctions and voluntary environmental audits, as well as certifications are effective safeguards, claims for the compensation and restitution of environmental damages internalise external cost if a price tag is attached to natural goods and an ombudsman appointed to file the claim. To save natural resources, companies should be encouraged to use recycled material, eco-balance-assessments and to take into consideration recyclability when designing their products. Governments can subsidise companies to develop and use eco-friendly technologies, for example e-cars, renewable energies or car-sharing concepts; they can impose eco-taxes, for example to incentivise the reduction of petrol consumption or carbon emissions; they can provide for feed-in tariffs for renewable energy producers. Regarding global challenges like climate change, a worldwide emissions trading scheme and a globally applicable international agreement to curb GHG emissions, stipulating standards and mechanisms and agencies for their enforcement, would be the adequate measure. As long as this is not achievable the optimisation of technologies to reduce emissions at the source, of regional emissions trading schemes and of energy saving programmes and the consequent increase of renewable energy production are instruments to reduce environmental impacts. This can be achieved via a mixture of regulation, financial incentives, education and corporate sustainability strategies. The EU Strategy 2011-2014 for Corporate Social Responsibility[13] follows such an approach. Companies may also be called upon to assist in the development of strategies for the negative impacts of climate change. Regarding nuclear energy, inter-generational justice may be only achievable with regard to the disastrous consequences of accidents and the still unresolved waste disposal issues

---

[13] COM (2011) 681 final.

when, as Germany has done and Japan is discussing, this technology is abandoned. A smart mix of regulation and enforcement, financial incentives, education, and corporate sustainability strategies on international, regional and state levels can form a coherent justice strategy.

5.   Sources and Further Reading

Ulrich Beyerlin, Thilo Marauhn, *International Environmental Law*, Hart, Oxford, 2011.

Christian Calliess, *Rechtsstaat und Umweltstaat*, Mohr Siebeck, Tübingen, 2001.

Udo di Fabio, *Wachsende Wirtschaft und steuernder Staat*, Berlin University Press, Berlin, 2010.

Ronald Dworkin, *Was ist Gleichheit?*, Suhrkamp, Berlin 2011.

Felix Ekardt (ed.), *Generationengerechtigkeit und Zukunftsfähigkeit. Philosophische, juristische, ökonomische. politologische und theologische Neuansätze*, LIT, Hamburg/Münster, 2006.

Felix Ekardt, *Theorie der Nachhaltigkeit*, Nomos, Baden-Baden, 2011.

Andreas Fischer-Lescano, Gunther Teubner, *Regime-kollisionen. Zur Fragmentierung des globalen Rechts*, Suhrkamp, Berlin, 2006.

Anthony Giddens, *The Politics of Climate Change*, Polity Press, Cambridge, 2009.

Hans Jonas, *Das Prinzip Verantwortung*, Suhrkamp, Berlin, 1979.

Michael Kloepfer, *Umweltgerechtigkeit. Environmental Justice in der deutschen Rechtsordnung*, Duncker and Humblot, Berlin, 2006.

Joachim Radkau, *Die Ära der Ökologie*, C.H. Beck, München, 2011.

John Rawls, *A Theory of Justice*, Oxford University Press, Oxford, 1999.

Amartya Sen, *The Idea of Justice*, Harvard University Press, 2010.

Birgit Spiesshofer, "Verbandsklagen im europäischen, deutschen und US-amerikanischen Umweltrecht", in *Studentische Zeitschrift für Rechtswissenschaft Heidelberg*, 2009, vol. 3, pp. 415–435.

Nicholas Stern, *The Economics of Climate Change. The Stern Review*, Cambridge University Press, Cambridge, 2009.

Rory Sullivan, *Corporate Responses to Climate Change*, Greenleaf, Washington, 2008.

UNEP, *Towards a Green Economy. Pathways to Sustainable Development and Poverty Eradication*, UNEP, 2011.

United Nations Framework Convention on Climate Change, available at http://unfccc.int/key_documents/the_convention/items/2853.php, last accessed on 1 October 2012.

Harald Welzer, *Klimakriege. Wofür im 21. Jahrhundert getötet wird*, Fischer Taschenbuch, Frankfurt a.M., 2008.

Harald Welzer, Hans-Georg Soeffner, Dana Giesecke, *Klimakulturen. Soziale Wirklichkeiten im Klimawandel*, campus, Frankfurt/New York, 2010.

Wissenschaftlicher Beirat der Bundesregierung Globale Umweltveränderungen, *Gesellschaftsvertrag für eine große Transformation*, 2011.

SECTION C: COUNTRIES IN TRANSITION

4.1.

Justice Sector Change Planning in East-Africa

Roelof Haveman[*]

One of the consequences of the international development aid framework is that developing countries have to formulate their policy with regard to the main determining issues, including the most important needs and priorities, as well as the goals to achieve within a given number of years to come. A common instrument to formulate this policy is the Strategic Plan. A strategic plan not only binds the sector or institute that formulates the plan, but also the development partners. In this think piece, three of the main potholes in the road towards implementation of strategic plans are discussed: the capacity of development workers; the agenda's and priorities of international development partners; and the lack of capacity in the developing country. The conclusion is that the implementation of change is an art, and requires well qualified development workers in order to reach the professional standards that may be expected.

1. Introduction

Strategic plans flourish in sub-Sahara Africa. The justice sector as a whole, Ministries of Justice, judiciaries, prison services, law schools, judicial training institutes, you name it and it has a strategic plan. Some are followed by action plans. Some again are followed by real action. Development cooperation seems to be an important motor behind these plans. Development partners often demand a clear strategy, written down in a document, and validated by the owner, before contributing to the development of the sector or institute. Development partners want to be convinced of the necessity of spending money in the sector, and are in dire need of tangible results in order to justify their aid.

Considering the number and variety of projects in the justice sector that are financed by international development partners, it is important to

---

[*] **Roelof Haveman** works as a Rule of Law consultant in Africa: Rwanda, Uganda, Côte d'Ivoire and South Sudan, supporting judiciaries and ministries of justice in capacity-building, strategic planning and institutional development.

underscore the framework in which international development aid is donated to developing countries: the Paris Declaration on Aid Effectiveness (2005) and the Accra Agenda for Action (2008).

Beyond its principles on effective aid, the Paris Declaration lays out a practical, action-oriented roadmap to improve the quality of aid and its impact on development. It puts in place a series of specific implementation measures and establishes a monitoring system to assess progress and to ensure that donors and recipients hold each other accountable for their commitments. Five principles are fundamental for making aid more effective:

- Ownership: Developing countries set their own strategies for poverty reduction, improve their institutions and tackle corruption.
- Alignment: Donor countries align behind these objectives and use local systems.
- Harmonisation: Donor countries coordinate, simplify procedures and share information to avoid duplication.
- Results: Developing countries and donors shift focus to development results and results get measured.
- Mutual accountability: Donors and partners are accountable for development results.

The Accra Agenda for Action was designed to strengthen and deepen the implementation of the Paris Declaration, setting the agenda for accelerated advancement towards the Paris targets. It proposes the following three main areas for improvement:

- Ownership: Countries have more say over their development processes through wider participation in development policy formulation, stronger leadership on aid co-ordination and more use of country systems for aid delivery.
- Inclusive partnerships: All partners – including donors, foundations and civil society –participate fully.
- Delivering results: Aid is focused on real and measurable impact on development.

One of the consequences of this international development aid framework is that developing countries have to formulate their policy with regard to the main determining issues, including the most important needs and priorities, as well as the goals to achieve within a given number of years to come. A common instrument to formulate this policy is the Strategic Plan.

For the international development partners one of the main consequences is that the needs and priorities as laid down in a strategic plan bind them in the expenditure of their funds. In principle the interventions of development partners should be in line with the choices made by the developing partner in the strategic plan. This clearly shows that strategic plans do not only bind the sector or institute for whom it has been drafted, but also development partners.

The theory is perfect. Reality is different. In this think piece, I will write about the reasons for this difference between theory and practice, illustrated by some examples of my experience in development cooperation in East-Africa: at the supply side in South Sudan, where we supported the ministry of justice and the judiciary, and at the receiving end of the table in Rwanda, where I worked as the vice rector academic affairs of the newly established post-graduate training institute for the justice sector.

2. Strategic Planning

A strategy is the overall process of having a clear understanding of the road towards a desired state of affairs. A strategic plan ideally has the following structure:

- Description of the current state of affairs:
  - A historical description.
  - A description of the external context in which the institute is operating, for example partner institutions, governmental policies, regional developments, global interventions (for example EDPRS). This contextual analysis gives the external preconditions for the well-functioning of the institute or sector.
  - The internal framework, such as management and organisation, infrastructure.
  - Existing financial framework, source of financing the institute.
  - The vision and mission of the sector or institute, as well as the values.
- Expected opportunities and challenges:
  - A SWOT-analysis: strengths, weaknesses, opportunities and threats. If possible on four levels: i) the framework of policies, laws and regulations; ii) the demand side, or: those institutions

that will ask services; iii) possible collaboration and competition, and iv) supply of inputs, for instance providers of electricity, catering, staff and infrastructure, as well as the relevant development partners. Resulting in the identification of challenges.

- Description of the desired state of affairs: where to go, considering the current state of affairs and challenges:
  o The strategic choices, in terms of goals or objectives, for the duration of the strategic plan.
  o The overall strategic objective: where should the institute be at the end of the duration of the strategic plan?
  o Specific objectives, determining more in detail – hence measurable – how to achieve the overall objective.
- The activities and infrastructure (physical and human) necessary to get from the current state to the desired state:
  o The expected results for each objective, together guaranteeing the achievement of the objectives.
  o An estimation of the financial consequences of the strategic choices.
  o General management, human resource management, financial resource management, infrastructure (buildings), ICT and library policy, necessary to achieve the objectives.
  o An analysis of the risks endangering the implementation of the strategic plan.
- The way to assess whether the desired state has been reached: Monitoring & Evaluation:
  o Instruments that inform managers on progress and allow them to take decisions and measures that aim at relevance, effectiveness, efficiency and sustainability, in order to achieve the overall strategic objective of the institute.
  o Systems within the institute, such as board meetings, management meetings, staff meetings, staff performance contracts, national or regional performance assessment commission.

A strategic plan defines the ambitions of the institute for the period of the plan as smart as possible, that is: specific, measurable, attainable, realistic, and time-based. This means that a strategic plan tries to be realistic, both in terms of what to achieve and with regard to the financial, human and infrastructural constraints. A strategic plan may be ambitious but not over-ambitious. A strategic plan prioritises and sequences the activities of the institute.

A well-defined strategy ensures that the institute remains focused on the issues that really matter – not distracted by everyday issues for the short term – and is able to allocate resources accordingly. This is particularly important for an institute that can be assured of never lasting attention from the side of international development partners who often have their own agendas that do not always concur with the agenda of the institute.

A strategic plan, containing in broad lines the strategic objectives, should be further detailed in an action plan, detailing the actions necessary to achieve the results, the person(s) responsible for the action, the timeline and the budget.

Reality does not always abide by these official rules. Not every strategic plan is a serious attempt to write down objectives and priorities for the near future. Some strategic plans are quickly stashed away in a deep drawer, never to see daylight again. But the real challenge starts with the implementation of the plan. A strategy means change, moving from an existing situation to a new, desired situation. Such a process has as many potholes and pitfalls as African roads. Strategic plans may be too generic to really guide the institute in its actions for the future. There may be a lack of resources or budget for the implementation. Everyday reality may take over from the strategic choices that have been made for the future. Those who have to implement the plan in practice were not included in the strategic planning process, hence do not own the strategy. There are many reasons for failure.

Below I will highlight three of what I consider to be the bigger potholes. The first one is the elephant in the middle of the living room that is often neglected while extensively discussing the mice in the kitchen: the capacity of development workers. Second is, that international development partners force their own agendas and priorities upon the beneficiary, despite the strategic plans. Lastly, lack of capacity in the developing country is not always recognised.

3. Managing Change

Strategic planning means change. No change without people who want the change. But very few people like change. A development worker responsible for the implementation of a strategic plan needs specific skills to make people change. It is my strong impression that very few development workers, myself included, know how to manage change. At best the strategic plan is implemented with a lot of *fingerspitzengefühl* and social skills. Managing change needs specific skills, two of which I consider crucial; those are leadership and seduction.

It is generally accepted that in order to bring about change, a strong change leader is important as the motor of the process. In development cooperation, however, "leadership" seems a contaminated word, in particular when linked to "strong". A strong leader is easily associated with authoritarian leaders, African dictators, who let the people work for them instead of serving the people. Good leadership then sounds more acceptable. A good leader has a vision, is an analytical thinker and goal oriented, inspires people, motivates, supports, sets the minds, creates commitment and ownership and guides. A good leader serves the people and may even be a bit autocratic. Change needs good leaders, at the top and throughout the entire institute.

A good leader knows moreover how to seduce the people s/he leads into change. During my first meeting at a law faculty where I would manage a development project, the oldest and most respected lecturer asked quite unexpectedly and snappy: "Why do we have to participate in this project? We are already too busy with our daily work". Then you realise that no one is waiting for you. That you have to continuously seduce each and every individual within the institute into change, even when the project has been designed by the institute itself, as it should be. I have the strong impression that the importance of building a close relationship with the southern partner and the time and energy that this takes is heavily underestimated. Ownership is not only something of the developing side.

This was perfectly well understood by a Dutch consultancy firm working at the Rwandan training institute where I was the vice rector of academic affairs. They were masters of seduction. By their clearly visible personal involvement in the institute and with its staff, asking the right questions at the right time, coaching where necessary, and consulting continuously, leaving the final decision with the institute – in short, because of their professionalism – they managed to get the confidence of the entire staff of the institute: creating ownership by showing ownership.

4.   Managing International Agendas

Development partners consider the Judiciary of South Sudan (JoSS) to be very difficult to work with. The reason is crucial to development cooperation, in the justice sector and beyond. The Director of Training of JoSS once formulated the contents of an MoU between JoSS and some international organisations. Four bullets, which for some of the international partners really felt like bullets:

- It is the southern organisation that determines the policy.
- It is the southern organisation that receives the funds.
- It is the southern organisation that determines which organisation may implement the prioritised activity with the funds received.
- It is the southern organisation that determines whether the money can be transferred to the implementing organisation, according to pre-determined plans.

It is this what makes the JoSS difficult to work with in the eyes of international partners, despite all beautiful principles about ownership, inclusiveness, accountability et cetera.

Already on the level of the first bullet, practice deviates from theory. In South Sudan, an international justice sector organisation developed a training programme for the judiciary and secured funding from UNDP, without ever before having discussed this with the judiciary. The JoSS, once informed, politely rejected the plan. In Rwanda, many organisations entered my office with beautiful proposals, plans that were interesting indeed but were not identified as objectives and priorities in the strategic plan of the institute. So we refused. That did not dissuade an American organisation working in a development project for the institute from telling us that they had other priorities for the institute, and that they would continue working on these other priorities. In fact this meant that they were undermining the Rwandan institute, creating sort of a second training institute, run by Americans, not Rwandans.

The second bullet – money – is an important cause of problems. The development partner does not always give a clear insight into the amount of money that is budgeted or spent on various activities. In Rwanda, we did not know whether there was 80,000 or 800,000 US$ for IT activities. The American development partner refused to tell us. In general, development partners are not eager to give an insight in the budget, if only for the simple reason that they then have to reveal the overhead of the project going to the international organisation instead of to the beneficiary.

The third bullet, the beneficiary determines who enters the institute as a consultant, advisor, or in whatever role. A truism but again, practice is different. Sometimes the best the beneficiary can get is that it has a vote in which organisation will implement a project. Individual consultants should be engaged on the basis of previously developed Terms of Reference for an activity. But too often, instead the ToR is written on the basis of the CV of a particular consultant related to the implementing organisation.

The fourth bullet, a summary of the previous three, again shows that it is the developing partner who decides. The developing partner has to agree for the full 100% with the project design and implementation. Why do we report to the EU, UNDP, INL or whatever donor organisation about the implementation of projects, and why not to the judiciary or the Ministry of Justice of the developing country? Aren't they the ones for who the work is done? Why do they not report to the donor?

The Judiciary of South Sudan is not difficult to work with. They know what the buzzwords of development cooperation really mean: *demand-driven*, *ownership* and *sustainability*. Those who are difficult to work with are the development partners who have the money and the arrogance to know better what is good for an institute than the institute itself. Development partners that insist on issues that have not been prioritised, sometimes are even not mentioned in the strategic plan which was written as a requirement for further assistance by that same development partner.

5. Managing Lack of Capacity

Lack of capacity in the developing country can be the cause of failing implementation of a strategic plan, in particular when this lack of capacity is not recognised by the development partner. Unfortunately that is quite often the case, which is strange, as lack of knowledge and skills is an important reason why development workers are in developing countries.

Sometimes the lack of knowledge and skills is striking, the writing of a simple letter for example, can be an insurmountable obstacle. I have seen consultants whom it took several days to realise the real capacity level, desperately looking for ways to bridge the gap between themselves and the persons that they worked for, and sometimes even leaving the project, considering this an impossible task. But at least these consultants recognised the capacity gap. It is worse when development workers fail to recognise the lack of capacity with those who are expected to make the change in the developing country.

The right response to this lacking capacity should be that that is what we are here for, we will have to support the institute in dealing with this challenge. However, more often than not, one can hear development partners complain about the lack of capacity, and blaming the southern institute for not performing as expected or for even being unwilling to cooperate.

This was an issue when I was the vice rector academic at the training institute for the justice sector in Rwanda. The vast majority of the staff had no working experience when appointed in 2007; most of them came fresh from school and university. This implies that when we started, every step to take was new for everyone. There were no manuals or standard procedures for the organisation of training. Computer skills were extremely low – no one at the institute could do the lay-out of a document; the financial director worked with Excel but did the calculations with his desk calculator. The lecturers had neither the skills nor the knowledge to teach. Administrative assistants had to learn how to write a letter. The number of staff members that spoke acceptable English were very few. Added to this lack of capacity in terms of knowledge and skills is a lack of capacity in terms of time – daily work continues, apart from the implementation of the development project – despite the extraordinary motivation of the staff to work 24/7 for the establishment of the institute.

The lack of active involvement of the institute as a result of these capacity constraints was for some international organisations reason to accuse the institute of unwillingness to work with them, and threatening to no longer collaborate with the institute. Some decided to take over the work of the institute, hence creating sort of a parallel institute, instead of supporting the institute in improving its knowledge and skills. International NGOs for example tried to force through their own training programmes without involvement of the institute, only very slowly and reluctantly accepting that the Rwandan institute had to develop as quickly as possible into *the* training institute for the Rwandan justice sector. The American organisation previously mentioned, meant to strengthen the capacity of the institute, instead managed within six months to generate doubt about the value of the institute among Rwandan justice sector partners. Partners in the justice sector were approached and asked for support against the institute. All faults and failures of the institute were publicly denounced instead of supporting the institute in building its capacity. Activities through which the institute could have strengthened its role in the justice sector were hijacked by the American project. With loads of money and – of course American – experts, they could easily win this competition with the Rwandan institute. Far from demand-driven, not sustainable, and even counter-productive.

6. Conclusion

Managing change is not an easy task. Maybe the easiest part is the writing of a Strategic Plan, which serves as the paper basis for desired change in a sector or institute. Implementation of the plan is much more difficult and requires specific skills on the side of the implementer. The required skills of development workers implementing strategic plans, hence promoting change, has to be thoroughly thought through. One cannot blame the developing partner for not having the capacity to implement strategies. After all, that is the *raison d'être* of development cooperation. However, one can blame development partners for not recognising this, and taking over the work of the institute in the developing country instead of supporting the institute in strengthening its capacity. A development partner that prefers to do the work itself and compete with instead of support the institute in the developing country is more working on its own capacity-building and sustainability than that of the developing institute. Further, the least one may expect of an implementing organisation or individual is that it does not deviate from the objectives and priorities of the strategic plan according to its own agenda, unless expressly authorised by the institute who's strategy is implemented. Last but not least, the importance of leadership and seduction is, in my opinion, heavily underestimated. Change management in developing countries is an art. The profession of a development worker is a free one though, without any qualifications with regard to knowledge and skills to enter the profession. The danger of this is that development cooperation does not reach the professional standards that may be expected. Developing countries deserve better.

4.2.

From the Bottom to the Top:
Supporting Local Defenders the IBJ Way

Karen I. Tse[*]

Over the past decade, extraordinary efforts have been made to develop legal rights around the world, an acknowledgment of their importance as a linchpin for economic growth and a stable society. However the emphasis tends to be only from the top down: improving the police, prosecutorial, and judicial authorities. Far fewer resources go where they are needed most: at the sharp end of the judicial system – the defense. This essay examines the problems, some of the recent progress and shortcomings, and describes a radical new justice strategy to foster legal rights. The method, pioneered by International Bridges to Justice, works from both the top down and the bottom up: partnering with governments and the local defender community to build the capacity and infrastructure for legal aid and defense to save people who are victims of embryonic or failed criminal justice systems.

1. The Invisible Victims

In 2003 in Moratuwa, Sri Lanka, policemen surrounded a thirty-six year-old woman named U.A. Somawathi and decided to "search" her. We shall say search, since that is the term used in the police report. They claimed to uncover five packets of heroin on the mother-of-three, and locked her up. Ms. Somawathi was held in Colombo's notorious Welikada Prison awaiting trail – and waited nine gruesome years. It took that long just for her to see a judge and plead not guilty. Moreover, Ms. Somawathi's story is one of the less ugly ones: she wasn't tortured, or raped or abused, which happens far more frequently than people want to admit. However, around the world every day, others like her – victims of broken judicial systems – usually face all this and more.

---

[*] **Karen I. Tse** is an international human rights lawyer and founder of International Bridges to Justice, a non-profit organisation which aims to eradicate torture in the 21st century and protect due process rights for accused people throughout the world.

Some four billion people "do not live under the shelter of the law," in the words of a United Nations-sponsored report of the Commission on Legal Empowerment of the Poor in 2008. In India two-thirds of all prisoners, or a quarter of a million people, are merely waiting for their day in court. Four people die from abuse in custody there every day. In Burundi, there were almost two thousand cases of prison torture recorded from 2002 to 2006 but only ninety qualified lawyers. In rural areas of Cambodia only one in five defendants receives legal representation. In China, which has made extraordinary progress building its legal system, defenders represent just four per cent of all lawyers.

Compounding these challenges is that the courageous defenders, working to help the accused, at times become the victims of what they are fighting against. They go to court and say their client was tortured. At the end of the trial, they are ordered handcuffed, brought to jail, and tortured themselves.

The good news is that the vast majority of countries have signed international conventions and passed domestic laws to safeguard citizen legal rights. The problem is that the letter of the law has not been upheld on the ground. Of the more than 100 countries that practice torture, the overwhelming majority prohibits it. Moreover, although political prisoners understandably captivate public attention, the reality is that almost all cases of brutal imprisonment and torture are not high-profile detainees but ordinary people.

I saw this first hand visiting Cambodia in the 1990's, as part of a United Nations mission. I visited a prison where I met a twelve-year-old boy who had spent years behind bars for attempting to steal a bicycle, whose scars from beatings were visible, and who had never been to court or even seen a lawyer. I witnessed something similar in Burundi, where I met a young mother in jail who had spent the previous two years in pretrial detention for stealing two diapers. When I begged the warden to get her in front of a judge, he agreed – but sadly explained that three-quarters of his two thousand eight hundred inmates were pre-trial detainees. What about them? The entire system needed help, not just this one woman.

After supporting a network of public defenders in forty countries on four continents, International Bridges to Justice (IBJ) has found that the sooner accused individuals have access to counsel, the more likely their rights will be respected. That means that they will be charged with a crime rather than be forgotten about in detention. They will be less likely to be mistreated or tortured for a forced confession. This is because in many developing countries, torture is merely a cheap form of investigation, freeing police and prosecutors from having to build a case based on evidence.

Sadly, the aid from much-needed assistance programmes to improve judicial systems is often severely unbalanced, aimed at the police and prosecutors rather than the defender community, the very part of the system closest to the victims of poorly functioning systems – and the part most able to respond, but most under-funded.

At International Bridges to Justice, we have experimented with a radical new justice strategy to foster legal rights. It works from both the bottom up and the top down. IBJ partners with the governments and institutions that do not have a strong record of upholding legal rights rather than acts as agitators against them. We also reach deep into the local defender community to give them the critical support they need. This combination of top-down "air cover" from national governments and official institutions, as well as bottom-up work at the grass-roots level, coupled with our role as outsiders without a vested interest, means that we can bring parties together, improve capacity and develop the infrastructure for legal aid and defence, in order to save people who are the victims of embryonic or failed public justice systems. This essay lays out the problems in criminal justice systems across the developing world and IBJ's strategy for dealing with them.

2.   Arresting Problems

Whilst assistance to improve legal systems did not exist at one time, it is now available as legal rights are being recognised as critical to the undergirding of society. However, whilst new initiatives may be welcome, funds have most often gone to police, prosecutors and judges, not to defenders. Furthermore, even on the rare occasion that aid actually does go to the defence side of the docket, it does not reach down into on-the-ground implementation, where it can do the most good because it's where the problems are greatest. For example, statistics show that pre-trial detainees constitute two-thirds of the prison population or more in countries like Bolivia, Haiti, India and Mali as well as Niger, and an astonishing ninety-seven per cent in Liberia. Moreover, many developing countries have a dearth of trained lawyers, with just one lawyer for every fifty thousand people in some countries.

The effects of this are both disastrous and widespread. In Nepal, a survey showed that between June 2008 and May 2009 nearly fifty per cent of individuals detained by the police were not taken before a court within the time limit established by law. In Nigeria, the average time spent in pre-trial detention is estimated to be almost four years. The detention facilities tend to be severely overcrowded. In Port Harcourt Prison (Nigeria), where ninety-two per cent of the detainees were awaiting trial, over two thousand detainees were held in a prison with the capacity for eight hundred, resulting in extremely poor physical and sanitary conditions. Strikingly, research shows that children whose mothers are detained have higher rates of educational failure and criminal activity. According to Martin Schönteich of the Open Society Justice Initiative, the "dependency ratio" in developing countries is around six dependents to each income earner, so the impact of pre-trial detention sometimes spreads well beyond the immediate family and can shake the entire community.

3. The IBJ Way

Dedicated to guaranteeing the legal rights of ordinary individuals throughout the world since its founding in 2000, International Bridges to Justice works to ensure every person the right to competent legal representation, the right to be protected from torture and other cruel and unusual punishment, and the right to a fair trial. IBJ's mission is global in scope, marshalling a global community of public defenders and legal rights advocates to support the work of defence attorneys in developing countries. What makes IBJ unique is its emphasis on working collaboratively with any sovereign government interested in effecting positive change in its criminal justice system.

The core of IBJ's work has consisted of in-depth programmes in six countries with challenging environments, including three scarred by genocide: Burundi, Cambodia, China, India, Rwanda, and Zimbabwe. IBJ pursues a top-down and bottom-up approach in each of these countries, working at both the national level to influence decision-makers to institute system-wide reforms, and on the local level, where IBJ fosters grassroots transformation through lawyer trainings, criminal justice roundtables, rights awareness campaigns, and representation of the indigent accused.

Believing that skilled defence attorneys, equipped with adequate training and support, are the key to unlocking the full potential of criminal justice reforms, IBJ prioritises increasing defender capacity. We provide training to new and experienced criminal defence attorneys, both increasing the number of lawyers taking criminal cases and improving each lawyer's ability to provide competent counsel.

Thus, in India in 2008, we conducted the first national defence training in partnership with the government's legal aid authority, reaching legal aid lawyers in all twenty-eight states. With the full backing of Zimbabwe's Ministry of Justice, we conducted a successful training in 2009 for 60 defence lawyers in Harare, including all the lawyers employed by the government-run Legal Aid Directorate. In Burundi, with a population of over ten million, we have trained more than half of the country's lawyers.

In addition, IBJ trains other stakeholders in the criminal justice system in best practices for safeguarding the rights of the accused. In China, we have trained over two thousand police officers in investigative techniques to reduce their reliance on coercion to compel confessions.

To promote respect among different stakeholders, IBJ also regularly convenes roundtable meetings where defence lawyers, judges, prosecutors, police, and prison officials can engage with one another and identify common ground. By providing a forum for justice sector stakeholders to communicate constructively, IBJ's roundtables foster institutional understanding of the role that defence attorneys play in a functioning criminal justice system.

IBJ's justice sector roundtables have been extraordinarily effective in resolving difficulties encountered by defence lawyers in Burundi. One example is a roundtable on excessive pre-trial detention that ended with participating magistrates promising to address this widespread problem.

A month after the roundtable, three IBJ lawyers travelled from Bujumbura, Burundi's capital, to the prison in Gitega Province. The lawyers met with the prison director, and together they scoured prison records and identified almost two hundred cases of irregular pre-trial detention. Of these, twenty-eight cases were viewed as especially egregious, requiring immediate attention. IBJ lawyers met with the accused, familiarised themselves with each detainee's circumstances, and prepared defence strategies. Gitega's prosecutor and magistrates who had attended the roundtable agreed to a special court session the next day to expedite these cases. The result was a resounding success: all twenty-eight detainees were immediately released.

IBJ also employs a variety of media platforms from posters to radio broadcasts to increase public awareness of legal rights. These rights awareness campaigns empower individuals with the knowledge they need both to assert their rights if arrested and to demand reforms of the criminal justice system. In China, IBJ has distributed nearly a million rights-awareness posters with the Ministry of Justice's logo. Additionally, through Defender Resource Centers (DRCs) in each programme country, IBJ-trained lawyers take hundreds of cases annually, increasing access to justice for the indigent accused and strengthening the country's pro bono culture. Thus, the DRCs provide a model for the implementation of a properly functioning legal aid system. In addition, they enable IBJ to complement its legal defence trainings with mentoring and one-on-one case consultations, opportunities for networking and skill sharing, and the provision of technical support for defence lawyers.

The impact of IBJ's case representation through its DRCs has been profound. In China, where most criminal defendants do not have lawyers until their trials, we have begun representing the indigent accused in the early "prosecutorial" stage of the criminal proceeding. Defendants in India who in the past would have languished – and been tortured – in pre-trial detention without access to counsel are being freed. Thus, an IBJ-appointed lawyer secured the release of a fifteen-year-old girl who had been sent to a juvenile detention facility without due process after the family she worked for accused her of stealing gold. IBJ-appointed lawyers secured the release of a man accused of stealing electrical wires after police inserted acid into his rectum to secure a confession.

Last year, a devoted team of thirty-five volunteer IBJ-trained lawyers provided representation to more than three hundred indigent accused in Rwanda. In Burundi, it is now standard practice for lawyers to move to nullify the tainted proceedings when torture is alleged. IBJ attorneys in Zimbabwe have persuaded several Harare judges to waive bail for many of the poor criminal defendants they represent.

Cambodia perhaps best exemplifies how far we have come in such a short period of time. As the only NGO there focused exclusively on criminal legal aid work, IBJ now represents indigent defendants in eighteen out of Cambodia's provinces. Indeed, we have provided representation to nearly two thousand indigent accused since 2008. In three provinces where IBJ has DRCs – Takeo, Pre Veng, and Pursat – investigative torture has nearly been eliminated.

We have implemented other pioneering initiatives, most notably our Justice Makers programme, in which IBJ selects enthusiastic defender activists throughout the world pursuant to online competitions and provides them with five thousand dollars in seed grants and a support network to enable them to implement innovative criminal justice reform projects in their communities, including defender trainings, justice sector roundtables, rights awareness campaigns, and representation of the accused. To date, we have completed three online competitions and funded thirty-three criminal justice reform projects in twenty-five countries from Colombia to Indonesia, including the project of Sri Lankan JusticeMakers Fellow Harshi Perera, which led to U.A. Somawathi's release.

As important, our JusticeMakers programme also functions as an online network that now connects more than six thousand lawyers and human rights defenders worldwide. The goal of this network is to enable these defenders to discuss the hardships and challenges they face in their work, to provide support for each other, and to create a sense of empowerment for defenders facing similar hardships and challenges. IBJ's vision is that this network will ultimately become so powerful, that it will create a tipping point that leads to transformative, grassroots change in criminal justice systems worldwide, including the end of torture as a police investigative tool.

4. Legal Rights Trickling Up

The only way that developing countries can ensure a stable society to support an emerging middle class is to provide a solid foundation for legal rights, so that citizens have confidence in their government. This foundation must provide safety – by providing detainees with the protection of early access to counsel to ensure their due process rights and, in particular, to end torture as a police investigative tool. Until now, however, few countries have laid this foundation.

A major problem with many formal rule-of-law assistance programmes that could help countries meet this responsibility is that the aid goes to the wrong place – the police, prosecutors, and the courts. Even when it goes to the defence side of the docket, this usually occurs in a way that is centralised and high-level, not on the ground where the abuses actually are, and where the resources can be better spent. Changes have to be implemented where the abuses take place. Anything else is just the pantomime of legal rights, not its substance.

In economics there is the "trickle down" theory, which suggests that economic growth for a society's richest will eventually make its way down and improve the lives of everyone else. A similar sort of thinking is applied to legal rights – that improving the system from up high will eventually be felt down low. However, from experience I can attest that it absolutely does not happen that way. Rather, a pernicious perversion takes place: the well-meaning assistance sometimes actually strengthens the hand of those most responsible for abuses inside the judicial system. In places where the police are untouchable, prosecutors are corrupt, and courts are barely functioning, strengthening these entities without strengthening the infrastructure for the defense risks setting back progress.

The IBJ way is a legal and justice strategy that is designed to transform this process. It consists of an approach that is both top-down and bottom-up. It replaces the existing top-down approach with one that engages justice sector officials to understand the challenges faced by defenders and implement reforms – most of which can be found in laws that are already in the books – to provide the due process rights that are vital to a stable society. In addition, IBJ's strategy adds a bottom-up approach that gives defenders the capacity and citizens the awareness that are crucial to weaving the rule of law into the fabric of society. In this way, legal rights, when implanted at the grass-roots level, trickle up.

By improving the situation on the ground, we achieve a system-wide benefit. Developing the infrastructure for defendant rights – by ensuring access to counsel, limiting pre-trial detention and torture, and guaranteeing fair trials – we can promote the rule of law in other areas as well, from intellectual property protection to commercial contracts. Moreover, whereas the economic success of emerging markets is plain to see, there hasn't been a similar development for legal rights, which are critically needed to embed these economic achievements in a stable society. As a legal and justice strategy, the "IBJ Way" thus makes an important contribution by building the institutional foundation of an accessible and predictable justice system that treats all individuals in a fair, impartial, and accountable manner.

What became of Ms. Somawathi in Sri Lanka, the thirty-six-year-old mother who languished in prison after being "searched" by a group of policemen? The tragic story ends well, or at least, as well as it might under the circumstances. IBJ JusticeMakers Fellow Harshi Perera learned about Ms. Somawathi's case and was sickened. However, she also knew that there was something that could be done. For this reason she filed a petition for Ms. Somawathi's release. On 22 February 2011, Ms. Somawathi and her proud attorney walked into a courtroom, and on that very day, after nine years lost to a broken system, she walked out free. Her story proves that it can be done.

5.   Sources and Further Reading

Barbara J. Myers, Tina M. Smarsh, Kristine-Amlund-Hagen and Suzanne Kennon, "Children of Incarcerated Mothers", in *Journal of Child and Family Studies*, 1999, vol. 8, no. 1, pp. 11–25.

Chitrangi, "Sri Lankan JusticeMaker Secures Somawathi's Release", IBJ blog post, 2011, available at http://justicemakers.ibj.org/2011/03/sri-lankan-justicemaker-secures-somawathis-release, last accessed on 25 August 2012.

Commission on Legal Empowerment of the Poor, "Making the Law Work for Everyone, Volume I", Commission on Legal Empowerment of the Poor and the United Nations Development Programme, 2008, available at http://www.undp.org/content/dam/aplaws/publication/en/publications/democratic-governance/dg-publications-for-website/making-the-law-work-for-everyone---vol-i/Making_the_Law_Work_for_Everyone.pdf, last accessed on 20 August 2012.

Gary Haugen and Victor Boutros, "And Justice for All", in *Foreign Affairs*, Council of Foreign Affairs, May/June 2010, pp. 51–62, available at http://www.foreignaffairs.com/print/66348, last accessed on 25 August 2012.

International Centre for Prison Studies, Prison Brief for India, 2007

Open Society Justice Initiative, "Justice Fact Sheet: Why We Need a Global Campaign for Pretrial Justice", 2008, available at http://www.soros.org/sites/default/files/pretrialjustice_20090903.pdf, last accessed on 25 August 2012.

Karen Tse, "From Fear to Hope", in *Innovations: Technology, Governance, Globalization.*, MIT Press, 2008, pp. 109–134, available at:

http://www.mitpressjournals.org/doi/abs/10.1162/itgg.2008.3.2.109, last accessed on 25 August 2012.

Ligue Iteka, Annual Report on the Situation of Human Rights in Burundi, 2007.

Martin Schönteich, "The Scale and Consequences of Pretrial Detention around the World", in *Justice Initiatives*, Open Society Justice Initiative, Spring, 2008, pp. 11–43.

National Human Rights Commission of India, Annual Report: 2006-2007, available at http://www.asiapacificforum.net/about/annual-meetings/12th-australia-2007/downloads/reports-from-apf-members/ APF%20Report%20-%20India.pdf, last accessed on 25 August 2012.

Open Society Justice Initiative, "Pretrial Detention and Torture: Why Pretrial Detainees Face the Greatest Risk," 2011, available at http://www.soros.org/sites/default/files/pretrial-detention-and-torture-06222011.pdf, last accessed on 25 August 2012.

The Global Campaign for Pretrial Justice, "Improving Pretrial Justice: The Role of Lawyers and Paralegals", Open Society Justice Initiative, 2012, available at http://www.soros.org/sites/default/files/improving-pretrial-justice-lawyers-paralegals-20120710.pdf, last accessed on 25 August 2012.

"The Right to Fair Trial in Nepal: A Critical Study," Advocacy Forum, Kathmandu, Nepal, 2012, available at http://www.advocacyforum.org/ _downloads/fair-trial.pdf, last accessed on 25 August 2012.

For more information about International Bridges to Justice, please see http://www.ibj.org.

4.3.

Towards Comprehensive Justice Reform Strategies in the Arab Spring Countries

Adel Maged[*]

This think piece sheds some light on the Arab Spring impact on the justice sector and attempts to develop a justice strategy for the Arab Spring countries, with special focus on Egypt, Libya and Tunisia. It is founded on the belief that without legal and justice strategies we cannot deliver efficient justice. It examines the components of such strategy and suggests a number of strategic goals pertinent to the Arab Spring countries. It also attempts to identify the main actors who should envisage, design and execute such a strategy and the manner in which this should be done. The final goal of this think piece is to articulate efficient justice reform strategies for countries in transition, based on their culture and traditions, and concludes, on a predictive note, that in countries which have suffered dramatic revolutionary changes after authoritarian regimes, justice reform strategies should adopt measures, based on the rule of law, that implement transnational justice and bring about redress for victims of serious human rights violations.

> [J]udge between them by what Allah has revealed and do not follow their inclinations away from what has come to you of the truth. To each of you We prescribed a law and a method.[1]

1. The Need for Justice Strategies

For decades, the Arab people in many Arab countries suffered corruption and abuse of power by authoritarian regimes that reigned with absolute power, and prevented them from meeting their aspirations to freedom and justice and to achieve economic and democratic reform. Arab regimes' failure to provide security and justice for their own citizens is a major fac-

---

[*] **Adel Maged** is Vice President of the Egyptian Court of Cassation (Criminal Chamber), the Supreme Criminal Court of Egypt.
[1] Qura'n, Surat al-Maidah, 5:48.

tor that led to the protests and revolutions that started in 2011 and that are still ongoing.[2]

The Arab Spring illustrates how Arab people aspire to win their freedom and achieve justice and prosperity within democratic regimes governed by the rule of law. Recognising that justice is one of the most important pillars for democracy and peace, comparative experiences have proven that the functioning of justice systems has become one of the key aspects for the success of any transition process. This requires measures of a transitional justice to restore public trust in the apparatus of the state.[3] It also needs reform of justice institutions so that they could establish the rule of law and promote legal certainty. In this think piece I will focus on the judiciary as the backbone of the justice system. The establishment of an independent, fair and efficient judicial system is a critical instrument for a country breaking with its authoritarian past. However, it should be noted that the strategy envisaged in the piece is meant to address the whole justice sector and is not limited to the judiciary.

> The legitimacy of the state itself and the inviolability of its institutions derive their strength from the power of justice, which is the cornerstone of governance system.[4]

Arab people come to believe that inefficient justice administration and delay will drain even a just judgment of its value. In addition, based on my own experience, the lack of coherent and coordinated strategic action in the justice sector constitutes an impediment to achieving justice. It paralyses the court system and hinders justice institutions in their planning and prioritisation of the use of the limited resources available to them. Therefore, an important modality to assist the Arab justice sectors is

---

[2] The uprising of the Arab people in many Arab States was mainly derived by the deterioration of the economic, political, social and security conditions. Protestors called specifically for change include: an end to martial law; the abolition of emergency laws and courts; a halt to the practice of torture; the eradication of corruption; the reform of Arab countries' legislations that is incompatible with freedom of thought and expression; and the full establishment and practice of the rule of law.

[3] See Hemi Mistry, "Meeting Summary: International Law and the Middle East Programme, Chatham House", Transitional Justice and the Arab Spring, 2012, p. 3, available at http://www.europarl.europa.eu/meetdocs/2009_2014/documents/droi/dv/1_chathamhouse_/1_chathamhouse_en.pdf, last accessed on 20 August 2012.

[4] Address by H.M. King Mohammed VI on the Occasion of the Commemoration of the Revolution of the King and the People and of the Youth Day, the Royal Palace, Tetuan, Morocco, 20 August 2009.

to adopt comprehensive reform strategies, programmes and action plans to implement such strategies.

2. Reform in Post-Authoritarian Regimes Requires Comprehensive Strategies

The Arab Spring countries are witnessing a sharp conflict between the out-dated political and legal regimes and the new social relations, created by the revolutions. These new relations are based on completely different principles and values, in particular regarding the rule of law. A comprehensive national reform strategy is needed to modernise the legal system and its courts to allow them to deliver efficient and prompt justice. This applies to both criminal and civil justice.

In Egypt, for example, it has been realised that in the field of criminal justice the current legal system is unable to address the type of serious crimes committed before, during and after the 25 January revolution. In Tunisia the first focus is also on transnational justice mechanisms. In Libya the goal is both to rebuild the justice system and to achieve transnational justice objectives at the same time. To be able to design any legal or justice strategy for a certain country, it is important to examine the components of the legal system as well as the state of the courts system. This process is important in assessing the quality of what is being delivered, identifying the deficiencies, recognizing the opportunities and threats, and finally in determining the priority areas for the strategy.

A primary challenge facing the new Arab Spring emerging regimes is the lack of in-depth research and evaluation. In order to overcome this, comprehensive, well-designed strategies are needed, matched with adequate resources. The evaluations would have to cover the following areas:

- The effectiveness of the justice legal framework governing the justice sector (the laws);
- The level of autonomy of the judiciary;
- The efficiency of the court proceedings;
- The weaknesses in the justice system;
- The capabilities of the stakeholders responsible for administrating the justice sector;[5] and

---

[5] Special attention should be paid to the core values affecting the delivery of justice, such as 'integrity' and 'professionalism'.

- The degree to which the 'customers' of the justice system – the citizens – are satisfied with the justice 'products' that the state is offering.

Based on such an evaluation the justice reform strategy should outline the basic goals that a comprehensive strategy should achieve. What are the key strategic goals that could be considered?

3.   Key Strategic Goals Pertinent to the Arab Spring Countries

Justice reform strategies in post-authoritarian and totalitarian regimes are different from those in stable and democratic states. I see three areas around which strategy is most needed in the Arab nations that have revolted: (1) building the rule of law; (2) fulfilling transitional justice requirements; and (3) combating corruption.

3.1.   Building the Rule of Law

The Arabic phrase corresponding to the English term 'rule of law' is *siyadat al-qanun*, which literally means, the supremacy of law. It occurs in constitutions as well as in legal and human rights writings throughout the Arab world. *Siyadat al-qanun* can be understood from different angles according to its impact on society. The rule of law concept is not alien to the Arab culture, as lessons in the application of the rule of law abound in the *Quran* and *Sunnah,* as well as in the historical legacy of Muslim rule during the peak-times of its glory, which lasted for centuries following the onset of Islam. Generally speaking, in the Arab world the rule of law mainly refers to prevalence of justice and equality, which are crucial norms derived mainly from the Holy Qur'an and *Sunnah*, which are the primary sources of Islamic *Shari'a.*

Box 1:   Rule of law in Arab culture.

There is a growing focus on the rule of law in post-conflict and post-authoritarian countries. However, there is little guidance on how to approach it, or how the adopted strategy should differ from that in non-conflict countries.[6]

Arab people have realised that the rule of law is a necessary foundation to achieve their demands as it paves the way for establishing social

---

[6]   Aika van der Kleij, "Legal and Judicial Reform in Post-Conflict Situations and the Role of the International Community", CILC Seminar Report, the Hague, 2006, p. 3, available at http://www.cilc.nl/Post_Conflict_Situations.pdf, last accessed on 20 August 2012.

equality, combating corruption and supports economic development and an open market economy. Unfortunately, however, the essence, and measures of the rule of law are still too ambiguous, despite the fact that Islamic *Shari'a* had introduced the essence of the rule of law and successfully put it into practice more than 1,400 years ago. However, in comparison to the Western modern civilization, it is submitted that consolidated systems of the rule of law have not yet been developed by current regimes in many Arab countries. And this, according to my own view, as mentioned above, was one of the factors that lead to the uprising and the revolutions in the Arab states are witnessing nowadays.

Key elements of the rule of law are separation of powers, access to justice, the independence of the judiciary, respect for the legality principle, and a fair and effective legal framework composed of rules to be known in advance and effectively enforced. Such legal framework should also ensure that conflicts can be resolved fairly and efficiently by an independent and credible judiciary, and that there are procedures for changing the rules when they cease to serve the purpose for which they were intended.

In order to maximise the chances of success when building the rule of law in post-authoritarian countries, interveners should build strategies in collaboration with national actors (see below, Section 4.). Strategies should acknowledge the complexity of the rule of law, be clear about what it is that they are trying to achieve, work on building a rule of law culture, and enhance local capacity.[7]

3.2. Fulfilling Transitional Justice Requirements

A feature common to the Arab Spring countries is the egregious human rights violations and other wrong-doings committed by the former regimes during their hold on power. Unlawful detention of persons and torture were standard practices to deal with opposition and those calling for reform or willing to fight corruption. In a desperate reaction to regain control and keep their grip on power, the former Arab regimes used all illegal means regardless of the cost. There were systematic attacks on unarmed people that resulted in the killing of thousands of civilians.

---

[7] *Ibid.*, p. 4.

The role of transitional justice is to enable these societies to move from tyranny to democracy and freedom and to determine how best to address the wrongs of the past when building for the future.[8] It is about societal reconciliation and addressing the plight of victims. This could be done through judicial and non-judicial forms. It requires the enactment of special laws.[9] Such laws help in establishing the truth and ensuring the non-recurrence of the past gross violations of human rights in the Arab Spring countries.

Some Arab Spring countries, for example Libya, Tunisia and Yemen, have taken considerable steps to issue laws on transitional justice. However, serious criticism is directed to those laws as they draw on foreign examples rather than implementing the Arab and Muslims values.

A successful modality to pursue transitional justice can entail investigative or truth-seeking processes through non-judicial mechanisms, such as commissions of enquiry, truth commissions and truth and reconciliation commissions with the main purpose to investigate past rights violations. By their very nature, truth commissions are quite pliable, and can be created in almost any shape or size, and to fit any number of agendas, depending on the circumstances and who holds the most influence over their design and operation. There must however be minimal standards for such a body to be considered a serious, good faith effort and respectful of those who will be affected by its work.[10] There are few examples of using truth commissions in the Arab region. The Moroccan regime appears to have taken the initiative to enact measures to address past human rights violations through initiatives such as a truth commission, and it did so before the onset of the Arab Spring. The Moroccan experience should be examined to see how successful such measure was and to what extent those measures constitute a genuine break from the past.

A key aspect of transitional justice is accountability of the perpetrators. This should be established in accordance with the rule of law. This approach is reflected in Islamic *Shari'a* through the principle 'no blood goes in vain in Islam'. Based on this, the perpetrators of such heinous acts

---

[8] See Mistry, 2012, see *supra* note 3, p. 2.

[9] By referring to special laws, I do not mean, of course, exceptional laws, such as emergency or martial laws.

[10] Priscilia Hayner, "International Guidelines for the Creation and Operation of Truth Commissions: A Preliminary Proposal", in *Law and Contemporary Problems*, 1996, vol. 59, no. 4, pp. 173–180.

against the peaceful protesters should be held liable for their wrong-doing, according to the highest international standards available. This is central in any legal and judicial strategy.

It is evident that existing national legislation in the Arab Spring countries is inadequate to prosecute such crimes. Any justice reform strategy should encourage the adoption of necessary amendments to laws to criminalise serious violations of human rights in the manner that many other countries had undertaken. It should also addresses the negative consequences of the lack of such legislation and find solutions to prosecute the perpetrators of serious human rights violations committed against the protestors. Such strategy should explore the modalities by which victims and their families could seek effective remedies and compensation through judicial proceedings. The existence of a functional independent and impartial system of justice would ensure that other institutions of government and individual leaders were held accountable for their actions.

3.3. Combating Corruption

Corruption is a serious hindrance to development, siphoning off resources meant for public services. One important implication of the Arab Spring is that it has exposed the former regimes to the public. However, no one imagined that corruption in those regimes was so prevalent, from top to bottom; characterised by powerful oligarchs who "captured the state". We have seen a handful of firms and business sectors controlled by small group of strong actors, surrounding the senior officials of the governing regime, manipulate the policy and legal environment of economy and business to advance and protect their own empires, at the expenses of the social interest, creating what is called a capture economy.[11] This collusion or marriage between government and business created patronage networks generating a form of grand corruption that is increasingly being recognised as the most pernicious and intractable problem in the political economy of reform.

It is not surprising, then, that the Arab Spring was fuelled in part by popular desire to weed out corruption. Transitional justice can also be

---

[11] See, Joel S. Hellman *et al.*, "Seize the State, Seize the Day: State Capture, Corruption and Influence in Transition", World Bank Policy Research Working Paper No. 2444, September 2000.

useful here by helping to organise accountability for corruption crimes.[12] A justice strategy in this field should be preceded by a comprehensive study of the root causes and forms of corruption and should focus on preventive measures, such as reporting mechanisms and awareness campaigns, targeting both the public and the private sectors. A common occurrence in the Arab Spring countries was the expropriation of public property, followed by sending enormous amount of assets overseas. Thus, justice strategies in the Arab Spring countries should contemplate a vision to implement efficient mechanisms to trace, seize and recover stolen assets.

4.   An Arab-Based Approach

Justice does not come from the outside, it should come from the inner values of the people and hence any type of justice reform should be developed by the Arabs themselves.

There is a consensus among practitioners in the field of rule of law and reform that use of local customary practices in promoting the rule of law and reform is crucial for developing communities. Accordingly, it is always advisable to make use of local agents of change and not to impose foreign norms and regulations on a society that does not readily accept foreign input. There can be no doubt that self-reform stemming from open, scrupulous and balanced self-criticism is the right, if not the only, alternative to efficient justice reform. Thus, justice reform strategies should be developed by Arabs to deepen the Arab-owned and Arab-led changes. There can be no doubt that self-reform stemming from open, scrupulous and balanced self-criticism is the right, if not the only, alternative to plans that have apparently been drawn up outside the Arab world for restructuring the region and for reshaping its identity.[13]

For the Arab countries, reliance on Islamic *Shari'a* principles for constructing a justice strategy is inevitable, as it constitutes the primary source of justice. Justice is one of the highest values in Islam and *Shari'a* played a great part in shaping it. It recognises the importance of the surrounding legal and justice culture in the context of the promotion of the rule of law and establishing justice. Bearing in mind that emerging regimes in countries like Egypt, Libya and Tunisia, which were able to put

---

[12]   See Mistry, 2012, see *supra* note 2, p. 3.
[13]   In the Arab Human Development Report (AHDR) 2002.

an end to longstanding authoritarian regimes, signal the rise of Islamic movements, we should expect that this will have an enormous impact on any future justice strategy that could amplify the core values of Islamic *Shari'a*. This will enable us to build reliable justice strategies that help emerging regimes in the Arab world in building their justice institutions and reforming their legal systems by employing those values.

5. How Should the Strategies be Developed and Implemented?

Any strategic framework requires combining the efforts of all agencies and institutions concerned, and the necessity for them to cooperate. The lack of such a coordinated strategy could entail the failure of efforts to improve the justice sector and to use available resources in an optimal manner. As said, such a strategy should consider the quality of the rule of law prevailing in the country and should seek to enhance it as an indispensible requirement to build efficient justice institutions.

When constructing a legal or justice strategy, it is important to consider the following policy requirements:

- apply the highest international standards in place in the field of justice reform;

- use as a guide the best national, regional and international practices in drafting and applying strategies, policies, action plans and programmes for justice reform;

- draft the elements of the strategy in a flexible manner that accommodates any future initiatives to execute the strategy;

- ensure that the elements of the strategy and related initiatives, plans, and programmes respond to the society's basic needs and aspirations and are tailored in a manner that fits the particular circumstances of the country;

- identify the obstacles and challenges in fostering legal and justice reform, and the means of overcoming them;

- specify the tasks and purview of the national agencies and institutions concerned with executing the elements of the strategy and identify the level of inclusion of civil society organisations in the preparation and implementation of the strategy;

- strengthen access to justice for all people;[14]
- enable the overall measurement of the efforts and effects of the work of the central institutions that contribute substantially to implementing the strategy and to reveal the strengths and weaknesses of such institutions;
- create budgeting and performance measurement capacities and establish a mechanism to monitor the implementation of the strategic goals and make assessments of their effectiveness and efficiency;
- assess the institutional resources available and secure the proper funding and effective use of resources to carry out the strategy;
- carry out continuous training for judges and other judicial officials to guarantee the development of a modern and professional staff specialising in judiciary management and administration;
- establish sustainable channels of coordination with law faculties to develop curricula that ensure resourceful preparation of the future leaders in the legal community and the judiciary.

Experience has shown that in countries in transition, political actors are usually interested in controlling the design of judicial institutions to accomplish their political goals. The designation of a credible justice strategy in the Arab Spring countries should avoid political interference or political influence by the government.

6. The Judiciary

There is no doubt that an independent, fair, impartial, transparent, and efficient judicial system, based on the rule of law, is crucial for building and maintaining a democratic state, ensuring the balance of powers and promoting economic and social development.[15] Turning back to building the rule of law, which I identified as a key area for strategy, I would now like to mention a few specific points that concern the judiciary. As stated above, a cornerstone for the rule of law is an independent judiciary and judicial authority, which enables the judiciary to adjudicate cases without

---

[14] To review required measures to strengthen access to justice, see, *e.g.*, Draft Strategic Plan for Ukrainian Judiciary, Working Group on Strategic Planning, presented at the International Conference of the State Judicial Administration of Ukraine on "Innovative Approaches in Court Administration", Kiev, Ukraine 10-11 September 2012.

[15] *Ibid.*

improper influence from other branches of government, private or partisan interests, and to render justice without fear that their decisions will have an impact on their career, compensation, or security. This independence should have a clear constitutional basis, honouring the principle of the division of power based on the checks and balances between the three branches, and guaranteeing the independence of the judiciary. This may require the amending of relevant legislation governing the judiciary in line with international standards and/or passing unified legislation for the judicial authority that regulates all work within the judicial bodies.

Regaining public trust in the judiciary is also important, especially in cases where the judiciary was subject to political interferences and sometimes direct attacks. In my view, the latter has occurred in Egypt after the revolution by counter-revolutionary powers with the aim to weaken the State's institutions. In some instances we have seen that the media is also part of this such as in campaigns attacking or criticising court decisions, which undermines the reputation of the judiciary in the eyes of the public. The level of trust and confidence in the justice system can be increased through collaboration with stakeholders in civil society. Therefore, it is very important to enhance public outreach and participation in the judicial process, mainly by adopting more proactive communications with the public and the media. It goes without saying that promoting integrity within the judiciary should be a strategic goal of the justice strategy. The development of and compliance with high standards of conduct and integrity, and transparency in informing the public sets a vital basis for the fair administration of justice, and secures members of the judiciary from improper influence, and also fosters public trust and confidence.[16]

Furthermore, Adequate infrastructure and human resource development, decentralisation, an effective case management system and legal awareness are the key priorities for improving access to justice and eventually increasing confidence in the formal justice system. Innovative use of technology should also be one strategy goal of the justice strategy. Justice reform strategies should encourage the use of modern technology for court and case management, research and communication and the utilisation of information technology and automated systems in judicial and courts proceedings through development and application of uniform automation technology. Reliance on new techniques of alternative dispute

---

[16] *Ibid.*

resolution is also imperative when the justice system is suffering backlogs of cases and delay.

Lastly, capacity building is important: strengthening the professional capacities of those who are working in the justice sector should be one of the goals of any judicial reform strategy. This will require well-designed training programmes targeting governmental and non-governmental actors.

7. Who Should Develop and Implement the Strategy?

Successful reform strategies require a holistic approach in creating them and multidisciplinary teams in their execution. Such multidisciplinary approach should encompass all stakeholders including the government, the judiciary and the civil society organisations. Effective coordination is a prerequisite to ensuring the success of any strategy. Preferably, each country should establish a committee of representatives of different institutions to carry out the responsibility for the implementation of the goals and activities envisaged in the strategy in a coordinated and harmonised manner. That committee should adopt effective measures to monitor the implementation of the strategy's policies and goals and evaluate their effectiveness and efficiency. Accordingly, such a committee should appoint experts or establish a database responsible for collecting the data required to evaluate the reform process.

Lessons should be learned from previous experiences. As transitional societies may simply not have the resources, infrastructure and capacity to respond to situations of potential mass criminality, or within a post-conflict society which follows severe destruction, accordingly there is nothing to prevent emerging democracies from seeking the assistance of international actors for material and technical support. Regional organisations such as the League of Arab States could play a great role in supporting the design of such a strategy.[17]

---

[17] According to its resolutions 801-25 of 19 November 2009, 840-26 of 20 December 2010 and 881-27 of 15 February 2012, the Arab Council of Misters of Justice has established a committee of experts of the Arab States Ministries of Justice to be responsible for drafting an Arab Strategy to Develop the Judiciary and Justice System and to Exchange Experiences in this Field.

8.   Conclusion

The discussion in this piece has shown that the Arab Spring has the potential to be a source of innovation in all fields of legal modernisation and justice reform. It has also proved that an efficient justice system is only possible when there is in place a coordinate and agreed strategy and a detailed implementation plan that is supported by all stakeholders. The lack of coherent and coordinated strategic action in the justice sector constitutes an impediment to achieving justice.

This piece has also illustrated that legal and/or justice strategies should be designed, developed and implemented according to each country's particularities. Any justice strategy in the Arab Spring countries has to be driven from Arab culture and from deeply-rooted faith, as the approach of Arabs to their daily life affairs is mainly influenced by cultural and religious aspects. Thus, a justice strategy should be envisaged, designed and implemented by local actors. Imposing a top-down approach is usually not recommended. It is also important to keep the objectives of transitional justice at the forefront of attention. Such strategy should be comprehensive, covering all levels of the justice sector, and should start with a profound analysis of the weakest areas in the system. It should also encourage the existence of a framework that ensures the promotion of the rule of law. This will ultimately support the judiciary in resolving legal disputes in a timely, efficient, and fair manner and increase public trust and confidence in the justice system.

The success of any justice strategy will depend on the existence of coherent and sound constitutional tenets that guide the nation and its institutions. Therefore, justice reform strategies in post-authoritarian regimes are best developed and adopted after the promulgation of a new constitution. The constitution must guarantee judicial independence. Finally, to ensure its success, a justice strategy should be supported by a monitoring and evaluation mechanism to ensure transparency and fairness of the functioning of the system. Conspicuously, the real test for gauging the success of such a strategy lies not so much in its blueprint, but rather in the ability to implement it. This requires the full mobilisation not only of the members of the legal profession, but of all state institutions, the civil society and indeed of all citizens.

9. Sources and Further Reading

Aika van der Kleij, "Legal and Judicial Reform in Post-Conflict Situations and the Role of the International Community", CILC Seminar Report, the Hague, 2006, p. 3, available at http://www.cilc.nl/Post_Conflict_Situations.pdf, last accessed on 20 August 2012.

Arab Council of Misters of Justice, Resolutions 801-25 of 19 November 2009, 840-26 of 20 December 2010 and 881-27 of 15 February 2012.

Arab Human Development Report 2002.

Hemi Mistry, "Meeting Summary: International Law and the Middle East Programme, Chatham House", Transitional Justice and the Arab Spring, 2012, p. 3, available at http://www.europarl.europa.eu/meetdocs/2009_2014/documents/droi/dv/1_chathamhouse_/1_chathamhouse_en.pdf, last accessed on 20 August 2012.

H.M. King Mohammed VI, Address on the Occasion of the Commemoration of the Revolution of the King and the People and of the Youth Day, the Royal Palace, Tetuan, Morocco, 20 August 2009.

Joel S. Hellman *et al.*, "Seize the State, Seize the Day: State Capture, Corruption and Influence in Transition", World Bank Policy Research Working Paper No. 2444, September 2000.

Priscilia Hayner, "International Guidelines for the Creation and Operation of Truth Commissions: A Preliminary Proposal", in *Law and Contemporary Problems*, 1996, vol. 59, no. 4.

Qura'n, Surat al-Maidah.

4.4.

Legal and Justice Strategies in the Arab World

Wassim Harb[*]

The Arab region has not witnessed pioneering experiences in strategic planning aimed at drawing up policies in the legal and justice
fields. This notwithstanding, there have been a few attempts in this
direction which have been partially successful. Such process may
be a result of several factors. Most probably, strategising in both
the legal and the judicial fields is considered to be a challenging
task, while at the same time requiring different inputs and following various processes. Developing strategies in the legal field differs significantly from developing strategies in the judiciary. The
former is viewed as being a stimulating task, requiring a comprehensive and holistic vision of development; it is mostly addressed
in governments' statements and sometimes in political parties'
agendas. On the other hand, strategies for the judiciary may be implemented at macro and micro levels, since the judiciary may be
seen as an entity encompassing several sub-entities, each with its
own mission, vision, objectives and results.

1. Introduction

This paper addresses the topic of strategising in the legal and justice
fields. It intends to cover the topic in general with a specific focus on the
Arab region, especially in the context of the Arab Spring and of the current waves of change that the region is witnessing.

'Strategic planning', also known as 'strategising', means planning
in every field, which entails the process of defining a strategy, or direction, and making decisions on allocating resources to pursue that strategy.
To do that it is necessary to understand the current position of the entity in
question and the possible path that may be followed in order to pursue a
particular course of action. Such processes also apply to planning and
strategising in the legal and judicial fields.

---

[*] **Wassim Harb** is Attorney-at-Law, and the founder and general supervisor of the Arab Center for the Rule of Law and Integrity (ACRLI).

Today's citizens call for a government that is able to respond to dynamic changes and socioeconomic challenges marking contemporary society, as illustrated by the recent – and still ongoing – Arab Spring movement. When governments fail to meet socioeconomic changes, laws become obsolete and the system becomes ineffective overall, leading to general discontent and mistrust amongst the public. Furthermore, when justice systems lack strategic planning and updating, accountability, efficiency and fairness do not have a chance to be monitored. To prevent (such) a similar situation in the legal and justice sectors, and in order to promote the rule of law, governments should engage in legal and justice strategic planning.

For the sake of clarity, the term 'legal' used in this paper refers to the legal system which is the structure that forms, implements and makes available a set of laws (legislative decrees, international agreements and treaties, regulatory texts, administrative decisions, circulars, administrative memoranda, *et cetera*). These, in turn, regulate the rights and obligations within a society. Thus it includes the *legal corpus* as well as the *legislative process*. Ideally, a legal system should be based on a fundamental belief in the rule of law, justice and the independence of the judiciary. As for the term 'judiciary', this is used in the paper to refer to the authorities/bodies entitled to serve the rule of law by interpreting and applying the laws created and implemented through the legal system to manage conflicts and enforce justice in society. Decisions of the justice system have the value of law and have the power and mandate to be enforced and respected.

This paper addresses the issue of Legal and Justice Strategies and is hence divided into two main parts: (a) Parameters of Legal Strategies and (b) Justice Strategies Platforms.

2. Parameters of Legal Strategies

Current laws and procedures need to be re-evaluated to fit citizens' needs and aspirations, in tune with the political, socioeconomic changes that nations undergo. In the context of the Arab world, legal corpuses are generally old, without comprehensive and appropriate updates. The legal environments thus remain inconsistent and unattractive to foreign investment.

In this light, and as defined in the introduction, planning in the legal field should be a priority. However, legal planning is not very common in the Arab region. In fact, legal strategies are rare and, whenever present, they are mainly embodied in governmental policies – namely in governmental statements. Such statements announce the legislative directives that will be applied and adopted during the sitting parliamentary or governmental term. Though this kind of planning is an enunciation of policies which normally do not follow the standard mechanisms of strategic planning processes, it nonetheless may be considered to be the sole source of strategising in the legal field.

Consequently, and for the sake of 'theoretical speculation', the paper elaborates on two areas where legal strategies can be applied: (1) the methodologies for drafting laws and regulations, and (2) the efforts to be made in accessing legal information easily and effectively.

2.1. Methodologies for Drafting Legislation and Regulations

In terms of strategy, a focus on methodologies for drafting laws and regulations allows for legal stability, as well as for the public cognizance of the law. When dealing with methodologies for drafting laws and regulations, the aim should be to provide the public with precise laws and regulations. Also, and importantly, a goal should be to standardise the process, leading to consistent laws and regulations of a given country. Provisions of the law or regulations should be limited to supervising objective circumstances. They should contain a clear and accurate statement of obligations, rights and duties. In addition to being clear and objective, the law or regulation should be consistent with the nation's constitution and with the fundamental principles recognised by the international community. In the event of a lack of strategising and planning with regard to the law, and if the law or regulation fails to meet these objectives, legal order and the authority of the legislators are undermined.

As mentioned, strategising and preparing methodologies for drafting laws and regulations not only facilitate consistency and uniformity in a nation's legislation; they also guide all those involved in the process of considering, drafting, and adopting the legislation. It is important to remember that legislators are not the only individuals who take part in the legislative process. These mainly include law drafters, civil servants who are responsible for the technical conception of the legal texts, as well as other state officials responsible for legislative planning and policy. Hence, strategising methodologies for drafting laws and regulations need to take all the individuals themselves into account; in addition they need to consider strategising methodologies as related to each actor for legislative consistency.

Strategising methodologies of drafting laws and regulations are not merely a matter of selecting appropriate uniform words or sentences. Creating such methodologies requires further efforts, in that legislative drafting usually addresses and regulates new circumstances and issues. Consequently, a new all-encompassing mind-set is required strategically to create successful reforms. Drafting technique and legislative procedure undoubtedly evolve, effecting, in turn, the way in which the legislation itself is drafted. There is no consensus on a common, generally accepted language, and this may change in time. Changes may also occur in matters such as the structure and competence of the public institutions or the way in which functions are implemented.

The above-mentioned are some difficulties that may arise when drafting laws. For such reasons, strategising methodologies constitute a difficult and at the same time stimulating task, with many advantages.

Methodologies and processes for policy/strategy development can be summarised in the following set of actions:

2.1.1. Legal Research

Legal research is the process of identifying and retrieving information necessary to support legal decision-making. Legal research generally involves tasks such as finding primary sources of law, searching secondary authority and non-legal sources. It also involves court judgments and academic papers. Although legal research is the first step, research needs to be conducted throughout the process of legal decision-making.

2.1.2. Compliance with International Treaties

Another element that should be taken into account is international treaties and agreements. Most countries are members of international agreements that regulate their actions, and hence newly drafted national laws should be in compliance with these international treaties and agreements.

2.1.3. Economic and Social Analysis

Countries differ. Reforms and transformations in a given country do not necessarily correspond to the same outcomes in other given countries. A given country has its own economic and social features and is influenced by the socioeconomic/security environment of its neighbouring countries. Therefore it is very important to analyse the economic and social environment and the potential impact of the law on both aspects.

2.1.4. Needs Assessment

Needs assessment is a systematic process for determining and addressing needs that may range between current and desired conditions. One good strategy for needs assessment consists of a public survey, where data are grounded on public opinion and perception.

2.1.5. Forecast of implementation

After the required research has been done, the forecast of implementation takes place. It involves predicting the implementation of law in terms of feasibility, practicality and acceptance.

2.1.6. Formulation of Legal Texts

After the above-mentioned steps have been taken, the very formulation of the legal text takes place. At this stage, the strategy should promote a structure that leads to clear, concise and uniform legislation. This should be available to be read to the general public in order to promote widespread awareness of laws. The drafters of the legislation would also need to use uniform language, so as to eliminate confusion and promote uniform interpretations of the legislation. In order to ensure absolute uniformity in drafting legislation, many governments have a separate department or ministry appointed for the drafting of the legislative text, following the policy development. In order to improve the uniformity of interpretation amongst lawyers, scholars, judges and the general public, governments could and should consider publishing an interpretation guide to legislation.

2.2. Access to Legal Information

Today, access to information is considered a basic human right. This is so as, without information, people are not able effectively to protect and promote their own rights. Access to information is a right that aims at effectively allowing public users to gain access to large amounts of legal information and, by doing so, to promote the rule of law. Through increased access to legal information, citizens are more aware of the law and, as a result, they are more prone to respecting the rights of others. Also, such a process may give the public the ability to exercise a certain influence on law-making and law-implementing processes and institutions. Finally and importantly, access to legal information is heavily related to the notion of *ignorantia juris non excusat*. This principle means that ignorance of the law does not excuse anyone infringing it. However, in the light of the current status of the ability to access legal information in the Arab world, the applicability of this legal principle remains challenged. In fact, such principle cannot be implemented unless there is a corresponding level of access to information in the countries of the region, which is not the case in the Arab region. In fact, laws which are published in legal gazettes are not made available to everyone. Also, laws and decrees that are published in gazettes or on websites are not comprehensive; public services such as electricity, water, general security and others issue regulations that are not even published in the legal gazettes and consequently unknown to the public. It is generally estimated that only 30 per cent of what is issued by public services is made available to the public in gazettes or on websites. As stated above, even if published, gazettes and websites are not easily accessible by a vast public.

To sum up, in our opinion states should and would need to develop strategies aimed at providing legal information that may be easily accessible to the public. A successful model that can be adopted could be the one introduced by ACRLI entitled National Legal Information Network (NLIN), which is a legal e-government networking add-on solution that gathers all the – currently scattered – legal data of the various governmental bodies such as legal texts, court decisions and advisory opinions issued by public institutions into one source channelled to the central government, thus constituting an open legal online source accessible to all users.

3.   Justice Strategies Platforms

The judiciary, which is one of the three main government branches, grounds its legitimacy and the reason for its existence on public confidence. This, in turn, is induced from several factors, amongst which are the quality of judicial services, the accurate interpretation and application of laws, neutrality, objectivity and various others. Hence, the judiciary is a body that should have plans for its successful functioning in the short, medium and long term.

Before the events of the Arab Spring, the Arab world had not witnessed systematic and systemic strategising in the field of the judiciary. Instead, attempts in this regard used to be sporadic and partial. Countries such as Morocco used to be advanced in this, while countries like Syria were less progressive. However, it can be said that plans based on clear standards and scientific methods of elaborating justice – which, in turn, include needs assessment, benchmarking, consultation, *et cetera* – used to be very rare, if not totally absent. This happened especially in countries affected by authoritarian regimes, in that rulers tried to retain the judiciary under their powers and control, thus undermining its independence and hampering it from playing its supposed crucial role in establishing the rule of law in societies where justice should prevail.

Nowadays, there is a general perception across many segments of society that the judicial system is not functioning properly. Such perception is particularly widespread amongst the judicial community of the Arab countries. Hence, Arab countries are invited to engage in significant steps to ensure the effective and efficient delivery of judicial services based on the principles of independence, integrity, competence and effectiveness. They should engage in this change by using the results of benchmarking and stocktaking processes as implemented by international and regional organisations, as well as progressive and innovative ways to strategise justice and to explore rule of law solutions such as, for example, the innovating justice platform.[1]

In fact, judiciary development can be seen at a macro and micro levels. The strategising process can be implemented at both levels: (1) the macro level focuses on the reform and development of the judiciary as a whole entity, whereas (2) the micro level focuses on the reform and de-

---

[1]   See Innovating Justice, available at http://www.innovatingjustice.com, last accessed on 20 August 2012.

velopment of a specific entity or entities that form part of the judiciary, such as, for instance, the Supreme Judiciary Council, Prosecution and investigation, Courts, Judicial Inspection Authority, judges and others.

3.1. The Macro Level Approach

Macro level strategic planning addresses changes in the judicial system as a whole, with the ultimate goal of making it independent, with integrity, competent, and effective.

In addition to ensuring that the improvement in the judicial system meets general global rule of law standards, the judicial system needs to be in tune with socioeconomic changes. For instance, macro-level strategic planning should take into account changes in demographics and technology. Accordingly, a justice plan may include the addition of translators to courts or the availability of judicial information in various languages, so as to meet the demands of a changing population. Since global access to technology and the Internet is improving, strategising may also include greater access to the judicial system via the Internet or mobile devices, etc.

If thoroughly planned and implemented, justice strategies are an effective mechanism for promoting good governance and good rule of law.

3.2. The Micro Level Approach

Micro-level approach strategies deal with the development and reform of one or more entities that end up constituting the judiciary. For instance, it could tackle judicial actors in their individual capacity; it could focus on improving their efficiency, professional performance and competence to satisfy the increasing number of litigants demanding judicial services. It is an evolving process rather than a randomly obtained outcome.

It is important to note that judicial micro-level planning should be also be based on a detailed plan that takes into account the legal system and the economy. Importantly, it should comply with the macro-level strategic plan, if developed and adopted.

To explain justice strategies at the micro-level better, we shall include a case study of justice strategy development for the judicial training institute, JTI, in Iraq.

3.3. Judicial Training Institute (JTI)

In 2010, the Arab Centre for the Rule of Law and Integrity (ACRLI) launched a project on "Provision of Legal Training Components for Legal Institutions of Iraq-LTI". The overall goal of the project was to increase the professionalism and accountability of justice actors belonging to Iraq's Government. As part of the project, strategic planning for the Judicial Training Institute (JTI) was implemented, representing in this case an example of micro-level planning, in that it was subjected to the same mechanisms as any strategic plan. The strategic plan revolved around the following points:

- Selecting the background and the extent of connection pertaining to the development of the whole judicial facility;
- Selecting the axes of development;
- Defining the general objectives;
- Setting specific objectives for the development of each axis, which end up constituting each one of the general objectives;
- Monitoring or identifying the projects and activities that could possibly achieve every special objective;
- Subsequently, identifying actions and mechanisms to be adopted for the implementation of each project;
- Monitoring the standards and the indicators of the measurement of success, or partial or complete failure in achieving each special objective;
- Monitoring the standards and the general indicators that would measure either the contribution to the judicial development as a whole or possibly its lack.

Special Objectives	Axis	Actions and Mechanisms	Projects and Activities	The Objectives' Measurement Standards and Indicators
Development of judicial body	Development of judicial training curricula in the Judicial Institute to have independent, impartial, competent and efficient judges	Building the capacity and efficiency of trained judges to practice with high quality and performance in accordance with the principles and standards of sound justice. Sound justice is based on the following principles and criteria: • Autonomy • Integrity • Efficiency • Effectiveness Contributing to the achievement of general and specific goals for the development of the judicial body.	• Capacity building for the efficient drafting of judgments • Building the capacity for managing cases and trials • Building capacity for communication with third parties • Capacity building for enhancing judges personality • Building capacity for enhancing judicial knowledge in basic legal principles • Building capacity for dealing with topics related to human rights, juveniles, family law, domestic violence and violence against women • To equip the institute with a library and adequate information technology tools.	• Quality of judgments • Rate of challenged judgments • The rate of reversed judgments by means of challenge • Rate of settled lawsuits • Lawsuit time and trial duration • Confidence in the judiciary • Complaints against judges • Media coverage for judiciary-related topics • Others

Figure 1: This chart was planned as a strategy to focus on micro-level improvements.

4. Conclusion

Legal and justice strategies are both being employed throughout the world as essential mechanisms to ensure the rule of law and good governance in the light of today's dynamic and changing society. However, the legal and justice sectors are encountering various challenges due to internal and external factors which, if not given careful consideration, may in turn hamper development. Amongst critical factors that may jeopardize development, a major one is the weakness of the legal and institutional infrastructures as part of the legal and justice institutions.

The main issues encountered by Arab countries in the domain of justice may include the weakness of the legal system, weakness of public confidence in the judicial institutions and adjudication procedures, weakness of the performance of the judicial institutions, weakness of means of communication with the public, *et cetera*. Besides the presence of weak or non-existent legislation, the legal sector is furthermore affected by stagnant electoral systems, lack of public participation, and centralised power.

Specifically in the current period of dramatic developments where deep-rooted authoritarian regimes have collapsed, new powers have arisen, while at the same time replacing the predominant "father" figure. Drastic changes have recently taken place in the direction of what we hope will be a more liberal and democratic society. It is worth noticing, however, that the first metamorphosis of this change led to the rise to power of various groups with religious ideologies, especially Islamists. Islam for these groups is as much a political ideology as a religion, and this ideology might entail the elimination of non-Muslims who are believed by some to be incompatible with Islam. Yet, justice is at the core of their ideology. Thus lies the very challenge of adopting a non-discriminatory approach *vis-à-vis* any minority or 'non-Muslim' groups in all areas. Such a non-discriminatory view should be adopted specifically in the arena of the judiciary. If the contrary had to happen, it would have absolutely negative and dramatic repercussions on several levels, including, importantly, efforts towards establishing the rule of law, together with fair and pluralistic societies.

The events of the Arab Spring provide us with a thorough example of how socioeconomic changes within a country have pushed legal and justice strategy planning towards implementation. A considerable share of the media's attention revolved round the efforts to reform electoral processes effectively, attempts to repeal stringent emergency laws, and to dismantle authoritarian governments. From the point of view of judicial reform watchers, an interesting development is the prominence of judicial independence as a key area of overall democratic reforms. Unfortunately, while significant steps have taken place in some of these areas, frustration has slowly but surely grown when relating to a structural and functional shift to judicial independence.

In conclusion, it may be argued that one of the greatest challenges for the success of the Arab Spring and the overall development movements will be the careful and thorough planning and implementation of legal and justice strategies. Also, it will be extremely important to see whether new rulers will respect the slogan adopted during the uprisings by the masses, namely asking for compromises between religion and the state (also a separation between the two), where every citizen should be respected regardless of his/her religion, gender or affiliation of any sort.

5. Sources and Further Reading

Colin Wright, "Justice Sector Qualifications Strategy", Skills for Justice, available at http://www.skillsforjustice.com/websitefiles/Justice_Sector_Qualification_Strategy.pdf, last accessed on 20 August 2012.

Islamic Republic of Afghanistan, "Afghanistan National Development Strategy", National Justice Strategy, available at http://info.publicintelligence.net/AfghanNJSS.pdf, last accessed on 20 August 2012.

Lawrence P. Webster, "Roadmap for Integrated Justice: A Guide for Planning and Management", SEARCH, The National Consortium for Justice Information and Statistics, available at http://www.search.org/files/pdf/StrategicRoadmap.pdf, last accessed on 20 August 2012.

Lynn M. LoPucki and Walter O. Weyrauch, "A Theory of Legal Strategy", in *Duke Law Journal*, 2000, vol. 49, no. 6.

Maurits Barendrecht, "Legal Aid, Accessible Courts or Legal Information? Three Access to Justice Strategies Compared", Social Science Research Network, available at http://papers.ssrn.com/sol3/papers.cfm?abstract_id=1706825, last accessed on 20 August 2012.

Organization for Economic Co-Operation and Development (OECD), "Law Drafting and Regulatory Management in Central and Eastern Europe", Sigma Papers no. 18, available at http://www.oecd.org/

officialdocuments/publicdisplaydocumentpdf/?cote=OCDE/GD%2897%2 9176&docLanguage=En, last accessed on 20 August 2012.

Pacific Centre, United Nations Development Programme, "Democratic Governance", available at http://www.undppc.org.fj/pages.cfm/our-work/ democratic-governance/accountability-transparency-frameworks/freedom -of-information/, last accessed on 20 August 2012.

Project on "Provision of Legal Training Components for Legal Institu The Arab Center for the Rule of Law and Integrity (ACRLI), available at http://arabruleoflaw.org/activitiesListing .aspx?postingID=362&categoryID=1&Id=196, last accessed on 20 August 2012.

Robert C. Bird, "The Many Futures of Legal Strategy", in *American Business Law Journal*, 2010 vol. 47, no. 4, pp. 575–586.

Strategic Plan, Republic of Turkey Ministry of Justice, available at http://www.justice.gov.tr/StrategicPlan.pdf, last accessed on 20 August 2012.

The Ministry of Justice New Zealand, "Justice Sector Strategy", available at http://www.justice.govt.nz/justice-sector/strategy, last accessed on 20 August 2012.

INDEX

A

access to information, 370
accountability, 69, 73, 80, 82, 125, 136,
    141, 149, 152, 159, 183, 188–189,
    216, 219, 223, 240, 286, 332, 337,
    356, 357, 366, 373, 377
administration, 12, 15, 28, 119–120, 148–
    149, 152, 178, 207, 221, 273, 352, 359
Africa, 62, 139, 141, 155–157, 161–164,
    242, 283, 295, 304, 331, 333
approach
    bottom-up, 344, 348
Arab Spring, 62, 159, 351–357, 360, 362–
    363, 365–366, 371, 375–376
Arab uprising. *See* Arab spring
Arab world, 354, 358, 366, 370–371
assistance programmes, 220, 247, 250,
    252–253, 257–258, 343, 347

B

Behaviour Modification Interventions, 54
behavioural mechanisms, 52
bureaucrats, 25, 69

C

capacity building, 189–190, 192–193,
    219–220, 222–224, 276, 278, 361
capitalism, 241–242
cassation, 120–121, 168, 174, 351
censura morum, 35
change management, 340
chaos, 12, 22
Chernobyl, 318, 323
child soldiers, 154, 155
climate change, 274, 279, 315, 317, 320,
    323–325
co-existence, 110
Cold War, 241
common law, 45, 271, 275
Commonwealth, 271–279
communications skills, 27

comparative law, 171–172
complementarity, principle of, 159, 164,
    177, 179–180, 183–184, 188–189,
    192, 194–195, 215–216, 219, 220,
    223–225
    positive, 150, 177, 189–191, 193, 218–
    219
complexity, 12, 15–16, 21–22, 24–25,
    120, 355
compliance, 15, 17, 57, 111, 116, 140,
    368
conflict resolution, 2, 21, 29, 130
consensus building, 272
constitution
    global, 75
constitutionalism, 41
control
    democratic, 119, 125, 266
core values and principles, 278
corporate social responsibility, 77, 325
corruption, 1, 16, 39, 52, 62, 159, 242,
    250–251, 253–254, 257, 332, 351,
    354–355, 357
Council of Europe, 107, 133, 247–249,
    251–259
Council of Justice, 33
crimes against humanity, 141, 144, 158–
    159, 180, 183, 186, 204

D

democracy, 21, 28, 29, 61–62, 67, 70, 79,
    127, 130, 242, 249, 250, 253–254,
    256–258, 271–273, 277, 286, 301,
    352, 355
    representative, 28
development cooperation, 331
direct effect, 168, 261–262, 266–267
Dutch Republic, 31

E

ECHR. *See* European Court of Human
    Rights

LIST OF CONTRIBUTORS

Krijn van Beek is Director of the strategy unit of the Dutch Ministry of Security and Justice. The strategy unit is designed to assist the long term focus and mission of the Ministry in its entirety, and directly advises the heads of the department. Previously, he worked as director for several think tanks: 2100, Council for Social Development and Infodrome. He started his career at the Netherlands Scientific Council for Government Policy, which is also a think tank. Van Beek holds a Masters Degree in Mathematics and a Doctorate in Economics.

Bernard Bot is Partner at Meines & Partners, a consultancy specialising in lobbying, public affairs and strategic communication. Bot was former Minister of Foreign Affairs of the Netherlands for the period of 2003–2007. He previously held a variety of diplomatic roles, including postings at embassies in Argentina and East Berlin in the 1970s. In the 1980s he was a deputy Permanent Representative at the North Atlantic Council in Brussels. He then went on to be the Dutch ambassador to Turkey. From 1989 to 1992 Bot was secretary general of the ministry of foreign affairs. He rounded off his diplomatic career by taking the position of Permanent Representative of the Kingdom of the Netherlands at the European Union in Brussels.

John Braithwaite is Professor and Founder of the Regulatory Institutions Network, Australian National University, and former Head of the Law Program of the Research School of Social Sciences. Restorative justice and responsive regulation have been major organising ideas for his empirical and theoretical work. Since 2005, he has worked mainly on peace building after armed conflict. This is the Peace-Building Compared Project. He was the first non-American to win the Kalven Prize of the Law and Society Association and has won all of the major international prizes in the discipline of criminology. In the late 1980's, he also worked with Philip Pettit in developing republican political theory, particularly in its application to criminal law.

Alex Brenninkmeijer is National Ombudsman of the Netherlands since 2005. As Ombudsman he aims to provide a complaint handling service that is easily approachable and confidence-inspiring for members of the public. In 2011, he was re-appointed by Parliament for a second term of six years. Brenninkmeijer was Professor of Constitutional and Administrative Law at the University of Leiden and held a Chair in Labour Law and Alternative Dispute Resolution (mediation). He also has occupied various judicial posts at district court level and as Vice-President of the Court of Appeal. Brenninkmeijer is a specialist in conflict analysis and methods of conflict resolution.

Kenneth Chan is a Ph.D. candidate in the research programme "Global Governance and Democratic Government", at the Leuven Centre for Global Governance Studies. As part of his doctoral program, he is examining the evolving legal norms surrounding the use of force and state failure. In 2010, he received his LL.M (advanced) in Public International Law at the University of Leiden, where he specialised in International Criminal Law, and has a LL.B (hons) from the University of Auckland, New Zealand. He has interned at the International Criminal Tribunal for the Former Yugoslavia and at the Coalition for the International Criminal Court. His main research interests are in international criminal law, international humanitarian law, and transitional justice.

Geert Corstens received his Ph.D. degree from the University of Amsterdam. After working as a public prosecutor in Arnhem and as professor of criminal law at Radboud University Nijmegen, he was appointed as Justice at the Hoge Raad (Supreme Court of the Netherlands) in 1995. Corstens became President of the Hoge Raad in 2008. He has written several books and articles in the field of criminal law and the judicial system.

Guy De Vel has a Diploma in Philosophy and Literature from St Ignace, Antwerp, 1962 and received a Doctorate in Law from the University of Leuven, 1966. De Vel has previously worked at the Council of Europe Secretariat General, Strasbourg from 1972 to 2006 in various departments to include, The Commission of Human Rights, Private Office of the Secretary-General; Directorate of Human Rights; Directorate of Legal Affairs; Head of Plan and Programme Division; Deputy Director of Political Affairs; Director of the Secretariat of the Committee of Ministers; Director-General of Legal Affairs and Legal Adviser to the Council of Europe Development Bank. From 2006 to 2012 he was member of the Management Board and Executive Board of the Agency for Fundamental Rights of the EU in Vienna, representing the Council of Europe.

Adama Dieng is Under Secretary-General and Special Adviser of the United Nations Secretary-General on the Prevention of Genocide, and former Registrar of the International Criminal Tribunal for Rwanda. He graduated in Law from the Dakar University and holds a Certificate from the Research Centre of The Hague Academy of International Law. He has also a Certificate on Homeland Security, Internal and External Security from the Paris Institute of International High Studies. Dieng has lectured on international law and human rights at institutes and universities around the world, and acted as a consultant for many organisations, including the United Nations Educational, Scientific and Cultural Organisation, the Office of the High Commissioner for Human Rights, the Ford Foundation and the African Union. Dieng is a former member of the Board of Directors of International IDEA, Africa Leadership Forum and Honorary Chair of The World Justice Project.

Mark Ellis is Executive Director of the International Bar Association (IBA) and leads the foremost international organisation of bar associations, law firms and individual lawyers in the world. Prior to joining the IBA, he spent ten years as the first Executive Director of the Central European and Eurasian Law Initiative (CEELI), a project of the American Bar Association (ABA). Twice a Fulbright Scholar at the Economic Institute in Zagreb, Croatia, he earned his J.D. and B.S. (Economics) degrees from Florida State University and his Ph.D. in Law from King's College, London. He has published extensively in the areas of international humanitarian law, war crimes tribunals, and the development of the rule of law. Ellis is a member of the Council of Foreign Relations and serves on a number of boards, including the DLA Piper "New Perimeter" pro bono project, and the Open Society Foundation.

Håkan Friman is Deputy Director-General in the Swedish Ministry of Justice (on leave), and former head of the division for international judicial cooperation and criminal cases. He is also visiting professor at University College London, Faculty of Laws, United Kingdom, and visiting scholar at George Washington University, Washington D.C., USA. Prior to this, he has been an Associate Judge of Appeal, Svea

Court of Appeal, Sweden, and E.o. Professor at University of Pretoria, South Africa. Friman has long been involved in international and national work in the area of international criminal law, including work within the European Union. He has published extensively in this field and is co-author to a leading textbook: *An Introduction to International Criminal Law and Procedure*, Cambridge University Press, 2nd ed., 2010.

Willem van Genugten is Professor of International Law at Tilburg University and Dean of the newly established The Hague Institute for Global Justice. He studied law and philosophy and graduated with honours and *cum laude* respectively. In the past he has been Professor of Human Rights Law at Nijmegen University (1991–2006). As of now, he also is an Extraordinary Professor of International Law at the North-West University, South-Africa, and Visiting Professor at the University of Minnesota, USA. In addition, he is the Chair of the Standing Commission on Human Rights of the Dutch government, Chair of NWO-WOTRO, Science for Global Development, Chair of the Royal Netherlands Society of International Law, Editor-in-Chief of the Netherlands Yearbook of International Law, and Member of the Committee on the Rights of Indigenous Peoples of the International Law Association. Some of his publications are mentioned in his think piece, under the section "Sources and Further Reading".

Linn Hammergren is an independent consultant specialising in rule of law, anti-corruption, and general governance issues. Until 2008, she was Senior Public Sector Management Specialist in the World Bank, and before that she spent twelve years managing Administration of Justice Projects for USAID. She has a Ph.D. in Political Science (University of Wisconsin) and taught at Vanderbilt University. Her research and publications focus on judicial politics and reform, public sector and judicial corruption, citizen security, and the politics of foreign assistance. Her publications include *The Politics of Justice and Justice Reform in Latin American: Peru in Comparative Perspective*; *Envisioning Judicial Reform: Improving Court Performance in Latin America*; a series of studies for the World Bank on "users and uses of justice" in Argentina, Mexico, Brazil, and Ethiopia; and a monograph on rule of law indicators for USAID.

Wassim Harb holds a Ph.D. in Law from Aix-Marseille University, France. He has been Attorney-at-Law since 1970. He held leading positions in the Lebanese university, among which Founder and Dean of the Legal Informatics Center , served as a consultant and as a senior expert for several International Organisations, including the UNDP and the World Bank and as advisor for several Ministries in the Arab region. He is the founder and general supervisor of the Arab Center for the Rule of Law and Integrity (ACRLI). He has several publications in the areas of Rule of Law, Good Governance and Institutional Development. Harb has more than 35 years of experience in the reform field at the regional and international level.

Roelof Haveman works as a Rule of Law consultant in Africa: Rwanda, Uganda, Côte d'Ivoire and South Sudan, supporting Judiciaries and Ministries of Justice in capacity-building, strategic planning and institutional development. Since its establishment in 2008, until 2010, he was the Vice Rector Academic Affairs of the ILPD/Institute of Legal Practice and Development in Rwanda. Three years previously he supported Rwandan law faculties in strengthening their capacity, including curriculum development. Since its establishment in 2002, and until 2005, Roelof Haveman was the Programme Director of the Grotius Centre for International Legal Studies at Leiden University's Campus in The Hague. Until 2005, he was Associate Professor of (International) Criminal law and Criminal Procedure at Leiden University. His scholarship concentrates on international criminal law, customary law, supranational criminology and victimology, comparative criminal law. He is the editor in chief of the series: *Supranational Criminal Law*, Capita Selecta, Intersentia, Antwerp, and co-editor of the electronic *Newsletter Criminology and International Crimes*.

Ernst Hirsch Ballin is Professor of Dutch and European Constitutional Law at Tilburg University and Professor of Human Rights at the University of Amsterdam. He is also Member of the Royal Netherlands Academy of Arts and Sciences. Hirsch Ballin served as Minister of Justice in the years 1989–1994 and 2006–2010, and as Minister of Interior and Kingdom Relations in 2010. He received his Doctorate in 1979 for his dissertation on Public Law and Policy. He was Member of Parliament (1994–2010), and, subsequently, Member

(2000–2003) and President of the Judicial Division of the Council of State (2003–2006). His publications deal with questions of national and international public law, philosophy of law and comparative law.

Akbar Khan is the Director of the Legal and Constitutional Affairs Division and Principal Legal Adviser to the Commonwealth Secretary-General. He is responsible for managing the Division of the Commonwealth Secretariat that promotes the rule of law in support of the Commonwealth's mandate to enhance democracy, good governance and development in member countries. He is a qualified Barrister-at-Law called to the English Bar and also the New York Bar as an Attorney-at-Law. Khan completed his professional training at the London Chambers of George Newman QC, and subsequently joined the United Nations Organisation followed by the British Diplomatic Service. He graduated from the Universities of Cambridge, Reading and the Rene Cassin Institute of International Human Rights, Strasbourg, and specialised at post-graduate level in Public International law and International Human Rights law. He is a Colombos Public International Law Prize Winner of Middle Temple Inn of Court and in 2011.

Reindert Kuiper is the Law Clerk (gerechtsauditeur) to the President of the Supreme Court of the the Netherlands, and to the President of the Network of the Presidents of the Supreme Judicial Courts of the European Union. He was a law clerk in the Court of Appeals in Amsterdam and in the criminal section of the Supreme Court of the Netherlands assisting several justices and advocates-general. He was also the Deputy-Secretary of the Hammerstein Committee. Kuiper wrote a comparative analysis on the subject of how procedural failures are dealt with in United States criminal procedure, which was published in the research memoranda series by the Dutch Council for the Judiciary.

Lousewies van der Laan has an LL.M. from Leiden University Law School and a degree in International Economic Relations from the Johns Hopkins University School for Advanced International Studies in Bologna. She was an elected member of both the European Parliament and the Dutch Parliament, where she also became party leader. She has worked at both the European Commission and the European Bank for Reconstruction and Development and until 2011 served as Chief of Staff to the President of the International Criminal Court. Van der Laan is currently Vice-President of the European Liberal Democrats and independent advisor on human rights, democracy and the rule of law.

Frans Leeuw is Professor of Law in Public Policy and Social Science Research at the University of Maastricht. He is also the Director of WODC, the Research, Evaluation, Statistics and Knowledge Management Institute of the Dutch Ministry of Security and Justice. Leeuw was previously Professor of Evaluation Studies at Utrecht University, the Netherlands, from 1992–2006, and worked as Chief Inspector at the Inspectorate for Education, the Netherlands, from 2000–2003.

Adel Maged is Vice-President at the Egyptian Court of Cassation (Criminal Chamber), the Supreme Criminal Court of Egypt. He was previously Judge at the Egyptian Court of Appeals and was also seconded to the Ministry of Justice of the United Arab Emirates as Legal Advisor on International (Criminal) Law and Treaty Affairs. He is also Visiting Scholar at the Department of Criminal Law, Rijksuniversiteit Groningen, the Netherlands and the Expert Advisor on Human Trafficking to the League of Arab States. His publications include articles on international criminal law in the Arab world, the ICC, international legal cooperation in criminal matters, terrorism and the rule of law. Maged is a member of the Editorial Board of the International Criminal Law Review, the World Justice Project MENA Group on the Rule of Law and the Hague Rule of Law Network and a Leader in the Innovative Justice Project of the Hague Institute for the Internationalisation of Law (HiiL).

Elaine Mak is Associate Professor of Jurisprudence at the Erasmus University Rotterdam. She holds law degrees from the Erasmus University (2001) and the Université de Paris 1 Panthéon-Sorbonne (LL.M. 2002; DEA 2003). Her doctoral thesis (Rotterdam 2008) concerned a comparative analysis of the role of classic 'rule of law' principles and 'new public management' principles in judicial organisation. Between 2008 and 2011, she conducted post-doctoral research on the changing role of highest national courts in the globalised legal context. Elaine has collaborated with HiiL and the Montaigne Centre at Utrecht University, and has been a visiting researcher in Berlin, Cambridge, Washington, DC, and Florence. She has published inter alia in Cambridge Law Journal and European Law Journal, and regularly speaks for academic and judicial audiences in the Netherlands and abroad. Her research interests include comparative constitutional law, legal theory and legal ethics, with a main focus on the functioning of national courts in western liberal democracies in an evolving legal context.

Sam Muller is the founding Director of HiiL. Before that, in 2002- 2004, he was Special Adviser to the Registrar on External Relations at the International Criminal Court (ICC), after having been interim Deputy Director of the Common Services Division and Acting Director of the Public Information and Documentation Section of the Registry. Between 1 July and 30 October 2002 he headed up the Advance Team to set up the ICC. Prior to the ICC, he worked as Senior Legal Adviser and head of the Legal Department of the Registry of the International Criminal Tribunal for the former Yugoslavia (ICTY) and as legal officer at the headquarters of the United Nations Relief and Works Agency (UNRWA) in Gaza. Between 1995 and 1996 he was Associate Professor and Programme Coordinator of the Public International Law LLM programme of Leiden University. Muller holds a law degree and a Doctorate from Leiden University. He has published and spoken extensively on various topics, focusing mainly on the law of international organisations and international justice issues. He serves on various Boards, including The Hague Prize Foundation, The Dr. Hendrik Muller's Vaderlandsch Fonds, The Hague Journal on the Rule of Law, and the Hague Institute for Global Justice. He is chairman of the Board of the Hague Academic Coalition.

Bert Niemeijer is Coordinator at the Strategy Unit of the Ministry of Security and Justice, and part-time Professor of Sociology of Law at the Free University of Amsterdam. Previously, he has worked as Deputy Director of the Research, Statistics and Documentation Center (WODC) of the Ministry, and at various universities. Niemeijer has published on a variety of subjects, recently on trust in the rule of law and legislative evaluation. His research interests focus on access to justice, courts, the social working of legal rules, internationalisation of law and legal policy.

Ana Palacio is a member of the boards of different companies, think tanks and public institutions. In 2011, she was appointed Senior Fellow and Lecturer at Yale University's Jackson Institute for Global Affairs. A lawyer by training, specialising in international and European law, arbitration, and mediation, Palacio was the first woman to serve as Foreign Minister of Spain (2002–2004), the most senior post ever filled by a woman in the Spanish government at that time. In March 2012, Palacio was appointed to serve as Member of the *Consejo de Estado*, the supreme consultative body on legislation and governmental acts. As Member of the Spanish Cortes, she chaired the Joint Committee on the European Union in the two houses of the Parliament. Palacio has served as Senior Vice-President and General Counsel of the World Bank Group and as Executive Committee member and Senior Vice-President for International Affairs of AREVA. As a Member of the European Parliament, Palacio chaired the Legal Affairs and Internal Market Committee, the Justice and Home Affairs Committee, and the Conference of Committee Chairs.

Fausto Pocar is Professor of International Law at the Law Faculty of the University of Milan, where he has also served as the Dean of the Faculty of Political Sciences and as the Vice-Rector. He has been Judge of the International Criminal Tribunal for the former Yugoslavia (ICTY) since 1 February 2000, and was the President of ICTY between November 2005 and November 2008. Pocar is the author of numerous publications on international law, including human rights and humanitarian law, private international law and European law. He has lectured at The Hague Academy of International Law and is a Member and Treasurer of the Institut de Droit International, as well as a member of several other international law associations.

Kimberly Prost is the Ombudsperson for the United Nations Security Council Committee pursuant to resolutions 1267 (1999) and 1989 (2011) concerning Al-Qaida and Associated Individuals and Entities, also known as the "The Al-Qaida Sanctions Committee". Formerly she was Judge of the International Criminal Tribunal for the former Yugoslavia (ICTY), and Head of the Legal Advisory Section within the Division of Treaty Affairs at the United Nations Office on Drugs and Crime in Vienna, Austria. She graduated as a gold medalist from the Faculty of Law at the University of Manitoba (Canada). She participated in the negiotation of the Rules of Procedure and Evidence of the Rome Statute for the ICC.

Michiel Scheltema was one of HiiL's founders, and since 2006, he has been Chairman of the Programmatic Steering Board of HiiL. He studied law at Leiden University (LL.M. 1964) and Harvard Law School (LL.M. 1965). He was Professor of Administrative Law at the University of Groningen from 1972 to 1997, except for 1981–1983 when he was under-Minister of Justice in the Netherlands. Since 1983, he has also been Royal Commissioner for the drafting of the General Administrative Law Act. From 1998 till 2004, he chaired the Scientific Council for Government Policy, a strategic advisory body to the government.

Boudewijn Sirks is presently Regius Professor of Civil Law in the University of Oxford. He was, formerly, Professor at the Goethe University Frankfurt am Main in German Private Law and Legal History, Reader and Acting Chair for Legal Techniques, University of Amsterdam (from 1989 to 1997), Lecturer for Legal History, and, later, he also became Senior Lecturer for Legal Techniques, Utrecht University (from 1978 to 1989). Sirks has published on Roman law, Antiquity and the 17th–18th century. His research interests include Roman and Civil Law, Papyrology, the History of European Private Law and the History of European Colonial Law.

Birgit Spiesshofer is Attorney-at-Law, and has been an Of Counsel at Salans LLP since 1 April 2010. Between 1993 and 31 March 2010, she worked at Hengeler Mueller, where, since July 1995, she holds a partner's position. Birgit Spiesshofer established the Gaemo Group – Corporate Responsibility International in June 2009. She is Chair of the CSR Committee of the Council of Bars and Law Societies of Europe (CCBE), Co-Chair of the CSR Committee of the International Bar Association and Member of the Constitutional Law Committee and of the Human Rights Committee of the German Lawyers Association.

Wilhelmina Thomassen is a consultant on fundamental law, Member of the Human Rights Commission of the Dutch Advisory Council on International Affairs (AIV), Substitute Member of the Venice Commission and member of several boards. From November 2004 to

January 2012, she was Justice of the Hoge Raad (Supreme Court of the Netherlands) and from November 1998 till November 2004, she was Judge of the European Court of Human Rights. Before that, Thomassen was Judge in the District Court and the Court of Appeal of the Netherlands and a Member of the Bar. She was also the Chair of the State Commission for the revision of the Dutch Constitution (July 2009 – November 2010), and Professor of Internationalisation at the Erasmus University Rotterdam (January 2006 – September 2009). Thomassen has published many articles on the relation between the national judges and international law and on international human rights law.

Karen I. Tse is an international human rights lawyer. She works with Rule of Law initiatives across the world. Karen Tse received her Master's degree from Harvard University School of Divinity, and received her J.D. degree from the University of California at Los Angeles (UCLA) School of Law. After graduating from law school, Tse worked as a San Francisco public defender. In 1994, she moved to Cambodia to train the country's first cadre of public defenders. There, she served as United Nations Judicial Mentor. Under the auspices of the United Nations Center for Human Rights in Cambodia and the Cambodia Defenders Project, she trained judges and prosecutors and established the first arraignment court in Cambodia. In 2000, Tse founded International Bridges to Justice, a non-profit organisation which aims to eradicate torture in the 21st century and protect due process rights for accused people throughout the world.

Robert K. Visser is Executive Director of the European Asylum Support Office. Before that, he held high-level senior management positions within the Dutch government. As Director-General for Legislation, International Affairs and Immigration (2003–2011), Visser was responsible for legislation and law drafting in the field of Justice and Home Affairs. In this same field he was also responsible for the international affairs. Further on, he was responsible for policy-making in the field of immigration as well as for several executive agencies in the field of migration. Before that, he held the post of Deputy Secretary-General (1998–2003) and Senior Adviser to the Prime Minister (1986–2003), Assistant to the Council of Ministers (1983–1986), and served as a Diplomat at the Royal Netherlands Embassy in

Madrid (1981–1983). He holds a Ph.D. in law from Leiden University and a Master's degree in both Law and History from Groningen University. He has published several articles on constitutional law, organisation of government and on European law and affairs. He is the author of a handbook on ministerial responsibility and parliament.

Erik Wennerström is Director-General of the National Council for Crime Prevention in Sweden, a Government agency under the Ministry of Justice. Until 2012, he was Principal Legal Adviser in International Law with the Ministry for Foreign Affairs of Sweden. His academic affiliation is primarily with the University of Uppsala, Sweden. He has a background with the Swedish Ministry for Justice, the European Commission and the Folke Bernadotte Academy of Sweden, and has been an adviser to countries seeking membership of the European Union on rule of law matters. Wennerström has been a member of his country's delegation to the Assembly of States Parties to the Rome Statute and to the United Nations General Assembly on Rule of Law matters from 2007. He has also been a member of various expert committees in his country, within the Council of Europe and the European Union and holds board memberships in several Swedish legal societies.

Jan Wouters is Professor of International Law and International Organisations, Jean Monnet Chair EU and Global Governance, and Director of the Leuven Centre for Global Governance Studies as well as the Institute for International Law at the University of Leuven. He is Visiting Professor at the College of Europe (Bruges) and Sciences Po (Paris), and has published widely (around 460 publications including 40 books and 80 international journal articles).

Stavros Zouridis is Professor of Public Administration at Tilburg University, the Netherlands. His research and teaching focus on the public administration perspective on the rule of law: in other words, how the rule of law affects the everyday decision-making processes, working routines, professional values, and organisation structures of public authorities; and vice versa, how the latter shapes the rule of law. For a number of years, Zouridis also worked for the Dutch Ministry of Justice as Director of the General Strategy Department. Next to his research and teaching activities, he currently acts as Vice-Dean for Education at Tilburg Law School.

ALSO IN THE LAW OF THE FUTURE SERIES

Sam Muller, Stavros Zouridis, Morly Frishman and Laura Kistemaker (editors):
The Law of the Future and the Future of Law: Volume II
Torkel Opsahl Academic EPublisher
The Hague, 2012
Law of the Future Series No. 1 (2012)
ISBN 978-82-93081-80-7

www.ingramcontent.com/pod-product-compliance
Lightning Source LLC
Chambersburg PA
CBHW050529190326
41458CB00045B/6762/J